ALPINE MANUAL

Acknowledgements

First Edition

This instructor's manual has been developed in response to an evolution in snowsports, and ski/snowboard teaching both in Britain and world-wide. Over the past few years, almost every aspect of the BASI training and grading system has undergone major revision, requiring a new manual which reflects the ideas, innovations and approaches which have been introduced.

These changes, and the manual which has developed from them, would not have been possible without the commitment and enthusiasm of the Trainers. Without the contributions and energy of all the Trainers and support staff over the years BASI would not have progressed so far.

Firstly, thanks must go to all those involved in producing BASI resources in the past, for giving us a starting point so rich with information and material.

Thanks are due both for their material contributions and their comments on the many drafts through which the document has gone. The structure of this manual has changed to answer calls from the membership for an updated, user friendly resource, with all relevant information in one manual.

Special thanks must go to the team of people who brought this project to fruition. Giles Lewis (Writer and Editor) and to the rest of the writing team for their contributions. Tom Saxlund (Teaching), Rupert Tildesley (Technical), Roy Henderson (The Mountain Environment), George Reid (The Mountain Environment) Dave Murrie (Biomechanics), Les Ward (Central Theme and Teaching), Kerr Stewart (Freestyle), Sean Langmuir (Central Theme). For their tireless work and enviable talent in design, Henry Meredith-Hardy, Paul Hammett. Also to Erica Meredith-Hardy, Henry Meredith-Hardy and Guy Coles for their excellent photography.

With a project of this magnitude, there are always people who have played a part and supported in many different ways, thanks to all those who have been involved no matter how small.

Paul Garner
Chief Editor and Writer

Foreword

BASI President's Foreword to the new BASI Manual

I'm pleased to be writing to you as President of this exciting and vibrant association and to bring you this first edition of the New BASI Alpine Combination Manual. Vital information contained in this edition will undoubtedly prove essential in your quest to become an instructor, at whatever level to which you aspire. Followed closely it will help you to develop your skills, improve your technical knowledge and highlight how to impart your valuable knowledge for the benefit and enjoyment of others.

During my term, I've witnessed the association's move into its own prestigious office building in Grantown-on-Spey in the summer of 2009. The installation of a new Chief Executive and the hosting of the ISIA conference in Aviemore in 2010. I'm now looking forward to the special celebrations in 2012 when BASI will celebrate its 50th year, with the international recognition from our fellow nations and a growing membership now in excess of 6,000 it is a credit to you all.

I know that you all play your part as international ambassadors for our association wherever you are in the world and I wish you every success in your profession.

Sir Clive Woodward
President

BASI Chairman's Foreword to the new BASI Manual

I saw the BASI Demonstration Ski Team skiing on an artificial slope at the London Ski Show in Earls Court during the early 80's. It was then that I decided that I was going to become a BASI instructor and make it into that team. At school whilst discussing with my careers advisor what job I would like to do, I told him that I would like to become a ski instructor with BASI. "No son, that's just a dream, off you go and get a proper job".

By reading this manual, it is the start of your dream. This manual will not only help you pass your BASI courses, giving you all the information on the technical and teaching, it will help to make you a great instructor, give you the knowledge and understanding so that you will be able to take your performance beyond your wildest dreams and will allow you to work all over the world. It will also help shape your own personal performance in life and business. Many people who have learned and put into practise the skills they have acquired through the BASI system have become successful in business beyond snowsports.

Many thanks go to all those BASI trainers and instructors whom I have met and supported me. You have all allowed me to have had a fantastic career and life in snowsports, which has allowed me to have and support my family, taken me all over the world as well as help me lead many different companies, including this association.

My thanks must also go to all the contributors to this the newest edition of the BASI Alpine Manual. By reading this, you too are taking your first step to making your dreams come true!

This book is not meant to be read once but is a reference manual and just like your skiing performance should be reviewed time and time again. This will help you to build larger foundations and allow you to grow bigger and better.

I wish you every success and can only hope that you also have the same great time and enjoy similar experiences that I have had in and with BASI.

Andrew Lockerbie
BASI Chairman 2006 – 2010

CONTENTS

Introduction & Overview

As the official instructors' manual of the British Association of Snowsport Instructors (BASI), this manual is designed to serve the needs of both trainee instructors and fully qualified snowsport teachers. As a learning tool for trainees, large sections can be studied in their entirety. As a reference tool, specific topics can be identified from the contents page, to help instructors and teachers find solutions to specific problems.

For ease of reference, the chapters making up this manual are divided into 4 parts, each relating to a specific subject area:

Part 1: Performance
Part 2: Teaching
Part 3: The Mountain Environment
Part 4: The Toolbox

In addition the appendices provide supplementary information on a range of topics.

Within each part, individual chapters address separate topics.

PERFORMANCE

In order to achieve good teaching and inspire effective learning, the content of the delivery needs to be accurate. For a snowsports instructor, technical understanding could be seen as a "hard skill" as opposed to softer skills such as communication, group management, understanding the learner etc, which are explored in the teaching section. It is essential to understand the nuts and bolts of our sport and how they fit together to produce skilful outcomes. We can start by identifying the fundamentals of skiing, these are the basic ingredients which are involved in skilful performances.

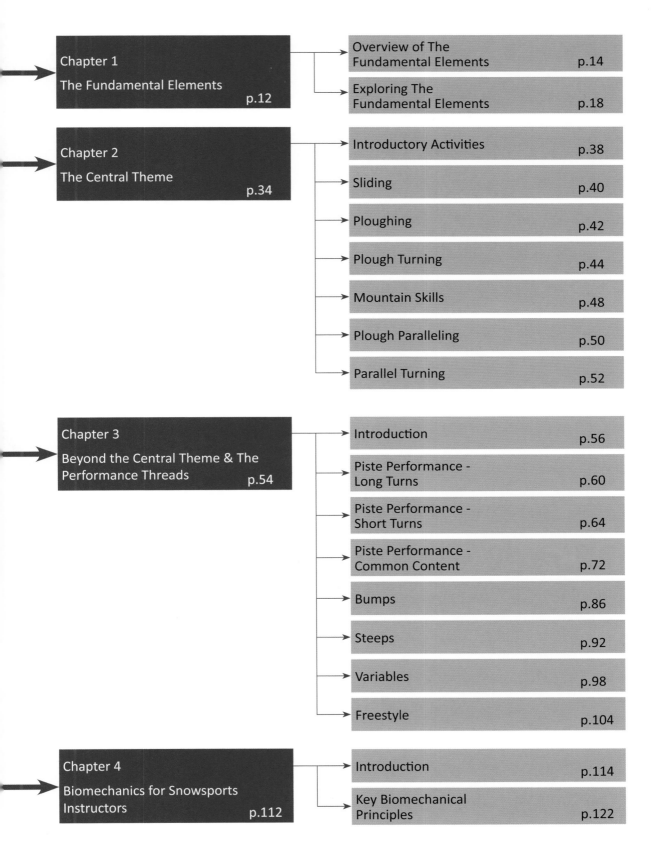

1. THE FUNDAMENTAL ELEMENTS

The Fundamental Elements - An Overview

The fundamental elements are the basic building blocks of technique and can be split into two sub-sections, those of input and outcome. For every outcome there are a set of required inputs and any given set of inputs will result in a particular outcome. Different outcomes in skiing occur in the context of the ever changing terrain and snow conditions and require constant adjustment of the inputs we use. These adjustments don't need to be considered separately as they involve all the other fundamental elements, all of the time.

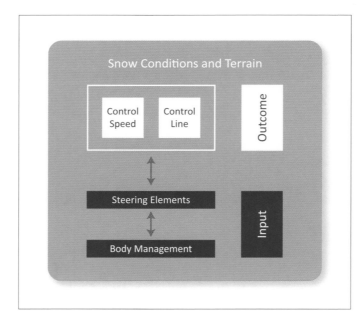

Figure 1.1:
The Fundamental Elements and how they interact

As this schematic shows, the Fundamental Elements are interlinked, all having an effect on each other. However, before we explore their relationship we will look at each element individually to ensure we have a sound foundation of understanding.

Body Management

How we manage the movements and positioning of our body in relation to the equipment, the snow and terrain, determines everything about our skiing performance. The first thing that a beginner learns is basic body management and how to stand on their skis. Although they are inter-related, BASI classifies body management into the following sub-headings.

Posture

How we align our skeleton and body parts over our feet impacts on our ability to steer and control our skis, to maintain and recover balance and to make whatever movements we choose. In short, good posture is our foundation for movement and balance, without it everything else is difficult.

Movements

Moving is fundamental to any sport and also integral to all of BASI's Fundamental Elements. Here we are concerned with the quality of our movements as this will determine whether we are effective on our skis.

Balance

In skiing we are constantly moving in order to create and manage the forces that enable us to turn. It is in relation to these forces that we need to be balanced. When we achieve this we can be accurate with our movements and are able to dictate what happens next.

Steering Elements

Three elements are involved in steering a ski around an arc, edge, rotation and pressure. They represent what we are able to do to the skis on the snow and are the result of the inputs that come from the Body Management family. As the skis interact with the snow and terrain they create the outcomes of speed, line and flow.

Edge – modulating the tilting of the skis onto their edges relative to the snow

In order to turn, edging has to be present. Even when the other steering elements seem to be dominant and the amount of edge used is very small, it is still required in order to turn. It is the grip from the edge and base of the ski that causes the ski to deflect around a curve. This is the case for any turn from very skiddy to fully carved. In short, without edge, grip is unachievable and with no grip there would be no turning force created between ski and snow.

Rotation – modulating the rotation of the skis on the snow

Every turn involves rotation as we are travelling around part of an arc and in many cases our main concern is controlling it. The rotation of the skis can also be described in relation to the turn itself. Do the skis turn faster than the turn itself – skidding, or do the skis turn at the same rate as the turn itself – carving.

Pressure – modulating the pressure of the skis against the snow

Pressure in skiing can be described as the feeling we get when the reaction force from the snow travels through our skis and is resisted by our bodies. We can distribute this pressure between the two skis evenly or by favouring one ski more than the other. When we are motionless pressure is dictated by the weight of the skier, however with movement we can influence the magnitude of the force we feel.

We can blend the steering elements to produce a variety of different turn types. It is important to recognise that the steering elements do not operate in isolation from one another, they are interdependent. By blend we mean the sequence, timing and magnitude with which the elements are applied.

Consider these two examples:

- Snowplough turning is often taught by emphasising rotary control – turning the plough shape around the curve. However, edge and pressure are both present in the turn. In a snowplough the skis are further apart than the hips, thus edging both skis and creating a turning force. This force is what we know as pressure

- A high-speed carved turn generally combines a high degree of edge angle with a large amount of pressure. The skis do rotate in this type of turn, but the rotation is at the same rate as the line of the turn itself. The rotation in this turn is sometimes described as passive

Control

Control is what we seek most when skiing. Without it we risk injury, emotional discomfort and reduced enjoyment. By making accurate tactical decisions as to how we blend the inputs we are able to manipulate the outcomes within the control family:

Control of Line – where we go

Control of Speed – how fast we travel

The outcomes of any performance are the visible end product of all the inputs made by the performer. It is important to remember that they need to be viewed in relation to an intended task. For example, if, when observing a performance it appears that the skier is failing to control their speed, we must first ask what they are trying to achieve. If they are trying to ski as fast as possible then perhaps the outcome is accurate and correct. Once we have a clear task we also have a clear intended outcome and something to aim for.

Flow

Flow is not a fundamental element in its own right. It is a way to look at existing elements from another (qualitative) perspective, as if looking at the same performance but through a different lens. A flowing performance is the difference between a mechanical disjointed performance which appears to have all of the elements present but doesn't have an effective relationship between the inputs and the outcomes.

To help us use flow we divide it into the following headings:

Managing the Forces of the Curve and the Snow/Terrain

Fluency and Ease

Co-ordination and Rhythm

Summary

The content above is intended to provide the reader with a basic understanding of the Fundamental Elements. Each element is introduced and explained. As our performance and teaching progress, however we need to develop a more detailed understanding of these essential components of ski technique. We also need to explore the relationship between each element to give us the best possible chance of achieving skilful outcomes. What follows will help you to understand the Fundamental Elements on a deeper level.

Exploring the Fundamental Elements

The fundamental elements are rarely used as separate entities. Each can have a profound effect and influence on another. For example body management elements influence the steering elements which in turn influence control of speed and line. This happens in reverse too, control of speed and line can be adjusted which requires changes in the use of the steering elements which in turn requires changes in the body management. The arrows on our schematic illustrate the ways in which a performer can use the fundamentals in order to develop performance, either using an input focus or an outcome focus. For a more detailed understanding of the relationship between input and outcome in relation to the Fundamental Elements please refer to the Teaching Section, Performance Analysis.

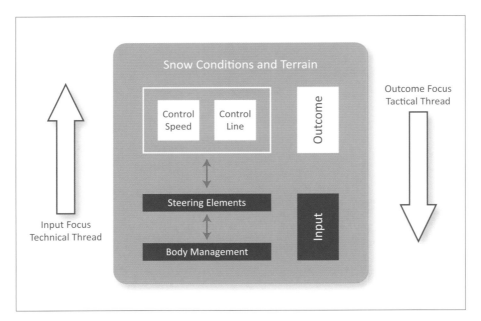

Figure 1.2:
The Fundamental Elements with an input/outcome focus

Body Management

Posture

A sound skiing posture is often described in terms of other activities – a 'runner's stance', the 'goalkeeper position', 'a tennis player waiting to receive serve'. Whatever the analogy, it is important to recognise that it is not a fixed, immobile position - rather, it is the 'home base' around which the movements of skiing are made.

Despite the dynamic nature of good posture there are several key features which can be highlighted:

Different movement qualities
A horizontal eye line
Arms away from the body to aid balance
All the skiing joints flexed, ankles, knees, hips
Able to balance over the whole foot fore/aft
Minimal muscular tension – skeletal alignment to support most of our body weight

Figure 1.3: (left) A skier showing good posture

Figure 1.4: (right) A skier showing good posture while carving

Skiing is a dynamic sport and as such our posture needs to be dynamic too. It is the link with movement and balance that defines good posture in skiing. Our posture needs to change and adapt as the forces acting upon us change when travelling downhill. While the postural features highlighted above are a useful starting point, it is not always possible or useful to maintain these when we're skiing.

There are large differences in posture when comparing the two photos and the second picture shows a lot of differences to the key points of posture listed above. However, the posture is effective and is allowing the skier to make the movements required to stay in balance from turn to turn. This is a good example of how aligning the body's skeleton allows the bones to take most of the force acting upon the skier. This is of less importance when the forces are smaller. When making a basic snowplough turn we don't need to align our skeletons to resist such a great force, we are more concerned with a posture that is stable and relaxed.

Movements

There are many ways that we can move when skiing. Amongst others we can flex, extend, rotate, abduct, adduct, supinate, and pronate different parts of our body. This will enable us to achieve different outcomes relevant to skiing such as tilting the skis onto an edge or moving vertically to jump the skis off the snow or absorb a bump. The location of the movement is one thing but the quality of the movements is also important. Below are the different qualities that we can bring to our movements. They will determine how effective those movements are overall.

Different movement qualities
Range
Rate
Accuracy
Smoothness/Timing
Muscular Effort

To move with agility and control is very different from moving stiffly and robotically. When skiers are practicing a new skill they often reproduce movements that are disjointed and clunky and need time to develop accuracy and smoothness (See Teaching Section, Skill Acquisition Model). Also, skiers often learn movements during teaching activities or drills but then fail to use these movements in their general skiing. There can be a number of reasons for this:

- A lack of confidence in the movements in a more challenging context
- A lack of athletic ability to implement the movements in a more challenging context
- The skier chooses the wrong movements for the given task. This happens when skills are learned in isolation and then used in the wrong context

Ensuring that the instructor works in relation to the performer's learning phase and has a robust grasp of how the fundamentals link together will avoid these problems

Balance

As is the case for posture and movements, balance is at the heart of skiing. However, it is important to realise that our understanding of balance in skiing differs from the dictionary definition, which requires the maintenance of our Centre of Mass (CoM) inside our base of support with minimal postural adjustments. This definition is applicable to a static system in which there is little movement but has limited application in a dynamic sport like skiing.

The BASI Alpine Manual

In skiing we are constantly moving in order to create and manage the forces that enable us to turn. It is in relation to these forces that we need to be balanced. When we achieve this we can be accurate with our movements and are able to dictate what happens next. We can influence the radius of the turn, start the next turn when we want, speed up and slow down. A poorly balanced skier does not create and manage the forces very well and may have to make extra movements and postural adjustments to avoid falling over. Consider the effortless, economy of movement demonstrated by a world class skier compared to the struggles of an average holiday maker.

To enable us to be good at managing our balance and the resultant forces, we need to remain alert to the changing terrain and conditions around us so we can respond quickly and accurately. It also helps to stay relaxed in the body parts that are not actively engaged. Without this we are likely to limit the quality of our movements and hence compromise our balancing abilities.

Steering Elements

When we go round a curve on skis the steering elements of edge, rotation and pressure are all involved all of the time. They allow us to create and manage the forces needed for the skier to turn.

Edge

To control how we use our edges, the skis and different parts of the body move laterally relative to each other. Depending on the circumstances of the turn we might focus on moving the body inside the line of the skis, whereas on other occasions it will be more effective to do the opposite and allow the skis to move away from the line of the body. Either way, the end result will be that the skis tilt onto an edge.

The lateral movement involved in creating edge tilt can originate in the following areas:

• The feet

• The knees (this is actually a rotation of the femur in the hip socket)

• Around the hips

• The waist and above (we can separate anywhere in the spine up to and including the neck)

• The whole body

A large lateral displacement of the skis relative to the rest of the body requires that the CoM of the skier travels inside the line of the skis. This requires higher speeds and is a feature of skiing beyond the Central Theme.

It is important to remember that the same movements that control the edge angles will also determine how far inside the arc the CoM travels through the turn. Increasing or decreasing edge angles without changing the position of the skier's CoM will have limited effect on the turning forces (pressure). Put simply, being balanced on the right amount of edge will make the ski grip, but the angle away from vertical of the CoM has a large effect on the turning force (think of a cyclist leaning into a turn, the further they lean in, the tighter they turn). Edge angle alone cannot influence the radius of the turn but also requires pressure and sometimes rotation.

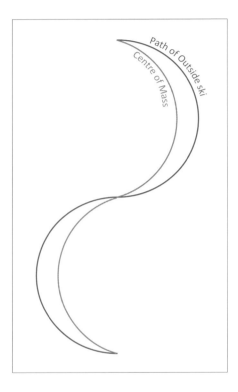

Figure 1.5:
The path of the Centre of Mass relative to the path of the skis

What is lateral separation?

When some parts of the body tilt with the skis and others don't, we call this lateral separation or angulation. Sometimes we will actively seek to separate laterally and other times it is a natural reaction to the movements we are already making.

Below are some points to consider when working with lateral separation:
- It takes longer to tilt the whole body than it does just a part of the body. For quick changes of direction, as when skiing narrow corridor short turns, it will be more effective to tilt the skis with the legs and keep the body more upright
- Separating laterally can put us in a weak position and may not allow us to maintain the balance and posture necessary to deal with larger forces. So for turns which generate large forces, like high speed carve turns in a wide corridor, we are likely to allow more of the body to tilt with the skis
- A single turn may contain sections with varying degrees of lateral separation. For example a skier may use full body tilt at the start of the turn to create edge angle but then separate laterally from above the waist later in the turn to aid the transition into the next

The BASI Alpine Manual

Rotation

Although rotation is ever present when we turn, rotating the skis alone will not produce a deviation in our line. If the skis remain flat on the snow with no edge grip, they will simply pivot and the skier will continue to travel in the same direction, as in a braquage turn. Although this can sometimes be useful, for the skier to be deflected from their original path, there needs to be some edge and pressure present.

To demonstrate this point more clearly let us use the simple analogy of a car turning. When the wheels of a car are rotated across the line of the car's momentum it will only turn if the tyres grip the road. If they fail to grip the car will continue to slide in the same direction much like in a braquage turn. Similarly, when we rotate our skis across our direction of travel, any edge grip will cause the skis to deflect from their path in the same way. Assuming the edges continue to grip then the more the skis are rotated across the line of momentum, the greater the potential turning force – or what we refer to as pressure. This is the case until they are rotated exactly perpendicular to the direction of travel at which point the skis and skier will decelerate and eventually come to a stop. This concept was originally referred to by the Canadians as "steering angles". In modern skiing, steering angles are also created by the sidecut of the ski, which means that even when edge is applied on its own, with no active rotation, a steering angle is already created. This makes modern skis turn more easily.

As the blend of rotation and edge changes the skis describe a whole spectrum of turns from skiddy to carved.

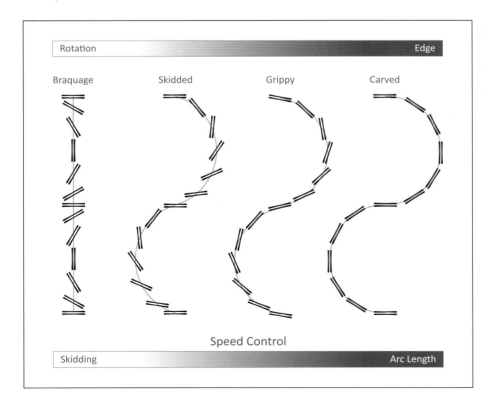

Figure 1.6:
Spectrum of turns ranging from fully carved turns to purely rotary based turns

Just as we do when we tilt the skis, we have a number of choices to make when we rotate them. Here are some of the ways we can rotate the skis:

- The feet rotate alone - minimal effect

- The thighs rotate from the hip

- Hips and below rotate without the upper chest

- The whole body rotates with the ski

These different ways of rotating affect the ease, speed and magnitude with which we can rotate the skis, and how easily we can switch the direction of rotation. Some points of rotation are particularly applicable to certain types of skiing, other points are less suitable.

When choosing which movements we use to control rotation it is useful to remember that not all parts of the body will take the same line down the hill. The upper body will often take a shorter, more direct route, meaning that it is necessary to have some degree of rotational separation even if it doesn't feel very active.

Figure 1.7:
A strong pole plant to aid rotational separation

Figure 1.8:
The skier separates the upper and lower parts of the body rotationally to move effectively into the next turn

What is rotational separation?

When some parts of the body rotate and others don't we call this rotational separation. Sometimes we will actively seek to separate rotationally and other times it is a natural reaction to the movements we are already making.

Below are some points to consider when working with rotational separation:

- It takes more effort to rotate the whole body than it does just a part of the body. This is why it will be more effective to rotate the legs and keep the body facing down the hill when trying to make quick changes of direction, as when skiing a direct line in the bumps

- Separating rotationally can put us in a weak position and may not allow us to maintain the balance and posture necessary to deal with larger forces. So for turns which generate large forces, like high speed carve turns in a wide corridor, we are likely to allow more of the body to rotate with the skis

- Rather than thinking of rotational separation as the upper body staying still and the skis rotating, rotational separation also describes any moment when the upper and lower body rotate at different speeds or times. For example: it can be useful to initiate a turn with a strong active rotation of the upper body. This can aid the flow of the body down the mountain and will be linked to lateral movements which help control pressure and edge. This active rotation of the upper body is often seen in the variable strand to help initiate turns. The timing and range of this movement must be carefully controlled to maintain balance

- In order to initiate or control rotation, the body needs some contact point with the ground. The pole provides the skier with an extra point from which to help him or her affect the rotation of the body and the skis

- Rotation always needs an axis about which to rotate. With the skiers body close to this axis the skier will rotate faster than when the body is further away. This concept can give the skier extra control over their rotation. Spreading the arms will give more control of the upper body (slowing rotation) than having them tight. Pulling the legs to the chest will allow a freestyle skier to complete a flip faster than remaining in an open elongated position

- Controlling existing rotation will require different movements to creating a new rotational force. A skier may be able to create more rotational momentum from a wide stance than a narrow one. A freestyle skier imparts rotational momentum before leaving the ramp with a wide stance but once in the air the stance may narrow to increase the speed of rotation

Pressure

How is pressure created? Pressure results from any action at the ski/snow interface that changes the speed or direction of the skier. We feel pressure when we are turning, when the terrain causes us to change direction (heading over a bump or through a hollow), or when we slow ourselves down using rotation and edge.

How to Control Pressure

- **Creating turns using rotation and edge** - Will lead to pressure, the greater the turning effect (or slowing effect) the more pressure we feel. This links with the simile used in rotation of the car turning its front wheels. As long as the skis grip then the more they are rotated across the direction of travel then the more pressure will be created and the tighter the turn will be

- **Distributing pressure between the skis** - This allows us to have more pressure on one ski than the other. This ability to change from one foot to the other helps us to move laterally and use pressure to initiate a new turn. This movement pattern, often referred to as pedalling, is used from the central theme right up to high level skiing. The movements of extension and flexion in the legs assist the skier to move laterally and change the distribution of overall pressure

- **Distributing pressure along the skis** - Changing where we stand along the length of the skis can have a huge impact on the pressure under the skis. As well as changing our basic posture and point of balance, having more or less pressure at the tip or tail of the skis can affect their performance. For example: On the piste, more pressure fore or aft will tend to cause that part of the ski to grip more at the expense of the other end. In deeper snow, fore/aft pressure can control where the ski travels within the soft snow, either dipping down or rising up

- **Moving the skier's Centre of Mass inside the arc** - As mentioned in the edging section, so long as the skier remains in balance the pressure will increase as the skier's Centre of Mass moves inside the arc of a turn. In the same way, pressure will decrease and return to body weight as the CoM returns over the feet. Whatever movements a skier needs to make in order to take the CoM inside the arc and stay in balance are therefore also pressure control movements. These movements will be in the lateral plane and will be similar to those used to control the edge angle of the skis

- **Controlling pressure directly through extension and flexion** - This is possible through a fast extension and flexion of the joints. Imagine standing on a set of analogue bathroom scales. You can make the scales read a higher weight by extending the ankles and knees quickly. However, do this quickly enough and you will jump, and when you jump the scales will read no weight. To do the reverse, stand on the scales as tall as you can and then flex quickly. The scales will read less weight until you reach the limit of flexion and then the scales will read a higher weight than normal. The limitation of trying to directly control pressure with flexion and extension is that you can only do it for a short amount of time and for it to be effective the movements need to be fast (they actually require an acceleration of mass). So although extension and flexion of the joints are common movements within skiing they do not necessarily control pressure. They may provide a useful means of controlling pressure in turns of short duration impulse but we need to be realistic about how much extension and flexion can directly control total pressure within turns of longer duration and certainly when performing the Central Theme

All these mechanisms control pressure, but they do not act alone. When they are used together they don't necessarily reinforce each other, it is the net sum of their actions that will determine the actual pressure on the ski.

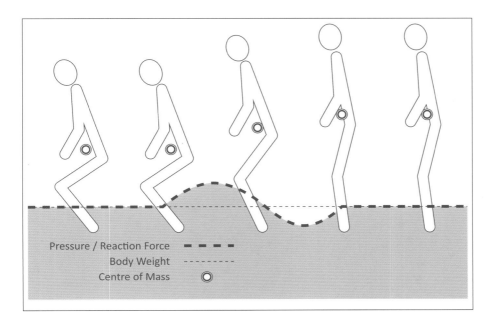

Figure 1.9: Pressure control through flexion and extension

Control of Speed

There are several ways which a skier can control their speed. We can think of the ones below:

Primary methods	Secondary methods
• Arc Length	• Modifying air resistance
• Skidding	• Use of the terrain or snow
• Checking	

Arc Length

One reason for turning is to steer the skis in the direction we want to travel (control of line). The other reason is to control our speed. On any given slope the fall-line provides the fastest route down the hill. All else being equal, the more we deviate from the fall-line the slower we will go. If we continue to turn round an arc far enough we will eventually go back up the hill and come to a stop. This method of controlling speed works regardless of the type of turn (skidded or carved).

Skidding

In a skidded turn we actively rotate the skis across the direction of travel whilst maintaining the amount of edge tilt. By doing this we create more resistance and reduce our speed. Reducing the edge angle will result in a skiddier turn with less deflection across the hill. Too little edge angle can actually decrease the resistance and take the skier in to a side slip. See figure 1.10.

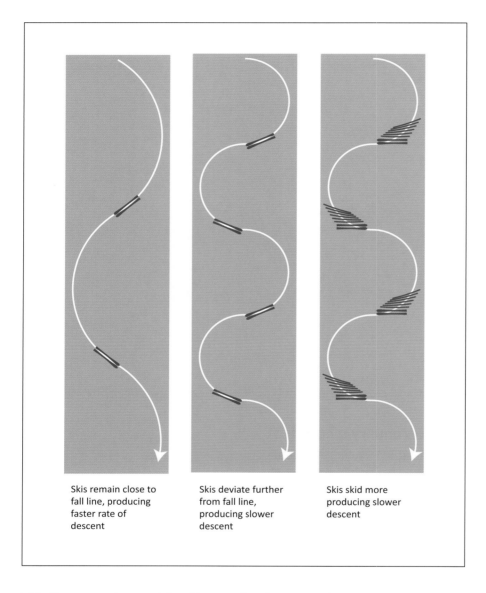

Figure 1.10:
Control of speed

Skis remain close to fall line, producing faster rate of descent

Skis deviate further from fall line, producing slower descent

Skis skid more producing slower descent

This illustrates the need for skiers to develop versatility, in order to vary the sequence, blend and timing of their movements to achieve the desired outcome. To control their speed skiers can use the methods of skidding and arc length at the same time or on their own. A purely carved turn relies on arc length to manage speed, whereas skidding the skis will control speed whether the arc length changes or not.

Checking

In some circumstances it is useful to control speed by setting the edges against the snow so that they grip and don't skid or side-slip at all. The edge set transfers some of the skier's momentum to the ground and this slows the skier down. It is important to consider the angle the skis are pointing in relation to the fall-line when checking, as the check will produce a reaction from the skis in the opposite direction. If a skier checks with the skis perpendicular to the fall-line so that the action is down the hill, the result will be a reaction back up the hill, bringing the skier to a stop (as in a hockey stop). However, if the check happens with the skis facing even slightly down the hill, the result will be that the skier travels in the direction the skis are pointing.

Checking is a method that can be applied at any suitable point during a descent but is rarely used in isolation. Most skiers will use turn shape and skidding to control the speed and will employ checking in addition and when necessary. Checking may also be used as a quick way to change direction as well as to control speed.

Modifying Air Resistance

The faster we ski, the greater the resistance or drag from the air. However, we can manipulate this by changing our aerodynamic qualities or the surface area of our body showing in the direction of travel. In practise, adopting a tuck and wearing tighter clothing will reduce drag and will increase the skiers' potential top speed

Use of the Terrain or Snow

We can use gravity to slow us down by skiing up hill. Often this is done at end of a turn as described above. Sometimes the terrain allows us to slow down without having to finish the turn, such as skiing up the side of a gully or heading for a minor rise in the terrain.

The resistance that the snow offers is governed by the combined factors of snow depth and the snow density. When skiing in deep powder the natural resistance offered by the snow means the gradient of the slope needs to be steep enough to overcome this. Equally a fast icy piste will provide faster racing conditions than soft new snow.

Control of Line

Corridors

There are only two reasons for controlling our line. One, is to take us where we want to go, the other is to control our speed. There are two key factors which determine the overall shape and size of a turn, its radius, and its arc length. The turn radius describes the size of the circle around which the skis travel. The arc length is the distance the skis continue round that circle before the new turn begins.

Take the example of someone who is trying to ski precisely within an imaginary corridor. They can achieve this in various ways: at one extreme they might make very long-radius turns, while keeping the arc length short enough to avoid over-shooting the margins of the corridor, at the other extreme, they might make very short-radius turns, but continue round each arc until reaching the corridor margins.

Two things distinguish these different lines: in the former case, the rate of descent is faster, and the vertical distance covered by each turn is greater. Many attempts by skiers to make 'short-radius turns' are actually long-radius, short-arc turns. This is the main reason why so many skiers have difficulty controlling their speed when skiing narrow runs. At the other extreme, many skiers have difficulty making long-radius, long-arc turns. Instead of allowing the skis to turn gradually, they make quick turns and then allow the skis to traverse before starting the next turn. This leads to a loss of rhythm, and makes each turn harder to initiate.

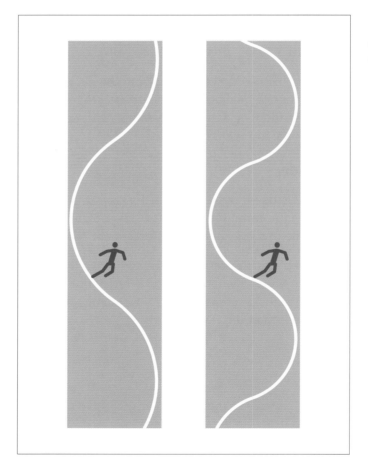

Figure 1.11: Different lines within the same corridor

We are not limited to skiing simple corridors and if we manage the inputs well we will be able to change the radius and arc length of our turns at will. This opens up the possibility of skiing an infinite number of lines. With only a few examples we can imagine variations such as funnels, cones, hourglass shapes and a diagonal step pattern. Being able to ski these different lines on smooth pistes is great for our skiing. Varying our line forces us to use the inputs of the fundamentals in different ways and develops our understanding of the way they link together. In the other strands our line takes on an even greater tactical significance as the terrain and snow conditions can change metre by metre.

Shape of the Arc

Although we talk about the radius of an arc, the line we ski does not have to be part of a circle. The radius can tighten through the turn or start tight and end up open. It is even possible to change the radius more than once in a turn for example start open, tighten at the fall line and open at the end. Opening the radius causes the skier to have a faster exit speed from the turn, tightening the radius after the fall-line will tend to cause the skier to exit the turn with less speed.

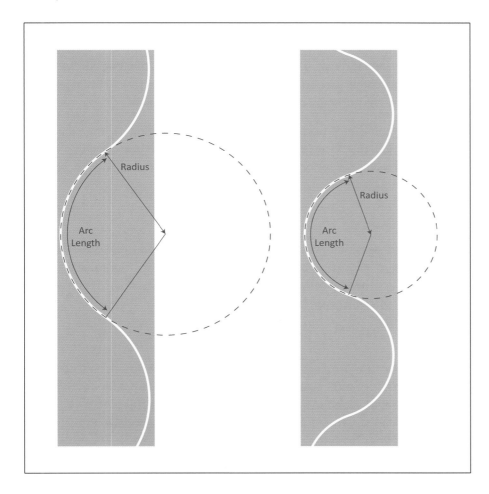

Figure 1.12:
Turn radius and arc length

Flow

As we have already mentioned we approach flow as if we are looking at a performance through a different lens. For this reason we group flow with the outcome elements because the qualities that it helps us to identify and develop are clearly visible in the outcomes of a performance.

Using and understanding what is meant by flow can help performers to train more productively and perform with more accuracy and sensitivity. It involves developing accurate inputs and responding to complexity.

To help us use flow we divide it into the following headings:

Managing the Forces of the Curve and the Snow/Terrain

To be able to maximize the effectiveness of the inputs that a performer has available, they need to be able to manage the forces involved in order to produce the line and speed desired. If the skier is making the expected movements but the outcome is not met, then the forces are not being managed well. Conversely a skier may not seem to be making the full range of movements expected, but the outcome exceeds the expectations of the task. This skier may have an exceptional feel for the forces and may be using them very effectively.

What ultimately governs the outcome of a performance is the forces acting on the skier. The inputs must be effective in relation to these forces, not in relation to a preconceived set of movement patterns. Feeling and using these forces accurately will enable the skier to achieve the desired outcome.

Fluency and Ease

Through increased relaxation and sensitivity a performer will become aware of where in the body the forces are being managed. Adjusting body management will allow the forces to flow more through the skeleton, and less through the muscles. This will allow the skier to be relaxed, alert and responsive, the movements will seem easy and natural.

Co-ordination and Rhythm

Co-ordination and rhythm describes the process of taking mechanical movements into a skilful flowing performance. A flowing performance will have the right movements present at the right time, with the correct magnitude and speed. One of the keys to achieving this is to move away from a cognitive organization of the movement patterns into a reactive responsive mode which focuses on the sensations and feelings from the snow through the body.

As instructors we have a choice of whether to work with flow or not because the fundamentals on their own can describe and develop any type of performance by linking input to outcome. However, flow provides us with an alternative path to identify and achieve the qualitative aspects of a performance that we are looking for in skilful skiing.

2. THE CENTRAL THEME

The Central Theme

The Central Theme is an evolving series of manoeuvres that is designed to help people learn to ski in a natural, progressive and simple way. It is not a complete lesson-plan, but rather a simple technical model for students around which lessons can be designed. The Central Theme is only one of many possible routes from first steps up to parallel skiing. Its whole purpose is to give less experienced teachers a clear and effective framework from which to work. As teachers gain knowledge and experience, they can move outside the boundaries of the Central Theme to cope with a wider variety of client needs and teaching environments. Ultimately, every route that is taken from plough to parallel should give skiers a sound and enjoyable foundation to their skiing.

The purpose of the Central Theme is:
- To help teach clients, from their first steps on skis to parallel skiing
- To develop the fundamental elements of skiing in a versatile way
- To progressively build skills, where each new movement builds on those previously learned
- To prepare the client to ski the whole mountain

In what follows, the descriptions of the manoeuvres can be thought of as a series of 'snapshots' of points throughout the skier's development. The learning process itself has a much more gradual, evolving character. Rather than the crude series of steps described on page 37, the learning process is best thought of as a continuum. The Central Theme progression simply selects some of the major stages along that continuum, and identifies the key technical points that are involved at these stages.

Each of these stages is presented in relation to a goal or intended outcome, such as being able to use a gliding plough to control speed. Each stage develops different aspects of the fundamental elements and the key elements are highlighted, although certain elements such as posture and balance actually occur at every stage. There are then a number of inputs listed that will help to achieve the goal. The terrain on which to base learning for each stage is also suggested. Finally, each stage is complemented with a Top Tips section and a Performance Beyond the Central Theme section. The former is designed to help when teaching the Central Theme, whereas the latter is intended to help make the link between the skills learned at this early stage and those required to ski at a higher level. Any movement we make when learning should have a reason which is relevant to skiing at any level.

Each stage of the Central Theme is covered in The Toolbox, Activities for the Central Theme.

The Central Theme – Development of the Fundamental Elements

Introductory Activities
To become familiar with the equipment and develop co-ordinated movements on skis

Sliding
To become familiar with the sensation of sliding and develop good posture and balance

Ploughing
To control the descent and lay foundations for learning to steer

Plough Turning
To control speed and direction by steering the skis

Mountain Skills
Development activities to help skiers move around the ski area

Plough Paralleling
To control speed and direction on steeper slopes and move towards parallel skiing

Parallel Turning
The start of advanced skiing in the strands

Introductory Activities

Goal

To become familiar with the equipment, the winter sports environment and the sensation of sliding with skis on

Terrain

Flat terrain

Key Fundamentals

Movements and Balance

Input to achieve this goal

- Create a safe, supportive environment so that learners feel at ease and ready to learn
- Choose terrain that has a safe run out, ideally an area that is in a shallow bowl
- Explain what learners should expect from their first experience of skiing
- Establish the expectations of the learners
- Remember new learners often know surprisingly little and will need help with everything from walking in ski boots to understanding the different items of equipment

Figure 2.1: Equipment can often be very alien to total beginners

See The Toolbox for developmental activities for The Central Theme

Top Tips

Skiers will slide on the slightest of slopes. In some cases if this happens unintentionally, confidence will be damaged at this very early stage

Once the students have an understanding of the equipment it is a good idea to start with activities that only involve one ski. This allows the other leg to be used as a balance aid and helps to build confidence and competence gradually

As an instructor, be very clear with your instructions. Once students are ready to move, it often helps to get them to follow you or a defined course, so that they can concentrate purely on their movements and balance

Sliding

Goal

Sliding on two flat skis whilst adopting a responsive posture enabling the skier to be balanced over the middle of the skis

Terrain

Gentle terrain with a safe run out or slight uphill section at the bottom of the slope

Key Fundamentals

Posture and Balance

At this stage, control of speed comes from the instructor's careful choice of terrain.

Input to Help Achieve this Goal

- Adopt accurate lateral alignment of the joints. For example, the knees should flex in line with the skis rather than inwards
- Use all the skiing joints - ankles, knees and hips when flexing and extending to remain balanced over the feet. This also promotes good fore-aft posture when viewed from the side
- Stand with the feet comfortably apart. This distance will vary between individuals, as a guide they should be hip width apart
- Hold the hands forwards and away from the body, at around hip level. When holding poles, the tips should diverge rather than point straight at the ground
- Look ahead with a horizontal eye-line to help balance

Summary: Adopt a ready, responsive position over the middle of the skis.

Top Tips

To help development, one option is to take ski poles away from beginners at this early stage. This must be balanced against the need for beginners to feel secure and continue to develop in confidence

It is useful to encourage skiers to stand with their weight balanced evenly over the whole foot rather than on the heels as is often the case when standing normally

A rounded back as opposed to a straight or hollow back gives the skier the ability to use all the skiing joints and keep the chain of movement working through the body and the equipment

It is preferable to adopt a responsive posture that promotes the ability to move rather than a fixed rigid position that is deemed 'correct'

To help skiers to relax, ask them to bounce gently on and off the front of their boots, which promotes movement of all the skiing joints

Performance Beyond the Central Theme

A responsive posture that allows the skier to move and remain in balance relates to every part of skiing. If the skier learns to use all the skiing joints at this early stage it will help performance in later development on all types of terrain. Learning to hold the poles with diverging tips affects how the skier can move and is important even at this early stage. Poles that point straight at the ground will inhibit lateral and vertical movement, especially in higher end piste performance turns

Ploughing

Terrain	**Key Fundamentals**
Gently sloping terrain with a safe run out	Rotation and Edge

Having developed good posture and balance, control of speed now comes from a combination of choice of terrain and a comfortable gliding plough that continues to promote sound balance and posture.

Input to Help Achieve this Goal

- Rotate both skis inwards to produce a gliding plough. The ski tips should almost touch
- Find a pivot point underneath the toe piece of the binding rather than towards the tips of the skis – although the feet will be displaced a little wider than the hips, pivoting from the feet will ensure the feet don't get pushed too far apart, resulting in too much edge
- Allow edging to occur automatically – at this stage it is very subtle

Summary: To begin ploughing learn to rotate the legs and skis inwards.

Figure 2.3: Sequence showing a gliding plough

Top Tips

Any mention of active edging at this stage is likely to result either in unnecessary lateral movements at the knee or an uncomfortably wide and unbalanced plough

When on terrain with no safe run out (e.g. entering a lift queue) you may need to displace the feet a little wider and use a braking plough in order to stop (see figure 2.4). Move progressively and ask people to concentrate on feeling the pressure build up rather than on simply pushing the feet wider apart

Performance Beyond the Central Theme

It is essential for good skiers to have the ability to keep the skis relatively flat. This is a key part of ploughing but is also a required skill to allow the skis to be rotated in the bumps, in short turns, on ice etc. In piste performance a common fault is to drop the outer knee inside the turn in an attempt to find extra edge. This is a weak position and inhibits the ability to rotate the skis to control speed and line

When making high performance short turns on a steep grippy piste, it is not uncommon to feel the skis judder. If the beginner tackles this when learning to plough the understanding of how to manage this judder will be learned at an early stage. An understanding of how edge control affects the feeling of the skis on the snow is relevant throughout all skiing

Plough Turning

Goal

To control speed and line

Terrain

Gentle beginner slope, flatter terrain

Key Fundamentals

Rotation and Edge

Having established the ability to move the skis into a plough, the learner now needs to develop the ability to make turns and control line.

Input to Help Achieve this Goal

- Rotate both legs and feet towards the desired direction of travel to allow the plough and skier to change direction. There will be a natural amount of edge and grip on the outside ski that promotes turning
- Keep the inside ski as flat as possible to allow the direction of travel to change and to prevent it from catching in the snow

Summary: To begin plough turning, rotate both legs and feet to steer the skis.

Top Tips

It can help learners to focus on rotating the flat, inside ski towards the desired destination, allowing the outer ski to follow

A common mistake is to use the upper body to initiate the turn. Remember it is the feet and legs that are closest to the skis and as such they will have a greater effect on turning. What happens to the upper body should be a result of actions lower down

Figure 2.5:
Sequence showing plough turning

Performance beyond the Central Theme

It is often the case that skiers focus too much on the outer ski and fail to steer the inner ski. This is often what happens when a skier has an "A-frame" in short and long turns

Developing Plough Turning

Goal

To control speed and line on steeper terrain or when travelling faster

Terrain

Beginner slope, steeper terrain or with more speed

Key Fundamentals

Rotation, Edge and Pressure Control

Input to Help Achieve this Goal

- With an increase in gradient or speed more pressure builds as the turn progresses. This pressure is created by the edge of the outside ski gripping on the snow and is what enables the skis to turn
- Turn shape becomes more important as a method of speed control. Pressure must be maintained and controlled throughout the arc in order to complete the turn and control speed
- Allow the inside leg to flex as the skis comes across the hill in preparation for the following turn
- When ready to start the next turn, gradually stretch the new turning leg, this will reduce the pressure build up on the old turning ski
- This stretch also brings the skier into a balanced position on the new turning ski, allowing the rotary movements to start again

Summary - Feel the pressure increase throughout the arc, regulate this build up of pressure by stretching the new turning leg once speed is controlled.

Top Tips

At this stage skiers start to experience a little more force and speed which can result in the Centre of Mass falling back. To help combat this ensure the hips are over the feet during the turn transition

It is important to remember that we are not trying to absorb or reduce pressure until speed is controlled. For this reason the outside leg will be more stretched than the inside leg.

The stretch and flex of the legs during the turn is a simultaneous action. It is often referred to as "pedalling"

A stretched leg is not a locked leg. We still need to be able to flex the outer leg if required during the arc, to maintain balance and react to the snow and terrain

Performance Beyond the Central Theme

There is a build up of pressure during any turn, which needs to be managed. A novice skier needs pressure at the end of the turn in order to slow down. When a more skilled skier performs high performance turns at greater speeds, the build up of pressure is released earlier in the arc so as to maintain or even increase speed. However, it is the same movement pattern as used when making a plough turn, the less weighted inside leg starts to stretch. This moves the skier's body across the skis and reduces the build up of pressure on the old outside ski

Mountain Skills

Now that skiers can make turns and control their line, they need some extra skills to help them move around the ski area more effectively. They need to access and move away from lifts, manoeuvre within the line up of a ski group etc. These skills need to be developed for safety reasons but are also useful throughout ski technique right up to the highest level. It is not essential to have learned these before moving forwards to more advanced turns but they will help with development.

Traversing

Goal
To travel across the slope in balance

Terrain	Key Fundamentals
Steeper slope than previously used	Edge

Input to Help Achieve this Goal

- Stand facing across the fall-line with the natural degree of edge tilt required to prevent sliding. The line of the shoulders, hips and knees will be at a similar angle to the slope
- To start traversing, either reduce the edge tilt equally on both skis or start to point both skis more downhill until you start moving forwards
- Balance on the edges of both skis, look forward and control the amount of edge tilt equally on both skis to continue traversing

Performance beyond the Central Theme
Controlling the turning edges of both skis equally and simultaneously is an essential part of parallel skiing. This is often the first time skiers feel the side-cut on the skis and can be a big step forward in their understanding.

Figure 2.7:
A skier traversing a slope

Top Tips

Too much edge angle will result in a carved turn back up the hill. Sometimes this is the result of too much lateral separation at the knee or hip and can also be a result of skiers "hugging the hill" through fear

To help us balance we need to ensure there is the right amount of weight on both skis. There will be less weight on the uphill than the downhill ski. This difference will be more pronounced on steeper slopes whereas weight will be more evenly distributed on shallower slopes

Side Slipping

Goal

To lose height without traversing across the slope

Terrain

A wide, quiet slope with a constant gradient

Key Fundamentals

Edge

Input to Help Achieve this Goal

- From the same starting position as when traversing, simultaneously release the edges and flatten both skis against the snow by moving the Centre of Mass down the hill
- This stops the skis from gripping and allows the skier to move sideways
- To slow the slide, re-engage the edges and generate grip by increasing the pressure and move the Centre of Mass back up the hill

Figure 2.8:
Skis rolling flat to
side slip

Top Tips

As the skis flatten to allow them to slide, move with the skis rather than leaving the upper body behind and falling out of balance to the uphill side

A common fault occurs when skiers fail to control the uphill ski which ends up rolling onto the big toe edge and catching in the snow. Ask skiers to focus on flattening the downhill ski rather than the uphill ski

Performance beyond the Central Theme

The ability to release both edges and stay in balance, with the skis flat on a slope is difficult but is also integral to a successful crossover in high performance turns. For example, in a short turn on a steep slope the skier will be caught back and inside if the body doesn't move with the skis and remain balanced in relation to the slope as the skis are flattened in the crossover. This unbalanced foundation leads to a reduced ability to control both speed and line

Plough Parallel

Goal

To improve control of speed and line by allowing the skis to come parallel at different stages of the turn

Terrain

Leaving the beginner slopes behind, moving towards green runs/easy blues

Key Fundamentals

Rotation, Edge and Pressure Control

Now that the learner can control speed and line in plough turns they are able to move onto steeper terrain. At this stage the skier will start to become more aware of the forces acting upon them.

Input to Help Achieve this Goal

- As speed increases, balance earlier on the turning ski, this allows the inner ski to be steered parallel, reducing the duration of the plough
- Stretching the outer leg helps to release the edge on the inner ski so that it can be rolled and rotated into the parallel position
- The pivot point for the inner ski should be underneath the toe piece of the binding, enabling the skis to become parallel
- Maintain pressure around the arc until speed is controlled, then stretch the new turning leg to manage the build up of pressure and start the new turn
- At this stage the skier's Centre of Mass remains inside the support of the feet during the plough phase but starts to move inside the base of support during the parallel phase

Summary: Balance early on the new turning ski, feel the inside ski change edges and rotate to become parallel.

Top Tips

The plough parallel is a progression in a person's skiing development. It doesn't have to be visited with every learner but to begin with, the parallel phase is likely to happen at the end of the arc. As instructors we should be aware of this in our demonstrations and not match the skis too early for the learner's level of skill

The timing of when we match the inner ski parallel depends on the terrain and the speed of travel. As the skier becomes more proficient, support from the outer ski and the matching phase both happen earlier. This is easier to achieve with more speed

A common problem is when the plough is too wide. This makes it very difficult to match the skis without changing the width of stance. Keep the plough narrow

Figure 2.9:
Sequence showing a plough parallel turn

Figure 2.10:
Sequence showing matching the skis later in the turn

Performance Beyond the Central Theme

Balancing early on the new turning ski is what allows the skier to progress towards parallel skiing by coming out of the plough as the arc progresses. It is this early platform that allows the skier to influence what happens to the skis in higher performance turns. For example, balancing early on the outer ski, when making fast open turns in variable snow, allows the skier to use progressive edge tilt to control speed. Without that platform the skier is likely to tilt later in the turn and hang onto a longer arc in an attempt to slow down or simply tilt and fall out of balance to the inside of the turn

Parallel Turning

Goal

To control speed and line whilst changing edges simultaneously

Terrain

Preparing to take on the whole mountain, moving onto blues/easy reds

Key Fundamentals

Rotation, Edge and Pressure Control

In order to move towards parallel skiing there needs to be an increase in speed. At this stage the skier's Centre of Mass starts to move inside the support of the feet.

Input to Help Achieve this Goal

- By balancing early on the outer ski the skier gains early support at the start of the turn
- Stretch the outer leg to move the Centre of Mass downhill and across the feet. This allows both skis to simultaneously roll onto their edges to initiate the new turn. At this stage the skier starts to feel a larger range of lateral movement when stretching the new turning leg
- Rotate both legs and feet smoothly and in unison to steer the skis parallel around the arc
- Plant the pole as the outer leg begins to stretch to provide support and an aid to timing as the hips cross over the path of the skis

Summary: Balance early on the new turning ski, roll both skis onto their edges to initiate the new turn and rotate both legs and feet to steer the skis parallel around the arc.

Top Tips

Before stretching the new outer leg, ensure that the skier is balanced over that foot. If this is not achieved the turning ski will lose grip

The pole plant helps with rhythm and co-ordination of the movements which is essential for a flowing performance. The pole planting movement should come from the wrist and not the shoulder

The width of the corridor has an effect on the blend of the steering elements and vice versa. It is worth being aware that a narrow corridor promotes greater use of rotary skills, whereas a wider corridor tends to result in more edging, which in turn leads to more speed

It is common for people to rotate the feet too quickly, creating an unbalanced skid. Steering progressively around an arc, like driving a car fast around a bend, will result in a more stable turn

Performance Beyond the Central Theme

In a parallel turn we balance early on the new turning ski rather than pressing it, which can result in the ski being displaced out to the side into a "stem". This can sometimes be the goal when skiing difficult snow or performing certain drills but for the most part it is not an effective outcome. We have a certain amount of pressure at our disposal, due to our body weight and the effects of gravity. How we distribute and position this pressure is more important than trying to create extra pressure. For example, if we try too hard to create pressure in a carved turn on soft snow, we are likely to loose grip and control. Equally, on hard snow, too much effort in creating pressure is likely to create judder and skid

3. BEYOND THE CENTRAL THEME
& THE PERFORMANCE THREADS

Introduction

In this section we will look at each strand in detail and discuss the principles involved to improve in each area. Presentation of each strand takes the following format:

- Outcome – the goals and outcomes we are aiming to achieve in each strand

- Input – what we need to do to achieve a given outcome in each strand

- Top Tips – coaching points to achieve a better performance

- Common Problems – pitfalls encountered whilst trying to achieve a better performance

This section is intended as a guide to supplement your work on the hill with your trainer, where the principles outlined here will be applied specifically to your performance. It does not offer a definitive structure of how to ski.

The Five Strands

The mountains offer an extremely diverse range of snow conditions, gradients and terrain that combine to make skiing a challenging and exciting sport. Whilst there can be an almost infinite combination of terrain and snow types, we are able to divide the mountain into five sections that cover most types of alpine skiing. We call them the strands:

- Piste Performance – Long-radius turns and Short-radius turns

- Bumps

- Steeps

- Variable

- Freestyle

Once confident in all these strands, the skier will have the basic tools to ski the whole mountain and the skilful skier will flow between the techniques required to ski each strand as the snow conditions, terrain and gradient demand.

The BASI Alpine Manual

The Performance Threads

In any sport a performer's level can be enhanced by looking at all the performance threads rather than just the technical thread. In most performances there will be a blockage in one of the threads outlined below that will hold back overall improvement If attention is not paid to the relevant thread, progress will not occur.

For example, if you are learning to climb and you are afraid of heights, no amount of technical input is going to improve your climbing since your performance will be blocked in the psychological thread, long before you reach your technical threshold.

Technical	Te	These icons appear throughout this chapter to indicate points in the text where a certain performance thread is particularly relevant.
Tactical	Ta	
Physical	Ph	
Psychological	Ps	
Equipment	Eq	
Environment	En	

Technical

This is specific to alpine skiing and details the techniques that need to be acquired to perform well in a given strand. A strong technical awareness and understanding is crucial to performing well in any strand, particularly with a view to subsequently teaching other skiers. Technical understanding will be enhanced on the hill during courses and if there are any technical misconceptions or holes in your understanding, you should discuss these with the trainer.

Tactical

Once the skier has a range of techniques at their disposal, careful tactical application of the relevant technique or physical intensity for a given situation, will improve overall performance. In addition, a good tactical awareness of what to focus on and how to practise during the practise phase will shorten the time spent in that stage of learning. References to potential tactical choices will be detailed throughout the technical text.

Physical

This thread covers a large range of variables from biomechanical accuracy to levels of fitness and physical application. References to the physical thread will be included in the text for individual strands and an appendix for further reading is available at the end of this manual.

`Ps` Psychological

This thread contains a large range of subjects from visualisation and arousal levels to psychological thresholds and long term mental preparation. This is an important performance thread, which has a foothold in most sports with the relevant application dependant on the sport. References to the psychological thread are included in the text for each strand but no attempt is made to cover all the aspects of this complex subject. An appendix is available at the end of this manual with a bibliography for further reading.

`Eq` Equipment

This thread covers everything from the hard technical gear of the skis, boots and poles to the software of clothing. If any of the equipment is deficient then the skier cannot be expected to perform well. Any deficiencies in the equipment may not only impair performance but could also affect the safety of the skier.

In terms of performance any specialist activity requires specialist equipment. This is true for performance skiing as it is for ski touring. Having the equipment in good working order affects it's ability to perform to it's potential and therefore allow the skier to reach their potential. Do not neglect this thread. More information on alpine technical ski equipment can be found in Appendix 4.

`En` Environment

This thread concerns itself with how the conditions may affect performance. This can be anything from the type of snow, the particular slope chosen, the weather or altitude. Differences in the environment will potentially have a big effect that will require the skier to make adjustments to the other threads – primarily to the tactical and technical threads. Choosing the correct environment will have a major impact on whether the task is appropriate and achievable.

More information can be found on the effects of the environment in the Mountain Environment section.

Summary

As is the case when breaking any sports performance down into categories, there is overlap. It is rare for one of the performance threads to be of importance in isolation. For example, there may be a technical response to fear (psychological thread), as a skier stems the start of a turn on a slope that is perceived to be too steep. Tactical decisions usually require a technical modification that can only be achieved when the skier is in appropriate physical condition. It is useful to understand the threads as separate entities but in reality it is more a case of prioritising their importance for a given situation, rather than focusing on one and ignoring the others.

Piste Performance - Long Turns

- Two clean lines in the snow
- Effective posture and balance throughout
- Ability to influence the turn radius

Input – How to Achieve the Outcomes

Te Two Clean Lines in the Snow

- Edge the skis evenly to use the sidecut/design of the ski to achieve an arc
- Move your body mass to the inside of the turn to create an angle with your skis against the slope and remain balanced. Use a combination of the main skiing joints (lower limbs, hips, whole body) in order to move inside the turn without losing balance.
- Avoid the temptation to rotate the feet, particularly at the start or end of the turn

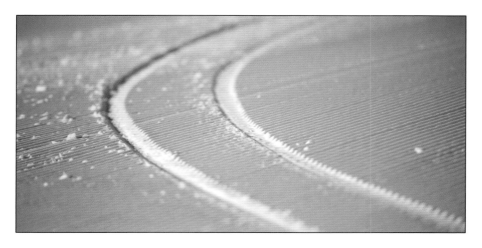

Figure 3.1: Two clean carved tracks

Figure 3.2:
This shows the Centre of Mass inside the arc of the skis. This allows the skier to balance against the resultant forces coming back from the snow.

- Long-radius carved turns use predominantly edging and pressure control from the steering elements, with active rotation almost non existent. The skis should turn along their length without any pivoting occurring
- Edge the skis sufficiently to grip and avoid drifting to the outside of the turn
- As the speed of the turn increases, the resultant forces increase proportionally. The skis must be edged enough and the Centre of Mass must be inside the turn enough, to balance against these forces and maintain a clean arc

Effective Posture and Balance Throughout

- This should remain similar to the basic posture and stance outlined in the central theme
- A posture that employs good skeletal alignment relies less on muscular tension to resist the forces that act upon the skier during the turn. A skeletally aligned posture is less tiring and helps promote stronger more powerful skiing. However, there may be a negative impact on agility which is often an important attribute in shorter radius turns, so the right compromise between strength and agility needs to be found
- Wide enough stance to provide stability at speed, not so wide that the skis tilt different amounts or that the edge change occurs sequentially
- Hip width apart is a good guideline, this may be slightly wider at very high speeds

Balance

- The skier must choose how much lateral separation and how much inclination they wish to use in order to take the Centre of Mass inside the turn without losing lateral balance. Inclination and lateral separation are not mutually exclusive and are used best in combination to find a solution that works for that skier at that speed for the desired turn shape
- A positive pole plant is still desirable for timing and support and can be useful when controlling the rotation of the upper body. Without this control the skier can overturn and/or compromise their lateral balance going into the next turn. However, the pole plant can adversely affect the skier's balance if it is too upright and the skier should be careful not to let this happen

Ability to Influence the Turn Radius [Te]

- Increase the amount of edge angle used beyond the minimum required to grip
- The further the CoM moves inside the skis, the tighter the radius of the turn (providing the skier remains balanced on the skis). A tighter turn made in this way will increase the pressure through the turn until the CoM starts to come back over the base of support
- Remain balanced against the outside ski to ensure that grip and the shape of the arc is maintained. Increasing the edge angle must not be done at the expense of lateral balance
- Use appropriate body movements to achieve the desired amount of edge angle whilst remaining balanced

Body movements that influence the amount of edge angle on the skis are:

1. Whole Body Inclination – The legs and torso incline in an even plane towards the inside of the turn. At high speeds this is a position of strength and good for resisting the pressure build-up that occurs. However, it is less agile and hence slower to go from one turn to the next. At slower speeds it can result in a loss of balance to the inside of the turn.

2. Lateral Separation – This can occur at the hips or above the hips, in the spine and, to a lesser extent, at the knees and involves tilting one portion of the body more than another. Depending on where it is initiated, a laterally separated position can aid agility and speed from turn to turn. It can also aid balance against the outside ski at slower speeds, whilst achieving an increased amount of edge angle. However, it is not as strong or skeletally aligned as inclining.

Inclination and lateral separation are not mutually exclusive and skiers need not choose one or the other. Skiers need to find a solution that works in terms of the outcomes, rather than trying to force a set of movements into the performance. For more information see the piste performance common content and clarification.

Common Problems

[Te] When the turn begins with a rotary movement of the skis or the upper body, the skis skid rather than carving cleanly. Try to replace the rotary movement of the skis with a simple tilt of the skis to the inside of the turn.

[Ta] [Te] A lack of edge angle results in insufficient grip. The skis drift sideways as there is not enough centripetal force to stop the skier from drifting to the outside of the turn. Either the edge angle needs to be increased or speeds need to be reduced during training.

[Te] A desire to influence the turn radius by moving further inside the turn, results in a loss of lateral balance and inaccurate carving. Use the appropriate body movements to come inside whilst remaining balanced against the outside ski. This might mean that the movement inside is performed more slowly or that lateral separation is used to help balance on the outside ski.

Top Tips

En Train on gentle slopes and at slower speeds to feel the edges of the skis gripping effectively without the complications of increased speed and resultant pressure.

Ps **Eq** Try to be open-minded to the radius and shape of the turn by simply edging and allowing the cut of the ski to turn you. If the turn shape is predefined in the mind of the skier, as is sometimes the case when copying others, rotary movements are likely to be made in order to steer the skis onto this predefined path. Edge the skis, trust them and see where they take you.

Ta As the speed builds up, decide where to finish the arc according to the speed you wish to carry into the next turn.

Eq **Ta** Set a corridor width that will suit your skis and the outcome that you are looking to achieve.

Figure 3.3:
Skier influencing the radius of the arc in a carved turn

Piste Performance - Short Turns

Outcomes

- Smooth rounded arcs within a defined corridor, skiing at an appropriate and constant speed
- Effective posture and balance throughout
- Ski steering along its length from early in the turn
- Effective use of the ski design to create a high performance turn

Input – How to Achieve the Outcome

Te **Smooth Rounded Arcs within a Defined Corridor, Skiing at an Appropriate and Constant Speed**

Ta
- Use an appropriate blend of edge and rotation of the ski to produce a round arc which fits inside the defined corridor. The blend of steering elements can vary whilst still achieving an accurate outcome. Different outcomes showing the relationship between the amount of edge and rotation and the resultant type of turn are shown in Figure 3.4
- Both ends of this rotation/edge spectrum can produce very skilful turns. Higher end performers should be looking to ski at the grippy/carving end of the spectrum as well as the skidded end
- Speed control comes from a combination of skidding and the shape of the turn. As the skier uses more edge there is less skid and so the speed control comes more and more from the arc length the skier chooses to make. A longer arc length at a given radius will result in a slower overall speed for the skier

Te **Effective Posture and Balance Throughout**

Posture and Stance

- The skiers posture and stance should remain pretty similar to that outlined in the central theme although there will be significant differences depending on the part of the turn in which it is viewed. Skiers may use a lower stance in order to transition. Lateral and rotational separation may also be used to create an effective turn. See piste performance common content

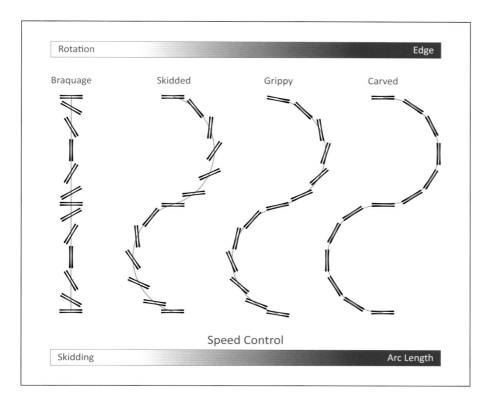

Figure 3.4: Spectrum of turns ranging from purely rotary based turns to fully carved turns

- A posture that employs good skeletal alignment relies less on muscular tension to resist the forces that act upon us during the turn. A skeletally aligned posture is less tiring and helps promote stronger more powerful skiing. However, there may be a negative impact on agility which is often important in shorter radius turns, so a compromise between strength and agility needs to be found

- Stance needs to be wide enough to provide stability at speed but not so wide that the skis tilt different amounts or edge change occurs sequentially. Hip width apart is a good guideline

Balance

- A positive pole plant is still desirable for timing and support and can be useful when controlling the rotation of the upper body. Without this control the skier can overturn and/or compromise their lateral balance going into the next turn

- During a short turn the skier has to choose how much they need to separate laterally in order to stay balanced. At slower speeds separation can help with lateral balance. It must be remembered that during a short turn the need to get out of the turn quickly means that using full inclination will inhibit the ability to get back out of the turn

- Fore-aft balance matching the terrain. As the skis turn down the hill they also tip with the slope. In the fall-line the skis are tipped down the slope to their maximum. The skier needs to ensure that in the fall-line they are standing near perpendicular to the ski, rather than vertically upright. (see Figure 3.5)

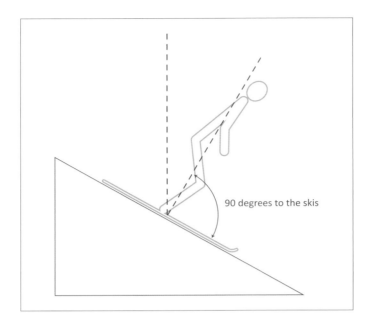

Figure 3.5:
Skier aligned perpendicular to the slope when passing through the fall-line

90 degrees to the skis

All these points above are valid but it must be remembered that the skier has to continually adjust their position relative to the terrain and the forces acting upon them. This dynamic system requires the skier to keep changing and moving. Balance is more about feeling than a picture.

Ski Steering along its Length from Early in the Turn

- Skiers should be aiming to steer around the arc with the tail of the ski following the tip, particularly when seeking to increase levels of performance in the turn

Te

Ta
- The skier needs to stand and balance on the outer ski early in the turn, to provide a platform to steer effectively through the arc. When steering, a tactical decision has to be taken as to how the steering elements will be blended and, depending on the desired outcome, which of these elements will dominate the early phases of the turn

Te We need to understand how the blend of rotation and edging affects the outcome of a turn. As a general rule, edging moves the skier towards the carving end of the spectrum and a higher level of performance whereas rotating has the opposite effect. (see figure 3.4). However this depends on when in the arc these movements occur. A skilful blend and a full understanding is required for good versatile skiing.

Te Consider the examples below to highlight the different effects of changing the blend of edge and rotation. Examples 1 and 2 demonstrate more of a blend whereas examples 3 and 4 use the steering elements in a more isolated fashion.

Example 1: Using predominantly rotation during the first half of the turn, with the edge biting once the skis have crossed the fall-line, will result in a lower level of performance and slower speeds. The ski is turned across the direction of momentum before any effective grip is applied or pressure is experienced. The rotation gives the skier direction, whereas the edge provides a braking effect.

Example 2: Using predominantly edge in the early phases of the turn will result in a higher performance and more speed. However this needs to be performed skilfully and in balance otherwise the edging will inhibit the skier's ability to turn the feet and steer later in the turn. The edge gives the skier more speed but the direction comes later with the rotary movements. See Figure 3.6.

Figure 3.6:
Short Turn sequence
relating to Example 2

Figure 3.7:
Short Turn sequence
relating to Example 3

Example 3: A small amount of rotation at the start of the turn can allow the skier to remain on their edges through the fall-line and exit the arc with a lot of speed. In this case the early rotation has given the skier just enough change in direction to then rely on edging to complete the arc. Too much rotation and the extra change of direction will result in the edge engaging after the fall-line and braking as in Example 1. See Figure 3.7.

Example 4: Relying on edge until the very end of the turn and then rotating will result in a fast entry into the arc and a slow exit. This is often a useful way to ski steeps and ice whilst trying to maintain a decent level of performance.

Effective use of the Ski Design to Create a High Performance Turn

- A modern ski has a sidecut and a flex pattern that contributes to the shape and intensity of the turn. At a high level, a skier needs to harness these attributes to attain the highest level of performance during the turn. Choosing a ski that is suitable for task and the skier, has a massive impact on the quality of performance

- When considering the blend between the steering elements, the ski design will play an important part. A longer-radius ski will require more rotation for the same radius arc than a shorter- radius ski

Figure 3.8:
Shows a skier in transition between short turns on a reasonably steep piste. Notice how in transition the hips are actually behind the feet, but the skier is coming forward as the skis tip down the hill. The tips of the skis are being tilted down the hill as the skier commits forward

Common Problems

Te **Ps** The skier is trying to force performance from the ski through muscular input. Too much physical effort can result in poor pressure control and a loss of balance. To generate a greater force the skier needs to allow the body to be further inside the line of the skis and then to resist the extra force created. By pressing hard on the skis, the skier can only create a force for a short duration and this can be hard to control. Once the skier is standing on the ski earlier, try increasing the speed of descent whilst maintaining the same levels of accuracy and grip from the ski. Then, by coming further inside the turn and resisting, the pressure is created by the turn itself and should be easier to control.

Te Often a skier will lose balance in the fore-aft plane when trying to increase the level of performance in short turns. This can be due to the skier failing to stay centred on the ski when the skis are in the fall-line. Remember that for every turn, the skier must stay in balance relative to the slope, which will see the body roughly perpendicular to the hill. If they don't then they will get caught out of balance with their CoM back. Fore-aft balance can also be lost if the skier flexes both legs simultaneously and rapidly removes all pressure. This often results in the skis shooting forwards with the skier's CoM getting left behind.

Top Tips

Ta It is not possible to follow prescriptive values on the amounts of edge/pressure/rotation required to produce a certain type of short turn. Therefore the overall outcome criteria should be observed closely when determining the validity of a given combination.

Ta When trying to grip early in the turn, try making a slightly longer-radius arc at first, to give the best chance of being able to steer effectively from above the fall-line. Once this has been achieved aim for the same outcome in a narrower corridor. Use funnel drills.

Te Listen to the sound that your skis make on the snow. A short checking sound made at the end of the turn suggests that most grip is during the latter phases. Try and start the sound earlier and thus have it last longer through the arc.

"Sam Snead was a famous American golfer. Golf pros often use the analogy of his name to improve the swing of their students. If a swing is short and snappy it makes a staccato sound in its rhythm - 'Sam'. If the swing is smoother and longer it is more effective and sounds like the longer syllable 'Sneeead'. The same is true of short-radius turns. A short sharp sound towards the end of the turn indicates that the effective part of the turn comes late and lasts only a short time – 'Sam'. Start standing against the ski from earlier in the turn and the effective steering will last longer – 'Sneeead'."

Te It is very easy to build up too much pressure at the end of the turn when trying to create a high performance short turn. Remember that pressure is often linked to the amount of edge angle, controlling this will help to regulate the pressure. So ask yourself "where in the turn do I have too much or too little pressure? What can I do to the edge angle at these points in the turn to affect this?"

Piste Performance - Common Content

This section deals with some of the commonly discussed concepts that feature in high-level piste performance. These concepts can be applied in the context of either short or long turns depending on the desired outcome. While there are often no clear answers as to which method to employ for any given situation, the main principles outlined offer pros and cons to give you some choice as to which inputs to make when aiming for different outcomes. This section is designed to complement the Piste Shorts and Piste Longs section of this manual. This section has a very technical focus, but remember, when applied to the real world and aiming for real outcomes, the technical thread is only important if the other threads allow it to be.

The concepts focus largely on 'Steering' from the Fundamental Elements and the related body movements which affect the steering of your skis. The main areas covered are listed below:

- **Edge Control** – what is it and what methods of control are available to us
- **Control of Rotation** – separate or not, and from where in the body
- **Pressure Control** – the methods used to control pressure
- **Turn Transitions** – How to use the steering elements to create different ways of moving from one turn to the next
- **Long Leg/Short Leg** – Appropriate leg length on the inside and outside skis during the turns

This section will also act as a reminder of the steering fundamentals. Some of the content is repeated from the fundamental elements section as a handy reminder.

Edge Control

To control how we use our edges, the skis and different parts of the body move laterally, relative to each other. Depending on the circumstances of the turn we might focus on moving the body inside the line of the skis, whereas on other occasions it will be more effective to do the opposite and allow the skis to move away from the line of the body. Either way, the end result will be that the skis tilt onto an edge.

The lateral movement involved in creating edge tilt can originate in the following areas.

- The feet
- The knees (this is actually a rotation of the femur in the hip socket)
- Around the hips
- The waist and above (we can separate anywhere in the spine up to and including the neck)
- The whole body

A large lateral displacement of the skis relative to the rest of the body requires that the CoM of the skier travels inside the line of the skis. This requires higher speeds and is a feature of skiing beyond the central theme.

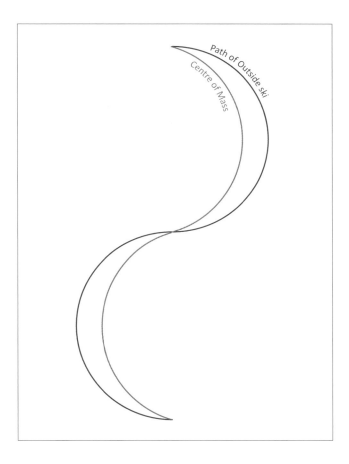

Figure 3.9:
The route taken by the is inside that taken by the skis

It is important to remember that the same movements that control the edge angles will also determine how far inside the arc the CoM travels through the turn. Increasing or decreasing edge angles without changing the position of the skier's CoM will have limited effect on the turning forces (pressure). Put simply, being balanced on the right amount of edge will make the ski grip, but the angle away from vertical of the CoM has a large effect on the turning force (think of a cyclist leaning into a turn, the further they lean in, the tighter they turn). Edge angle alone cannot influence the radius of the turn but also requires pressure and sometimes rotation (see Pressure Control).

Lateral Separation

When some parts of the body tilt with the skis and others don't, we call this lateral separation or angulation. Sometimes we will actively seek to separate laterally and other times it is a natural reaction to the movements we are already making. Often a lack of lateral separation is called inclination and the skier uses all the joints to move inside the turn.

Figure 3.10: Skier showing lateral separation

Figure 3.11: Skier showing inclination

Below are some points to consider when working with lateral separation:

- It takes longer to tilt the whole body than it does just part of the body. For quick changes of direction, as when skiing narrow corridor short turns, it will be more effective to tilt the skis with the legs and keep the body more upright

- Separating laterally can put us in a weak position and may not allow us to maintain the balance and posture necessary to deal with larger forces. So for turns which generate large forces, like high speed carve turns in a wide corridor, we are likely to allow more of the body to tilt with the skis

- A single turn may contain sections with varying degrees of lateral separation. For example a skier may use full body tilt at the start of the turn to create edge angle but then separate laterally from above the waist later in the turn to aid the transition into the next

- A skier who is separated laterally can also incline

	Less lateral separation	More Lateral separation
Benefits	Strong position Good for resisting pressure at high speeds	Quicker from edge to edge Can aid agility Can aid ability to balance against outer ski
Problems	Less agile Can lead to loss of balance to the inside of the turn or a difficulty exiting a turn	Structurally weaker/less well aligned Too much, too early can limit the ability to tilt inside progressively through the turn

It is perceived that there is a choice for a skier to either incline or to separate laterally. This dichotomy is a false one. Skiers can choose which joints to use when moving laterally. They also choose the timing of those movements. Skiers should use the appropriate movements to control the forces and maintain balance.

Figure 3.12: In this example a skier uses less separation at the start of a turn and increases the lateral separation at the end of the turn as he heads into transition.

Control of Rotation

Although rotation is ever present when we turn, rotating the skis alone will not produce a deviation in our line. If the skis remain flat on the snow with no edge grip, they will simply pivot and the skier will continue to travel in the same direction, as in a bracquage turn. Although this can sometimes be useful, for the skier to be deflected from their original path, there needs to be some edge and pressure present.

To demonstrate this point more clearly let us use the simple analogy of a car turning. When the wheels of a car are rotated across the line of the car's momentum it will only turn if the tyres grip the road. If they fail to grip the car will continue to slide in the same direction much like in a bracquage turn. Similarly, when we rotate our skis across our direction of travel, any edge grip will cause the skis to deflect from their path in the same way. Assuming the edges continue to grip then the more the skis are rotated across the line of momentum, the greater the potential turning force – or what we refer to as pressure. This is the case until they are rotated exactly perpendicular to the direction of travel at which point the skis and skier will decelerate and eventually come to a stop. This concept was originally referred to by the Canadians as "steering angles". In modern skiing, steering angles are also created by the sidecut of the ski, which means that even when edge is applied on its own, with no active rotation, a steering angle is already created. This makes modern skis turn more easily.

As the blend of rotation and edge changes, the skis describe a whole spectrum of turns from skiddy to carved see figure 3.13.

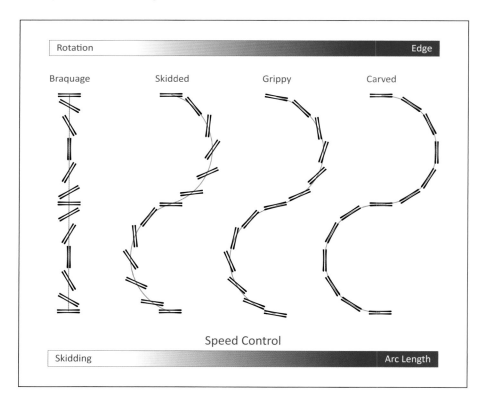

Figure 3.13: Spectrum of turns ranging from fully carved turns to purely rotary based turns

Just as we do when we tilt the skis we have a number of choices to make when we rotate them. Here are some of the options as to how we can rotate the skis:

- The feet rotate alone - minimal effect
- The thighs rotate from the hip
- Hips and below rotate without the upper chest
- The whole body rotates with the ski

These different ways of rotating affect the ease, speed and magnitude with which we can rotate the skis, and how easily we can switch the direction of rotation. Some points of rotation are particularly applicable to certain types of skiing, and other points less suitable.

Rotational Separation

Until now we have limited our examination of rotation to the action of the skis. However, our bodies are turning as well as our skis and this too requires our attention.

When some parts of the body rotate and others don't we call this rotational separation. Sometimes we will actively seek to separate rotationally and other times it is a natural reaction to the movements we are already making.

Below are some points to consider when working with rotational separation:

- It takes more effort to rotate the whole body than it does just a part of the body. This is why it will be more effective to rotate the legs and keep the body facing down the hill when trying to make quick changes of direction, as when skiing a direct line in the bumps
- Separating rotationally can put us in a weak position and may not allow us to maintain the balance and posture necessary to deal with larger forces. So for turns which generate large forces, like high-speed carve turns in a wide corridor, we are likely to allow more of the body to rotate with the skis

Figure 3.14:
The skier separates the upper and lower parts of the body rotationally to move effectively into the next turn

- Rather than thinking of rotational separation as the upper body staying still and the skis rotating, rotational separation also describes any moment when the upper and lower body rotate at different speeds or times. For example: it can be useful to initiate a turn with a strong active rotation of the upper body. This can aid the flow of the body down the mountain and will be linked to the lateral movements as well, which help control pressure and edge. This active rotation of the upper body is often seen in the variable strand to help initiate turns. The timing and range of this movement must be carefully controlled to maintain balance

- In order to initiate or control rotation, the body needs some contact point with the ground. The pole provides the skier with an extra point from which to help him affect the rotation of the body and the skis

- Rotation always needs an axis about which to rotate. With the skier's body close to this axis the skier will rotate faster than when the body is further away. This concept can give the skier extra control over their rotation. Spreading the arms will give more control of the upper body (slowing rotation) than having them tight. Pulling the legs to the chest will allow a freestyle skier to complete a flip faster than remaining in an open elongated position

- Controlling existing rotation will require different movements to creating a new rotational force. A skier may be able to create more rotational momentum from a wide stance than a narrow one. A freestyle skier imparts rotational momentum before leaving the ramp with a wide stance but once in the air the stance may narrow to increase the speed of rotation

Figure 3.15: Strong pole plant aiding rotational separation

When choosing which movements we use to control rotation it is useful to remember that not all parts of the body will take the same line down the hill. The upper body will often take a shorter, more direct route, meaning that it is necessary to have some degree of rotational separation even if it doesn't feel very active.

Staying square to the skis means maintaining the basic stance (see sliding pictures in the Central Theme) relative to the skis, no matter what arc the skis describe. Any turn that is not fully square therefore has some element of rotational separation in it at some point (skiers are often square in one part of the turn and separated in another).

Separation at Lower Limbs	
Good for	• Straight line bumps • Short turns on flat slopes with very narrow corridor
Encourages	• Fast rotation • Small rotational deflections
Discourages	• The ability to deal with a large rotation of the skis or large forces through the skis

Separation at Hips	
Good for	• Shorter turns of medium radius • Squeezing a little more edge angle through the middle and latter part of a long turn
Encourages	• Medium rotational deflections. It can allow a skier to get the hips further inside the turn through the middle and end of a long turn • Can encourage a leading inside ski (split stance) which negatively affects fore-aft balance
Discourages	• The skier from being in a strong aligned position • The ability of the skier to rotate the skis and tilt the lower limbs so freely

Separation above Hips	
Good for	• Faster more powerful turns in a wider corridor
Encourages	• The hips to stay in a strong aligned position
Discourages	• Fast rotations of the skis, the ability to create lateral angle at the hip if the skier stays very square

Totally Square	
Good for	• Closed turns controlling speed through line
Encourages	• Maximum strength • Full closed turns using more width across the hill
Discourages	• Early transitions, fast rotations, line change

Figure 3.16: The advantages of rotational movements originating at different parts of the body.

Common Problems and Coaching Tips - Rotational Separation v Remaining Square

- Turns made in a narrow corridor give us less time to rotate the large mass of the upper body one way and then the other. It makes sense to use more separation
- In tight-radius turns, keeping the body square to the skis will result in the body also having to rotate quickly. It is difficult to control this rotation sufficiently to move into the next turn
- Even in long turns the body does not have to be square to the skis and some rotational separation may help the skier make the transition into the next turn and allow the CoM to travel a shorter distance
- Rotational separation can happen in the lower legs, the hips and from above the hips

Pressure Control

How is pressure created? Pressure results from any action at the ski/snow interface that changes the speed or direction of the skier. We feel pressure when we are turning, when the terrain causes us to change direction (heading over a bump or through a hollow), or when we slow ourselves down using rotation and edge.

How to Control Pressure

- **Creating turns using Rotation and Edge** - Will lead to pressure, the greater the turning effect (or slowing effect) the more pressure we feel. This links with the simile used in rotation of the car turning its front wheels. As long as the skis grip then the more they are rotated across the direction of travel then the more pressure will be created and the tighter the turn will be
- **Distributing Pressure between the Skis** - This allows us to have more pressure on one ski than the other. This ability to change from one foot to the other helps us to move laterally and use pressure to initiate a new turn. This movement pattern, often referred to as pedalling, is used from the central theme right up to high-level skiing. The movements of extension and flexion in the legs assist the skier to move laterally and change the distribution of overall pressure.
- **Distributing Pressure along the Skis -** Changing where we stand along the length of the skis can have a huge impact on the pressure under the skis. As well as changing our basic posture and point of balance, having more or less pressure at the tip or tail of the skis can affect their performance. For example: On the piste, more pressure fore or aft will tend to cause that part of the ski to grip more at the expense of the other end. In deeper snow, fore-aft pressure can control where the ski travels within the soft snow, either dipping down or rising up
- As mentioned in the edging section, so long as the skier remains in balance the pressure will increase as the **skier's CoM moves inside the arc** of a turn. In the same way, pressure will decrease and return to body weight as the CoM returns over the feet. Whatever movements a skier needs to make in order to take the CoM inside the arc and stay in balance are therefore also pressure control movements. These movements will be in the lateral plane and will be similar to those used to control the edge angle of the skis

- **Controlling Pressure directly through Extension and Flexion -** This is possible through a fast extension and flexion of the joints. Imagine standing on a set of analogue bathroom scales. You can make the scales read a higher weight by extending the ankles and knees quickly. However, do this quickly enough and you will jump, and when you jump the scales will read no weight. To do the reverse, stand on the scales as tall as you can and then flex quickly. The scales will read less weight until you reach the limit of flexion and then the scales will read a higher weight than normal. The limitation of trying to directly control pressure with flexion and extension is that you can only do it for a short amount of time and for it to be effective the movements need to be fast (they actually require an acceleration of mass). So although extension and flexion of the joints are common movements within skiing they do not necessarily control pressure. They may provide a useful means of controlling pressure in turns of short duration impulse but we need to be realistic about how much extension and flexion can directly control total pressure within turns of longer duration and certainly when performing the Central Theme.

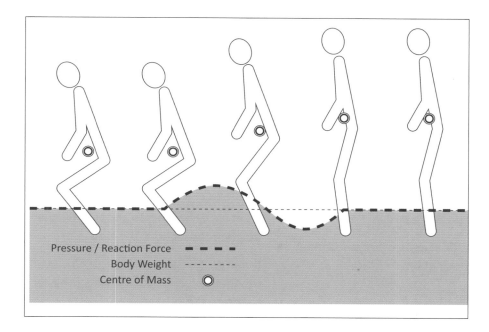

Pressure / Reaction Force
Body Weight
Centre of Mass

Figure 3.17: Pressure control through flexion and extension

All the above mechanisms control pressure, but they do not act alone. When they are used together they don't necessarily reinforce each other, it is the net sum of their actions that will determine the actual pressure on the ski.

Common Problems and Coaching Tips

- It is often suggested in modern skiing that we stand on both skis equally in piste performance. Whilst we are looking for two clean tracks in long turns and like to see the skis turning equally at the same time in long and short turns, it is not true that we spread the pressure equally between the two skis. The way the pressure is spread between the skis depends upon the snow we are skiing and the gradient of the slope. Generally, the harder the snow and the steeper the slope, the more important it becomes to favour the outside ski

- Resist the temptation to always try to control pressure through extension and flexion movements. This section shows how pressure can be created and controlled through a variety of different mechanisms and a single approach to this steering element is not sufficient

Turn Transitions

To get from one turn to the next the skier needs to be able to change the steering elements so that the skis go from one set of edges to the other. The pressure in one turn needs to be released so that it can build in the new turn and the skier needs to be able to use rotation as and when necessary.

There are different ways to make this transition from one turn to another but there are some common outc omes that help us to achieve performance skiing in the piste performance strand:

- Standing in balance on the new outer ski early in the turn
- Adopting a suitable posture so that the movements required to edge and rotate the skis are easy to execute and come from a suitable joint

	Low Transition	High Transitions
Benefits	Faster edge change Flexing the legs at the end of the turn allows the skier to take the edge angle off the ski more easily There is less unnecessary movement in the vertical plane	Slows down the edge change and can make building a platform at the start of the turn easier It encourages skiers to adopt a stronger position throughout the turn It makes it easier to keep the hips over the feet, which in turn makes it easier to rotate the skis If done deliberately, then a fast and vertical transition can unweight the skis which will allow the skier to rotate the skis very easily
Problems	Hard to build a platform and stand on the ski at the start of turn Flexing the legs too fast at the end of the turn means the pressure is often released too fast, making the transition difficult to control	If done too fast or in the wrong plane, then a high transition can lead to an unwanted unweighting This type of transition can encourage movements that are extraneous to movements in a lateral plane

Figure 3.18: Table showing the differences between low and high turn transitions

Often the transition is talked of in terms of high transition (cross-over) or low transition (cross-under). In reality the skier has a choice as to how high or low they stand during transition, but for our purposes we will look at each of the extremes to gain an understanding of their benefits

Overall, we can summarise that the skier is looking for a change in the lateral plane to execute the transition. If movement in the vertical plane begins to hinder an effective transition then the skier has probably gone too far to one end of the spectrum.

Long Leg/Short Leg

From the plough turning phase of the central theme there is a movement pattern which can be described as pedalling or an alternate flexion and extension of the legs. This movement pattern helps skiers to make the transition from one turn to another.

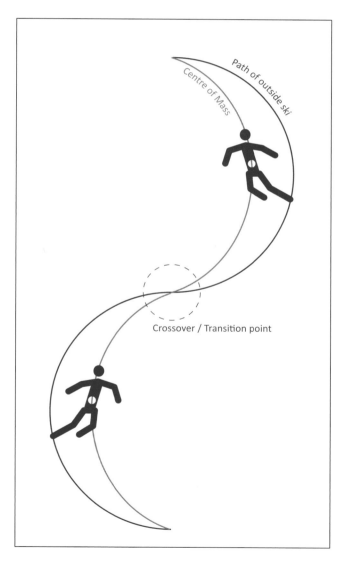

Centre of Mass

Path of outside ski

Crossover / Transition point

Figure 3.19: Turn transition when skiing at speed, with the path of the skiers Centre of Mass relative to the path of the skis

At speed, when the skier tries to influence the radius of the turn, the edge angle becomes higher and the skier allows their body to come inside the turn to a greater degree. It is necessary that the inside leg becomes shorter and the outside leg stays longer, as it is required to resist most of the force. However, if the leg is straight or braced, then the skier loses the ability to make small adjustments vertically to keep the skis tracking cleanly (like the suspension on a car when running over a slightly bumpy surface). Having a straight leg also means the ability to use the lower leg to vary the edge angle is restricted, and so the skier is limited to using the hip or the whole body. A long leg, not necessarily a straight leg.

Figure 3.20: Skier showing the Centre of Mass well inside the arc using a blend of the skiing joints

Conclusion

This chapter has looked in more detail at some of the concepts and words commonly used in performance skiing. It refers specifically to the piste performance strand but the concepts themselves are relevant to all the stands and will be used across the mountain.

Hopefully, by going in to more depth on these topics, we will have a better understanding of the terms we use and a greater understanding of the link between inputs and outcomes. By understanding this link, we are able to find our own solutions to performance skiing and can base our skiing and teaching on a solid platform of knowledge, rather than a shaky platform of dogma and unquestioning repetition. With this in mind, we should aim to build our knowledge so that any gaps are filled and any errors corrected. The contents of this manual should be subjected to your review and not just accepted without question. This way our knowledge and understanding will continue to grow.

Bumps

Outcomes

- A continuous speed
- The ability to ski a variety of lines including a fall-line descent
- Maintain effective balance and posture that allows the skier to match turns to the terrain
- Flow from one turn to the next no matter what task is set

Input – How to Achieve the Outcome

A Continuous Speed

There are at least four different ways to control speed in the bumps. The ability to use all of them as appropriate will allow the skier to chose any speed they wish, on any line, in any bumps field and is likely to result in a flowing performance. However, it must be remembered that not every method of speed control will work in every bumps field. For every bumps field it is a major tactical skill to be able to choose the correct speed control method for the correct place, whether skiing open bumps or in a rut line.

Speed Check

- To achieve this, the skis need to be rotated across the direction of travel and then the edge applied quickly in order to slow the skier down quickly. In some circumstances the skier may be able to use the soft snow of the bump itself to control the speed, in this case the edges are used less and the base of the ski impacts the soft snow. The skis can only rotate easily where there is space for them to turn without making contact with another bump. Typically a skier will use the top of the bump, the face of the bump, one of the shoulders or the col in between troughs. Care must also be made to stay in balance over the skis laterally, so that the skier does not fall into the mountain with this rapid decrease in speed. It is also important that the skier separates rotationally, so that the skis can quickly be turned back down the hill in order to continue with the run

- Skilful skiers will be able to apply a speed check that does not interrupt the overall speed and flow of the performance

Skidding Down the Back of the Bumps

- This is similar to the edge check method of speed control but involves a less sudden application of edge. This time the edge is applied very gently, so that the skier begins to slide down the back of the bump with the skis across their direction of travel. Again, the ability to rotate the skis easily is determined by the skier's position on the terrain. By pivoting the skis in suitable places and then scraping down the steep shoulders of the bumps, it is possible for the skier to travel very slowly. Occasionally it may be necessary to traverse or side slip at an angle, in order to reach the next appropriate place to pivot the skis

Arc Length

Ta
- Just as arc length can control speed in piste performance, it is also a major method of speed control in the bumps. In open bumps it is possible for the skier to make an arc all the way around a bump and begin to come back up the hill. This controls speed in the same way that it does on the piste, the longer the skier holds on to the arc, the slower the skier will travel

Pressure Control

Ph
Ta
- Skilful use of pressure control needs to be employed to strike a balance between absorbing the bump and slowing the skier's progress through muscular resistance. Imagine running down the stairs or a steep hill. A braking effect is achieved on each step by using muscular resistance as the pressure builds. This slows the progress of the CoM down the hill. This method is mostly used in high speed bumps skiing, where the pressure experienced is higher. The skill level, physical strength and timing needed to achieve this is considerable

Ps
- Whilst these are the main ways of controlling the speed in bumps, they are rarely used in isolation. A skier does not have to pick one method of speed control and stick to that. As skill levels increase and as the skier becomes psychologically more confident, the desired speed will increase. This is likely to require a mixture of these methods to enable this higher level of performance

Ta The Ability to Ski a Variety of Lines Including a Fall-line Descent

Figure 3.22 shows the variations on a direct line through an open bumps field. Depending on the size and spacing of the bumps, the skier can choose between any of the lines and switch between them if they are tactically aware of the line ahead. Below the key features of each line are highlighted

Direct Line Descent

Ph
- This is a fast line that uses predominantly pressure control to manage speed. It is difficult and physically demanding

Ph
- The timing of the flexion and extension movements used to control the pressure needs to match the terrain

Figure 3.21: The sequence above shows a high level skier taking the direct line

- It is important to note that whilst the line of the skier's feet down the hill is direct, the skis are still turned across the fall-line to a degree to match the terrain and offer some degree of speed-control. A direct line does not mean the skis take a straight line down the hill. See Figure 3.22

- There is a large range of movement with flexion in ankles, knees and hips. The feet and the body are travelling in separate directions (rotational separation). Speed control is through pressure control and a quick check on the face of the bump

- Full and rapid extension in time with the terrain and speed. The skis travel a path that follows the terrain up and down, even if the skis lose contact with the snow. There is some lateral displacement of the skis, even on this straight line

- The skier regains a position ready for another impact, the feet are slightly forwards and across the hill

Outside Line

- The skis move in a wider arc, out from and back across the body

- The skis follow the trough or the outside camber of the rut, rather than descending the back of the bump

- Even within a fall-line descent or a rut line, there is the possibility to use a little bit of skid in order to stop the skis accelerating as fast as they would otherwise. This uses a little of the skid method, so that the ski is slightly across the direction of travel and a little of the arc length method, so that the skier begins to move laterally across the hill. As the line becomes rounder, the skier can actually steer the skis to avoid the deepest part of the trough, which as a consequence makes pressure control easier

Inside Line

- The skier turns high on the bump inside the main trough and uses the back side of the bump as an opportunity to skid and scrape. Skidding is the principle method of speed control. The skier still finishes the turn on the front of the next bump in the same place as when taking a round line but approaches from inside the arc. This line is generally less smooth but offers more opportunity to control speed

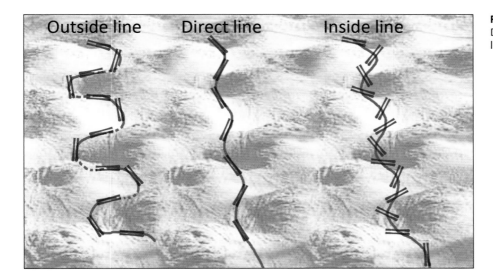

Figure 3.22:
Different options of
lines in the bumps

Non Fall-line Descent

- It is possible to ski any set line through a bumps field, from a giant slalom line to an hourglass shape, to funnels and cones. The difficulty of the task will depend upon the speed of the descent and the size and spacing of the bumps. Pressure control and choosing where and how to change edges will be some of the major tactical and technical decisions that the skier needs to make

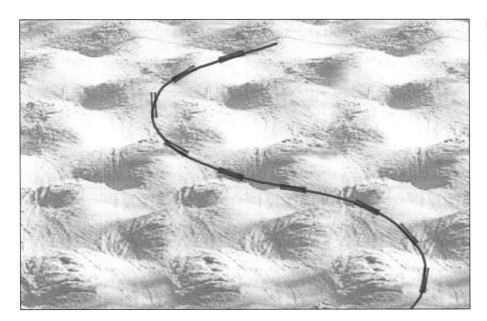

Figure 3.23:
Non fall-line descent
in the bumps

Maintain Effective Balance and Posture that allows the Skier to Match the Turns to the Terrain

Posture and Stance

- From the basic stance and posture of the Central Theme, the skier may wish to use a narrower stance to aid the speed at which the skis can change edges and to ensure that the skis don't encounter vastly different terrain to each other
- The skier needs to be standing in a balanced position on the skis to be able to flex in every joint with a large range of movement. The skier may require a straighter back and a position that allows the feet to come up in front of the hips
- Pole plant is essential. Be careful where on the bump you plant your pole. Planting on the face of the bump can knock the skier off balance when travelling faster

Fore-aft Balance

- Once the skier is making contact with the bumps in a bumps field, fore-aft balance becomes a lot more interesting. The skis will no longer be travelling along a plane slope but will need to match the contours of the bumps themselves. The skier must allow this to happen through flexion of the main skiing joints at the ankle, knee and hip. These movements also allow the skier to control the pressure that builds up as they make contact with another bump on their journey down the hill
- Fore-aft balance can be maintained through skilful steering. It is as important to keep the feet under the CoM when moving, as it is to keep the CoM over the feet

Lateral Balance

- Whilst bumps skiing often focuses on fore-aft balance and the movements associated with this, many skiers lose balance in the lateral plane. As mentioned above, there are lines that are ski-able in which lateral movement is very important. Just like on the piste, to make a lateral displacement the skier needs to be subjected to a force that moves them laterally and then to deal with this force. This means that when making arcs in the bumps, a lot of the technical content for the piste performance must not be forgotten. See Figure 3.25

 Flow from One Turn to the Next no matter what Task is Set

- Flowing from one turn to the next requires us to match technical performance to the tactical approach. It is easier to flow if the skier is confident in the bumps and enjoys skiing in this strand. It is also easier to flow if the method of speed control does not just involve the checking approach or the full skidding and scraping approach

Figure 3.24:
From side on it is clear to see the flexion in the knees and hip whilst maintaining an upright upper body. The feet are slightly in front of the body to achieve this

Figure 3.25:
Showing lateral movement in the bumps requiring balance and movements more associated with piste skiing

Top Tips

Te A closer stance has a few benefits within this strand. It increases agility, can allow faster edge changing and prevents the skis running separately over very different terrain, which makes controlling both skis at the same time difficult

Ta Using skidding and checking as the major ways to control speed does not favour a flowing, smooth performance. Try not to limit yourself to these methods of speed control

Te A strong pole plant is a great way to aid balance within the bumps strand. Make sure that it is helping and not hindering the performance. Play with the timing and positioning of the pole plant. Try delaying the pole plant until reaching the top of the bump or even the back side, this can aid timing and smoothness through any line that you ski

Te Accurate body management is important to offer the best chance of staying in balance. Keep the limbs within an imaginary rectangle around the body, with the arms in front, (not being left behind) and avoid extreme lateral or fore/aft movements with the legs

Common Problems

Ta Not picking an appropriate line for the terrain ahead

Ta Thinking that a fall-line descent means that there is no turning involved

Ph Skiing a line that is too physically demanding for that skier. This is both a tactical mistake and a lack of physical ability to achieve the chosen line. Rounder lines, even within a fall-line descent require less range and a slower rate of flexion and extension movements, although there does have to be a greater range of lateral movement

Steeps

Outcomes

- Flowing performance showing good control of speed and line
- Effective posture and balance throughout
- A high degree of ski performance

Input – How to Achieve the Outcome

Flowing Performance Showing Good Control of Speed and Line

In many ways the technical and tactical approaches to skiing steeper terrain are similar to those used on the piste. The methods of speed control are the same as those highlighted in the Fundamental Elements section. However, a steeper gradient demands an increased awareness of speed control:

- Skidding is a good option on the steeps. To achieve this we must use an accurate blend of steering elements. Looking at the diagram featured in short turns piste performance (see figure 3.13) the safest option is to start at the skidded end of the spectrum, using predominantly rotation at the start of the turn and only move towards the carved end if the speed is still controlled

- Checking is another method of speed control, often employed on steep terrain during higher levels of performance. Checking involves rotating the skis across the skier's direction of travel and then quickly increasing the edge angle. The skier needs to be very accurate, with the skis being perfectly across the direction of travel. If they are not then the skis will accelerate. Checking will slow the speed of the skis, but the body should continue to flow down the hill across the skis, facilitating the next edge change

- Depending on the gradient the performer will need to consider how to initiate the turn. A primary goal is to turn the skis sufficiently and early enough to avoid picking up too much speed

- At a basic level when the skier has a low level of technical ability or is psychologically anxious, they can initiate the turn with a stem which involves rotating the outer ski before the inner ski. Although it will inhibit a flowing performance, it is safe and can be used at any level to get the performer out of trouble

- If the snow is hard and smooth, the initiation can look similar to the initiation of short turns on the piste. The rotary steering element is likely to dominate the initial phases of the turn and the skier may choose to change edges in the air, either through jumping clear of the snow or retracting the legs to initiate the turn. Either way the skier will place the skis back on the snow on the new set of edges

- If the snow is heavy or cruddy, the need to employ an airborne edge change increases, since it becomes harder to rotate the skis on the snow

- If the gradient is particularly steep, there is no real need to jump up to gain air underneath the skis, the performer only needs to jump out from the slope. This can be aided by jumping from the top foot and retracting the lower leg to gain extra height if needed

The approach the skier has to a steep slope both tactically and psychologically will determine the outcome achieved. Getting this approach right takes a clear head and some experience.

Ta

- If the performer chooses to ski with a high degree of ski performance, they run the risk of the skis accelerating from underneath them. At lower skill levels, skiers can over-edge the skis in the illusion that this will slow them down. In fact a ski that grips early in the arc will accelerate especially on a steep slope. In these instances the performer may have the technical skills to ski skilfully down the slope but is tactically naive

Figure 3.26:
It is important to remain in balance whilst airborne, to ensure control when landing

- Conversely if a skier uses too much braking, they may not be skiing to their full potential and will need to focus on a different thread to raise their level of performance on steeper terrain

- Because steep slopes can be intimidating, skiers are often psychologically inhibited which can have a significant effect on performance. Instinct can often cause a skier to lean back, or rotate the upper body into the hill in an attempt to grip. Skiers need to be mentally prepared to ski a steep slope

Effective Posture and Balance throughout

Posture and Stance

- As in other strands, the performer must be relaxed, alert and responsive, which is reflected in the stance. A wider stance may help the skier to feel the edges grip whilst remaining stable on steep terrain
- Agility is an important factor on the steeps and there may well be increased amount of flexion and extension to change edges and land softly. A stance which finds the right balance between agility and stability is essential in this strand

Balance

- When performing short-radius turns, rotary separation at the hips or waist will occur, this will allow the legs to turn independently of the upper body. This is important to ensure the upper body remains quiet and relaxed and avoids any balance issues caused by poor control of rotation
- A positive pole plant will offer support to the skier, both physically and psychologically, whilst descending a steep piste
- Fore-aft balance can be maintained through skilful steering. It is as important to keep the feet under the CoM when moving as it is to keep the CoM over the feet. To achieve this, the skier must skilfully blend the steering elements, too much edge too early in the arc will allow the ski to accelerate and risk leaving the skier in the back seat, too much braking can result in the upper body pitching forward over the skis
- On hard snow the skier will need to focus on keeping the weight on the downhill ski at the end of the turn. This will probably require some lateral separation. This is less important in soft snow as the weight can safely be spread between the skis

A High Degree of Ski Performance

Once the skier has sufficient control over their speed and line, it is time to increase the level of ski performance to get the most from the run. This is done in a similar way to short turns, with the performer standing against the ski earlier in the turn using edge to grip earlier. Here are some key considerations for high performance short turns on the steep:

- The edge change may be airborne, so the skier must place the skis on the snow accurately before any effective edging can take place. The earlier they can regain contact with the snow, the earlier the option of achieving grip

- The skier will need to use skilful control of rotation in the early phase of the turn, more so than on a shallow gradient
- Because of the gradient a skier will naturally edge the skis more at the end of the turn, relative to the slope which is falling away underneath him. However, this edging needs to be married to the right amount of rotation, to ensure the skis are turned sufficiently across the fall-line to control speed
- Any increase in descent speed with a subsequent deceleration will increase the amount of pressure in the system. The skier must therefore be prepared to make moves that will control pressure loading as smoothly as possible. A greater range of flexion and extension movements can control pressure directly if necessary and will allow the edge angle to be varied at will, further controlling the pressure build up and allowing a smooth entry in to the next turn

Common Problems

Ta **Te** Over edged skis that accelerate from under the performer. This could be due to a lack of tactical awareness, technical inability to flatten the skis and skid, or as a consequence of anxiety. Whatever the cause, if the skis grip early in the arc or unexpectedly, without the skier making the requisite movements to stay in balance, it will leave the performer in the back seat. Time spent recovering balance before the initiation of the next turn will spoil the flow of the descent

Ps The flow of the performance is inhibited through hesitancy. Often the first turn is the hardest to execute and once momentum is taken from one turn to the next, the edge change is made easier. If the performer is anxious they can often hesitate between turns, effectively making each turn like the first one. In this instance, it is important to stress to the performer that the turns do not need to be any faster, they just need to flow from one to another

Ph **Te** Inability to separate. Control of rotation is a key skill for skiing the steeps and performers who are rotating the whole body to turn the skis, risk turning into the hill, which often results in a loss of balance and a delay at the start of the next turn. Control the upper body

Ps Leaning into the hill. For psychological reasons, skiers can often 'hug' the hill and lean their upper body into the slope. This can result in a loss of grip on the lower ski. Don't do it, especially on hard snow. Find a positive way to achieve this. Instead of trying not to lean in, maybe concentrate on actively leaning out. Narrow the focus of the skier so that the fear does not take hold

Top Tips

Ps Ensure that you have the necessary skill sets before putting yourself in the pressured and often intimidating environment of steeper terrain. Typically this will involve the ability to rotate your skis accurately and separate in a rotary plane. Ensure that you are confident at skidding, checking and everything in between

Ta If unsure of the slope, it is often a good tactical approach to start with a fairly conservative blend of the steering elements (more rotary skiddy turns) and increase the degree of ski performance as the run progresses

Ps Be psychologically prepared. Raise your arousal level to a suitable point and mentally rehearse or visualise your descent. Having a strong focus of attention is also important (see psychology section)

Ta Good skiers looking to make a flowing performance should be aware that too much side slipping or checking, makes it harder to achieve a flowing run. Aim for rounded turns

En **Te** **Ta** All skiers should be aware that on steep terrain, away from the piste, the snow is likely to be changeable. Skiers should not expect to make the same movements in every turn and will have to adapt to the terrain and the snow to maintain control

Variables

Outcomes

- Ski curve to curve using a variety of turn radii
- Effective posture and balance throughout
- A high degree of ski performance

Input – How to Achieve the Outcome

Ski Curve to Curve using a Variety of Turn Radii

To achieve this outcome in the variable strand, a lot of the technical content is very similar to piste performance, especially when the snow is hard and smooth. On this type of snow we can use a similar technical approach as we do on the piste and make any shape of turn from short turns to long turns.

Te When the snow is softer the technical approach will have to change in order to match the consistency of the snow:

- In the soft snow, the skis can tilt up and down within the snow pack along their own length. Letting the tips tilt down in the snow pack may result in a submarine effect and a fall forwards, tilting the tips up may lead to the entire ski coming out of the snow and the skier skiing on their heels. Whether this is appropriate or not really depends on the steepness of the slope and the depth and heaviness of the snow. Keeping the tips slightly out of the snow can allow the skis to run a little faster

- In soft snow the skier does not have to be so precise in building a platform, before moving inside the turn at the top of the arc. The forces coming back from deeper snow are less immediate than when on a hard piste, therefore the skier can afford to move inside quickly without the pressure building up too suddenly as it might on the piste

- If the skier decides to have the skis edged and away from the body (as described in the point above) before building a platform, then it is possible to perform transitions that would result in a loss of grip and balance, if performed on the piste. Two types of turn transition commonly used in variable conditions are, changing edges in the air from a rebound and an airborne edge change from retraction

En • In soft snow, very often bumps will start to form, which can also offer more opportunities to make different types of edge change. Jump turns off terrain features and compression turns over the top of the bumps can be achieved more easily than on a smooth piste

Ta • If the skier is capable of the different approaches to turning as outlined above, then it comes down to a tactical choice as to which type of turn to perform and at which point in the run. Matching the turn to the terrain is one of the greatest skills of an experienced and strong variable strand skier

• Because the deeper snow found in the variable strand exerts forces on the skis in different ways to those found on the smooth piste, skiing the variable strand can be a very physical experience

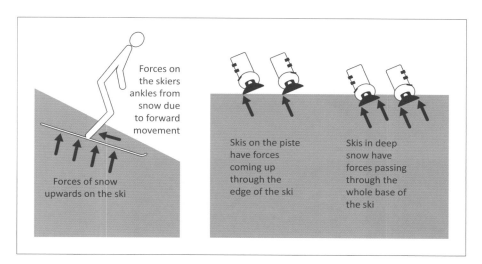

Figure 3.27: Diagram showing some of the forces experienced by a skier in soft snow

Ps Being able to resist and overcome these forces will allow the skier a greater choice of turns using all of the steering elements. Time spent in the correct conditions, as well as a good level of specific fitness, will allow skiers more time and ability to work on the technical issues

Te ## Effective Balance and Posture Throughout

This will depend upon the forces that are affecting the ski and the type of snow the skier is skiing through. However, generally the same principles apply in the variable strand as they do in piste performance

Posture and Stance

• This will be similar to the basic stance and posture from the Central Theme. The feet can be closer together if the snow is soft, as explained later. The skier may also feel the need to move their CoM towards the heels in the boot, especially in heavy snow at slower speeds

Fore-aft Balance

- If the snow is heavy and the gradient low, the skier may need to lean back in order to get the skis to travel a little faster. This will result in a weaker posture due to poor alignment of the joints, and the skier will quickly become tired. A better option would be to make a tactical choice to ski a straighter and faster line, assuming the skier is psychologically happy to do this. At a faster speed the skis will float more easily and the skier will be able to come back to a centred position and adopt a more effective posture

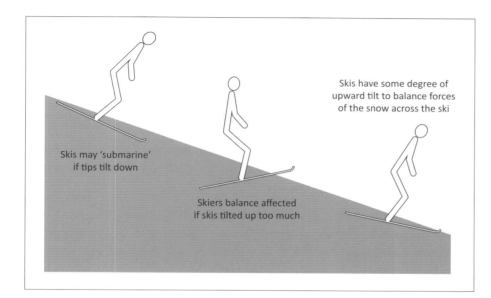

Skis have some degree of upward tilt to balance forces of the snow across the ski

Skis may 'submarine' if tips tilt down

Skiers balance affected if skis tilted up too much

Figure 3.29: Fore-aft balance in deep snow

Lateral Balance

- To balance on one ski in soft snow is difficult at slow speeds, as the single ski will tend to sink into the snow pack. This makes managing the steering elements very difficult. To avoid this, the skier may need to spread the weight between the two skis and try to keep the skis at a similar height in the snow pack. Generally there is less emphasis on the outside ski in the soft snow as the skis will grip easily and the forces required to turn a skier do not have to come from a hard edge but can come through the base of the ski as well. As the speed increases, the skier may feel confident enough to place more emphasis on the outside ski and adopt a technique closer to those used on the piste

- A narrower stance can help in soft snow, especially at slower speeds. It will help the skier spread their weight evenly between the skis, ensuring the skis remain at the same depth as each other in the snow pack. This is important for effective lateral balance

- A pole plant will help enormously to maintain balance and initiate the turn

A High Degree of Ski Performance

Eq This comes from using the ski as it is designed to be used, as explained in detail in the piste performance section. Using the sidecut and distributing the pressure accurately along the length of the skis will help to get the most out of the equipment. The design of the ski will have a large influence on the proportional sizes of the forces generated in variable conditions. For example a wide ski will result in more float, a narrow ski less so.

Top Tips

Ps **En** For skiers less used to skiing variable or soft snow, it is really important to choose the terrain properly so that there is enough speed for the skis to float but not so much as to introduce too much fear

Ta When the surface underneath is lumpy, try to feel the bump underneath to help you time your turns, don't fight the terrain

Ta Remember that deep, soft snow will make it difficult to rotate the skis. Carry a little speed and drive the skis around the arc rather than turning them so fast that a lot of snow has to be pushed sideways by the whole length of the skis

Te Better to do a little a lot rather than a lot a little. Although it is necessary to spread the weight between the two skis to remain in lateral balance, the spread of this weight is subtle and subject to constant variation. It is better to make a lot of little movements rather than wait too long to make an adjustment and then make really large movements

Te If you need to get the skis out of the snow to change edges, then pushing down quickly will often result in the skis coming back out of the snow easily. The rate at which this movement is performed depends on the depth and consistency of the snow. If the skier then turns the skis as they re-enter the snow and drives them around the arc with the pressure increasing, the rebound will again happen for the next edge change. Keep doing this and those elusive rhythmical short turns are yours

Ta To keep the feet and skis doing the same thing at the same time in the soft snow, try to leave a single track in the snow, not two

Eq Big baskets on powder days

Common Problems

Eq For lower-level skiers in the awareness and early practise phases, using the appropriate equipment can make a big difference. In soft snow the wider the ski the more flotation the skier will have and the easier it will be for the skier to turn

En As the terrain changes, the skier needs to predict what will happen to their speed and to the forces that are acting upon them, so they can be ready to change their position on the skis and maintain balance

Ps To cope with all the adjustments necessary during a descent, it helps to be strong in the core. A weak middle means that the extremities are more likely to be out of control

Freestyle

Snowsport instructors work in a global market, freestyle is proving to be a large part of that market and BASI instructors are expected to be able to lead recreational skiers safely in to this area of the sport.

Freestyle encompasses activities for the park and pipe, flatland and open mountain skills. The Fundamental Elements are as valid in the freestyle strand as anywhere else. Freestyle is characterised by large ranges of body movement and high levels of agility. Breaking down the movements needed to create a trick, using sound biomechanical principles, means that freestyle should not be an area into which we are scared to venture.

Most freestyle activities are specialised and require appropriate training and a clear progression for learning. The vast majority of the activities are easily learned and can add a lot of fun to any skier's day, who has reached a performance level beyond the Central Theme.

The aim of this section is to introduce freestyle's basic themes and to give some guidance on how to approach freestyle for yourself and your clients. Freestyle skiing will improve your all round performance and increase what you can do on a pair of skis.

The structure and layout of this section is a little different from how the other strands are presented. As freestyle remains an area where most instructors have a shortage of teaching experience, this section focuses more on teaching and teaching progressions, than is the case for the other strands.

NB: Twin tips and protection for the Park will make it more fun and safe for all.

Flatland

Outcomes

Flatland is about performing a variety of tricks on a smooth slope. This is an important part of freestyle in its own right but also serves as excellent preparation for both the Park and the Pipe.

Input – How to Achieve the Outcomes

Ollie

Use strong fore-aft movements. Rock fore-to-aft and then use the spring from the tails to pop up. Use a strong core, push and pull up from the legs to pop higher.

Nollie

Use strong fore-aft movements. Rock aft-to-fore and then use the spring from the tips to pop up. Use a strong core, push and pull up from the legs to pop higher.

Nose Press/Butter

Rock forwards onto the tips (lifting the tails off the snow). Keep the legs together and fully extended. To butter (spin): pre-wind by turning the upper body in the opposite direction you intend to spin, and as you rock into the nose press rotate into the spin.

Tail Press/Butter

Rock backwards onto the tails (lifting the tips off the snow). Keep the legs together and slightly bent. To butter (spin): pre-wind by turning the upper body in the opposite direction you intend to spin, and as you rock into the tail press rotate into the spin.

180

Scissor the legs and feet by sliding one backwards and one forwards and allow the hips and shoulders to turn side on. If the left leg is behind, spring up and allow the legs and lower body to rotate 180 to the left. Try to land flexed and low over both skis. Shoulders and head shouldn't need to move from where they were side on. (Scissor right to 180 right).

Switch 180

Scissor the legs and feet by sliding one backwards and one forwards, allow the hips and shoulders to turn side on. If the left leg is behind, spring up and allow the legs/lower body to rotate 180 left. Try to land flexed and low over both skis facing forward down the hill. (Sissor right to switch 180 right).

360

Make a small plough shape. pre-wind by turning the upper body in the opposite direction you intend to spin and then push strongly off the inside edge of that leg. Rotate the upper body as you push up, tuck up and allow the head, shoulders and legs to come round 360 degrees.

Park - Jumps

Parks feature man made jumps of varying shapes and sizes that are used by snowboarders and skiers. The jumps are designed with a take-off and landing area, to make taking air safe. The most common shapes are listed below:

Tabletop - a flat area that must be jumped over to reach the landing following the run in. A tabletop can be any size but the important aspect is to jump far enough to reach the landing slope.

Gap - this is similar to a tabletop but instead of having a flat area between the take off and landing, a gap is dug out. This means that you will hit a wall if you do not cover the distance between take off and landing.

Hip or Spine - imagine a Toblerone packet lying on the snow directly down the fall-line, the end that faces you has a take off. You choose whether to land on the right or left side, or even at the far end. Hips are safe to jump as the landing is long and you can choose to go a short distance or a long distance.

Quarterpipe - this is one wall of a half-pipe, designed so the rider jumps and lands on the same slope. It can be placed down the fall-line like a half-pipe wall but is often found at the end of a park so that you hit it straight on.

Guidelines for Jumping

It is important that we can introduce our clients to jumping in a safe and controlled way. These guidelines outline some simple principles to follow when introducing people to jumping. Go and have a look at the jump with the client and discuss the following:

a) how far they must travel in air
b) knuckle of jump
c) landing slope

The run in speed - Ski in a straight line from the point above the jump, where you will be travelling fast enough to clear the gap to the landing zone. The client doesn't need to jump but it is important that they are psychologically prepared to run in at the correct speed in a relaxed manner.

Take off ramp - Have the client look at the amount of "kick" (how much the jump will throw them backwards on take off). Have them take off their skis and face uphill on a slope roughly the same angle. Then get them to practise hopping up hill and landing balanced again. If they jump "on the spot" they will fall back on landing – this is what is likely to happen on the jump unless they react. You need to "pop" (jump) up and forwards to compensate for the kick off ramp you are jumping off.

Air time - to remain balanced in the air ask the client to push their arms/hands forwards and tuck up. This will keep them stable in the air. Get them to practise doing this with skis off or by pulling up one leg at a time with skis on. Emphasise that they should look for the landing zone whilst in the air.

The knuckle - Point out the point where the gap/table finishes and the landing zone starts and stress the need to clear this to land safely.

The landing - Landing softly is key, extend the legs out and then absorb by bending and staying centred.

Watch some other park users on the jump and point out all the above points. Wait until the client is ready, feel free to ski away and come back later if they are not confident.

Do's for Jumping

- Ensure there is a clear landing beyond the jump
- Make sure that you have a friend to make sure it is clear to land on the other side
- Ensure there is a suitable run-out after the landing area

Don'ts for Jumping

- Stand and explain everything on the top of the jump
- Wait beneath a jump
- Attempt a blind Jump

Safety for Jumping

At all times safety is a priority. It is easy for a group of clients to become too ambitious and over excited, leading to increased risk. Ensure you set safe boundaries for all teaching sessions, activities and post session practise recommendations.

Figure 3.30: A well performed jump requires a balanced position at take-off, in the air and on landing

Inputs for some Basic Jumps

Straight Air

Watch some other skiers and judge the run in speed. When you run in stay flexed, don't turn, as this will allow you to judge whether you need to start from higher up or lower down on the next attempt. Push up/forward off the transition "pop" and tuck your legs up. Keep arms forward and look at where you will land. Extend legs before landing and absorb on impact.

Grabs

Pull up with your legs so they come in close to your body. You should not have to reach down too far – if you do you'll lose balance in the air. At first, just try grabbing the ski anywhere and holding on until you need to let go to land. When performing any grabs with the legs to the side, use the other arm to counter balance whilst in the air.

180

Ski into the jump in a scissored position (see flatland). Pop off the lip on your edges and this will help the spin to start immediately. Allow the legs to come around as you spot the landing – turn the shoulders and head at end to land facing back up at the jump.

Switch 180

Ski into the jump in a switch scissored position (see flatland). Pop off the lip on your edges and this will help the spin to start immediately. Allow the legs to come around as you spot the landing. Push the hands forward and absorb landing with legs/body.

360

Ski into the jump in a small plough shape. Pre-wind and then push strongly off the inside edge of that leg (i.e. pre-wind right / push off right leg). Rotate the upper body as you push up, tuck up and allow the head, shoulders and legs to come round 360 degrees.

Park - Pipe

Outcome

Pipes are U-shaped gullies built in the snow like skateboard ramps, they were originally built for snowboarding. The idea is to take air out of the top and make a trick. The beauty is being able to link several tricks on one run down the pipe.

Pipe Terminology and Etiquette

Pipes are built in different shapes and sizes but all have the same basic components:

Flat Bottom - The base of the pipe.

Transition - The curved part that links the bottom to the wall.

Vert - The vertical section of the wall that ensures you go up and not out of the pipe.

Coping or Lip - The edge at the top.

Pipe Etiquette

- At the top of the pipe, wait your turn and call 'next' or 'dropping in' to signal you are entering the pipe
- Try to avoid destroying the vert/coping by entering the pipe lower down and skidding or falling on it
- If you fall, continue your run but be aware of riders coming down behind you. You should let them pass if they are close to you or moving faster
- Do not begin a run in front of someone who has called out his or her intention to enter the pipe

Inputs for a Progression to Taking Air out of the Pipe

Ride the Walls of the Pipe

Aim to take a line down the pipe and ski up the wall on your edges. Hold the carve until you feel the line up the wall slowing you down. Keep pushing against the wall, feel the skis flatten and turn the shoulders down the pipe. Let the turn happen on the wall, change edges and ride down the wall and across the flat bottom - repeat on other wall.

Pumping Transition

Push the skis forward and through the curved transition at the bottom of the wall. Keep extending legs into the wall so you don't compress. This will start to help you accelerate through the transition and maintain speed.

Getting Air Above Lip

Take a line down the pipe and ski up the wall on your edges. Pump the transition and hold the carve all the way up the wall. As you reach the lip keep the legs strong and move the shoulders/body down the pipe wall. If you have enough speed you will now be airborne. Keep the legs tucked and look for where you want to land back on the pipe wall. Extend, land and ride pipe wall as before.

Dropping In

The key to really getting air is dropping in. Ski on the top of the pipe wall with some speed. Lift the ski nearest the pipe wall and step into pipe. Try and push yourself forward and land close to the top of the wall. Keep your line and momentum down the wall and across the pipe. You'll now have more speed to take air out of the pipe.

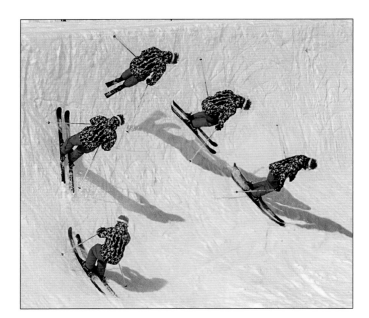

Park - Boxes & Rails

There are boxes and rails in the park, of all sizes and shapes. There are lots of different tricks we can perform but a good place to start is with a basic grind.

Outcome

To grind rails and boxes in balance.

Inputs – How to Achieve this Outcome

Begin by finding the "green" level box that should be flat to the ground and wide enough to fit both skis onto easily in a straight run. You should explain to your clients how easy it is to slide on, plastic top of the box. There will be no chance they can grip with their edges for balance. At first take some straight runs over the box (known as "50/50") and ensure the client skis parallel. kids will want to snowplough, make sure they know to keep the skis together!

Once they've been over the boxes a few times like this, you can introduce a basic "grind" where the skis travel sideways across the box instead. The key to a grind is to rotate the body from the under the ribcage. So the hips and legs turn and the hips and feet can stay square. With this movement you can then stay flat on the skis and balanced over both feet without falling back. It may look as though a lot of skiers try to edge when grinding but you must ensure the client aims for flat skis. You can practise this on firm snow, ridges of snow, anywhere really so they get a feel for jumping into this position. Get them to try and lift the uphill ski and still be able to slide on the downhill ski. They are going to want to lean away from the box, get them prepared to reach forward and stay over the downhill ski.

- When they are comfortable with the previous step, practise jumping onto the box and landing with skis 90 degrees across the box. You don't have to slide along the box just land in balance. Pull the client along with their pole and get them to sink and feel the right position to balance

- Gradually increase the speed of the run in – this will dictate how far you slide along the box

- If things go wrong, explain that they can ski off the box in the direction they are facing, by hopping up and turning the skis into the fall-line. BUT if they feel themselves continuing to spin on the box simply point the feet uphill and come off backwards

Grinding boxes and rails is all about the "balance" you have on the box or rail. Avoid the thinking initially that – "the faster I go the easier it will be" - as the lack of grip on the box or rail will only serve to have you fall back… onto the box or rail!

Once you are happy on an easy wide box, use the same technique for the other boxes or rail features. The only major difference will be the need to balance better under foot and adjust to the shape of the box or rail.

4. BIOMECHANICS FOR SNOWSPORTS INSTRUCTORS

Introduction

Biomechanics can help us understand, analyse and teach snowsports technique with more accuracy, authority and confidence, focusing on function not style, and mechanism not method. Presented here is an introduction and overview of this useful ski science.

Skiing and riding can be thought of as a control and guidance activity, sliding down on a varying surface. The challenge is to play with gravity and the snow, using our riding equipment, so that we positively affect and control where and how we move. We need, by learned experience, to change and control our speed and direction effectively, by creating and managing external reaction forces from the snow, the snow is what turns us. Biomechanics can give us the understanding of how we do this, how we, as individuals, interact with our equipment, the snow and gravity to create and control our speed and direction. With modern equipment it is much easier to carve and we

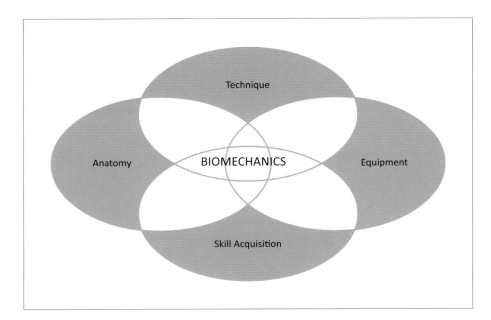

Figure 4.1: Biomechanics can be divided into four aspects, each one interacting with the other

have increased the forces acting on our bodies but, the fundamental technical principles were and still are basically the same. The best skiers make the same fundamental movements, the laws of physics and human anatomy have not changed. We extract from the snow the reaction we need, to change direction and balance against to ride.

Biomechanics is the scientific study of the structure and movement of the human body, using of structural & functional anatomy and mechanics, the branch of physics that involves analysing the actions of forces. Put simply it's the science of sports technique and its acquisition, and is therefore something that underpins everything that we talk about as snowsport instructors.

How is a Sport Analysed Biomechanically?

There are two approaches used to study biomechanical aspects of sports movement, quantitative and qualitative. The quantitative approach is more scientific and is concerned primarily with measurements.

Figure 4.2: Example of a quantitative biomechanical assessment – Foot pressure and forces recorded quantitatively, measured in real-time, combined with video recording during skiing

Biomechanics looks to provide objective information through the use of mathematics, 3D computer simulation, telemetry and other technical data gathering devices. Access to accurate data helps to eliminate the subjective assessment associated with the qualitative approach and provides a more precise analysis. The qualitative approach is used extensively in basic coaching and during the teaching of sports skills. It relies on the coach or instructor's accurate understanding of how the body moves and works.

So what use is Biomechanics to you?

Many sports coaching and educational systems identify biomechanics in their documents and training but often this involves using examples from sport to try to teach science. It is in the interest of coaches to use biomechanics to help explain their sport rather than using their existing sport specific knowledge to explain biomechanics. It is important for sports instructors explain why we use a certain technique rather than using that technique to demonstrate a certain biomechanical principle. As a coach or teacher you will be expected to explain to your clients why a particular movement pattern will help performance. You will need to be able to interpret technical ideas and articles and see beyond a doctrine of do it this way because that is our way.

It is the responsibility of the teacher or coach to understand how the equipment as well as the body works to reduce the likelihood of injury, and to improve performance. This also requires a commonly understood and agreed terminology so that terms such as inclination, separation and angulation bear the same meaning and implication from one individual to the next. The ability to think clearly and visually and to then use accurate language and clear descriptions is what enables the teacher or coach to impact on performance. Consequently, as teachers or coaches, we need to develop our appreciation of how biomechanics affects performance in our sport and increase our understanding of how our body works when subject to different forces. However, what is also essential, is that we do not automatically start using scientific terms and make delivery overly complex. The science is there more for the teacher than the client. Quality coaches and teachers have a depth of technical understanding and are able to communicate important ideas in an effective way, without using complicated language.

Now, to change direction effectively we need to be able to change from using the skis/board tilted on one side of us to the other we need to change edges skilfully. In biomechanical terms, the start of a turn is when the body crosses the skis. The turn is divided into 2 phases – when the lateral, ground reaction forces are downhill and when they are uphill - with an approximate ratio of 40/60. Interestingly, long term training has the effect, on experienced skiers, of minimising the difference between the quality of turns to the right and left, but lateral dominance still equips most people with better control of one side of the body. The dominant side in people is around 90% right-handed and 2.5% ambidextrous, with over 80% favouring their right leg. Consequently, when asked, most skiers say they prefer to turn to their left, with the right leg being the dominant one in completing the turn and dealing with the highest loads. So, when even national team members of the Czech Republic were tested on a symmetrical carving course, the duration of the right turn was seen to be considerably shorter, with a longer initiation and shorter steering phase (and with less forces) than in their left turns. The preferred side was consistently used for both speed control and direction where the turn on the non dominant leg was used for direction only, even at this level.

Technique knowledge is one thing, but the capacity to see through baggy clothes, habitual movement patterns, accepted practise etc. is when biomechanics and a deeper understanding of movement analysis come to the fore. The most important body segments to be aware of are our feet and legs operating effectively on the boot / binding in order to use the boards, as this is where we transmit and manage forces. Of course skiers can also press ski poles against the ground and these actions can affect our movement too – for good or bad.

Because the board base is so slippery, the reaction from the snow, the reaction force, will generally be at right angles to it, so being able to balance and move in & out of balance, in this plane when inclined, is very important.

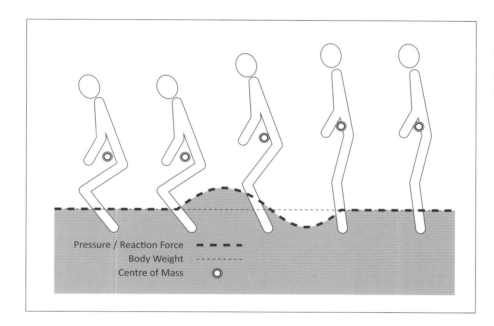

Figure 4.3: Reaction force change, in relation to body-weight, with simple leg-extending

Within the figure:

Pressure / Reaction Force — — — —
Body Weight - - - - - - - -
Centre of Mass ◎

How is Biomechanics being used in Snowsports Today?

The term (bio) mechanics has been used in snowsport instruction for some time. The British team has used biomechanical analysis to improve performance and the subject is something of a growth area in sport in general. However, in common with most sports, biomechanics has largely been either left out of coach education, or has been limited to a learning of definitions and facts that nobody really uses effectively in their teaching.

Too often "biomechanics" is used as a fashionable tag to explain sport techniques in an attempt to justify existing systems and ideas. This is using biomechanics as a drunk uses a lamp post – for support, not illumination. With a little knowledge it is possible and human to argue for your belief or assumptions as fact. It is also easy to claim biomechanical ideas support opposing views and for instructors to get things back to front. Here is an example, the principle of action and reaction encapsulated in Newton's 3rd law will show contrary effects if the performer is not in contact with a supportive resistive surface (the ground) compared to if they are. Hence, rotating the arms after take-off on a snowboard or skis will have the opposite effect to if the same action had occurred before take-off.

There are many traditionally used but mythological facts that are handed down from coaches to trainee coaches to performers and even to the general public. For example, tall people cannot

Figure 4.4: Instinctively swinging the arms anti-clockwise in an attempt to check/slow down rotation of the body/skis which are rotating in the same direction

accelerate as fast as short people, short people are inherently more stable than tall people, gravity will make larger riders go faster, or even that there are four planes of movement. To quote Bode Miller, "Just because everybody believes it and keeps repeating it doesn't mean it is true." A quality coach or instructor should approach information with an open mind but also with a degree of scepticism. We should be myth-busters rather than following blindly what is passed down by others.

The Austrian reverse shoulder or counter-rotation technique in alpine skiing, or the French projection circular have a basis in finding or enhancing forces to assist the turning of relatively long, poorly shaped skis with low torsional stiffness. They are also techniques born from emulating the best gate-racers of that time. This early type of biomechanical analysis is another example of fitting biomechanics to a technique rather than using the science to understand and develop an effective performance model, useable by all. Using the current world champion as a model template requires care. The world's best are not generally average or normal but often have extremes in their make up such as Usain Bolt's physique or Hermann Maier's strength that lesser mortals would be ill advised to try to copy. There may also be certain style elements that are not significant to performance and effort to change could be counterproductive e.g. Paula Radcliffe's nodding head. The two historical national techniques mentioned above have some justification, but to teach these movements as a technique for all could lead to overuse of the upper body. The fact that something is observable does not necessarily mean one should tell people to actively do it. We should be striving to effectively manage the forces that act upon us, this requires an understanding of how we create and react to these forces.

What the Research says about Biomechanics in Snowsports

Injury Prevention

The average fall rate is 1 in 5 jumps during freestyle snowboarding, with an increased fall rate found for spinning manoeuvres, especially backside spins. A key factor to be aware of here is landing with the board not orientated to the fall-line and catching the opposite edge, leading to a violent trip and head injury risk. Studies have shown that children and adults fall twice as often as adolescents and young adults, with falls of 32% and 24% respectively in terrain parks or half pipes. Interestingly, although the downhill-arm has been found to be the most commonly injured upper-limb in snowboarding generally, the up-hill hand is the most common body part to make first contact with the ground during falls from jumps (a consequence of the high proportion of jump falls being in the direction of the tail and heel-side edge of the board).

The change in ski equipment from traditional, to carving skis, seems not to have significantly influenced injury occurrence in skiing generally although male experts have suffered a slight increase in knee injuries. It is possible that the shorter and more manoeuvrable mass-market skis have benefited slower skiers.

Knee injuries though comprise approximately a quarter of all ski injuries, and 10% of all injuries in snowsports are injuries to the ACL, with women more susceptible than men. In a comparison of the top 30 skiers, an injury rate of 50% for ACL injuries during 25 years of competitive skiing was found. Also 26% of Austrian, female racers age I5-18yrs, have had at least one ACL injury. Performing sensory-motor (balance control) training, actually in ski boots (fixed ankle joint) has recently shown to enhance early and more powerful, protective activation of muscles around the knee (especially the important hamstrings) in the event of forces that are tending to displace the knee forwards.

There is no evidence base though that aerobic fitness per se is significant in performance or injury, or that skiing skill is founded on traditional conditioning factors, but knee injuries have been related to deficits in muscular strength. There is moreover, some evidence that eccentric muscle strength is important with increasing speed, and in beginners. This was more recently refined to proportionate strength and coordination of the muscles crossing the front and back of the knee. Even in GS ski turns the eccentric phase for knee extensors lasts twice as long as the concentric phase and the eccentric action of the outside leg exceeds that of the concentric activity. Modern slalom technique produces minimum knee angles of less than 60 degrees and high muscular activity corresponding to low knee angles. Moreover, recent studies suggest that the muscle activity in slalom and GS are much closer than expected, suggesting the efficacy of recent ski regulations needs further thought. Maximum eccentric contraction by knee extensors may in fact be a limiting factor for the speed at which gates can be passed in racing.

It may also be interesting to note that, currently, in boarder cross the start is a critical, factor in the race (similar to short sprint races). In this case, power in the core (particularly in women) and the arms, for the start technique have been shown to be important, but otherwise high levels of fitness and strength have not been shown to be the determinants of competitive performance.

Race Turns

With modern equipment technique has changed subtly compared to the days of traditional straight skis. This has impacted on coaching and training methods and has allowed athletes to generate larger forces when turning.

One recent aim in ski racing has been the equal loading of both skis during turns to optimise glide and minimise the decelerating effects of friction. However, the ground reaction forces are not necessarily or normally equal. In fact modern skis do not require us to share our weight evenly between the two, during most of the turn there will be more force acting on the outside ski. Before we can attempt the relatively difficult objective of optimising glide we need to make sure we can balance effectively on the outside ski. There is a greater emphasis in using both skis with modern equipment in terms of steering rather than pressure. Equal edge angles are often the goal of good technical skiing but this should be considered a way to help improve performance rather than a requirement of good skiing. The edging angles of the inside and outside skis are not normally identical during a carved turn, and the outside ski is more bent in deformation. On the outside ski the centre of pressure is in front of the binding and more forward leaning causes a higher deformation (which in turn may overload the shovel cutting the surface resulting in increased friction and slowing the skier). In a study, Norwegian Europa cup racers were found to be positioned (centre of gravity) approx 10cm behind the outside ankle joint at turn start, and rapidly move forward to approx 18cm forward of the ankle joint through the initiation, but move back prior to the gate and through to turn end.

In race turns, the phasing of the turn is advanced relative to the positions of the gate marker flag and the turn shape is more like an ellipse or a parabola in GS. The GS race turn is a turn getting tighter (the theoreical maximum carved radius is approximately equal to the Side-Cut Radius) or less tight, i.e. it is not a long circular turn. The widest part of the turn is above the gate with a rapid rolling off the edge on passing the gate, which allows the turn to open out rather than continue to tighten (see Figure 4.5). Recently, as ski regulations for racing have changed and courses cannot be cleanly carved throughout, some old skills (steering and drifting) have again become more important.

Good performers deliberately topple and flow from one turn into another. As indicated initially, turns are normally evaluated by the teacher/coach using a visual estimate (body geometry and desired outcome), often augmented by (2D) slow motion video analysis, according to the teacher's education and experience. The view of the teacher or coach is often from the perspective of the bottom of the run, with most performers dependent on guidance from these evaluations. The question is, from this perspective, how precisely can one evaluate the true technical effectiveness of the skier?

A study of the variables used by ski coaches in GS to analyse an individual turn and its speed, tend to be, inclination of the body, angle of the shoulders, heights of the hands, hip angulation, outer lower-leg angle, ski distance apart, distance of the inner ski from the gate. By measuring these accurately in 3 dimensions it was found that the faster turns did exhibit the following qualities, when considered at the point the skiers head was aligned above the turning pole: greater inclination of the body (and shoulders), greater angulation, smaller outer leg angles and larger ground distance between the skis.

Figure 4.5:
Herman Maier,
World Cup GS,
Adelboden

So what Biomechanics do you need to understand as a Coach or Instructor?

Recent experience in instruction and instructor education has shown there is a need for clear appreciation and emphas s on the following areas in alpine skiing:

• Assessing posture and functional alignment

• Releasing and increasing edge angles (tilt)

• Accurately blending tilting with flexion

• Thigh and hip rotation (with appropriate upper body balance / complimentary movement)

• For-aft movement of the feet through the turns

For example, when, where and why would you teach inclining versus angulating and what do these terms actually mean? Freestyle coaches in particular, will need a good biomechanical appreciation of considerations like `moment of inertia` and impacts in jumps, twists and somersaults. The following is an overview of the biomechanical concepts that underpin BASI's technical and teaching courses and those you will come across in technical literature.

Key Biomechanical Principles

Your segmented body provides you with opportunities to use muscles and bones as levers to create and control your movement. Holding ourselves rigid with fear, inexperience or in a pose is against how the body was designed as a vehicle for movement. However, the freedom and opportunity to move, that your non-rigid body provides, requires that you develop the ability to control this movement. This is why the learning of sound movement patterns (technique) and the appreciation of some core stability is important to riders. Here are some concepts that inform snowsports technique.

Posture and Stance

Keep in mind most that people do not have perfect posture or perfect symmetry. Posture in riding will be effective when you use your skeleton and muscles to best apply forces and manage the forces built up during sliding and turning. This will be a dynamic (changing) posture. Being well aligned or "stacked" helps you to remain effective and safe, but it is not a position. In snowboarding we might say it is the arrangement of the body parts so that the forces from the snow tend to pass through the centre of gravity and produce an intended movement. Generally speaking, the body is most efficient and stronger when in a taller stance, where the spine and legs can transmit most of the forces through our bones with the minimum work for the supporting muscles.

In skiing turns, especially on steeps this will mean some use of countering with the upper body, although being overly flexed, bent and twisted at the waist, or indeed rigid, is neither most effective, efficient or safe. If the performer is tense the hips or the upper body may have to produce the rotation required to turn.

Stability

Your stability will vary and can be manipulated. It depends on five factors:

1. The size of the base of support (bigger is more stable)

2. The height of the centre of gravity above the base (lower is more stable)

3. The position of the centre of gravity over the base (centred is more stable)

4. The amount of grip you have (more is better)

5. The size of the mass (more is harder to move)

Being centred over the base in a wide stance and flexed provides stability (e.g. a speed skier on the Flying Kilometre) but this is not always the goal when riding. Being overly stable can seriously compromise your agility. There is a constant trade off and decision process at work between the ability to move quickly and the ability to remain stable. In general terms you use a wider and lower stance for stability and a narrower stance for changing direction (although this does not always equate to the narrowest stance, would a goalkeeper stand for a penalty with feet together?).

Figure 4.6: A well aligned stance, where the structure of the lower skeleton provides much of the support for the forces acting against the skier

Centre of Gravity

The term centre of gravity refers to the simplified model of the body shape, representing the whole body as a single point where the force of gravity can be assumed to be acting. Although gravity is the motive force that pulls us down the mountain, keep in mind there are important forces that are acting away from the centre of gravity. For example there are key forces at work where the skier makes contact with the snow that allow us to balance, slow down, change direction and stop.

Forces

A force can be thought of as a push, pull, strain or exertion from one object on another. In BASI we often talk about pressure rather than force. You are already familiar with the force called your weight, as a consequence of the pull of gravity and centre of pressure along the ski/board, but equally as important are the reaction forces that are at work all the time when riding and your feel for them. Reaction force is a key concept in snowsports, it is the response exerted by a second body on the first e.g. the snow slope against the board/ski. Skiing and riding is about manipulating the ski/snow and pole/snow reaction forces. Any reaction is equal in size but opposite in direction to the applied force. Simply put, the more you press on the ground, the more reaction you will get in the opposite direction, so long as the surface you are pressing on is resistive enough. We need to be able to compress the snow to support us and gain enough grip not to break the contact. In snowboarding the rider can twist the board to extra positive effect, as well as tilt, rotate and apply pressure.

Figure 4.7:
The reaction to any action is equal in size and in the opposite direction – Newton's 3rd Law

Internal Forces

These are the forces operating inside the rider system, inside the body, the boot, the binding and the board(s). The skier can use muscles to press their feet against the boot and skis and press poles against the snow to create external forces on themselves. The muscles of the foot and ankle in the boot are heavily relied upon as are the muscles which protect the knee and back. The effective use of the hip joint, with its accompanying internal and external rotator muscles for thigh turning is equally important. To ensure the forces are transmitted and managed effectively and efficiently there is a need for strength in and around the joints which links to the significance of appropriate core strength. On steep terrain the tendency is for anxiety to create a stiffening of the legs, making flowing into the turn very difficult. In snowboarding for example, anxiety can cause the rider to turn and lock into a heelside position with the board well up on edge. To release, the rider needs to move the centre of gravity across the board, usually by having to use an extreme movement of the upper body as the legs are too tense to subtly release the edge and move into the new turn.

Skiing Muscles

The tibialis anterior (shin muscle) and the gastrocnemius (calf muscle) are very active in the lower leg for fore-aft balance. All of the major muscles of the knee (the quadriceps and hamstrings) are key players in knee flexion and extension during turns, especially in bumps. An important guideline that helps to protect against the commonly occurring injury of the anterior cruciate ligament (ACL), is that the strength of the hamstrings should be upwards of 70% of that of the quadriceps. Further, the gluteus and core muscles are used for stabilizing the pelvis and spine during turns. These then are the muscles that create internal forces to apply to the ski and to effectively manage external forces.

Momentum

Momentum is a measure of how much motion there is. It is the product of the mass of the body and its velocity.

Mass is a measure of matter (substance) and indicates the amount of inertia, which is the resistance to change of a body's motion.

Velocity (as opposed to speed) is a measure of the speed and the direction of the body.

Momentum is what we call a `conserved` quantity, it is constant (unchanging) until some force acts upon it. Gravity is at work to increase momentum as we travel down the hill. Larger or faster skiers/riders have more momentum and need more force (and thus strength) to change direction or stop than smaller or slower riders/skiers. The body's acquired momentum acts against the turning ski/board pressing it into the snow and requires the performer to control this reaction.

Net External Force

In mechanical terms, there are two interactions to consider, one between the board(s) and the slope and one between the board(s) and the skier. But what actually turns the board(s) and performer? Well, the performer can rotate the board(s) underneath them, but to create/ride a curved path, the snow has to produce the lateral forces to turn the whole system, by appropriate management of contact between the board(s) and the slope. The net external force is the overall force or the sum of all the forces on the body. In a schuss, for example in the Flying Kilometre, the effect of gravity will keep accelerating the skier down the slope until the air resistance becomes large enough to equal this external force and then the skier will stop accelerating, reaching what we call terminal velocity. At this point there is no net external force as the forces all balance out.

Angular Motion

This refers to simple motion around a curved path. This could be a freestlyer spinning around their own axis, or a skier on a curved arc. During a carved turn there are ways you can influence the curve by varying the size and direction of the reaction force using edge and pressure control. When moving slowly angulating becomes important to create grip at greater edge angles while still in balance. Compare turning on a bicycle at slow speeds versus leaning over at higher speed with and without turning the handlebars.

Centripetal Force and Centrifugal Effect

A net external force is needed to keep something moving in a circle or along a curve. This creates a centrifugal effect which is a sense of being thrown to the outside of the turn. You create the centripetal (literal meaning "towards the centre") force through the interaction of the ski with the snow, and by moving your centre of gravity inside the turn whilst tilting the skis on edge.

Figure 4.8:
The main external forces at work when skiing

If the net reaction force you generate is directed through your centre of gravity then you are `balancing` through the turn. The degree of inclination / angulation you need to adopt will depend on the speed and radius of the turn. In simple terms, if the force providing the centripetal effect is removed then the body will continue in a straight line – visualise the release of a sling shot. In riding (skiing or boarding) it is a little more complex, because your centre of gravity is away from where the ski forces are applied. If you suddenly release your edges completely and remain balancing, you will slide in a straight slide.

During a turn and as you accelerate down a slope you need to continue to incline your centre of gravity inside the path of the skis/board, otherwise you will not maintain the centripetal force required to keep you moving in a curve. It follows that when you desire to end one turn and start the next, you need to remove the centripetal force that is producing the current turn, flatten the outside skis/board and start the process again in the opposite direction. Without the edge gripping in the snow it is impossible to create centripetal force and hence impossible to turn around an arc. It is worth considering here what happens when a skier/boarder uses pure rotation (no edge at all) to turn. This is the aim of braquage turns or can sometimes be the chosen technique in certain types of mogul skiing or even when in a very narrow gully. In this instance there is no arc and arguably no turn. There is simply a pivot which changes the orientation of the equipment.

Acceleration

A change in velocity is referred to as acceleration whether it is speed, direction or both that changes. In racing there is little point in having the fastest speed gun reading if your line (direction) means that you are the slowest to the bottom of the hill. Consequently speed and direction must be optimised. Our velocity is affected by the direction in which we release the body's mass at the transition of a turn (when we change the reaction force). A common problem in high performance skiing is when the racer releases too late and fails to harness the full benefits of acceleration via gravity and the slope. This means the direction of movement is overly across or back up the hill as opposed to the usual goal of down the hill. With the intermediate performer, a more common problem may be to release too early and not `finish` the turn, this will result in a lack of speed control.

Impulse

Impulse is a combination of the amount of force exerted and the length of time the force is applied (F x t) and is equal to the change of momentum (motion) that occurs. Safety padding on lift pylons is there so that if you happen to crash into them, the duration (t) of the impact (force) is increased. Impulse is also a relevant concept in moguls. By flexing effectively and by spreading out the work through the turn (being active earlier and longer) you also spread the impact forces while still getting the changes in momentum. This smoothing out of the forces saves your lower back, and knees. Blending different impulses requires skill and precision and will enable you to respond seamlessly to changes in conditions and make smooth transitions between turns.

Moment of Inertia (swing weight)

Moment of Inertia is the spinning equivalent of body mass, it is the measure of the tendency to resist changes in spinning motion. This depends on both the size of the mass and how it is distributed in relation to the axis about which it is rotating. Longer skis have generally larger swing weights. Perhaps the easiest way to understand moment of inertia in context is to consider when we make short, quick turns down the fall-line. Here you will need to use more rotational separation between the upper and lower body, so that you do not have to rotate your whole body from side to side. Rotating the whole body (large inertia) will require large forces applied repeatedly and quickly in order to keep this large amount of angular momentum changing direction. However, by keeping the upper body quiet and rotating the feet via the hips joints we are only working against the moment of inertia (resistance) of the lower body. Basically there is less angular momentum to be created and controlled. Consequently you will be quicker, more effective and more efficient with your turns.

Once airborne (remember Herman Maier in Nagano) the skier cannot create a net external force to change the angular (circular) momentum that he/she has – there is nothing to really press against to get a net external turning-force (torque) before you hit the ground. So if you want to perform a somersault or a twist you need to know how to generate this at take off. There are ways that the angular momentum you have can be managed though. For example during an aerial spin, if you tuck in your arms you will rotate faster. This action reduces your moment of inertia whilst spreading your arms before landing will slow the rotation as this change of mass distribution increases your moment of inertia.

Figure 4.9: Finishing the turn, and preparing to release the mass of the skier across the skis

Summary

This chapter was designed to give you an insight into sports biomechanics, help you better understand technical discussions and information, be familiar with technical terms used in BASI courses, and be better equipped to analyse and develop snowsports performance.

TEACHING

In order to be a skilful teacher there are several very broad but key attributes that need to be in place. Teachers need to understand their subject, they need to be in full command of safety considerations and they need to be able to deliver what they understand in an effective way.

The three chapters in the teaching section are:

• Understanding

• Delivery

• Safety

Just about everything else that we consider to be important qualities of good teaching can sit under these headings. Areas such as enjoyment, learning, communication skills and the acquisition of skill are all covered in what follows. The order in which the information is presented is intended to flow towards an end goal, that of an effective delivery.

It should be noted that although the Performance Section is important in its own right, it also sits inside the teaching section. Without this knowledge the requisite understanding will be missing and hence the quality of teaching will suffer.

5. UNDERSTANDING

Understanding Performance

Performance Analysis

Introduction

Performance analysis is one of the most important skills we can have as an instructor or a coach. It is the essential link between our understanding of all aspects of performance and the content delivered in our teaching or coaching sessions. If we are not able to analyse performance accurately then our knowledge is useless and our delivery misses the chance to improve performance. Performance analysis is not just about finding out what is wrong with a performance, but also finding an effective way to improve it.

This section sets out a model for performance analysis which gives instructors or coaches a framework within which to operate. The goal is to have a foolproof system which makes our teaching and coaching as effective as it can be. The model is presented first in a very simple format for less experienced teachers who need to get the basics in place and the second half of this section expands upon the model to integrate the Fundamental Elements and the Performance Threads to create a comprehensive and detailed framework that more experienced instructors can use.

A Simple Model - TIED

Our approach to performance analysis can be simplified in to these four stages:

- **T**ask – Setting and performing the task
- **I**nformation – Gathering information
- **E**valuate – Evaluating performance
- **D**evelop – Making decisions and interventions to allow the performer to develop

This model links sequentially, taking the result from the previous process and then applying it to the next. It is worth looking at each stage in this model more carefully.

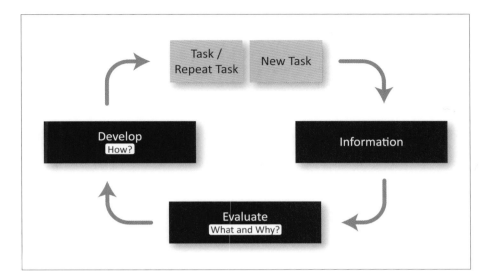

Task

This is the starting point for the model, the task must be as clear to the performer as it is to the instructor. The task may be a part of a larger goal that has been set between the instructor and performer, but the only thing the instructor should be focussing on is the current task in the current context. The context in which the task is performed will include things like: the slope, the snow conditions, the weather and anything that is specific to the performer, like their physical ability, tiredness or equipment.

Information

As long as the task is clear then the instructor and or student can gather information on the performance. There are many ways in which this can happen from observing, to feeling, to using timing equipment. This is covered in more detail below. During this part of the learning process the emphasis is on noticing things and becoming aware of what is happening. It is not about making judgements on quality or effectiveness – that happens next.

Evaluation

The information is used to make a judgement on how well the skier performed the task. We compare the performance to a template of how we would like the performance to be and thus establish if there is anything missing or if there is anything wrong with the performance compared to the expected or desired performance. Another way to think of the evaluation process is to ask these two questions:

1. "**What** would I change in the performance if I could?"
2. "**Why** is the performance not as we would like it?"

Develop

The develop stage of the model is where the instructor and learner agree on how they are going to achieve the desired performance of the same task or if it is necessary to try a different task. These are some of the possible results from the develop process:

After a successful outcome:

- The task is repeated in order to allow positive re-enforcement of the skills required. It is important to remember that there is value in repeating a successful outcome
- The task is changed in order to make it harder for the performer to achieve a successful outcome. Maybe initially it was too easy or after completing the task it is simply time to move on

After an unsuccessful outcome:

- The task is repeated whilst trying a different approach which will hopefully lead to the improvement in performance required. "Try it again and see if you can make the following change"
- The task is changed in order to make it easier for the performer to achieve a successful outcome

Task	A second week skier who is competent on blue runs attempting to ski steeper terrain. The skier is a gung-ho lady and is not intimidated by the task
Information	On steeper terrain the skier loses control of line and speed and tends to fall over backwards as the skis accelerate away down the hill. The inside ski lifts at the front and seems to get stuck on an edge at the tail
Evaluation	The skier does not maintain for/aft balance through the fall-line of the turn. It is probably not a mental issue
Develop	The instructor talks to the skier and suggests moving forwards at the start of the turn so that as the skis tip down the hill, the posture remains relative to the skis and the skier maintains balance. The instructor explains, demonstrates and encourages the student to assimilate this movement in to the transition and top of the turn
Task	The skier tries this on the same terrain, but if unsuccessful the instructor would probably try the same thing on slightly easier terrain before returning to the original piste

Figure 5.2:
An example of using the simple TIED model

Whichever course is chosen during the develop process, there will be another task to observe, whether it is the same task or a new one. This task must be treated in the same way: information must be gathered and evaluated in order to assess the effectiveness of the previous intervention. The model is used again and again to help us improve performance.

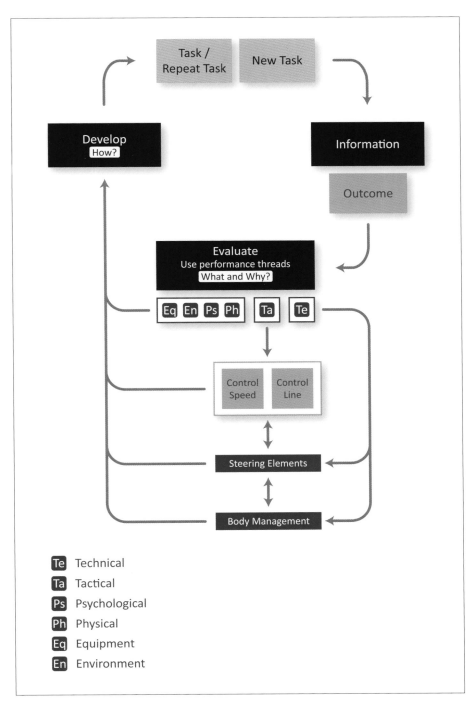

Figure 5.3: In-depth performance analysis model - TIED

The in Depth Model – TIED

Here we expand on all the stages of the simple model and integrate both the Performance Threads and the Fundamental Elements. This makes the model much more specific to BASI and snowsports. It also encourages the instructor to go to a greater depth in his or her analysis.

Task

The task remains the starting point for the model. The task may be part of a longer term goal. However, the task in this model should be limited to the actions upon which you can gather relevant information, the task may stretch over a series of runs or just a single run.

Information

Observation Live by Instructor/Coach

- Observe on varying snow and terrain
- Make sure you watch all the runs so that you don't judge a performer on one run
- One mistake can be a one off. Repetition of a mistake is likely to have a common cause
- Don't rush in to evaluation and action. Allow the athlete to perform again without trying anything new
- What do you gain from viewing from different angles? From below, above, the side

Observation by Video

- Is the video representative of the live performance that you saw? If not, don't use it
- Remember the task and environment in which the performance took place
- Make use of slow-mo to look for more detail, but remember that full speed is important to see flow Elements
- Don't get so focussed on one aspect of performance that you ignore the bigger picture. Think performance threads
- Remember the limitations of a two dimensional image. E.g. it is hard to see fore-aft movement from below. Video from different viewpoints

The Athlete or Performer

- Essential to work with the performer to establish which thread is likely to be the most effective starting point
- Check that the performer understands the task and is trying to achieve it
- Check what the performer thinks compared to your observations. Performers are not necessarily a reliable source of information about their performance. This changes with the ability and experience of the performer
- What learner phase are they in? Does this affect how much you trust their input on their own technical skiing? How does this affect how you will structure practise

The Snow

- Observe the line that the skis/board leaves on the snow
- Remember that this represents the line of the skis/board and not the skier/boarder's CoM
- What can the tracks tell you about the steering elements during the turn? For example:
- Can you see judder ruts, indicating a bouncing edge?
- Can you see both skis changing edge at the same time?
- Do skis/board ever run flat?

Timing

- An objective source
- Very OUTPUT focussed

Evaluation

The two questions used above are still valid here:

1. "**What** would I change in the performance if I could?" - The answer is likely to be in terms of things in the outcome, like the line, the speed or flow. If the answer is in terms of an input, then the instructor needs to be sure that they can link this back to the desired outcome. E.g. "I would like to see more edge angle" is not enough on its own. To complete this evaluation the instructor needs to link how insufficient edge affects the performance.

2. "**Why** is the performance not as we would like it?" - This second part of the evaluation is where we can use the Performance Threads to help us be more accurate and efficient in our coaching.

In the model the Performance Threads are laid out in order with environment, equipment, physical and psychological, coming first. We very often jump straight to the technical thread, neglecting the others in the process. If any of the other threads are thought to be the root cause of the failure to complete the task satisfactorily then they need to be addressed before technical and tactical.

For example, with beginners, if a student is too frightened to make a plough turn on the nursery slope, then the psychological thread needs to be addressed before attempting the same task again. Having made this evaluation the instructor could: work on a breaking plough so they know they can always stop, use visualisation to help the student see themselves succeed, work through some imagery to help them commit. The instructor may even decide to move to easier terrain in order for the learner to get the idea first before coming back to the original task. By moving to easier terrain the instructor is in fact setting up a new task as outlined in the performance analysis model.

Whilst the non technical and tactical threads should be dealt with only when the other threads allow, we can be limited by time and terrain so that the only practical option is to work in the technical and tactical threads. That doesn't mean we should ignore the root cause of any blockage and the thread that is responsible. The threads do not operate independently of each other. e.g. technical changes can make less suitable equipment work better (think of slalom skis off piste, keep the tips up a bit and don't over rotate the feet), or different tactical approaches can be used to give performers options of how to deal with a task (don't try to grip on ice, go for skiddy turns with less edge) and this can build confidence in the psychological thread. In a perfect world we would tackle the appropriate thread head on, but this is often not possible, especially in ski school teaching rather than coaching.

When we do use the technical and tactical threads, we can evaluate the performance in terms of the fundamental elements. Remember that the fundamental elements are all linked so that a change in the inputs (Body Management and Steering Elements) will affect the outcomes of (Line, Speed and Flow.) Equally a different outcome requires a specific set of inputs to achieve it.

If it is thought that the difference between the expected outcome and the real outcome is due to a tactical problem then line and speed can be developed directly without reference to the other Fundamentals. If this tactical approach does not work (re-run the model for a repeat of the task), the Fundamentals offer us the opportunity of working through the inputs in order to achieve the outcome.

Some instructors like to work directly with movements. The link between the Fundamentals allows us to guess what effect this will have on the Steering Elements and then the resultant effect on the outcome. Working directly with inputs is effective as long as the link between input and outcome is not lost.

Develop

By this stage we know what we wish to achieve and how close to achieving it we are. We have also decided as best we can why the performance is not as good as it could be. The develop stage is how we make the performance meet the expectations of the task.

The develop stage can be very short and involve a quick decision to repeat the task with a different focus (based on a performance thread) or change the task. However, there may be other developments which could take a long time to achieve, whether this is finding a psychological approach which allows a good technical skier to tackle steep slopes, or developing a physical program to allow a racer to last 1 min 30 secs and still be effective. These longer development times will still allow the performer and instructor/coach to come back and repeat the task and use the model to check that development is happening, it will just take a little while. Almost certainly there are other areas to be worked on in the mean time (new task).

Summary

Please note that these models are here to be used by instructors or coaches. They incorporate the terminology and concepts familiar to BASI. They are also circular in nature, if you start the model at the beginning and follow the steps, then eventually you will come back to the start again. This is important because it means that there is always a check between inputs and outcomes. The results of development are always compared using up to date information and an objective evaluation. Genuine progress will be made if the model is followed and the instructor does not get stuck in a rut, tied down by outdated and inaccurate dogma, committed unthinkingly to repeating the mistakes of the past. Using a model with a link between the inputs and the outcomes gives us freedom to experiment and try different approaches because if it doesn't work the model gives us the chance to try again.

The following pages have 2 examples of using the in depth model.

Top Tips

Make sure the performer and the coach know exactly what the task is

If you don't have the right information to use the model, don't try

Use technical and tactical threads only if the others are not inhibiting performance

Using the tactical thread before the technical thread can save the need to venture in to inputs.

If your evaluation leads to you trying something different, then go for it. The model allows for an experimental approach and you can always re-set the task if it doesn't work

If the performer achieves the task, then run the evaluation anyway. What, in terms of the performance threads, allowed the performer to achieve the desired outcome? This will develop your understanding of performance analysis in general

When in charge of a group, there may be more than one person who cannot achieve the set task. Each person has to be treated individually to find a solution that works

Example 1 of the in depth TIED model

Task	An advanced skier attempts to shorten the radius of the turn in long radius carved turns whilst leaving clean lines in the snow. The snow is firm, the piste is fast and reasonably steep
Information	Live observation and the instructor uses a video to analyse the outcome with the performer
Outcome	The skier is struggling to achieve the task, they are losing balance to the inside of the turn and the outside ski is losing grip
Evaluation	The instructor notices that the performer's skis are designed for back country freestyle and may not be allowing the skier to grip on this snow and terrain (equipment)
Develop	The performer changes skis to a pair of piste skis
Task	The performer attempts the same task again
Outcome	Whilst the skis grip more than the previous time there is still some loss of balance to the inside of the turn and the skis do not cut a clean arc
Evaluation	Whilst the skis have helped and were part of the problem, there must be another thread involved. The skier is travelling fast and is happy to travel much faster when free-skiing, so the instructor suspects it is not psychological

During the video session it is noticed that the performer is over-inclining to the inside of the turn and uses little lateral separation when building an edge angle and taking the Centre of Mass inside the arc. Linking the fundamentals together the instructor suspects that the performer's movements lead to him being over committed inside the turn without being balanced on the outside ski. This has the result of the ski not gripping properly. This is a loss of line and so the outcome criteria of the task are not met. Changing the way the skier moves laterally is a technical solution

When looking at body management and movements the excess inclination stands out as being the movement which causes the loss of balance. It is important to realise that this has an effect on the skis (technical) |

Develop	To address the issue, the coach can focus on the movements in the Body Management family of the Fundamental Elements and suggest that the performer achieves their increased edge by using some degree of lateral separation as well as inclination. The legs are still tilted the same amount to achieve a considerable edge angle but the upper body remains more level and is not over-committed to the inside of the turn. This should allow the task to be completed. The instructor may suggest: Trying to separate laterally on the same terrain. If the skier is not able to do this then the instructor needs to find suitable terrain where the skier can enter the associative phase of learning Different ways of separating laterally. Which one works best for the performer? Which way will allow the skier to complete the original task The time it takes for the performer to achieve the original task will vary between individuals. Some skiers will be able to implement the changes straight away but many will go through the stages of skill acquisition more slowly and only return to the original task after a good deal of work. How the instructor delivers and structures this will depend on the skier and the time available
Task	There may be many interim tasks before the original task is repeated. Both the interim tasks and the original task will also need to be subjected to the methodology in this model in order to get accurate and effective performance analysis

Example 2 of the in depth TIED model

Task	An intermediate to advanced skier is attempting to ski a fall-line descent through the bumps
Information	Live observation by the instructor and feedback from the performer
Outcome	Skiers struggle to achieve the task and keeps exiting the line. Because they cannot achieve the desired outcome, skiers are said to have insufficient control of their line
Evaluation	This is treated as a tactical thread issue. The speed is too fast, the line cannot be maintained and this creates the outcome problem
Develop	If performers were to slow their descent speed they would stand a better chance of staying in the line. If this suggestion works then they have achieved the task by doing nothing more than controlling their speed and going slower. To check if this works they repeat the task
Task	As before, with a tactical focus for the performer
Information	As before
Evaluation	The performer is still struggling to control the speed and line. The instructor may decide that the problem is more than just tactical and requires a technical approach. It may be that they cannot control their speed because they are not skidding effectively, one of the recognised methods of speed control in lower level bumps skiing
Develop	Attention is then placed on the skier's ability to rotate the skis and skid to control their speed at appropriate places in the line. The instructor may suggest: Some training out of the bumps in order to establish the movement patterns and feelings required to implement this in the bumps especially if the performer is in the cognitive phase Once in the associative phase the skier takes the new skills into easier bumps and develops versatility and confidence in the skill. (The structure of this practise will be dependent on the progress of the performer. Further performance analysis may be required during this development phase before returning to the original task (1 run, 5 runs, 2 days later?))

Task	The performer then attempts the fall-line descent again
Information	As before
Evaluation	The performer meets the expectations of the task. It is worth running through the evaluation stage here to re-enforce the successful outcome, and to learn from the changes made by the performer and the resultant changes to outcome
Develop & Task	After a successful outcome the develop and task stages offer the chance to either stick with the current task and repeat the successful outcome, or to change the task in some way. This change in task may be to add versatility to the performance, increase the speed or change the environment. The decision made here will be largely affected by the overall goal setting between the performer and instructor/coach

Understanding Learning

Understanding Learning

Great ski teaching is about helping clients learn effectively in a stimulating and safe environment. There are many factors that contribute towards good teaching. At its core however, an understanding of learning and the learning process will help provide a framework through which we can structure and deliver great teaching. An increased understanding of learning will also help us develop our own teaching ability and skiing performance. This chapter is about developing an understanding of learning. It looks at how we as ski teachers may choose to define learning and what constituent parts are required for effective learning to take place.

The Learning Process

Understanding learning can be a challenging topic. Much has been written, yet there is no commonly agreed definition of what learning is or how the process works. Looking to the fields of education and psychology, learning is often explained as a process combining cognitive, environmental and emotional influences to create changes in skill or understanding. Kolb (1984) suggests we learn through experience in a cyclical set of learning activities. Honey and Mumford (1982) identified different learner typologies, or preferences. This has been popularised through learning types such as doer, thinker, feeler and watcher.

At times, learning in skiing may be very easy to observe. A client may not be able to perform a certain skill, say parallel turns on a blue run. After a lesson, the performance has changed (hopefully!), and the client is skiing happily down the same blue run with skis parallel throughout. From this skiing example, one could describe learning as a positive change in performance. But what occurred during the lesson that made the change happen?

TIED Model and Learning

Several learning activities are vital to enable effective learning. The performance analysis model

(TIED) used earlier in the Teaching section highlights four sets of activities necessary to develop performance:

• A task is set and attempted

• The instructor and perhaps also the learner collect information about the performance

• This information is then evaluated and analysed

• From this, further developmental steps are decided, and the next task may be suggested

The TIED model can also be applied successfully to the learning process itself. This is perhaps best explained with an example:

• Imagine having a go at a skiing task (e.g. simultaneous edge change in your parallel demos)

• Whilst skiing you collect information about your performance (e.g. in turns to the left, your inside ski changes edges before the outer ski)

• At some point you reflect on this information and evaluate what happened (e.g. you are rushing the movements when you turn left)

• To develop further, you decide to do a few runs on easier terrain so you can really focus on both edges, changing at the same time in your turns to the left. You may also decide to ask someone to video it, or ski behind you to provide further information and feedback about your performance

The four learning activities form the fundamental building blocks of learning and development. In structuring and delivering lessons it is helpful to reflect on how well we as teachers include these learning activities to facilitate a sound learning process. The TIED learning model forms a simple framework to help us understand the learning process. The model suggests that there are broadly speaking four "learning activities" learners and teachers could engage with to create learning that is both effective and efficient. Building on common views about learning, it is possible that learners and teachers will show strengths and preferences for some of the activities, whilst they might have less of a preference, or even dislike for some of the other learning activities.

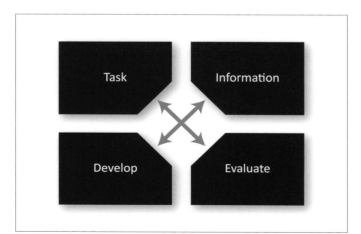

Figure 5.4:
The learning activities involved in the TIED model. In any ski lesson, it is useful to include a blend of the learning activities to enable clients to progress effectively

Task

To develop skiing performance, we need to have a go at skiing. In a learning context, this is obviously fundamental. If it is true that we learn through experience, getting miles under our feet is going to be helpful. People who are strong at this learning activity are often characterised by:

- Willingness to give new things a go
- Not particularly bothered by what others may think of their performance
- Enjoy experimenting
- Happy to try things out without needing to know much about how the task is performed

Information

By performing a task, we can gather information about the performance. Having some information about a performance or task will help us begin to analyse what is happening and make decisions about what to do next. The source of information can be internal (what the leaner notices about their performance through their senses), or external (from observers or other sources e.g. video, tracks in snow etc).

People who are strong at this learning activity are often characterised by:

- High sensory acuity
- Good at focusing attention on what is happening, rather than what they think should happen
- Confidence in own ability to pay attention and notice

The quality of information gathered makes a potentially big difference to the quality of the ensuing analysis and evaluation of the performance. Much time can be spent helping clients gather sensory information about what they are noticing in their own skiing performance. It is after all the learner who has to make the changes in skiing performance, and not the coach...

Evaluation

The information needs to be evaluated. Without some kind of performance analysis, any information we get from skiing will be of little use. In a learning situation, skiers often expect the "expert" or teacher to take responsibility for the evaluation. However, learning can often be more effective if the learner also engages in this process and links the evaluation with the information collected during the task performance.

People strong at the evaluation activity are often characterised by:

- Questioning
- Analytical
- Prepared to change perspective
- Trust their own judgment and not just leaving it to others

The better the learner has been at noticing what happened in their own performance, the more effectively they can engage with the task evaluation. Effective task evaluation will often lead to obvious decisions about what needs to happen next.

Development

This learning activity is about making decisions concerning what should follow the evaluation. What conclusions did the evaluation draw out? Sometimes it may be really obvious, "try the task again". Other times it may be really useful to let the learner decide. They may come up with something different to what the teacher was considering, but this can sometimes mean it is even more important.

People who are strong at this learning activity are often characterised by:

• Faith in their own judgment

• Taking responsibility for their own learning

• Open and decisive

As we develop as instructors, it is useful to keep returning to the four learning activities and consider how we include them in our lessons. We should also be thinking about how much responsibility we give our clients for each learning activity. Finally, it is also useful to be aware that it is all too easy to structure our lessons according to our own learning preferences rather than those of our clients. This may happen at a subconscious level.

With all models, it is important to remember that they are only a model! The TIED model is not the truth. It is only a framework to help us describe the learning process in a simple and understandable way.

Using the TIED Learning Model in Practise

Here is an example of how the TIED learning model can help us as ski teachers.

Imagine a group of blue run skiers. During the first session, the instructor asks everyone what they want from the week and what their developmental goals are. After some discussion (and good questioning/listening from the instructor), there is a general consensus that people want a general MOT on skis, and they would like to be able to ski with confidence down red runs. Having got some ideas about the clients' goals, the instructor suggests "we ski a gentle warm up run to find our feet and enable me to have a little look". This allows the instructor to check on current performance. At the bottom of the run, the instructor decides it could be useful to work on skidding and turn shape to aid speed control. He talks about how controlling speed is critical on a steeper run, and would it be useful if we started by "checking our brakes" so that we are happy everything is working?

At this point, the instructor has suggested a task activity. He needs to ensure the clients are aware of what they are doing, so asks them to notice the speed at which their skis twist or change direction through the turn. It can either be smooth and gradual or sharp and quick.

This helps clients focus on the information they might collect during the task. Once people have had a go, the instructor asks what they all noticed.

This allows the learners to reflect and evaluate their own performance. Through discussion, the instructor draws out that some clients are aware that they turn their skis quite sharply. He can augment clients' intrinsic feedback by adding what he saw. This is a good check to ensure clients are becoming aware of what is happening during their own skiing.

Once this awareness has been raised, the discussion moves towards what we each need to do next (development). In some cases the instructor may prescribe a drill or exercise, whilst in other cases he may encourage clients to help decide themselves what they want to do next to continue developing their speed control skills. He might get answers such as:

- "I'd like to follow in your tracks, because you always ski smooth turns"
- "I'd like to watch a clear demonstration of sharp and smooth turns first"
- "I'd like to spend the next ten minutes just getting miles doing it right. I know when it's right or wrong myself, so I just need to practise doing it right"
- "I'm not sure, what do you suggest?" Upon which the instructor suggests a drill or exercise

Learning Styles and VAK

Having looked at a model for learning we need to consider how individual learners may differ. We all collect information through our senses but different people have different 'modes' through which they prefer to operate. For example, some people rely more on vision, others on sound and others on feeling. It's not simply that each spends more time watching or listening or feeling, rather, each person tends to use their own preferred senses to help represent what they are thinking about or doing. Having some understanding of our own learning style preferences and those of our clients can help us as teachers.

For practical purposes, we can identify 5 different learning styles or modes - watcher, thinker, feeler, listener and doer. In terms of learning, each type of person tends to want something different.

- **Watcher -** Works best with demonstrations, pictures, visual analogies and visual imagery
- **Thinker -** Tends to want detailed technical explanations and descriptions rather than a particular sensory input. This is the classic 'left-brain' learner
- **Feeler -** Uses body-awareness as a major source of information, works best with descriptions of what an action feels like
- **Listener -** Uses sounds and rhythms to aid learning
- **Doer -** Wants to simply get on and try it

So in order to tap into our pupils' preferred learning styles, a useful approach is to give them a model for the task which relies on more than one sensory channel. This does not mean overloading them with extra information, but rather providing a more 'all-round' picture of the action.

This approach is sometimes known as 'VAK', which stands for Visual, Auditory and Kinaesthetic. In its simplest form, it can mean giving an explanation of the task (auditory), a demonstration of the movements (visual) and a description of how it should feel (kinaesthetic). Take the example of teaching beginners how to create a snowplough:

- "Stretch and rotate your legs to create an 'A' shape with the skis"
- Demonstrate the movement
- "Feel the resistance of your skis pushing against the snow as you begin to plough"

Skilful performance relies on the learners' ability to tailor their actions to the situation. That requires good awareness, both of the movements being made and of their effects. Using the VAK approach, we can also draw pupils' attention to the information available from different sensory channels as they are performing.

Visual

- Watching your shadow to monitor body shape
- Keeping both hands within your field of vision
- Looking at a fixed point to monitor upper-body movement
- Looking back at your tracks

Auditory

- Listening for the edge-set in short swings
- Relating sound to snow-texture
- Investigating which part of the turn is quietest
- Listening to squeaky boots, to monitor ankle movement

Kinaesthetic

- Judging speed of travel
- Feeling when the body crosses the path of the feet
- Keeping the head level when travelling through bumps
- Performing with the eyes closed

Imagery can also be used to increase awareness of this information.

It can be helpful to consider the TIED model and the learning styles described above. How will this affect the way you interact with clients and the way you deliver your sessions? How effective are you at noticing your clients' learning style preferences? Do you pick up on the client who always wants to go first and the other client who always wants to watch your demo before he has a go himself?

Learning Styles – Honey and Mumford

Honey and Mumford's work on learning styles encompassed four key styles or stages. Again, it can be helpful to think of these types when working with the TIED model.

Activists

Activists enjoy the here and now and are happy to be dominated by immediate experiences. They are open-minded, not sceptical, and this tends to make them enthusiastic about anything new. Their philosophy is: "I'll try anything once". They tend to act first and consider the consequences afterwards. Their days are filled with activity. They tackle problems by brainstorming. As soon as the excitement from one activity has died down they are busy looking for the next. They tend to thrive on the challenge of new experiences but are bored with implementation and longer-term consolidation. They are gregarious people constantly involving themselves with others but in doing so, they seek to centre all activities around themselves.

Reflectors

Reflectors like to stand back to ponder experiences and observe them from many different perspectives. They collect data, both first hand and from others, and prefer to think about it thoroughly before coming to any conclusion. The thorough collection and analysis of data about experiences and events is what counts so they tend to postpone reaching definite conclusions for as long as possible. Their philosophy is to be cautious. They are thoughtful people who like to consider all possible angles and implications before making a move. They prefer to take a back seat in meetings and discussions. They enjoy observing other people in action. They listen to others and get the drift of the discussion before making their own points. They tend to adopt a low profile and have a slightly distant, tolerant, unruffled air about them. When they act it is part of a wide picture which includes the past as well as the present and others observations as well as their own.

Theorists

Theorists adapt and integrate observations into complex but logically sound theories. They think problems through in a vertical, step-by-step logical way. They assimilate disparate facts into coherent theories. They tend to be perfectionists who won't rest easy until things are tidy and fit into a rational scheme. They like to analyse and synthesize. They are keen on basic assumptions, principles, theories, models and systems thinking. Their philosophy prizes rationality and logic. "If it's logical it's good". Questions frequently asked are: "Does it make sense?" "How does this fit with that?" "What are the basic assumptions?" They tend to be detached, analytical and dedicated to rational objectivity rather than anything subjective or ambiguous. Their approach to problems is consistently logical. This is their "mental set" and they rigidly reject anything that doesn't fit with it. They prefer to maximize certainty and feel uncomfortable with subjective judgements, lateral thinking and anything flippant.

Pragmatists

Pragmatists are keen on trying out ideas, theories and techniques to see if they work in practise. They positively search out new ideas and take the first opportunity to experiment with applications. They are the sorts of people who return from management courses brimming with new ideas that they want to try out in practise. They like to get on with things and act quickly and confidently on ideas that attract them. They tend to be impatient with ruminating and open-ended discussions. They are essentially practical, down to earth people who like making practical decisions and solving problems. They respond to problems and opportunities "as a challenge". Their philosophy is: "There is always a better way" and "If it works its good".

Goal Setting and Learning

Most people are familiar with the SMARTER approach to goal setting. This mnemonic sets out a structured approach to setting goals and can be a useful tool for teacher and student alike (the SMARTER approach is taken from work initially done by George T. Doran (1981) in business management, it has been adapted and described in the Goal Setting section later in this chapter). In terms of learning and the learning process, goals are critically important and most attempts at improving performance will fail if the objectives of the session are not clearly identified at the outset. Goal setting also links in really well with any performance analysis methodology (see Performance Analysis chapter).

To enable learning and positive change we need to view a performance goal or desired outcome in relation to a current level or performance. This gives us perspective and allows us to fulfil many of the principles outlined in the SMARTER model. Having established where we are and where we want to get to, we can evaluate and analyse the gap that exists between these two places. It is this analysis that allows us to clarify the performance areas that need changing and developing to reach the end of the journey. The TIED model that was presented earlier in this chapter provides us with a structure for how we then go about making these changes happen.

In summary the goal setting process provides the context for effective learning. It provides the teacher and learner with information to help focus on the appropriate content necessary to improve performance. Without this focus learning may happen but the relevance and usefulness of this learning to the student is left to chance.

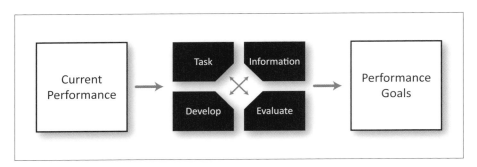

Figure 5.5: Performance development and learning as a journey

Skill Acquisition

Skill can be defined as the ability to perform a task well, usually through training or experience. It helps to think of criteria we could use to judge which of two performers is the more skilful:

- **Effectiveness -** The ability to achieve precisely the outcome that is intended
- **Efficiency -** The ability to do so with minimum expenditure of time, energy or both
- **Consistency -** The ability repeatedly to achieve the desired outcome

In other words, skill refers to the quality of a performance, not the performance itself. In the same way as a surface may be described as smooth or rough, a performance may be described as skilful. While movements and techniques may be performed skilfully, they themselves are not 'skills', any more than particular surfaces are 'smooth' or 'rough'.

For example, identical movements might be performed on two separate occasions, but depending on their appropriateness to the circumstances, one performance might be much more skilful than the other. This point is eloquently made by John Shedden in his book Skilful Skiing (Crowood Press 1982).

It is often said that dribbling in soccer is a skill, but, if someone is barely able to dribble attempts to do so against an active opposition, then what results is not likely to be a skill, it will be 'dribbling done badly'.

In conclusion, it must be emphasised that skill and technique are complementary rather than opposing ideas.

Skill Acquisition Model

In 1967 Fitts and Posner presented a skill acquisition model which proposes that the learner is subject to three phases when acquiring skill. (This model has been well accepted in the academic world and is often applied in sports coaching.) The distinction between the phases is a little artificial as one phase merges into another as learning progresses. However, each phase builds on the experience of the previous one, with the early phase building on past experiences in related activities. It is useful to look at the implications of each stage for the learner and the teacher. The original names for these phases are not very self explanatory and for practical purposes more easily-understood names can be used, these appear below in brackets. However it is important to understand the real meaning of the original words before substituting less precise words in an attempt to make understanding more accessible.

Early or Cognitive (Awareness) Phase – Getting the Idea

At this stage of learning, the pupil concentrates mainly on understanding the task. As suggested by the word cognitive, the learner is required to think and process information that will often result in a disorganised performance. The emphasis is on understanding and visualising the task rather than on performance. In fact an attempt at achieving the task will usually produce a fairly crude version of the template. As skill development is mostly a process of building on existing skills it is important during this early phase to make the link between the new skill and activities that the learner has tried before.

Implications for Learner and Teacher

- Building on existing experience is important to facilitate understanding at this stage. Relating skiing movements to other activities such as pedalling a bike, skating on roller blades or the principles of steering a car are often used as ways of giving the learner a starting point from which to acquire a new skill

- Building on previous experiences is also a useful way to adapt existing skills to achieve different tasks rather than having to learn something new. In this case the performer spends time in the cognitive phase in order to understand how to match existing skills to a different outcome. Once this new usage of already learned skills is understood, the performer can often travel through to the autonomous phase fairly quickly

- In some cases, depending on the learning style, it can work for learners to try a new task with minimal explanation. However they will still need a template on which to base their efforts, this may come as purely visual information through demonstration. If this happens then the learner can pass very quickly into the associative phase and begin to practise. However, it should be noted that when the demands on performance are greater a better understanding may be needed in order to maintain levels of skill. In this case the learner would need to revisit the cognitive phase and more external input may be helpful

- Most tasks related to skiing are relatively complex. Consider a gliding plough, the skier needs to rotate the skis inwards, manage how close the tips are to each other, keep the skis flat enough to prevent the edges from gripping too much. There are balance issues as the skier starts to slide, snow and terrain to adjust to, new equipment and a new environment. In this stage of learning it can help to break the task down so that the learner can understand parts of the overall task. The instructor might explain how to rotate the skis inwards. Explaining how to make certain movements can be a difficult task for the teacher and it helps to understand how the student learns. Some people will want a detailed breakdown of which muscles are used, while others may prefer an analogy. In this case something like imagining their feet are on old record player turntables. This is a very input focussed way of teaching and it is important to recognise the value of attending to the inputs before trying to shape the outcome

- The learner is not necessarily aware if they achieve the task. The teacher will speed up the skill acquisition process by confirming this with the learner, regardless as to whether the teacher goes further and aids the development of the leaner

- At this stage the learner is unaware of how a successful performance will feel, the teacher may choose to draw attention to certain sensations to help develop some basic kinaesthetic feedback, "stand still and try to rotate one ski towards the other, try to feel as little pressure as possible under your feet, we don't need to dig the edge in, just let the tips come together". Without an understanding of this kind of feedback the learner fails to create an experience on which to build and relate to in the future

Intermediate or Associative (Practise) Phase – Putting it All Together

Here, the overall action is understood and can be performed, although in a fairly crude form (wrong sequence, poor timing, poor relation of cues to response, poor co-ordination of movements). The main focus is now on creating associations between the parts of the task or sub-routines and the whole, or end goal. If we take the example used above of the gliding plough, it is now time to put the action of rotating the ski inwards into practise whilst sliding. Now that the task is understood and a template can be pictured by the learner, there is something to practise. It is this association between the nuts and bolts and the finished task that gives this phase its name.

Depending on the nature of the task and on the learner, this phase will last for varying lengths of time. However, in order to become skilful and make enduring associations between the parts and the whole, it will often be a long process. As such we should not rush learners through this phase.

Implications for Learner and Teacher

- How exactly we practise a task is of paramount importance during this phase. This is covered in more detail in the Structure of Practise chapter later in this section, but as teachers we need to ensure that practise is effective. Choosing between practicing the whole task or breaking it down into component parts, will depend on the ability of the performer. The teacher should ensure that the performer is able to feel some level of success during practise. Most studies have found, that a varied structure to practise is more effective than continuous massed practise

- The old adage of "practise makes perfect" is not strictly true. Imperfect practise will lead to imperfect performance, so perhaps a better way of looking at it is "practise makes permanent". We should do everything we can to ensure that accurate procedures are being practised. This is where the teacher adds value to a practise session. When it is established that the learner needs time to practise, the teacher needs to be on hand to monitor the accuracy. If the learner is a long way from the intended template it is sometimes necessary to go back to the cognitive phase and check or modify the level of understanding. On the other hand if the teacher can see that the learner is on the right track but needs longer to make the link between the nuts and the bolts and the end result, then it is more appropriate to employ patience and simply encourage and motivate the learner

- The teacher needs to bear in mind, that the goal is to travel through the associative phase and into the autonomous phase. To help the learner make this journey the focus on input and thinking should gradually decrease as the skill is practised and becomes better organised. As instructors there is often perceived pressure to continue giving our clients new information, "isn't that what they are paying for?" However, this approach will continually move the learner back to the cognitive phase and at best will ensure they never stop practising. When skiers feel their performance has reached a plateau, it is often due to the lack of direction towards non cognitive or outcome based tasks. In order to achieve the elusive goal of a skill happening without thinking at some stage we need to structure our practise to reflect this intention

Final or Autonomous (Acquired) Phase – Doing it Without Thinking

At this stage, the action is learned and can be performed without deliberate concentration or thought. The action occurs like a reflex and is less subject to interference from other activities or environmental factors. For example, when an instructor has become so skilful at making parallel turns that the action becomes autonomous, they can continue to perform accurately in white out conditions or whilst watching their students. Although the skill is learned, performance still improves during this phase as long as the performer retains motivation. Tactical considerations start to form a bigger focus, where and when to use certain actions, how to remain skilful in different conditions etc.

Implications for Learner and Teacher

- As the learner is now performing the task without having to think about it, it can be detrimental to re-introduce a cognitive focus. If a skier is skiing the bumps to a high level but wishes to go faster, thinking about the sequence and blend of the steering elements during each turn is likely to reduce the performer back to the cognitive stage of learning. This is likely to result in a clunky, non-flowing performance. However, if the teacher suggests focussing on a different line, a tactical focus, then the performer can allow the skill of skiing the bumps to continue autonomously whilst focussing on the different line instead

- As we have already mentioned, the acquisition of skill is largely a case of building on past experiences or old habits. These old habits can be remarkably persistent, when the performer is placed under stress. These habits are likely to resurface and become components in the learner's performance again, even if previously the skill was performed autonomously with no overt errors. Teachers need to recognise this phenomenon in order to maintain motivation. Returning to the practise phase can be seen as a positive step if it results in the performer developing the ability to perform autonomously in more challenging situations

Teaching Styles

The way in which people learn has a direct impact on how we teach and equally how we teach will affect how people learn. There are many styles in which we can put across information or teach our pupils. This choice offers the teacher different ways in which to cater for their learners needs, and to manage the learning process. Much of the original work on teaching styles was done by a researcher called Muska Mosston. The ideas were originally developed in the 1960s, and are currently described in Teaching Physical Education by Mosston and Ashworth (1994). It identifies a 'spectrum' of teaching styles, each with its own distinctive features. As a teaching tool these different styles are of great use, however, they are presented here as a collection of styles rather than as a spectrum. There is no order in which they should be used, a skilful teacher may choose to incorporate more than one style into a session and will see the benefits of using one style with another.

The Discovery Threshold

Although these teaching styles are of equal value in their own right, they can be categorised into two sub-groups, those before and those beyond the discovery threshold. The discovery threshold indicates when the learner starts to take responsibility for discovering solutions for themselves, rather than replicating actions previously shown and explained to them by the teacher. Non-discovery based styles lend themselves to developing performance, while those beyond the threshold encourage the development of understanding (as well as potentially developing performance). Although the styles beyond the discovery threshold are often seen as the territory of more experienced teachers, we shouldn't get caught in the trap of thinking that clever teaching only uses these styles. Learning in an environment that is constantly open-ended and nothing is wrong, is as unconstructive as working within a purely command style approach. For that reason, skilful teaching will often use styles from both sides of the threshold in unison, to provide pupils with balanced learning. Put simply, in order for learning to be effective, we need to spend time at each of the bases on the TIED model. If we focus on gathering information and evaluating new approaches, we must also allow time to develop performance and redefine the task. The teaching styles presented below help us to attend to each of these bases.

Command

Command is classified as a teaching style, however, it is also a way of communicating. Most of the other teaching styles will involve some form of "command" even if it is to set up a discovery based session. It is also used when there are any safety concerns – the teacher steps in and takes charge. This style sees the teacher take all the decisions, the learners have no responsibility whatsoever. It is commonly used with total beginners or in potentially dangerous situations where to give the students responsibility would be counter-productive and potentially dangerous.

Practise

The structure of the session is controlled largely by the teacher, however the student is given some responsibility to make choices such as:

• Where to practise the task (within an area defined by the teacher)

• When to set off on each attempt

• How many times to repeat the task (within the overall practise period set by the teacher)

The teacher still chooses, explains and demonstrates the task, sets the level of difficulty and evaluates and provides feedback on performance.

Practise is a vital part of skill development and involves the pupil spending, sometimes considerable time, in the development stage of the TIED model. Using the practise style is the perfect way to complement a discovery based session. It allows time and experimentation for the skier to incorporate into their performance, any new ideas or approaches, that have been discovered during the information and evaluation stages of the learning process.

Inclusion

This style is very similar to practise, however here the teacher gives the pupils a choice of levels or degrees of difficulty. Each pupil then selects their own individual level at which to perform the task. This extra layer of responsibility that is placed upon the pupil promotes self awareness and encourages the learner to evaluate their own skill level. In this way the learner not only develops performance through practise but also their understanding.

The concept of 'inclusion' is perhaps best explained with reference to its opposite - exclusion. An exclusive task is one which ultimately excludes some pupils - for example, seeing who can get all the way down a bumps field or slalom course without bailing out or losing the line. Because some pupils may fail at the task, it is classed as exclusive.

Self-Check

The teacher defines the task and gives the pupils guidelines on how they should evaluate their own performance. Only one aspect of the performance should be monitored at a time, and the criteria which are used to evaluate it must be clearly identified. The primary aim of self-check is to increase pupils' intrinsic awareness. This helps to wean pupils away from a reliance on extrinsic feedback (mostly provided by the teacher) and encourages them to start tuning into intrinsic feedback.

It is the job of the teacher to help pupils to be accurate with their evaluations. For this reason it is useful to set a goal and give them some means of measuring their success. Rating scales are one way to achieve this, take the case of pupils who are learning to absorb bumps while on a traverse.

To begin with, you might simply ask them to monitor the trajectory of the head:

"As you traverse the bumps, try to feel whether your head moves up and down, or stays on the same level all the way across".

Essentially this is a very simple 2 point (yes/no) scale. As the pupils gain greater awareness, you may incorporate a scale with more variation.

"Try to feel how much vertical movement your head makes as you traverse the bumps. This time, see if you can tell me how many centimetres your head moves up and down".

Another way to help the pupil is to use imagery to make the task clearer (see Communication Skills section).

"Imagine there's a ceiling over the slope, at just about head height. Try to gauge your head movement relative to that imaginary ceiling".

Self Check Key Features

The teacher must monitor the accuracy of each pupil's self-check, at least over the first one or two attempts

This style is only appropriate with pupils who have already gained some proficiency with the action being performed. Pupils should at least have entered the associative stage of learning (see Skill Acquisition Model) before attempting self-check methods

Reciprocal

The structure of the session is controlled largely by the teacher, however the students are given some freedom and responsibility within clearly defined boundaries.

The pupils work in pairs, with one practising the task while the other observes, evaluates and provides feedback, at intervals, the roles are reversed. There should be a single aspect of performance to be observed, with clear criteria for how that aspect is to be evaluated. If the criteria are not clearly established by the teacher the pupils feedback and focus are likely to drift into other less appropriate areas of performance, often with inaccuracy.

Here is an example using traversing as an exercise to develop edge awareness:

- The task is to traverse a moderate slope without the skis slipping sideways. Working in pairs, each skier traverses across the slope while the other observes. Each then tells the other whether their partner's skis slipped during the traverse

- To make the observer's task easier and more accurate, the teacher can suggest they look specifically at the tracks in the snow (the outcome) rather than just at the action of the skis

- The teacher should initially monitor the quality and accuracy of the feedback which is being given, and if necessary clarify the criteria being used by the observer

Reciprocal Key Features

When in a group, pupils receive more frequent individual feedback than where this is provided by the teacher

This style offers good team building potential as well as an opportunity to develop performance and understanding

Feedback provided by technically weaker pupils can be of equal value to that given by the stronger group members. This helps build self-esteem of less confident pupils

By acting as an observer, people look more closely and critically at what is being performed. As a result, pupils gain a clearer picture and understanding of the manoeuvre or task

The Following Teaching Styles represent a Shift Across the Discovery Threshold

Guided Discovery

This style involves a problem solving approach and is a great way to build rapport within a group if used well. The pupil is initially unaware of the intended goal and so experiences the outcome of the process as a discovery or insight. The learner develops their understanding as they progress through a series of questions posed by the teacher that require exploration and experimentation. By going through this process of discovery and revelation, new information is likely to be more memorable and hence more easily reproduced, than if it was simply handed to the pupil on a plate.

Here is an example of Guided Discovery in teaching a class of beginners who can already perform a gliding plough down the fall-line. What follows is presented as a series of questions asked by the teacher. But rather than the pupils simply answering them directly, their answers are the result of going and finding out. That is, each question sets a practical task, where the pupils have one or more runs to establish the answer:

Q: "When you plough straight downhill, do you have the same amount of weight on each ski?"

A: "Yes".

Q: "What happens if one ski has more weight on it than the other"?

A: "You turn".

Q: "Which way do you turn if your left ski has more weight on it"?

A: "To the right".

It should be noted, that while this example serves to illustrate the idea of guided discovery, it is very unlikely that a real class would move so quickly and smoothly along the discovery pathway.

Guided Discovery Key Features

The process is guided by the teacher from start to finish. The teacher asks a question or sets a task to start the pupils off towards the intended discovery, if at any time a pupil appears to be moving off course, the teacher must ask an additional question, or re-define or clarify the task so that the pupil moves back on course

As pupils progress towards the intended discovery, the teacher should confirm that their actions or answers are taking them in the right direction. Detailed feedback is not usually necessary

The pupils are not told what the intended answer or outcome is - they must discover it for themselves

This style places demands on the teacher's own understanding and ability to think and respond quickly. Although the outcome is planned, the pupils may respond in ways which were not expected. The teacher may therefore have to make significant adjustments to the process at short notice

Divergent

This style is similar to Guided Discovery. However, it differs in that the teacher's specific objectives for the session are not pre-planned. One question or problem is posed to the pupils who are then given free reign to explore the subject in any direction they choose. The pupils may well come up with legitimate solutions to the problem which were not anticipated by the teacher and in so doing further their understanding and analytical skills. This style only works if the pupils have a good grounding of knowledge and experience in the area to be explored.

As an example of this style, consider a group of experienced skiers trying to make grippy short turns on a steep piste. Several of the group are losing grip towards the end of the turn with the tails of the skis washing out. To develop their understanding the teacher splits the pupils into smaller groups and sets them the task of resolving this problem.

From this point on, the pupils are free to pursue their own investigations and experiments, for the period of time allocated by the teacher and within the designated area. The teacher's role during this period is simply to remain available for consultation and to deal with questions. The teacher should not suggest solutions to the problem but may need to reassure some pupils that their proposed solutions are valid or at least worth trying. This is the most important part of teaching in this style. Pupils should try using the solutions they have found. This is often called experiential learning and sees the feedback come from the success or failure of the task rather than from an external source.

In this example one solution maybe to ski a wider corridor to give the skier more time to deal with the pressure build up. Another may be more input focussed requiring the CoM to move back slightly to try and get the tail of the ski more weighted. Someone might even suggest snowploughing the start of the turn and trying to grip more at the end as a developmental drill. None of these are right or wrong until the pupils try them out to see what works.

The teacher still has an important role when using this style and needs to be able to look at the learning process as a whole. Sometimes pupils will come up with valid solutions that they either can't demonstrate through lack of ability or can't explain effectively through lack of experience. Here the teacher can help and ensure the idea is not lost. Another vital role for the teacher is taking the results of the session and structuring a follow-up session that completes the learning cycle. This way of unguided learning is a valuable way of improving understanding and analytical skills, it is also a good way to redefine tasks so that learners set new goals. However it doesn't tick the development or practise box. If the learners discover new information they then need time to put this into their performance. That is why the discovery based styles rarely work well in isolation and need the guidance, either during or after the session, of an experienced teacher.

Learner Design

In this style the teacher takes on the role of facilitator and allows the pupil to choose what they want to work on. The teacher establishes an initial performance area such as skiing bumps but the pupil decides where he or she feels they need to focus their development. For example the pupil may wish to ski the bumps in control with more speed, this goal is not set by the teacher. The pupil is also left to suggest ways in which they can approach their training, drills that have worked in the past, ideas they want to try, they are encouraged to problem solve for themselves while the teacher acts more as a consultant.

The pupil may well have a role they want the teacher to play, "can you tell me whether I am hitting the bump before or after I plant my pole"? or "can you give me your thoughts on how I might blend the steering elements differently to speed up"? or even "can you ski the bumps and act as my pace setter"? Obviously this kind of approach requires the pupil to have a high level of understanding and considerable experience. Although this teaching style is unlikely to be used in many ski school scenarios, it is the perfect way for ski schools to train their instructors or indeed for instructors to train each other during their free time.

Learner Initiated

As the name suggests this style is fully learner led, the advice and help of the teacher is sought out by the learner, the subject matter, nature of the training etc. is all the decision of the learner. To illustrate the difference between learner design and learner initiated consider the following scenario.

A senior instructor runs a staff training session on piste performance for more junior instructors within a ski school. Given the freedom to decide the content of the piste performance training this could run as a learner design session. However, a learner initiated session might be the result of this session with a junior instructor approaching the senior instructor a few weeks later to ask for a follow up session on a specific point that came up during the initial session.

The situations in which this style is most likely to be used is in long-term personal development - whether the ongoing training of an instructor supported by a colleague, or that of a competitor assisted by a coach.

Self Teach

When operating within this style, the roles of learner and teacher become merged, pupils assume full responsibility for their own learning.

Responsibility Spectrum

It is clearly the teacher's responsibility to keep clients safe in the hazardous winter mountain environment. However, when it comes to learning and responsibility, a spectrum can be identified. Sometimes a teacher will take responsibility for much of the activities and decisions during a session. These sessions are often dominated by the teacher doing lots of telling and giving instructions to the learners. At the other end of the responsibility spectrum, the teacher will act much more as a facilitator and support person. In these sessions the clients will make most of the decisions and the teacher will be asking questions to help people reflect and work through things themselves. Social constructivist theory suggests that we learn better when we take responsibility for our own learning. Whilst neither the autocratic nor abdicratic teaching approach is superior, it is really important to consider how much responsibility is appropriate for the learners as we help them develop.

Learner

RESPONSIBILITY

Instructor

Figure 5.6: Spectrum of responsibility for learning

Often, teachers with less experience will be more comfortable delivering in a more autocratic way. There is less uncertainty and the teacher can "stick to the plan" more easily. The EDICT model is a good example of teaching in this way.

- Explain – The teacher explains the new task
- Demonstrate – Then he demonstrates it
- Imitate – Next the students have a go at the task
- Correct – The teacher observes and provides corrective feedback
- Trials – Finally the students try again

Although the EDICT approach provides a safe, predictive and straightforward framework for less experienced teachers, it may not be the most effective. Sometimes, "things" happen during a session and it may be useful to allow it to flow according to what happens and not just what was planned. This may demand more skill and experience from the teacher. During BASI courses it is not uncommon for a student teacher's session to go wrong, because the clients didn't behave or learn according to the student teacher's predetermined plan!

Mosston's different teaching styles include varying levels of responsibility between the teacher and students. To facilitate deep learning it is essential to help learners develop awareness of their own performance and not just rely on information from the teacher. This suggests that learner responsibility is important. Good teachers are able to decide how much responsibility it is appropriate to hand over to the learner in each given situation. Sometimes it may be better to just tell the client to lean forwards, whilst other times it may be more effective to ask the client to notice where they are balancing over their feet whilst they ski.

Structure of Practise

As we know, practise is a fundamental part of learning. In most sessions there will be some practise involved unless the students are continuously trying a new task. The teacher has a choice as to how this practise is structured and this choice should be based upon the learner's needs in terms of ability and skill level.

Typically a learner in the cognitive phase (e.g. task has just been presented) should have the chance to perform the task in an environment as uniform as possible. By minimising variables, the students are able to focus on the task itself and hopefully achieve the task at least in a rough form (early associative phase).

Once in the associative phase of learning it is useful to build in some more variation. The environment may stay fairly uniform but the task can be practised with a variety of speeds, rhythms and lines, if appropriate. The students should be encouraged to feel what it is like to perform the task with this variability and know when they get it right.

In the late associative and autonomous phase of learning the variation can be increased. The terrain can change as well as the speed, timing and line. The performers should remain challenged and test the robustness of their skills. At some point the practise may be so different to the original task that a new solution is used to achieve it. This may be considered a new task and the process can begin again.

Variability of Practise

Changes to the nature of practise helps to develop a skill through adaptability and also helps to prevent boredom. Some of the factors that can be varied are:

• The speed, range and timing of the movements

• The speed of travel and small variations in line

• The steepness of the terrain and the variability of the terrain

• Texture of the snow

Distribution of Practise

It is possible to change the duration and timing of practise sessions throughout a session. This can have an affect on the rate of skill development for the learner

• Distributed practise involves relatively short practise sessions which are interspersed with periods of rest or another activity

• Massed practise involves the task being repeated over an extended period and any rest periods are shorter than the practise periods

Generally it is found that distributed practise allows for better skill development and retention than massed practise although this has been found to vary, depending on the nature of the task (Dail, Teresa K. Christina, Robert W 2004).

It is thought that the potential for boredom and fatigue impairs skill acquisition within massed practise and as teachers we should monitor the students for signs of both. It is also true that if we use variety in our practise, as described above, then the potential for boredom will be less and the amount of useful practise can increase.

The amount of practise needed to hone a skill will depend on the complexity of the task and the ability of the learner. Some skills can become autonomous very quickly (within a few minutes) whilst other skills may never reach an autonomous stage. Practise helps to groove an action and increase the chance of repeating the same action. It must be remembered that practising a bad habit is potentially worse than not practising at all. Practise therefore requires some kind of feedback loop in order to ensure that the practise is useful. BASI use the TIED model for performance analysis (see Performance Analysis section). Practise sessions feature in the development stage of the model, and must be used within the context of the TIED model to ensure that there is useful progress being made.

Task Presentation

How the task is presented to the learner has a direct effect on how people learn. There are essentially three ways that we present tasks, "chaining", "shaping" and "whole-part-whole". Each is explained below.

Chaining and Shaping

When teaching a new movement or action, it can be presented in a variety of ways. For example, movements can first be broken down into smaller parts, and the parts then re-combined to create the end product. Alternatively, the action can be taught as a whole from the outset - beginning with a fairly crude version, and gradually refining it with practise. These two processes are often called 'chaining' and 'shaping'.

Example 1 - Learning a New Piece of Music

- Learning a new tune on a musical instrument is often done by chaining: first, the opening few bars are learned, once that is done, the pupil moves on to the next section, which is then added to the first. The process continues until the whole tune has been built up out of smaller pieces. This is chaining

- Alternatively the musician might sight read the whole piece from start to finish and then keep repeating the whole section whilst trying to improve the quality of the performance. This is shaping

Example 2 - Learning the High Jump in Athletics

- The process of learning to high-jump is often done by shaping. By starting with the bar set low, the pupil can use a fairly crude action to get over it. As the technique is gradually refined, the height can progressively be increased, all the while working on the complete manoeuvre. This is shaping

- Equally, the high jumper can break down his sport in to sections and work on those individually. He or she could initially work on the run up section and get that part right. Then they may work on the take off but without using a bar, finally they would work on the movements required in flight to clear the bar. At the end all these parts are put together to make the whole performance. This is chaining

In both the above cases the way these tasks are learnt is not fixed and we have a choice how to present them. The way they are presented will depend on the task and the learning phase of the student.

Chaining Key Features

Chaining can be used to break down very complex actions in to more simple parts and allow the athlete the chance of success in at least some of the task

In chaining it can be easy to lose sight of the end goal. The instructor has a responsibility to keep the smaller tasks in context or ensure that the progress is swift enough that the students can understand the overall purpose of the session

Often, there will be a key step to any chaining which is more important or more difficult than the others. The instructor should ensure that this step has more attention given to it than the others

Practising a section that can already be achieved is not as useful as working on the difficult section of the task

Chaining is more associated with the cognitive phase of learning and early associative phases and fits well with setting intermediate goals as a progression towards a longer term goal

Shaping Key Features

Shaping has the benefit of allowing the performer the chance to attempt the whole task. Maybe the task is very achievable for that performer and chaining is an unnecessary delay before attempting the whole thing. A shaping approach can be more time efficient than chaining if the task is achievable or nearly achievable for the performer. It also allows the performer to work on combining movements to achieve the whole task rather than working on isolated movements which later have to be combined with other movements

Shaping is more associated with learners in the associative phase of learning

Whole – Part – Whole

Between the two approaches of chaining and shaping there is a third way to present the task which allows the instructor to tailor their approach to the needs of the student. The task would be set and the student attempts the entire task. If the attempt is successful enough that the student is in the associative phase for the whole task then the instructor would continue to shape the performance. However, if the student is still in the cognitive or early associative phase, then the instructor can revert to a chaining approach, picking the part(s) of the task that the student is struggling with and working on those. Ultimately the whole task is attempted again and the benefits of the chaining work can be evaluated in the whole performance.

Whole - Part - Whole Key Features

The instructor must be able to recognise the difference between a learner in the cognitive phase and a learner in the associative phase

Students have the chance to prove that they can complete the task in its entirety. This can save time and avoid chaining sections which they can already complete

From viewing the original performance it is easier to decide which section is proving to be most difficult and then focus more on that

This approach allows the instructor to view the whole group and then fit an approach for the individual. Some may move to chaining, some may continue with shaping the whole

The students are more likely to view any chaining sections in the context of the complete task and therefore motivation for chaining tasks will be maintained

Summary

The way the task is presented and attempted has a large impact on the structure of the session. There are choices to be made by the instructor as to which one of the methods above is used. This decision must be based on knowledge of the learner. It must also be remembered that choosing one method initially does not trap an instructor in to continuing down that path. The instructor should be able to react to the group's performances and adapt accordingly.

Goal Setting - SMARTER

We have already looked at goal setting when viewing its importance in relation to learning and the TIED model. Here we look at the practical process of goal setting and in particular the SMARTER model (Doran 1981). Whether happening on a conscious level or not, virtually all of our actions are directed towards particular goals. Our goals not only shape our actions, they also affect our sense of satisfaction and achievement.

At the end of a lesson, the pupils' satisfaction largely depends on whether and to what extent they've achieved their goals. They might not have been the goals they arrived with, but if they haven't achieved anything they wanted, they're unlikely to go away on a "high".

It is worth being aware that peoples' goals will vary dramatically depending on the individual. When teaching skiing you may come across people with the following kinds of goals:

- Having a good time
- Looking like Alain Baxter
- Learning to ski parallel
- Getting the hang of powder snow
- Getting down a black run
- Forgetting work for a week
- Meeting new friends
- Seeing if they like snowsport
- Enjoying the mountains in winter
- Drinking strange liquids and falling over a lot
- Keeping their partner/parents/ children happy
- Re-discovering the magic sensation of that one perfect run

Having looked over the list of goals, consider them in the light of the following questions:

- Which goals can you as a teacher help them to achieve?
- Are the goals to do with learning or improving technique?
- Might any of them turn out to be unrealistic?
- Are any of them incompatible with each other?
- Are there any you wouldn't want to help them to achieve?
- How do they compare with the goals you set for them as their teacher?

The chances are that if you had a class who collectively shared the above list of goals, you'd have your work cut out trying to keep everyone satisfied. Even if it wasn't that extreme, you might well have to do some negotiating to reach a compromise that everyone (including you) was happy with. If you are able to reach a compromise then you need to set about putting a program together to meet those goals.

Setting SMARTER Goals

To help us with the goal setting process we borrow a system commonly used in sports coaching that has been adapted from a model that originated in the world of business management, known as the SMARTER model. It states that well-chosen goals should be:

Specific - they should express a clear, simple objective
Measurable - it should be clear when they've been reached

Achievable - within the time and resources available

Realistic - within the capabilities of the individual

Time-phased - divided into a sequence of shorter steps

Exciting - it should be fun getting there and represent an appropriate level of challenge

Recorded - as a reminder of what was decided

We use the SMARTER model as a checklist to ensure that we have set the goal up correctly and that we will give our students the best chance of meeting those goals.

Establishing and Negotiating Goals (SMAR)

A key process is to establish your pupils' goals. Just a few minutes at the start of the lesson is all it takes, to ask everyone what they want out of the session, that day or the week. Having established that information, you might need to do some negotiating to ensure the goals are not:

- **Unrealistic** e.g. a raw novice keen to learn to ski/ride powder that week
- **Non specific** e.g. "I would like to be better on the piste". "Ok, but which pistes? The steep ones, ones you can carve on? What do you mean by better"?
- **Incompatible with the group** e.g. one pupil can't stand cruising and wants to concentrate on skiing steeps, another doesn't like steeps and wants to cruise
- **Unachievable** e.g. pupils want to run gates, but the facilities aren't available

The negotiation process usually involves further questioning and discussion. The communication skills of the teacher are obviously crucial at this stage (see Communication Skills section). It is often possible to achieve certain goals by means the pupils may not be aware of. For example many of the skills needed to ski off piste can be developed on the piste with the right drills and guidance. This can be a useful tactic when trying to make different goals within the group more compatible.

Long Term and Intermediate Goals (RT)

Apart from making sure that peoples' goals are realistic and achievable, it also helps to think of a progressive way to achieve them. That means dividing the goal into intermediate steps.

Example 1 - A snowplough turner who wants to ski parallel. Some of these steps might be:

- Improved posture
- Developing rhythmic movements
- Greater confidence at speed
- Learning to skid to a stop
- Learning to steer the inside ski
- Better edge control

The basic principle is to divide a long-term goal into a series of shorter-term steps. Looked at as a single hurdle, a longer-term goal can quickly become disheartening. Approached step-by-step, it takes on much more manageable proportions. Even if you don't discuss these steps with the group, it is a good way of helping plan your lessons to ensure the objectives are achieved.

Example 2 - A basic parallel skier whose goal is to learn to ski bumps. This is potentially a much longer term goal than the first example. While they might achieve it within the week, failure could be a real disappointment. Even worse, as the week progresses, the goal might seem increasingly unattainable, leading to a progressive loss of motivation. As a first step, we'll break the main goal down into smaller steps:

- Reading a line through the bumps (without necessarily managing to ski it)
- Using the convex areas of single, isolated bumps for initiating turns
- Improving the pole-plant to help stabilise the upper body
- Avoiding over-turning the skis when initiating turns on bumps
- Linking 2 (then 3, 4, 5, etc.) turns together over a series of small bumps
- Absorbing small bumps while traversing the slope
- Absorbing a single bump while turning over it
- Linking 2 (then 3, 4, 5, etc.) compression turns together over a series of small bumps

These intermediate goals should be clearly agreed with the pupil as the main stages they need to go through to achieve their main goal. Assuming both the pupil's aptitude and the conditions are reasonably favourable, many if not all of these intermediate goals might be achieved within the week. The nature of the delivery will have huge influence on how much fun it is to achieve these goals and how close to the end goal the leaner gets.

Goals and Motivation (ER)

The ways in which people are motivated can be classified into two categories intrinsic and extrinsic motivation. Some people have a genuine, personal desire to do something for its own sake (intrinsic), while others are motivated by wishing to please someone else or attain tangible rewards (extrinsic). In ski teaching it is common to have people in the same group who are motivated in these two opposite ways. How many times have you had a couple in a class, where one of the pair is really keen to get better and lives for the annual ski holiday, while the other is only there to keep their partner happy?

Extrinsic motivation is much more fragile than its intrinsic counterpart. Someone who really wants to participate will usually put up with a fair level of discomfort or frustration before completely losing heart. But for someone who is extrinsically motivated, the slightest setback can often be the last straw. While there isn't an easy answer, just recognising the nature of the problem is a useful start. If someone isn't motivated by the activity, the technical objectives held by others in the class will have little relevance to them. Rather, being helped to get by with what they've got (a tactical approach) can be more useful. It may even be possible to offer alternative activities within the session, such as missing out a bumps field or having a coffee stop option for anyone who wants one. By being aware of everyone's goals from the start of a session (and negotiating different ones where appropriate) a good teacher is able to do their best to facilitate everyone meeting their own specific goals.

Through setting goals carefully we can ensure that learners experience both ENJOYMENT and SUCCESS. Making a ski lesson enjoyable is central to the learner centred approach to ski teaching. Each goal that is achieved represents a success.

Summary

Setting and re-setting goals is a key part of being a successful teacher. Without having a goal to aim for it is impossible to start the process of planning and delivering a session. As long as the goals are shared by students and teachers and have been negotiated to everyone's satisfaction, then the teacher can focus their attention on meeting those goals using the other tools at their disposal.

Finally, it is worth noting that the teacher's goals may initially be very different from those of the pupils, these should not be allowed to over-ride those of the class.

6. DELIVERY

To deliver sound teaching sessions that are enjoyable and where progress is made quickly and safely, ski teachers require a blend of knowledge and understanding, as well as the practical skills of planning and delivering. At the same time attention must also be given to all the other factors that affect the potential for learning.

On BASI teaching courses, student sessions are ultimately reviewed and assessed according to how well the student teacher actually enables real learning. To do this well, successful teachers show clear planning around agreed objectives. This allows the session to be properly structured and contain content relevant to the learners. As teachers become more skilful they will review and adapt the session as it unfolds, thus enabling learner centred lessons that flow and reach

their objectives. Over time it is important to train ones teaching skills with as much attention as we place on training our performance skills. To deliver really effective teaching that comprises accurate knowledge of ski technique and of learning, takes practise and experience.

The delivery section is meant to be very practical. It is about what happens on the hill in our sessions. There are two parts, firstly the Learning Environment, and secondly the Planning, Content and Reviewing.

The Learning Environment

Imagine two different lessons running side by side. They have the same technical content, structure and progressions, the same students and the same teacher. Yet, observing the two sessions there are still huge differences between them. In the first lesson there is less energy, the students seem less interested and the teacher looks less confident and engaged. The second lesson has much more energy, people are laughing and having a good time. There is lots of activity and as the observer you want to join in.

Many factors affect the learning environment. Some of them we can influence and shape on purpose, such as the activities or the terrain we choose. Others are outside our control such as the weather or the make-up of characters within a group, although we may be able to limit negative factors to some extent.

Teaching a sport that takes place in the mountain environment brings its own set of challenges that may affect our clients' ability to learn and progress.

Here are some, you can probably think of more:

• The weather and snow conditions
• Clients' familiarity with the mountain environment
• The group dynamics
• Level of challenge in the sessions
• How engaged and cared for clients feel
• Our communication skills
• How we deliver feedback
• Our choice of teaching styles and delivery
• Our client sensory acuity (ability to observe, examine and interpret clues from clients)
• Snow

It can be very challenging to manage all these factors, yet by doing so we actually deliver much more impact.

Climate Setting

Good teachers will influence the learning environment on purpose. They will make choices and shape sessions to support and assist clients' learning as much as possible. Imagine a session where one or two clients always want to go first and ski behind the instructor, they seem insensitive to the other members of the group. Tension grows as the two extra keen clients are beginning to feel held back, whilst everyone else feels rushed. Picking up on this, the teacher changes the plan and moves the group to a shorter run served by a drag lift. Here the teacher sets up a series of round robin activities that allows each group member to work at their own pace. During this part of the lesson it is possible to speak to the two faster clients one to one and tactfully suggest that they may be moved up a level for tomorrow's session. The teacher asks them respectfully to help get today's session to a successful close by supporting the slower members of the group. There are many other ways in which good teachers pick up on cues from the group dynamics and shape the lessons accordingly. In this way a positive learning climate can be maintained.

The climate or group dynamics have a large effect on the ability of students to learn and enjoy their sessions. It will affect their motivation, their willingness to try new ideas, their willingness to make mistakes and their ability to take on new information. What is perhaps most useful to us as teachers is that with practise we can manipulate the climate to effect different outcomes. We can see climate setting as the tool (input) by which we manage the learning environment (outcome).

The climate within a group will depend on the individuals within it, but the instructor has a responsibility to control the climate themselves. The tools to achieve this are covered in the "teaching tools" and the "communication skills" sections, but it is important to remember that it is not just what we say and do but our manner of communicating that will affect the climate. The energy with which you talk, the enthusiasm of your delivery and demonstrations, the nature of your feedback to students and even the instructors willingness to look silly or make a mistake, all these things will affect the climate of a group.

Climate setting is a metaphor borrowed from classroom teaching, and describes the "conditions that promote the growth and development of students" (Knowles 1980). This approach has developed in classroom teaching, through the years to mean a climate in which there is mutual respect, openness to learning, a shared responsibility between student and teacher as well as a responsibility and degree of support between the students. Learning is encouraged through exploration and discovery more than telling and listening. (Starr 2004) These values are shared in BASI'S approach to teaching, but BASI also see the climate as something that can be manipulated and deliberately changed in order to maximise learning. Other climates that maybe useful:

relaxed	intense	motivational
inclusive	competitive	exploratory
supportive	serious	light hearted

Setting the climate is achieved with communication skills, body language, animation, content and the structure of the session. Above all the climate set should be useful and ultimately enjoyable for the learners and if it is not then the instructor needs to recognise this and change it. The theory behind climate setting states that children will need a different climate to adults. It is also true that whether adult or child, students within these two groups will require and respond better to some climates than others.

Often instructors will tend to set a climate which suits their personality and will do so by default unless they actively seek to do otherwise. The ability to change the climate does not mean changing one's personality. Unless you are a very skilful actor, it is much better to rely on your own natural strengths than to attempt to emulate someone else, as Polonius said, although admittedly not referring to ski teaching, "to thine own self be true".

Whatever your personality, it is important to tailor your delivery to suit the group. For example, an approach which is too extrovert and 'jokey' can easily overpower some pupils. On the other hand, teachers who are naturally quiet and reserved may need to learn to project their personalities more strongly.

Enjoyment

Without enjoyment any learning is likely to be marginalised and certainly the student is unlikely to come back for more. There is something wrong with our delivery and approach to teaching if in striving to use a learner centred approach we fail to make a lesson enjoyable. However, enjoyment is not simply about having fun, it is something that can be experienced in various ways, a sense of satisfaction or achievement, a new discovery or enlightenment. Since different people enjoy different things, understanding the learner is the key to delivering an enjoyable session (see "learning Section, Leaner). The instructor will need to tailor their approach for the individual, even within a group lesson. The following headings list some factors that affect pupil's enjoyment.

MCA Maximum Class Activity

At the most basic level we can assume that people wishing to learn to ski will want to have a go at skiing at some time. There will be exceptions to this rule, but generally the more skiing people get to do, the more chance they have to enjoy themselves. This principle is enshrined in the acronym MCA, if there is the chance for the class to be doing something, take it. If, for example there is enough space available to allow beginners to have two lines attempting their central theme on the nursery slope, then the instructor should set up the session accordingly and maximise MCA. Making a group ski down one at a time on the piste takes a lot of time and does not encourage MCA. The instructor ought to be able to justify doing this for another reason (see Planning a Session).

Achievement

Achieving something is an enjoyable experience. Each learner will want to achieve their own personal goals, and through careful negotiation and planning the instructor can help to set and achieve those goals. By achieving those goals the pupils will feel rewarded themselves, but should also be congratulated by the instructor. Some people will appreciate a physical reward for their efforts. Children's ski badges are designed to do this. Giving the learner responsibility for setting and achieving their goals can hugely increase the sense of reward when they are achieved.

Do not be afraid to use competition for those who are motivated by that. Competition can be a big driver of motivation and enjoyment for sports participation (see Goal Setting, Planning a Session).

Climate Setting

Setting the climate in the group will affect how people learn and how they enjoy themselves. The energy, supportiveness, friendliness, and seriousness of a group will suit some learners more than others. It is not always possible to have a climate that suits everyone as each person will prefer something different. However it is important to be able to modify the climate and over the course of a session or series of sessions, meet everyones' needs.

Sometimes the instructor needs to give their energy to the group in order to set the climate and other times the group will provide a lot of that energy themselves. Being able to influence and set a particular climate can allow the group to work better and increase enjoyment. Being able to recognise, set and adjust the climate of the group takes good communication skills and a good understanding of the learners. A good understanding of the teaching tools and how they too may affect climate or require a particular climate will give the instructor more options for delivery (see Climate Setting and Communication Skills).

Enjoying the Whole

If you know your pupils well enough you will find that their enjoyment does not just come from skiing and getting better at skiing. Being in the mountains, breathing fresh air, enjoying each others' company and other factors are all part of the enjoyment of a ski holiday. An instructor should allow pupils time to enjoy these parts of the sport too. By knowing the names of the local mountains, being able to spot and name the local flora and fauna and being able to book a table at a good restaurant, the instructor can add value in these areas too. This is part of being a good professional.

Variety

A lack of variety in teaching will lead to boredom and loss of interest. There are a number of things that the instructor can change to mix up teaching and learning and keep it interesting. The task itself can be varied, although time should be allowed for development when necessary. The terrain and part of the resort in which the lesson takes place can provide different challenges and views. We can change how we structure practise sessions, how we use the teaching styles, affect the climate, and choose to communicate. It is important for the teacher to feel motivated too, the mood of the leader will always rub off onto the group, variety keeps everyone fresh not just the students.

Varying the pace of the lesson is another good way to manage levels of enjoyment. If the instructor senses boredom or apathy towards the task, changing the focus even for a short time can get people back on track. Equally if things are going really well and everyone is having a great time, don't change it. if the instructor adds in another drill or exercise and kills the energy in the group it can be very difficult to get that "feeling" back.

Variety need not be used for the sake of it, the learner's needs are of paramount importance but with a little bit of imagination and experience there are a multitude of approaches and methods to keep it interesting for everyone (see Structure of Practise, Teaching Styles, Communication).

Summary

Considering the factors above and using them in combination with the rest of the teaching content will help you to deliver enjoyable sessions. Enjoyment is what drives us to ski and is what drives our profession. A happy client will want to come back.

Feedback

The way we manage feedback will affect the learning environment. Feedback in sports coaching often means the information delivered to the learner about their performance. The instructor might say "that was a great run" or a video analysis session might provide some information on a technical issue. However, in the wider world feedback has a deeper meaning. Feedback is more than just delivering information to the performer on what they did, it requires that this information is then used to change (improve) the original situation (performance of task). Whilst feedback will continue to mean any piece of information relayed back to the student on their performance, the deeper and more useful meaning in terms of an entire feedback loop are embodied in BASI's teaching philosophy.

In fact the whole of the TIED model can be seen as one large feedback loop in which the performance is being changed based on information gathered from a previous performance.

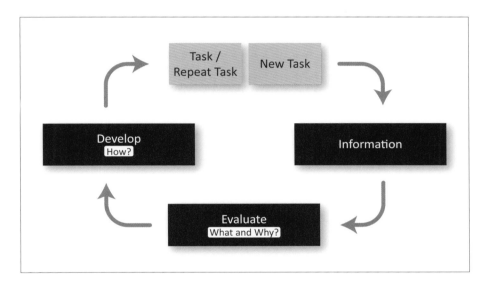

Figure 6.1:
The TIED model as a feedback loop

In the narrow view of feedback this process can get stuck at the information stage. It may be impossible to evaluate the information itself due to its nature ("your hat really stands out as you come down there") or the instructor and pupil fail to use the information in the rest of this model to improve performance or achieve the task. The information contained in the feedback must be used to evaluate and develop the performance so that the performer has a chance to improve. The teacher takes the role of managing all stages in this feedback loop even if the teacher does not perform one of the stages themselves.

Information used in Feedback

The information can come from a variety of sources. Often these sources are categorised from the perspective of the learner in to intrinsic and extrinsic sources. Intrinsic feedback comes from within the performer whilst extrinsic information comes from outside the performer.

Intrinsic Feedback

The senses provide the learner with information about their performance:

- **Vision** – What did they see as they performed? Were they looking where they were going? Did they go where they wanted to? Did they see their hands? Where on the bump did the pole plant land?

- **Hearing** – What did they hear as they performed? Could they hear the ski making a noise? Did that noise relate to a skiddy turn or a carvey turn?

- **Touch** – Feeling the pressure coming through the foot. Did you feel the shin on the front of the boot through that turn?

- **Proprioception and Kinaesthesia** – These two terms are used almost interchangeably. There is no agreement on their mutually exclusive definitions although there is a tendency for kinaesthesia to be used more in relation to movements through space. Together they describe the body's ability to tell you where your body parts are in relation to each other and where you are in relation to the environment around you. These terms also cover the body's ability to determine whether it is in balance or not

Some of these senses will provide information that is not available to the conscious mind, but other senses will give the performer a lot of information relevant to their performance. Often the senses will provide information in combination and the performer will not be able to separate the source of the information. This doesn't really matter.

As an example, a skier turns their feet across their direction of travel and applies some edge to the ski, they may notice several things:

- Greater pressure under the feet, running up through the body
- Visual information that the rate of travel is decreasing
- Increased sound from the skis on the snow
- Proprioceptive information about any changes in the positions of the joints or limbs as a result of the extra force being applied to them
- A feeling of deceleration. This will come from vision and sound, but also from the balance organs in the inner ear

Using Intrinsic Feedback

Intrinsic feedback will always be available but may not always be recognised by the performer. The instructor can encourage and help the learners to recognise this information so that it can be used as part of a successful feedback loop. Once recognised, the information needs to be evaluated accurately in relation to the task. Often for learners in the associative phase they are not able to evaluate intrinsic information. For example, a skier may try to widen their stance whilst performing short turns. The performer feels that their legs were as wide as possible, at the edge of their range. The instructor can see that the legs were still within hip width apart. The skier may say, "I felt my skis were wider than last time." Here the instructor is able to help with the evaluative process by calibrating the intrinsic feedback by adding "yes, your feet were a couple of inches further apart". After receiving this augmented feedback, the performer will be able to evaluate the performance (she knew that the task involved getting the feet about 6 inches apart, so she has to go further) and can set a plan for development in order to achieve the task (she goes back up and has another go, with the same focus but improved intrinsic awareness). This is known as augmenting the feedback.

There are some key points for the instructor to remember when delivering feedback that augment the intrinsic feedback:

- If the instructor augments on a particular aspect of performance (e.g. stance width) then the student should be aware that this is the focus of the task
- Augmented feedback should be as specific as possible. E.g. "your feet were about 3 inches wider" as opposed to "yes, your feet were a bit wider"
- Feedback should be restricted to the task set. If the task is a wider stance, then pole plant is irrelevant
- The instructor should use the PAT principle. PAUSE to give the student time to reflect and review their own performance, ASK questions to direct attention to elements of performance that you think are relevant. TELL only once intrinsic feedback has been reviewed

Using rating scales is a way to improve a performer's intrinsic feedback. For example, on a scale of 0-5 where 5 is the maximum edge angle, and 0 is no edge angle, the performer can be asked to rate their edge angle. The teacher has the chance to augment this informative feedback. The scales may need to vary and need not be numerical e.g. "where do you stand on your feet, front middle or back"? Scales should be agreed with the performer first so that they can use them happily. Instructors can use imagery to help with theses rating scales so that the pupil is able to relate to them more easily. For example in a children's' group an instructor may ask what type of fruit they could squash under their feet when they make turns, can they squash fruits of varying firmness, a grape, or an orange, what about an apple?

Using these rating scales allows the pupil to develop their intrinsic feedback. They suit the self check style of teaching very well. By agreeing the desired result on their scale and comparing with the achieved result, the student and teacher move through the evaluation stage and are ready to move in to development.

Being able to link the intrinsic information back to a more objective evaluation of performance is a key element of the learning phases. As the learners move from cognitive to associative and late associative they will get better at calibrating the internal information and it will become more useful in the overall feedback loop.

Extrinsic Feedback

This is often thought to come largely from the instructor, but it can also come from another member of the group (as in the reciprocal teaching style), a video camera, the snow (looking at the tracks) or from timing equipment. When it comes from a non-human source, feedback provides objective information which is less effected by opinion or dogma, this can be very useful when trying to convince people that something is happening in their performance that they can't feel intrinsically. Extrinsic information is used to evaluate performance without reference to the performers' intrinsic information. In order to close the feedback loop the instructor must come up with a plan to develop the student's performance. Often the plan for development will be designed and agreed upon in conjunction with the student and at this stage the student may augment the extrinsic feedback with their intrinsic information. It is rare that one type of feedback, either intrinsic or extrinsic works alone.

The Nature of Communication when Working with Feedback

The goal of feedback is to close the feedback loop and improve the chances of achieving the task. Communication to the pupil does not have to try and meet all the stages of this process at once and can be broken down into three types.

Informative statements - Give facts about the performance but do not evaluate the performance or suggest ways to develop it. This may be deliberate, in order to allow the student to calibrate their intrinsic information, or to allow the student to go through the process of evaluation on their own.

The following statement, "You were using a bigger range of leg extension and flexion on that run" gives the pupil information about their movements and augments their intrinsic feedback. Depending on the context this remark could also have an evaluative and corrective purpose too, but for now we will focus on the informative aspect.

This statement could be more helpful by using a rating scale. For example if 10 is maximum range and 0 is no movement the teacher could say "your leg extension was a 4 that time compared to a 2 the last time". This will improve the accuracy and sensitivity of their intrinsic feedback.

Evaluative statements - Judge the performance based on the expected outcome. They do not suggest a pathway for development. Often evaluative statements are given to motivate the student, encourage the student or confirm their own evaluation of performance.

Statements like, "that was about as much use as a chocolate fireguard" maybe raise a laugh from the group but are not especially helpful. It only evaluates performance in terms of good or bad, rather than highlighting what aspect of performance is bad or encouraging the performer. "You matched the skis really well but then lost balance sideways which stopped the outside ski from turning. How will you stop that next time?" This statement is more specific and includes encouragement. The corrective/developmental action required is opened up to the learner to encourage understanding and taking the responsibility for learning himself.

In order to make useful evaluative statements whilst maintaining a positive approach, an instructor can use the "Big Mac" approach. A poor element of performance (the meat) is highlighted but is surrounded by positive aspects of the performance (the bun). For example "I thought you did turn your feet more across the hill that time, nice one, however the skis still split a little at the end of the turn, we need to do some more work on that, however your speed was more controlled that time".

Corrective/Developmental - Feedback tells the learner what aspect of their performance needs to be improved. It fulfils the develop stage of the overall feedback loop.

Quite often we use all these ways of communicating feedback within one statement, it is not a case of deciding which type to use and then sticking with it. Consider the previous statement which refers to the example given in the informative section.

"Although you thought it was a 10, I would give it a 7. There is more movement available and you need to be about a 9 to keep the skis on the snow. Have another go".

This statement is now informative, evaluative and corrective/developmental.

The teacher needs to know whether their communication fits in to any or all of these categories as it will then affect the overall feedback process. There are good reasons for the communication not to fulfil all or any of these categories, but the instructor needs to be sure that the overall feedback loop represented by the TIED model is eventually met.

Other Qualities of Communication when Related to Feedback

Be Specific – "Good edge set" is better than "good"

Be Positive – Try to point out what it good in a performance and try to make sure that corrective communication is constructive rather than destructive. This gives better guidance for development and is likely to motivate the pupil more.

Be Relevant – Make sure communication is in relation to the task set and in relation to the focus within the task. If the focus is on the result of the task, like leaving two clean tracks in the snow, then the feedback should focus on this result first, rather than the movements used to achieve the results. If a student is asked to make a snowplough shape with their skis and achieves it, then this should first be praised (evaluated). Comments about which movements the skier used to make the snowplough can come later.

Be Sparing – Students need to develop their ability to gather intrinsic information. They need to be able to evaluate their own performance and understanding so that they can potentially find their own developmental solutions. By communicating too freely and taking away responsibility from the learner during the feedback loop, an instructor will inhibit the pupil's development in the long term. Students should be educated not to expect feedback at every moment of a lesson and should be encouraged to take responsibility themselves.

Summary

The whole teaching process is one large feedback system enabling the current performance to influence future performance. This loop of cause and effect is described in the TIED model. Communicating or delivering feedback to a performer is just one part of this model and alone does not necessarily close the loop. It is feedback within the whole process presented by the model that ensures we are effective in achieving the goals of the learner.

Top Tips

Let the pupils know that their intrinsic feedback is important

Set up a feedback contract with the group and let them know that the bigger feedback loop is more important than having a piece of information every time

Be positive. Even an evaluation that means there is a lot of work to do, means that there is a lot of room for quick and enjoyable improvement

Do not hide behind intrinsic feedback. Your evaluation based on observation may still be valid, even if it contradicts the intrinsic information from the learner. You should seek further information

"How was it for you?" is not as useful as a more specific question that helps the learner manage the information they have. "Did the ski grip around the whole arc"?

If you didn't see the performance, then admit to it

Communication Skills

The ability to communicate effectively underpins the usefulness of just about everything in this manual. Effective communication needs to be clear, unambiguous and understood by the recipient. Communication is a two way process and the goal is for the sender and the receiver to understand the same information (and meaning). If the meaning of the message becomes distorted, it will lead to frustration and a break down in the communication process. Below is a simple illustration of how we communicate. We will use the stages highlighted in the diagram to structure this section.

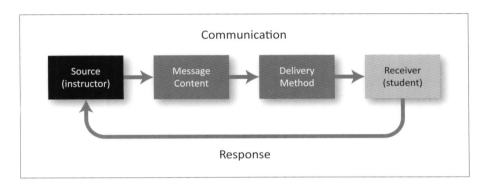

Figure 6.2:
The process of communication

Source

The source is where the message originates. In most cases for us this is the instructor although the students can obviously initiate communication too.

Message Content

How we structure the content of our message is covered in the Content and Structure section of the manual, however, a key consideration, specific to communication skills is how we can minimise the distortions and interference to our message. Very often in ski teaching students have preconceived ideas or are subject to misunderstandings based on content from a third source.

To eradicate this type of interference it helps for the instructor to talk to their students and get to know them. This might sound obvious but focussed questions about the students learning history can be more useful than the normal small talk that often happens on chairlifts. Experience also helps, by being aware of the kinds of misunderstandings and preconceived ideas that may arise, the instructor can attend to these issues early and avoid having to back track during the lesson.

Another consideration is that we shouldn't under estimate the power of using people's names. It can be difficult to memorise the names of your group on the first day but by doing so you show your students that you are interested in them as individuals, that you care and that you are professional. They are also more likely to listen to your message. There are many ways to help commit names to memory but one simple tactic is to repeat someone's name as soon as possible after having been introduced.

Finally, remember to make the content of your message interesting and relevant to the audience.

Delivery Method

This part of the communication process is what we usually think of as "communication". The skills associated with how we deliver a message are related to reducing the possible interference that can occur and maximising the effectiveness of delivery.

In the Understanding Learning section we expand on the different types of learner and how they think and learn in different ways. This is simplified in to the VAK approach, we need to cover all aspects of VAK if our communication is to be effective for all types of learner.

Visual

Demonstration – One of the most important ways that we communicate visually when teaching snowsports is by demonstrating the intended task. For communication of this type to be effective our demonstrations need to be easy to see and accurate. Take your time when demonstrating, make sure you have finished speaking before setting off and have a clear plan in your head of what you are going to show the students. It is also important that demonstrations are not always conducted with the same orientation. Ski towards your group, away from the group and past the group to ensure people see what is happening from different perspectives.

Body language – We send messages with our bodies all the time and it is important to be aware of how these might be interpreted by our students. When meeting a group for the first time an open, welcoming demeanour will set an open and welcoming climate. Other climates can be created with help from body language. Below are a few examples:

Climate	Communication Traits
Closed	Crossed arms, frowning
Open	Eye contact, smiling, arms open
Attentive	Ignoring distractions, showing patience
Bored	Looking away, making repetitive actions (tapping pole), yawning
Domineering	Standing too closely to people when talking to them

How the teacher positions themselves in relation to the group will also have an effect on the climate and how the delivery of the message is received. For example if the instructor always has the group lined up in front of them the climate is more formal than if the students are gathered around the instructor in a huddle. If the instructor is to then squat down onto their haunches in the middle of the huddle and look up at the group, this creates another climate, it is non-threatening and suggests a togetherness or humility.

Imagery – Whilst the spoken word is by definition auditory, the teacher is able to communicate better with all learning through the use of imagery, metaphor and simile in their delivery language. The extension and flexion of the legs can be like riding a bike, the skiers are asked to try and float down the off piste section making light touches in the snow and not breaking the egg shells under foot. By painting pictures for people when explaining often complex activities we are able to communicate better with visual learners.

Auditory

Volume – Firstly we need to speak loudly enough. This doesn't mean we need to shout for people to hear us. A good communicator can engage their audience and encourage them to listen without raising their voice. Face your audience and look them in the eye. If you mumble at the ground your message is likely to get lost and you will lose the attention of your listeners.

Clear and Concise – Try to use simple words with accurate meaning. Structure your message in such a way as to say what is important without too much prattle. It is a skill to be concise and still get across the relevant information. National and regional accents add character and interest but if too strong they can confuse a message. Too many colloquialisms can have the same effect. We should make an extra effort to communicate in such a way as to ensure our audience can understand what we say.

Tone – The tone of your voice can have an important impact on your audience. Is it encouraging, condescending, warm, mocking, concerned etc? Often you won't be aware of this but it can have an effect on the learner, especially if they are in a nervous or vulnerable state. The tone of your voice goes some way to telling the listener what you are thinking, it is an important tool for the teacher when considering how to motivate students, ensure discipline and cope with anxious learners.

Intonation – The rise, fall and the pitch of your voice will also have a bearing on whether your audience listen and buy into what you say. Maintaining attention will be difficult if your message is delivered in a monotone. Allowing a passion for what you are teaching to come out in your voice is a great way to inspire people. This doesn't mean you have to jump around like a children's TV presenter, different people will have different ways of sounding interested in what they are saying.

Questions – Asking a good question involves the audience in the delivery – to keep this simple we can look at two types of question, **open** and **closed**. An open question has more than one answer and helps to bring new information into a discussion, "What would you change to prevent you from losing your edge grip on your left leg turns"? A closed question will usually result in a yes/no answer and is more useful for focussing on specific points or clarifying information, "did you lose your edge grip on your left leg turns"?

Asking questions is a great delivery method if done skilfully. If the instructor can elicit information from the learner by asking the right questions then the learner can move across the discovery threshold (see Teaching Styles). As we have already discussed when introducing the Teaching Styles this is not always appropriate but it can be a useful way to achieve certain objectives. Asking good questions can:

- Help the student feel a part of the learning process
- Check understanding

- Encourage the student to evaluate their own performance and develop their analytical skills
- Promote learning that is memorable
- Give the instructor time to think

If performed badly, questioning is a waste of time that creates frustration and boredom in the listener. Don't ask questions for the sake of it, use them to make communication more effective.

Kinaesthetic

For doers and feelers a kinaesthetic approach will help get the message across. Some learners may not understand the message until they have had the chance to try it, others will benefit from referring, through communication to physical feelings or images of movement in order to help them relate to the message.

Imagery – This can work for visual learners or kinaesthetic learners, either people use the picture in their minds eye or they imagine themselves doing the action. For example imagining compressing springs attached to the soles of the feet, with one spring compressed (outside ski) and the other open (inside ski), might work better as a kinaesthetic approach than simply pedalling. Either example has its merits and will help visual and kinaesthetic learners.

Simulation – Another way to communicate with kinaesthetic learners is to get them to simulate the movement you are asking them to make before setting off on their skis. This can make use of other parts of the body. Use the arms as if they were legs and simulate the action of flexing and extending during a turn. Ask students to practise jumping with the skis off to feel the pop of take off and the flexion required on landing.

Receiver

Knowing your audience will help to ensure that the message you deliver is received in the way you intend. Their existing knowledge level and past experience should be established as early as possible and taken into consideration. Over time the instructor will also get to know the learner type of their students. This will allow the instructor to shape his delivery and focus on different aspects of VAK accordingly.

Response – Once the message has been delivered there is likely to be some kind of reaction from the receiver. This may be verbal or non-verbal but it will provide an opportunity to check whether the message has been understood. This response from the learner closes the communication loop. If there has been a misunderstanding then the message can be delivered again taking into account whatever feedback comes from the receiver.

Being a good listener is a key part of communicating. Listening and understanding what the learner is saying in response to your instructions or ideas is what guides your delivery and allows you to meet the needs of the learner. There are other ways to deal with the response of the learner such as watching their behaviour and their performance. However, it is through conversation that we glean most of the information we need for effective communication, conversation that flows both ways.

Top Tips

If you want to develop your ability to speak concisely try running a practise session where your class loop on a drag lift. Position yourself in the middle of the slope near to the lift. Prepare what you want to say to each student as you watch them ski down the slope and deliver this information as they pass you on the lift. This will give you 5 seconds maximum to deliver your message

Reviewing Skills

The ability to manage and facilitate reviews well is often a key skill exhibited by great teachers. Reviewing is about helping learners think better and deeper about the information available to them. Reflecting, analysing, evaluating and deciding can all be influenced by how well the instructor leads the review. It is easy to think of reviewing as something that only happens on BASI teaching courses. However, reviewing forms an important part in all good learning sessions.

When working through the TIED model reviewing is the process that helps learners to evaluate their own performance. It helps learners take responsibility for their own learning which can sometimes be difficult for us as teachers because it often means we have to resist the temptation to " just tell them what to do" all the time.

More often than not it is the teacher who will lead the review. It is important to know what the objectives of the review are beforehand. Why are you doing a review? There may have been a lot of skiing activity with the clients working in pairs. You might not have been able to check in and watch each pair. A review will help bring everyone together to share their findings.

Listening to other people's findings and ideas may help individuals add perspective and deeper understanding to their own learning issues.

Reviewing often means not skiing. Sometimes learners (and the teacher) can get so engrossed in the review discussion that times flies by. Be aware of this and manage time appropriately. You should think about managing each person's contribution in the review. Rarely will each person in the group wish to speak the same amount as everyone else! Using a round robin system, where everyone knows they have to contribute, is one way to pull all the members of the group into the discussion.

It is also important to keep the review positive. Sometimes we need to give people critical and constructive feedback. After a weaker student led teaching session on a BASI teaching course, there may be some critical development points to be made. Asking the other students to give the student teacher one positive developmental point to "help make the next session better", sets up positive "do" rather than negative "don't" do statements. This makes it more likely for the recipient of the feedback to accept and take on board the information in a productive and accepting way. By maintaining an open and honest environment when reviewing as a group, people who contribute to the process are likely to feel valued and respected. This is an important part of how the reviewing climate is managed. We must be careful not to disregard comments even if we as the reviewer feel they are of little use or relevance. Rather we should encourage the comment maker or the group as a whole to continue sharing their thoughts until useful information starts to come to the surface. For example:

"Great, that's an interesting point, so what else do we think might help James to be more succinct in the future".

When leading a review, it can be useful to have a review structure, whilst still being prepared to explore other areas as they may arise. Asking holidaymakers to compare the differences between two skiers they are watching can be a good way to help them develop technical understanding. Asking BASI students to review a peer's lesson in terms of the TIED model, may be a good way to help students focus on certain strengths or weaknesses in a teaching session. As you learn and develop your reviewing skills, it can be good to have a couple of back up approaches in case things don't go the way you planned. Here are a few examples:

Round Robin – Keep, Stop, and Develop

Set the review up so that everyone knows they have to comment. Ask them to comment on a performance in terms of what they think should be kept (strengths), what should be stopped (weaknesses) and what should be developed (areas to work on).

Put the Learners in the Teacher's Shoes

When a review highlights something that needs to be stopped or developed it can help to ask the group to share their thoughts on how they would approach the situation if they were in the role of the person being reviewed. This will often generate a host of ideas that can act as options or choices for the performer.

Keep Drilling to get the Useful Information Out

Firstly the reviewer attempts to get general information out of the group such as "what did you like in Peter's lesson"? Once people start contributing thoughts about what they liked in Peter's lesson, you keep asking for more, "ok, thanks, and what else did you like"? It is surprising how many times a "what else" questions will continue to generate new content and ideas. Once you have captured the main points, you may decide that one or two need investigating further. You now ask "ok, so you all said you liked how Peter was so specific in his technical feedback, what was it about that, that you really liked"? or "how did that help the session"? Perhaps people thought Peter's session was great fun. In this case you may decide to drill down a little further by asking "what was it that made Peter's session such fun"? once you get an answer, you may continue drilling down by asking a further question such as "and what was it about that made it fun"? Again, it can be surprising how many times you can repeat the same question and get more and better information to help everyone take more from the review.

Customer Care

The Importance of Good Customer Care

Many of the attributes that create good customer care are covered in other sections of the manual. Communications skills, feedback, enjoyment, climate and goal setting to mention just a few. However it is worth considering our delivery from the perspective of the client to ensure we meet the high standards of professionalism that we expect as BASI qualified snowsport instructors. Putting the clients satisfaction at the centre of the experience not only guarantees happy clients, but is also a necessity to generate that vital part in any business – the return customer.

Developing a first class reputation for customer care doesn't come without hard work and an attention to detail. In order to maintain that reputation it is necessary to maintain these high standards. There is no room for complacency, a lack of professionalism or a failure to work in a client friendly way, will lead to unhappy customers and the likely distribution of bad press. Word of mouth is a powerful medium and can be as destructive as it is useful.

The Basics of Good Customer Care

As a starting point we should strive to always employ basic traits of human decency, such as treating our clients with respect and empathy. A true professional will not allow personal preferences to dictate the nature of a relationship with a customer. The old adage, "the customer is always right" has stood the test of time and provides a worthy foundation for the way we approach our work. On the occasion that the customer is not right the manner in which you let them know this is crucial. Below are some ideas that will help us to employ good customer care.

Listen to the Customer

It is essential that we understand what our customers want, a few open questions to start the conversation will allow you to listen and then show that you care about the experience they are going to have whilst in your company. By making eye contact as you listen, you engage with them and show them that you are trying to understand their needs. This is when the customer will form their first impression of you and is a vital part of the relationship building process (see Communication Skills).

Agree on the Goals of the Session

We need to establish some agreed outcomes. These can be as varied as the people we meet but in order to look after our customers we need to help them to achieve these goals, so it is essential that they are skilfully negotiated to avoid disappointment or dissatisfaction (see Goal Setting).

Create Rapport

This plays a fundamental role in the enjoyment for the client and for the instructor. The ability to engage, entertain and understand our clients ensures that we build rewarding relationships. There are many qualities that can be highlighted as ways to create good rapport, honesty, sincerity, openness, empathy, it all boils down to treating the customer the way you would like to be treated if the roles were reversed.

Showing an interest in the customer is a better tactic than talking purely about you and this brings us back to the ability to be a good listener. By listening actively you will begin to recognise the warning signs of anxiety or frustration in your clients and will be in a better position to react and steer proceedings in the right direction.

Humour can be a great ally in building relationships. You don't have to be the world's best comedian trying to get laughs all the time but a lightness of spirit works wonders. Show people that you are enthusiastic for them to learn. Make sure that you always laugh with them and not at them. The best instructors combine the necessary practical skills with the best principles of customer care delivered with their own unique personality and style.

Professionalism

This should go without saying but your professionalism will impact on how the customer reacts to the lesson. Punctuality and personal appearance set the tone for the relationship between instructor and client. If you arrive late, with a dirty uniform and bad breath you are not showing much respect for the client. They have paid for your services and expect to enjoy a lesson with someone who takes a pride in what they do and displays this pride from the word go.

Behaving in a manner appropriate for the customers in question is also an important consideration, you may need to change your behaviour if teaching a group of adults to when teaching a group of teenagers. However, remaining polite and respectful towards the people in your care and to other professionals in the resort is something that should never change.

Dealing with Customer Problems

Although we try to keep our customers satisfied all the time, it is inevitable that problems will occur. It is possible to minimise the likelihood of problems arising by striving to achieve good customer care as outlined above, however we should be prepared to handle potentially awkward situations.

Risk assessment has become standard practise in today's health and safety driven world, yet it should not be consigned to form filling and box ticking. Assessing risk is something that we should do continually as we work with our customers, managing that risk skilfully is one way to reduce potential problems. For example avoid using certain runs at the end of the day when they will be crowded and prone to cause collisions. Be aware of the signs of tiredness in your customers and stop for a drinks break rather than pushing them too far.

If, despite your best intentions, a complaint does occur, there are some guidelines for how to manage the situation.

Behaviour

- Remain calm and in control to avoid a problem escalating
- Try not to argue, rather listen and look for a solution
- Calmly ask questions to find out the exact nature of the person's complaint, if someone is agitated they can sometimes make little sense and fail to express the real problem

Approach

- Look favourably on the customer's motives. Don't be too sceptical or cynical about their reason for complaint
- Remember that you may not be able to completely satisfy each and every customer
- Do not take complaints personally, try to be concerned with what is right rather than who is right

Policies and Procedures

- Be aware of company policies and procedures for handling complaints
- If you don't have the authority to deal effectively with the complaint, refer it to someone who does and let the client know what you are going to do
- Follow-up on complaints to ensure there is an acceptable outcome for the client
- When appropriate thank the customer for bringing the problem to your attention

Planning a Session

This section is designed to help you put into practise all the knowledge that you have as a snowsports professional. It provides you with a step by step guide to planning a session. Firstly we look at the structure of a good lesson and the different parameters we need to consider. Secondly we look at the meat of the session - the content. By better understanding the key content areas of a lesson, the instructor will be able to use the information presented in this manual and their existing knowledge in a skilful and effective way. Finally we will look at how to review the plan before delivering it, to ensure that it will flow and address the key areas effectively.

Structure

The effective performance of any complex task depends on good planning. Teaching snowsports is certainly no exception. With practise, teachers may be able to deliver high-quality lessons without formal planning. However the structure of such lessons draws on the teacher's knowledge and previous experience. For novice or inexperienced teachers, formal planning is vital.

The best approach is to plan the lesson on paper - either a blank sheet or a standard prepared form. The main advantage of the latter is that it acts as a reminder of the key points which need to be included. An example of a suitable lesson plan is shown opposite. A full-sized version is reproduced in the Appendix, and may be photocopied freely by anyone wishing to use it.

How we structure our session is firstly dependent on the parameters outlined in the lesson plan. Here we consider each one in turn.

See Appendices for example lesson plan.

Number of Clients

Class size has a strong bearing on how a lesson is structured.

Large Groups

- Here safety issues are potentially more complex and need to be thought through in detail (see Safety, Group Management section)

- MCA is more difficult to achieve and needs thorough planning. Assuming safety is not compromised, the way in which we structure practise within any of the teaching styles can help to keep a group moving. It is rarely necessary to have one person skiing down at a time, whilst the rest of the group wait for their turn. The location of the session and the nature of the terrain are crucial. If there is a short lift where the top and bottom of the slope is visible from the middle this would provide a perfect place to get the group looping, individually, in pairs or in small groups. Working on activities while the whole group is on the move also allows a much higher level of activity than practising one by one

- A greater range of potential faults will occur with a larger group. This needs to be planned for with different activities and solutions

- Dealing with feedback needs more planning than with smaller groups. This can be done as a group so that everyone listens and learns from each other's feedback or it can be done individually. Care needs to be taken when working through feedback individually for the process not to take too much time. A chairlift or cable-car can sometimes be a great place to talk to people individually when working with large groups, it is a tactic that helps make the most of the time available in the session

- There is often more skill needed from the instructor when setting goals with the group. It is worth planning a few different goals that could be suggested to the group that can be worked upon in the same session. The students can still be part of the process but may be given options rather than a totally open remit. For example, "piste short turns, steep runs or bumps? We can work on skills (inputs) that will help in all these areas and then go to a piste that has all those terrain options available. Then you can choose which strand you practise in." This is really tough to achieve and takes a lot of experience in group management to meet everyone's needs. It should only be attempted by very experienced and confident instructors. Alternatively the instructor can set the terrain and the strand for the session and then work individually with the pupils to meet their goals

Small Groups or Individuals

- When working with small groups or in one-to-one sessions there is a danger of the session becoming too intense. Plan for extended practise sessions and allow for time to experiment

- Plan to keep the teaching content to the slopes and allow time for normal chat on the lifts, this will break up the intensity of the lesson

- With smaller groups the goal setting process can be a lot more open. In terms of planning it is important to anticipate a wide range of topics

Age

Different age-groups have different teaching requirements. For example, the main focus in children's lessons should be on learning through play, with very little explicit emphasis on technique. On the other hand, adults may wish for much more technical content and detail. Some clients like to know what they will be doing in advance, others are happy to be surprised. Do not assume that the older clients do not like surprises or that younger clients are happy to have things thrown at them. Treat each client as an individual and change your approach based on knowledge rather than assumptions.

Until you get to know your group, the use of an inclusive teaching style can be very valuable.

Gender

In general, the learning process is the same for both males and females. However, there may be differences in strength, confidence and attitude that are, to an extent, gender specific. These can influence the pupil's approach within a lesson and are important considerations when planning a session.

Just as men tend to be physically larger and more powerful than women, so they tend to differ in their response to challenge. Men are more likely to rely on strength and commitment to overcome any limitations in technique. Conversely, women often tend towards greater caution, preferring to rely on technique rather than commitment or strength. Neither of these tendencies is intrinsically better than the other and gender does not guarantee that a pupil will fit in to either category. The "can do" approach enables clients to attempt a wider range of speed and terrain at a given technical level but often falls down by eventually resulting in poor technique. On the other hand, being more cautious has the advantage of usually encouraging greater sensitivity and technical accuracy.

Children and Adolescents

When teaching children, there are no significant differences between the sexes until puberty. During adolescence however, males and females often start to respond differently. Because energetic physical pursuits are sometimes seen as intrinsically masculine, adolescent girls may be more reluctant to engage in them. This is truer of those who are taking up the sport for the first time than for those more experienced.

As young people develop their sense of identity, they may benefit from seeing appropriate role models of their own sex, whether recreational, instructors or competitors. Equally, it may be useful to highlight the more challenging or competitive aspects of the sport for some pupils, while emphasising its more aesthetic features such as gracefulness and rhythm for others.

Specific Needs and Requirements

While many pupils are happy for the teacher to make most of the decisions about what to do and where to go, some have very specific needs and requirements. In order to plan effectively, you need to find what these are. Regardless of whether or not you have received information about the group in advance, it is important to check for any specific requests at the start of the lesson.

Some may be quite simple, such as staying only on blue runs, or improving their mogul skiing. Others may be less so, such as a pupil who has to avoid making particular movements due to a damaged knee ligament. Even more difficult judgements may be involved where a pupil suffers from a more serious medical condition such as a heart complaint or epilepsy. Whatever the clients' needs, they must be given the opportunity to express them, either in the group or privately.

Another category of needs and requirements is that of clients with disabilities or learning difficulties. This is a much more specialised field and is outside the scope of this chapter. There are separate courses to train teachers to work with clients with such requirements. Known as Adaptive Ski Instructor Courses, further information can be obtained from the BASI.

Standard and Experience

Your clients' technical standard and level of experience may be established either by direct questioning or by observation of their performance. Many recreational skiers have a fairly limited understanding of technique. For example, pupils may say that they can ski parallel. In practise, this may mean anything from their being at the earliest stages of plough parallel turning up to being confident skiing all over the mountain.

When relying on verbal information, the number of weeks' experience is often a more accurate guide than the stated technical level. In general, it is preferable to observe pupils' performance directly in order to obtain an accurate picture.

Even in a group that is supposedly of the same standard there are often splits in ability or ambition. It is helpful to plan different options for where a session might go for the group or for certain individuals. This may be difficult on day one but once you know the group it becomes easier to anticipate how quickly people will progress and what challenges they will welcome or shun.

Motivation for Attendance

In part, pupils' aims and interests may already have been established in "Specific Needs and Requirements" above. You may however, still need to find out their reasons for being there. Do they want to be there for themselves, or are they there to keep somebody else happy? (see Goal Setting, and Motivation section).

With intrinsically motivated students, planning is easy as the pupils wants to learn. Where motivation is extrinsic, the reasons for being there may be very diverse, and planning the lesson may require careful thought. Such pupils may still want to learn, but this is unlikely to be the most important aspect. Feeling safe, staying warm, having lots of coffee stops, enjoying the mountain scenery - all of these may play a much more significant role than becoming a better skier or snowboarder.

Lesson Duration

Good time management is essential for good teaching. Within the duration of the lesson, the structure and content must be gauged to make best use of the time available. For example, a task which takes 45 minutes practise to achieve may be appropriate for a half-day lesson, but not for a 1 hour private lesson.

Whatever the lesson's duration, the following elements need to have time allocated to them:
- Revision (**develop**)
- Core lesson content (**task**)
- Feedback and fault correction (**information** and **evaluation**)
- Practise and consolidation (**develop**)

Approximate timings for each of these stages should be considered during the planning of the lesson, with enough time allocated to the practise period to give the learner an opportunity to actually improve their performance and develop their skills (see TIED model, Structure of Practise and Skill Acquisition model).

State of Fitness

As well as their technical suitability, activities should be appropriate for the clients' state of fitness. Tasks which are within people's capacity will enhance both performance and sense of achievement, those which are physically too demanding can result in injury or demoralisation.

When planning, consider the effects of terrain, snow conditions and weather, in relation to the physical demands of the activities.

Terrain

Having ascertained as much information about the group as possible it is useful to plan where the session will take place. The choice of terrain is crucial for managing most of the variables already presented and has a huge effect on the learner's rate of development.

From the Known to the Unknown

Before looking at the content of the lesson, there is one key principle to be borne in mind: that of always going from the known to the unknown.

The willingness to try something new – to explore the unknown – depends largely on pupils' confidence and commitment. Timid or less enthusiastic learners are usually more reluctant. But even the most committed pupils generally have more success where a new task builds on what has already been learned. Not only is confidence likely to be greater, the learner will also have a clearer picture of the action or task to be performed. Building on past experience is fundamental to skill development as seen in the Skill Acquisition chapter.

For example, the Central Theme illustrates this principle. Throughout the progression, each new movement builds on those which have gone before. Even where a new activity does not relate directly to what has gone before, the principle can often still be used. In an introductory lesson, there are no previous skiing activities to which the tasks can be related. However, virtually all of the movements of snowsports can be related to other, more familiar activities. Such similarities often underlie the use of imagery (see Communication Skills section) in teaching:

- Standing like a runner/goalkeeper/tennis player for basic posture
- Pedalling to describe the action of standing rhythmically on alternate skis

So even if there are no 'known' skiing activities on which you can build, try to find points of reference in the learner's previous experience. In that way, the learning process will be strengthened by moving from the known to the unknown.

Content

In order to be accurate and effective with the content of a session, much of the information in this manual needs to be addressed. In many ways this section is the culmination of the BASI product through from the performance section, to understanding learning. The content needs to include appropriate safety considerations and create the right learning environment. It is the meat of the delivery section and if delivered well, is ultimately what will make the difference to the learner.

Having established the different parameters of our lesson in the Structure section, here we look at the different content areas of a good lesson. A lesson can be seen as a story that has a beginning, middle and end, with this in mind it is helpful to break the lesson down into the following stages:

- Introductions
- Goal setting (Introduction)
- Warm up activities
- Revision activities
- Session activities
- Cool down
- Conclusion

The BASI Alpine Manual

Introductions

This is a very important part of the session. First impressions count especially with a one off lesson. Think carefully about how your behaviour will affect the climate, how the student(s) may be feeling. Often they will feel more nervous than you and it is your job to put them at ease. It is a skill to make small talk interesting but this is often what needs to happen when meeting a group for the first time. As you wait for other members of the group to arrive, it will be your role to lead the conversation. Anything from current affairs, recent sporting occasions, where people are staying in resort, how their journey to the mountains was, where they last skied etc. will help to get things flowing. If this doesn't come naturally to you, it is possible to plan some topics to break the ice.

Goal Setting

The content of a session must be relevant to the learner in some way, this is usually in relation to the goals set by the learners and instructor together. The instructor will often need to negotiate these goals so that there is general agreement within the group as to what is the motivation for the session. Even after this process it must be recognised that goals within the group will probably differ, it is the instructor's job to ensure that all the goals are met. While we assume this is the instructor's own underlying goal, they may well have other goals of their own, separate to those of the students.

Here are some examples of over all goals and how they might relate to the people involved in the session:

1. To make the move from plough turning to parallel skiing (individual goal).

2. Helping a group of first-week snowboarders to ride all the way from the top of the mountain back to the village (group goal).

3. Helping a group of disheartened learners to regain a sense of enjoyment and satisfaction from the sport (instructor goal).

Depending on how long the instructor has with the group, these over all goals may need to be achieved in one session or over a series of sessions. Whether happening over the course of a week or 3 hours, it will usually help to set intermediate goals as stepping stones to achieving the over all goal. Here are some examples of intermediate goals that follow on from the examples above:

1. Raising the speed at which the individual is confident, improving their ability to stand on the outer ski, introducing basic edge-awareness activities.

2. Revising ways of coping with difficult terrain, improving everyone's ability to follow an accurate line, ensuring that pupils understand what to do if they get separated from the group.

3. Establishing what everyone enjoys most and least about the sport, revising activities which everyone enjoys and is able to achieve, focusing pupils' attention on their strengths rather than their weaknesses.

When planning a session, setting both over all and intermediate goals is key for ensuring success and for developing a flowing lesson (see Goals Setting section for further information).

Warm up Activities

The warm up is how we prepare for what is coming in the main part of the session. It needs to prepare body and mind and is a good way to reduce the risk of injury. (For more in depth information see Physical Thread, Reading List, Appendix 5)

Make the warm up appropriate:

- To the situation - There is no point warming up at the bottom of a chairlift to then spend 20 minutes getting cold on the way to the start of the first run. Warm up to prepare for action. This may involve working through activities on the way to the area chosen for the main part of the session or warming up at the top of the slope to be used for the session

- To the conditions - A cold January day will require more of a physical approach to increase blood circulation and raise the body temperature. On a warm Easter afternoon it may be more useful to spend longer tuning people into being balanced or increasing mobility

- To the nature of the session - If the main part of the session is going to be based around plough parallels, build some ploughing and skidding activities into the warm up. If you're planning to ski bumps, get students jumping and skiing short turns to firm up the muscles in the same way they'll be used in the bumps. Balancing exercises relate to any type of skiing, so getting students to tune into being on one ski or lifting the tail of a ski are great ways to move a warm up towards what is coming next in the session

- To the group - A group of kids will get pretty bored doing the same warm up that you may run with a group of adults. Kids want to play games and can warm up without even knowing that is the purpose of the activity. Games of tag, relay races, snow ball fights anything that gets them moving is a good idea. A similar approach can be taken with skis on, activities that involve them using a full range of movement, jumping, touching the snow, hopping, shuffling, balancing on one ski etc

With adults there can be more of a structure and an explanation as to why you are warming up in a certain way. Relate the activities to the forth coming tasks or to the conditions.

Revision Activities

This provides students the opportunity to move from the known to the unknown and link the warm up to the main session by practicing skills and activities that are already familiar. Depending on their stage of development and any time constraints (number of sessions remaining etc.) this stage can continue for a long time and end up forming the main part of the session, with the instructor there to work with people individually as they practise. Equally, it can be a short revisiting of material covered the day before that helps to build confidence and put everyone in a good frame of mind.

Session Activities

This is the main body of the lesson and is aimed at achieving the intermediate goals agreed at the start. What happens here has to be relevant to these goals, the students should not be in any doubt as to why certain activities are happening unless the instructor is purposely using a discovery method of teaching.

The session activities are shaped by how the instructor chooses to use the tools presented in the Understanding section and should also take into account the differences between the learners. Here are some examples of how this information might be used when working with skiers moving from ploughing towards plough parallel:

- The phase of learning that each student is in might not be the same for each skill or activity. The task may need to be presented in a different way using chaining rather than shaping. For example: Move the skis from a plough to parallel on a shallow traverse without changing direction (chaining) or focus on standing earlier on the new turning ski to enable the inner ski to be steered parallel (shaping)
- The phase of learning of each student will also affect the nature of the feedback used. In cognitive and early associative phases the learner will require more extrinsic guidance whereas in the later associative and acquired phases the learner can rely more on their own information and evaluation. In any case the instructor needs to ensure the whole feedback loop is closed (see Feedback and TIED model)
- There may be learners who are predominantly visual learners and others who are real thinkers, so a good demonstration and clear explanation will be necessary
- As new information is introduced, the command style of teaching may be appropriate for a short time followed by a practise or reciprocal style part to the session. Introduce how to steer the inner ski parallel and then allow the group to practise. Reciprocal work could be to work in pairs and feedback to each other on how wide the plough is – too wide and steering parallel will be more difficult
- It may work well to introduce some discovery style teaching where you ask the group to try matching the skis parallel whilst standing still. Ask the question: "is it easier with the ski you are trying to match flat against the snow or tilted onto an edge"?
- During practise it might be useful to include some self-check for students who are progressing well and working in the late associative phase. "Start the turn in a plough but see if you can actually lift the inner ski off the snow, this will show you that you're balanced on the outer ski ready to steer it parallel"
- The practise sessions may make use of steeper terrain on a different part of the piste so as to make it more varied and appropriate to the goals

Cool Down

Just as we warm up to ready ourselves to perform it is a good idea to cool down before finishing a lesson. This can be a literal cool down where the intensity of the activity drops so that people actually cool down. It can also involve a mental cool down, where students are given time to digest the main part of the session. During this stage people should be given the freedom to choose what to focus on, the environment should be open and non judgemental so that people are happy to question and experiment with what they have learnt.

Conclusion

Finally, any good session needs to have a definite end. Before saying goodbye to your learners try to conclude the session by conducting a short review of the lesson. "Let's just recap on the lesson. What will you take away from this morning that has worked for you? What do you feel you need or want to work on tomorrow"? This kind of ending can really help with the warm up and revision part of the next session.

Review

The final part of planning a session is to review your plan, before using it. This is slightly different from the process of reviewing presented in the Reviewing chapter of the Learning Environment section. There are various considerations that affect the outcome of a lesson that will highlight any weaknesses or inconsistencies in the plan. The easiest way to review the planned session is to ask pertinent questions.

How does the Lesson Flow?

This can be viewed in a similar way to flow in the fundamental elements (Performance section). It helps us to identify the outcomes of a good session and is the result of skilfully used inputs. The inputs at our disposal include everything else in this manual and the sum of our existing knowledge and experience. This may sound rather daunting but in fact it can be simplified as it is in the content section above.

For a flowing lesson make sure:
- That the lesson has a beginning, middle and end
- That each of these parts relates to the others. Sometimes this is known as the storyline of the lesson
- That over all goals are met by setting int ermediate goals
- That the session as a whole relates to the goals of the learner

Does the Session Achieve the Goals?

The goals of a session are so integral to the content that it is worth reviewing these and asking the question, does my session achieve them? The goal will fall into one of the categories highlighted in Figure 6.3.

By reviewing the session in relation to these categories we are able to get a better handle on how and whether the session is likely to achieve the goals set.

Achieving the Task – The session will be focussed on achieving tasks of one kind or another. The instructor needs to check that the attempted tasks relate to the goals set out at the start of the lesson plan.

The next two headings represent a decision for the instructor. "Am I going to better achieve the goals of the session by focussing on developing the individual or the team as a whole?" Get this decision wrong and the content of the lesson is unlikely to successfully achieve the goals of the individuals, of the group or of the instructor.

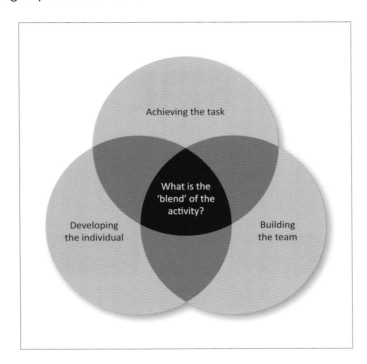

Figure 6.3: Action centred model

Developing the Individual – Does the session allow for the development of the individual? Each pupil may need a slightly different approach. Differences in confidence, learner types, physiology, learner phase or ability need to be addressed. Developing the individual may mean than some people in the group actually perform a slightly different task to the rest. Some beginners may be skiing plough parallel whilst others are still plough turning. By focussing on the individual and allowing the pupils to work at their own level, it is more likely that individual goals will be met.

Building the Team

Does the session develop the team? Building a climate of trust, openness and support that allows the students to work together is often a good way to encourage learning for individuals later in the session or in the week. Equally, building the team for its own sake may be the best way to achieve the desired outcomes of a session. Making friends, ensuring the group help each other and have a good time, guiding the group to a new area of the resort or section of off piste, these could all be examples of achieving the goals of a session without attending to the specific needs of the individuals.

By reviewing the session according to these three categories it gives the instructor a chance to check that all the needs of the group are met and that the goals of everyone have a chance to be fulfilled. (This material is adapted from a leadership model by John Adair (1988)).

How is Responsibility Managed within the Session, who took the Lead?

In order to effectively manage the goals it is helpful to review the lesson plan and look at who will be the key decision takers at different times in the session. This will have an impact on the outcomes of the session and will affect how successfully the goals are achieved.

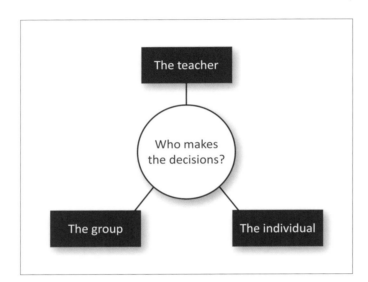

Figure 6.4:
Decision centred leadership model

By allowing different people or groups of people to steer the session, different outcomes will result. Take example 2 from the goal setting section.

Helping a group of first-week snowboarders to ride all the way from the top of the mountain back to the village (group goal).

If the instructor makes all the decisions this may achieve the goal of reaching the village, however if the instructor allows some of the responsibility for decision making to fall to the group, then the goal of building the team is also likely to be achieved. These decisions may include allowing the group to decide on the procedure for keeping everyone together, do they buddy up, have a back marker, arrange a meeting point for lost skiers, descend in two smaller groups, put certain people nearer the front etc?

Finally, if the instructor allows the individual group members to choose the area of skill they feel they need to improve in order to reach the village, and then works with each group member individually in a practise session before descending to the village, then the individual will be developed more than the team.

How the instructor decides to manage this responsibility is dependent on whether the over all goal for the group is to get to the village all together or to primarily improve their performance with a view to getting back to the village, irrespective of whether the rest of the group manage to do so.

The way in which the instructor chooses to manage the decision making process will also, to an extent, dictate the teaching style.

In the above example the session may start with the instructor, setting the intermediate goals for the session, to improve performance to a level whereby all the group members have the necessary skills to reach the village (command). The individuals might then be asked to choose what area of technique they wish to work on in a practise session (practise, self check, inclusion). Following this skill development session the instructor decides to set the group the task of working out and defining the safety parameters before setting off on the descent to the village (guided discovery, divergent). Finally, as the descent ensues the instructor once again takes charge and implements the safety guidelines agreed upon by the group (command).

What Climate will be most Useful?

Having reviewed the whole session the instructor needs to ask what climate will work best for each section of the session. Do the tasks allow that climate to be set? What changes in communication style will I employ in order to set the most useful climate?

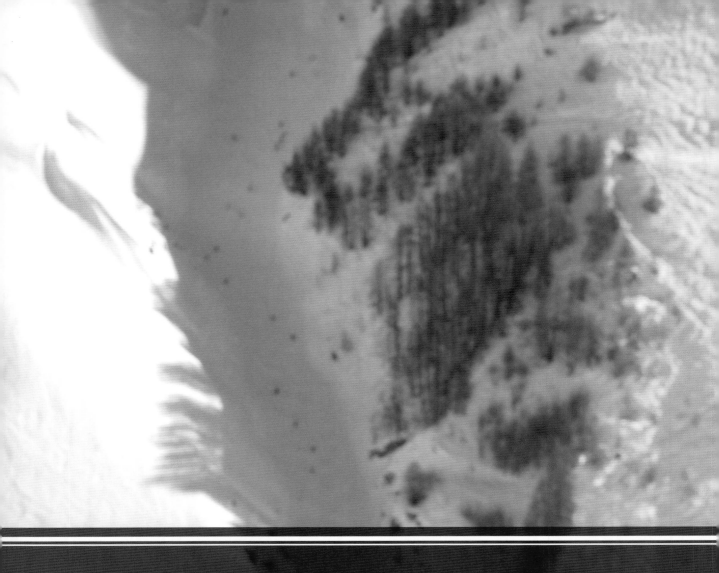

7. SAFETY

Having looked in detail at what it takes to gain a thorough understanding of performance and learning, and then at what it takes to ensure an effective delivery, we must not forget the essential place of safety. Although this chapter sits at the end of the Teaching section it is of paramount importance, without a safe environment in which to work, the delivery will be at best ineffective and worst dangerous, and all the understanding in the world will be of no use.

The Mountain Environment section which follows covers the mountain hazards part of this chapter, it also provides more detail on safety considerations in the mountains.

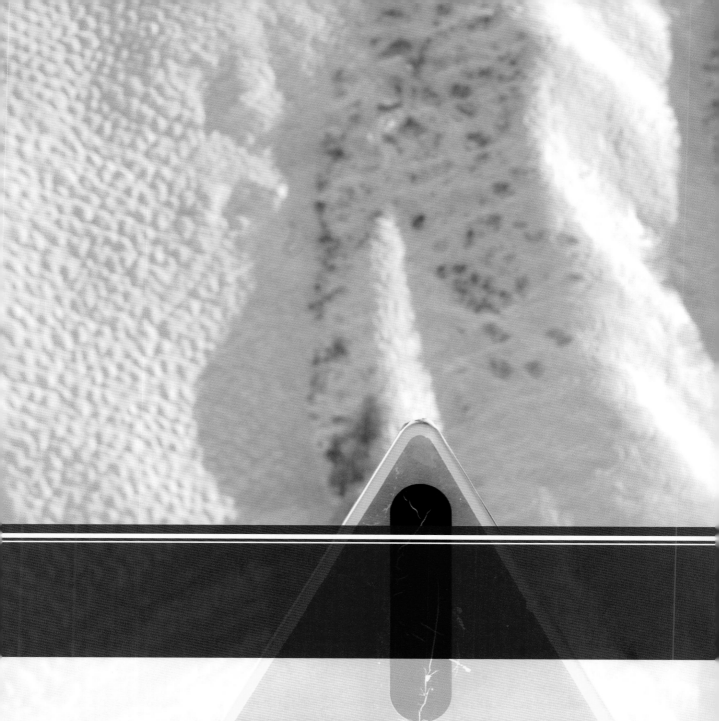

Principles

The Ski Way Code is an internationally-recognised safety document produced by the Fédération Internationale de Ski (FIS). Its official title is The FIS Rules for the Conduct of Skiers. While its main purpose is to advise skiers on the principles of safe conduct, it is also increasingly used as the basis for assessing liability in legal cases involving skiing accidents and injuries. The following section lists the rules themselves, along with the official FIS comments giving guidelines on their interpretation. It should be noted that the wording is taken from the original FIS document, and uses the terms "he", "his" etc. to refer to skiers of both sexes. The general comments on the rules start with the following statement.

Skiing like all sport entails risks. The FIS rules must be considered an ideal pattern of conduct for a responsible and careful skier, their purpose is to avoid accidents on the piste. The FIS rules apply to all skiers. The skier is obliged to be familiar with them and to respect them. If he fails to do so, his behaviour could expose him to civil and criminal liability in the event of an accident.

The Ski Way Code

Rule 1: Respect for Others

A skier must behave in such a way that he does not endanger or prejudice others.

Commentary: Skiers are responsible not only for their own behaviour but also for their defective equipment. This also applies to those using newly developed equipment.

Rule 2: Control of Speed and Skiing

A skier must ski in control. He must adapt his speed and manner of skiing to his personal ability and to the prevailing conditions of terrain, snow and weather as well as to the density of traffic.

Commentary - Collisions usually happen because skiers are travelling too fast, out of control, or have failed to see others. A skier must be able to stop, turn and move within the ability of is own vision. In crowded areas or in places where visibility is reduced, skiers must ski slowly, especially at the edge of a steep slope, at the bottom of a piste and within areas surrounding ski lifts.

Rule 3: Choice of Route

A skier coming from behind must choose his route in such a way that he does not endanger skiers ahead.

Commentary - Skiing is a free activity sport where everyone may ski as and where they please, provided that they abide by these rules and adapt their skiing to their own personal ability and to the prevailing conditions on the mountain. The skier in front has priority. The skier skiing behind another in the same direction must keep sufficient distance between himself and the other skier so as to leave the preceding skier enough space to make all his movements freely.

Rule 4: Overtaking

A skier may overtake another skier above or below and to the right or the left, provided that he leaves enough space for the overtaken skier to make any voluntary or involuntary movement.

Commentary - A skier who overtakes another is wholly responsible for completing that manoeuvre in such a way as to cause no difficulty to the skier being overtaken. This responsibility rests with him until the overtaking manoeuvre has been completed. This rule applies even when overtaking a stationary skier.

Rule 5: Entering and Starting

A skier entering a marked run or starting again after stopping must look up and down the run to make sure that he can do so without endangering himself or others.

Commentary - Experience proves that joining a piste or starting to ski again after stopping are the sources of accidents. It is absolutely essential that a skier finding himself in this situation enters the piste safely and without causing an obstruction or danger to himself or others. When he has started skiing properly again – even slowly - he has the benefit of rule 3 as against faster skiers coming from above or behind.

Rule 6: Stopping on the Piste

Unless absolutely necessary, a skier must avoid stopping on the piste in narrow places or where visibility is restricted. After a fall in such a place, a skier must move clear of the piste as soon as possible.

Commentary - Except on wide pistes stops must be made at the side of the piste. One must not stop in narrow places or where it is difficult to be seen from above.

Rule 7: Climbing and Descending on Foot

Both a skier climbing or descending on foot must keep to the side of the piste.

Commentary - Moving against the general direction poses unexpected obstacles for the skiers. Footprints damage the piste and can cause danger to skiers.

Rule 8: Respect for Signals and Markings

A skier must respect all signs and markings.

Commentary - The degree of difficulty of a piste is indicated in black, red, blue or green. A skier is free to choose whichever piste he wants. The pistes are also marked with other signs, showing direction or giving warnings of danger or closure. A sign closing a piste, like one denoting danger, must be strictly observed. Skiers should be aware that warning signs are posted in their own interests.

Figure 7.1: Examples of warning signs

Rule 9: Assistance

At accidents, every skier is duty-bound to assist.

Commentary - It is a cardinal principle for all sportsmen that they should render assistance following an accident, independent of any legal obligation to do so. Immediate first aid should be given, the appropriate authorities alerted and the place of the accident marked to warn other skiers. FIS hopes that a hit-and-run offence in skiing will incur a criminal conviction similar to a hit-and-run offence on the road and that equivalent penalties will be imposed by all countries where such legislation is not already in force.

Rule 10: Identification

Every skier or witness, whether a responsible party or not, must exchange names and addresses following an accident.

Commentary - Witnesses are of great importance in establishing a full and proper report of an accident, and therefore everybody must consider that it is his duty as a responsible person to provide information as a witness. Reports of the rescue service and of the police as well as photographs are of considerable assistance in determining civil and criminal liability.

FIS Rules for Instructors

In addition to the Rules for the Conduct of Skiers, another FIS document has special relevance to ski instructors. Entitled The FIS Rules for Safety in Winter Sports Centres, it specifically lists the responsibilities of instructors in ensuring skiers' safety. It contains the following rules:

- The ski schools, instructors and guides must teach pupils how to ski safely, which means teaching the technique of skiing and the rules of conduct for skiers
- The ski schools are responsible for placing their pupils into different classes according to their standard of skiing
- The ski schools, instructors and guides must never allow their pupils to take any risk beyond their capability especially taking into account the snow and weather conditions
- The instructors must remind their pupils that during instruction they have no particular priority on the piste and that they should at all times respect the rules of conduct of skiers

In other words, not only should you adhere to the Ski Way Code while teaching, you also have a duty to ensure that your pupils understand its principles. Rather than a single 'sermon', this should be an on-going process reminding them of safe practise while skiing. As resorts become more crowded, it is increasingly important that skiers understand the need to show consideration for others, and know how to ski in a safe and responsible manner.

For more information see www.fis-ski.com

People

People are unpredictable, put that together with a constantly changing mountain environment and a risk associated sport, and the possibility for accident and injury is always there. The manner in which the instructors manage their groups will have an important impact on minimising these risks. There is also a duty for instructors to educate their customers in matters of safety so that safe conduct can continue away from the lesson.

Group Management

The rules of the Ski Way Code apply to all snow users, whether they are skiing or snowboarding individually or in a group. Whenever you are in charge of a group, whether teaching, leading or guiding them, there are a few additional principles to which you should always adhere:

- Stopping – Always ensure that they stop below rather than above the group, and that where possible, they enter the line from behind rather than in front
- Parking – Always ensure that the group stop in a visible position which does not obstruct other snow users (Ski Way Code rule 6)
- Setting Off – Always ensure that the group know the order in which they are setting off, to avoid collisions
- Following – Always ensure that group members maintain a safe distance when following, and that the principles of safe overtaking (if allowed) are understood (Ski Way Code rule 4)
- Lost Skier – If leading the group for any distance, check regularly that everyone is still following if appropriate, nominate a back marker. Ensure that everyone knows what to do if they get separated from the group. It is often useful to nominate a meeting place in case a skier gets separated from the group
- Accident and Injury – Always ensure the safety and well-being of the rest of the group as well as the injured skier, when dealing with an accident
- Counting – Always remember to count your group: "Count them out and count them back"

Injury Prevention

Modern binding technology has significantly reduced the incidence of below the knee injuries. Further improvements are as likely to come from improved skier education as from technological developments alone. In particular, instructors can reduce the probability of certain types of injury by teaching pupils the safest ways to fall.

The most disturbing trend in skiing injuries is the risk of tearing the anterior cruciate ligament. The evidence suggests that even bindings with upward-releasing toe pieces may not be able to respond fast enough to loads on the knee to prevent injury. However, evidence from the USA indicates that by following a number of key principles (below), the probability of ACL damage can be significantly reduced. Essentially the ACL is most likely to be ruptured by the back of the boot forcing the shin bone forwards and tearing the ligament. This occurs in one of two ways:

Boot-induced Tear

This injury is caused by the skier's shin being pushed rapidly forwards by the rear spoiler of the boot. Generally it occurs when landing on the tails of the skis from a jump, and is especially likely if the skier lands with an extended (straight) leg. Immediately after the tails touch down, the skis are slammed back onto the snow surface, driving the boot spoiler forwards and tearing the ligament.

This injury may be combated by:
• Ensuring that skiers are competent to execute the jump
• Avoiding situations where skiers may land off-balance
• Teaching skiers to land on both feet with legs relaxed and knees flexed
• Emphasising that skiers should never attempt to recover from such a fall

'Phantom Foot' Injuries

The term 'phantom foot' was coined by the American ski safety researcher Carl Ettlinger. It refers to the fact that this type of injury is best understood in terms of the tail of the ski acting as a rearward extension of the skier's foot, creating leverage forces which produce the injury.

It generally occurs when a skier falls backwards and into the hill. Ettlinger identifies 6 elements which are generally associated with phantom foot injuries:
• Uphill arm back
• Uphill ski un-weighted
• Skier off-balance to the rear
• Weight on inside edge of downhill ski tail
• Hips below the knees
• Upper body generally facing downhill ski

As the skier's weight moves onto the inside edge of the downhill ski, it grips and 'carves'. This acts as a lever, causing the rear cuff of the boot to push and twist the tibia until the ACL tears. This type of injury is more difficult to prevent than the boot-induced tear. However, when losing balance, the following points can significantly reduce the risk of injury:

- Bring the arms forwards
- Move the hands over the skis
- Bring the skis closer together
- Never try to recover in mid-fall

Protecting against other Injuries

There are two additional measures which can reduce the likelihood of injury. The first is to protect the fingers and hands, the second to minimise the general risks of leg and knee injury. These points apply in all skiing situations, but are especially relevant on artificial slopes.

Finger and Hand Injury

If a skier uses their hands to cushion a fall, they should be encouraged to 'trail' their fingers so that they are pointing behind them, i.e. away from their direction of travel. This minimises the risk of fingers becoming trapped or twisted.

Leg and Knee Injury

When falling, skiers are often told to relax and let themselves go, rather than tensing up and fighting the inevitable. Overall, this is good advice. However there are two further steps that can reduce the risk of leg injury:

- When falling, try to keep the legs close together
- Immediately the body touches the ground, extend the legs sideways while keeping the feet off the surface

This minimises the risk of the skis catching and acting as a fulcrum, applying leverage to the legs and knee ligaments.

General Injury Prevention

While it is not possible to eliminate all skiing injuries, we have a duty to minimise the risks faced by our pupils. In addition to the above, the following three general principles should always be borne in mind.

Class Management and the Ski Way Code

In relation to the risks of injury, your prime responsibility is for the safety of your clients. It is vital that you always follow the Ski Way Code and the principles of safe class management outlined above. For their own safety and that of others, your clients should themselves understand the

Ski Way Code and the reasons for its rules. Observing these rules significantly reduces the risk of collision injuries, whether due to impact with another skier or a solid object.

Clothing and Equipment

When instructing a class, you must also take some responsibility for ensuring that your clients are appropriately clothed and equipped. Clothing should be suitable for the conditions, with no loose items which might get entangled in lift machinery. This is particularly important on non-overhead cable lifts such as rope tows.

It is also important that everyone has appropriate eye protection such as goggles or sunglasses, and that sunscreen is applied regularly (see The Mountain Environment). Apart from exceptional circumstances, instructors should not themselves attempt to adjust clients' bindings. However, it is good practise to visually check everyone's equipment at the start of the lesson, and refer them to a technician where adjustments are required. As an instructor it is your duty to notice any obvious defects in your pupils' equipment.

Preparation

One further step in preventing injuries is to ensure that the class is adequately warmed up at the start of each lesson. By doing so, the risk of injury is considerably reduced.

Accident Procedure

As part of their qualification, all snowsport instructors must hold a valid First Aid certificate. This training not only helps save lives, but is vital in preventing a casualty's condition from worsening. The first principle of such training can be summarised as "do no further harm".

The following section does not deal with detailed first aid procedures, but simply gives additional information on dealing with a casualty in a mountain environment. You should therefore also refer to your first aid training for the additional procedures involved.

Your first action following an accident or injury should be to assess the situation. This includes the following questions:

- Is it safe to approach the casualty? If they are in a hazardous location (e.g. off piste), you might put yourself at risk by approaching them. If so, await the assistance of the ski patrol
- Is the rest of the class safe? Remember your responsibility is for the safety of the entire class, not just the injured person
- How serious is the injury? If it is a small bump or scrape, there may be no need to call the ski patrol. But even a seemingly minor knee injury may become much worse if the casualty attempts to ski on it. If in doubt, call for assistance. If the injury is serious enough to require medical attention, call the ski patrol straight away

In most resorts, accidents are usually dealt with promptly and efficiently. Meanwhile, the instructor's main responsibilities are to:

- Keep the casualty as safe, warm and comfortable as possible
- Give the ski patrol the casualty's precise location
- Ensure that the rest of the class are safe and warm

Unless help will take some time to arrive, you should only attempt treatment where the injury is potentially life-threatening – for example, in cases of unconsciousness, severe bleeding, or where there are no signs of breathing or pulse. In these cases, immediate treatment should be attempted.

Key Points of Accident Procedure

In order of priority, the key points of accident procedure are:

1. Ensure that the casualty is in no further danger. Make sure that they cannot be hit by other snow users (see 2 below), and that they are secure from sliding further downhill.

2. Warn other people of the casualty's position by sticking crossed skis in the snow at least 10 metres uphill. This also helps the ski patrol find the site. This may be delegated to another person while you deal with the casualty.

3. Check for life-threatening injuries, and immediately take the appropriate steps:

- If the casualty is unconscious, ensure that their airway is clear and put them in the recovery position.
- If the casualty has stopped breathing, apply mouth-to-mouth resuscitation
- If the casualty has no pulse, apply cardiac massage
- If the casualty is suffering serious loss of blood, apply a pressure-pad to the wound

4. Check for signs of spinal injury. If the casualty has damaged their spine, any further movement may cause additional injury, including permanent paralysis. If you suspect this, avoid moving them except to deal with life threatening injuries.

5. Keep the casualty warm, and try to reassure and comfort them prior to the ski patrol's arrival. Support and immobilise an injured limb. Where the lower leg or foot is injured, never loosen or remove the ski boot.

6. Summon the ski patrol via the nearest emergency telephone, lift station or café. If possible, stay with the casualty and send a message (preferably written down) with two or more experienced people1. If possible, give the following details:

- The nature of the injury
- The name or number of the run
- The identifying number of the nearest piste marker or lift pylon
- Any other information on the casualty's precise location

7. Ensure that the rest of the class are kept safe and warm. Assemble them at the side of the run, or send them to the nearest café or shelter. Bear in mind that the incident may have affected their confidence and state of mind.

Conclusion

As an instructor you are ultimately responsible for the safety of your pupils. You may influence this directly during lessons, but just as importantly by teaching them about safety for when they are not in class. While snowsport carries inherent risks, you must take all reasonable steps to minimise these. Remember that in the event of an accident or injury, you may be called upon to justify your actions in a court of law.

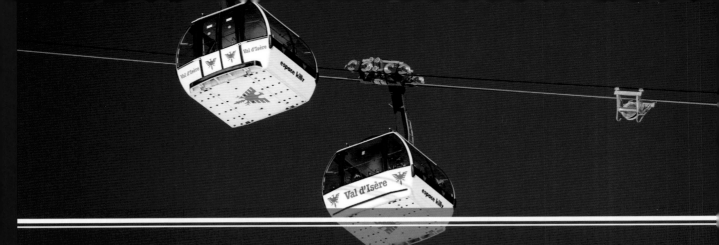

Equipment and Lifts

Although familiar to the seasoned skier, very often the equipment and lift system is approached with a fair amount of trepidation by less experienced winter sport enthusiasts. To beginners everything is alien and something as seemingly unachievable as riding a drag lift can divert attention away from the learning the process. The equipment section of this manual can be found in the appendices and the relevant safety information can be found there. Here we focus on ski lifts and how to use them safely.

In most cases, the first type of lift which skiers will ride while wearing skis is a button-lift or T-bar. The most appropriate time to introduce this depends on the situation. A very gentle, easy lift may be used even before starting plough turning, whereas if the slope or lift is more difficult it may have to be delayed until everyone can turn reasonably well. Where access to the nursery area is by chairlift, the problems can be greater. Pupils may have to use the chair before gaining any experience of balancing and sliding on skis. In this case, they should if possible go up the lift carrying their skis rather than wearing them. In any case, the attendant should be informed, so that the lift can be slowed down and your class helped to get on safely.

Before anyone first attempts to use a lift, they need a clear understanding of what is involved. This can be done both by explanation and by watching others using the lift. In the case of drag-lifts, practise exercises can also be done to prepare them for how to get on and off.

Safety on Ski Lifts

Whatever the means of uphill transport, the first priority is safety. Apart from ensuring that pupils understand how to use the lift, there are several other key points when using ski lifts:

- Make sure that no-one has any loose clothing (belts, scarves, etc.) which might get caught in the lift. Long hair should also be secured, especially when using rope tows or lifts with low level cables
- Explain that the class should assemble at a spot well clear of the top of the lift to avoid creating an obstruction

- On drag-lifts, explain that skiers should immediately roll clear of the track in the event of a fall. Ensure that pupils know where to re-join the class in the event of a fall from a drag-lift (e.g. wait where they are, ski to the bottom of the lift, climb to the top of the lift, etc.)
- The instructor should always go up last, so as to know the location of anyone who has fallen off and to offer advice or assistance if necessary

Button-lifts

The first difficulty skiers face on button-lifts is staying in balance during the initial take-off. Before their first attempt, you can prepare your pupils on the flat. Stand the class on a level area of snow, then push each person firmly forward. Place your hands against the pupils' hips, and push them smoothly forward with enough force to make them continue sliding for a   metre or two.

Once everyone is comfortably able to maintain balance in this exercise, they should next learn how to dismount at the top. The key is getting the skis quickly into a herringbone position to avoid sliding backwards downhill, then stepping across the slope to move out of the way of following skiers. Having made the above preparations, there are four points which skiers must clearly understand before first getting on a button-lift:

- When moving uphill on a drag-lift, skiers must stay balanced over their feet rather than leaning or sitting back against the button. While they may need to lean back slightly at the very start, especially if the lift take-off is rapid, skiers obtain no balance support from the lift once they are in motion
- When travelling uphill, the skis must be kept around hip-width apart for balance, and kept pointing directly up the track. Skiers may sometimes clamp their thighs around the bar in an effort to avoid dropping it. Instead, make sure the bar is pulled high up between the thighs, so that the legs and feet can be kept apart
- In the event of a fall, skiers must move off the track as quickly as possible. Before gathering equipment or getting up, a fallen skier should try to roll sideways out of the path of following skiers
- After dismounting at the top of a lift, skiers must move quickly away to guard against being hit by buttons released by those coming up behind. Always make sure that the class gathers at least 10 metres away from the get-off area to avoid creating a bottle-neck

Initially it is preferable for pupils to discard their ski poles. If these are needed for the descent, they can be carried up by the instructor. When pupils are ready to carry their poles, they should be held in one hand, mid-way between handles and baskets. For the first attempts, the instructor or lift operator should stand beside each pupil to help them get the button into position. As the lift takes off, additional reassurance and support can be provided by jogging alongside the pupil for the first few metres.

T-bars

Exactly the same preparation and procedures should be followed for T-bars as for button-lifts. Initially it is preferable for pupils to go up alone until they are used to getting on and off and can steer and balance effectively. Alternatively, ensure that each pupil is accompanied by an experienced skier. When pupils are ready to go up in pairs, the following additional points apply:

- Ensure that when poles are carried, they are held in the hand away from the other skier
- Once in motion, skiers should lean gently towards each other. In this way, the skis are less likely to get caught up with each other, and overall stability is increased
- Skiers should dismount one after the other rather than together, so that they can both move off to the same side without difficulty or delay
- Depending on the layout at the top of the lift, one of the pair may have to take responsibility for ensuring that the bar is released safely

Chairlifts

When teaching pupils how to ride a chairlift, the key points are as follows:

- When poles are being carried, hold them in one hand mid-way between handles and baskets, keeping them clear of other skiers
- As soon as the preceding skiers have departed, move promptly and accurately into position ready for the approaching chair
- Look back and place the free hand against the front edge of the seat as it approaches, to minimise any impact against the backs of the legs
- Sit down and lower the safety bar, making sure that skis, poles etc. are not in the way
- When approaching the top station, raise the safety bar and keep the ski tips high so that they do not catch in the snow
- Keep the skis parallel as they touch the ground, then stand up and push gently forwards away from the chair
- Move well clear of the dismounting area before stopping and re-grouping

THE MOUNTAIN ENVIRONMENT

It is easy to forget with all the facilities of modern snowsport resorts that the mountains can be an unpredictable and hostile environment. As well as the risk of avalanche, the environmental conditions have a strong influence on our safety and welfare.

Mountain weather can be both unpredictable and severe, and the hazards are compounded by the effects of altitude. Even in good weather, several factors must be borne in mind when looking after ourselves and our clients. This chapter is not just for the off piste traveller and ski mountaineer but has many relevant sections to help the snowsports professional stay safe and in turn look after their clients.

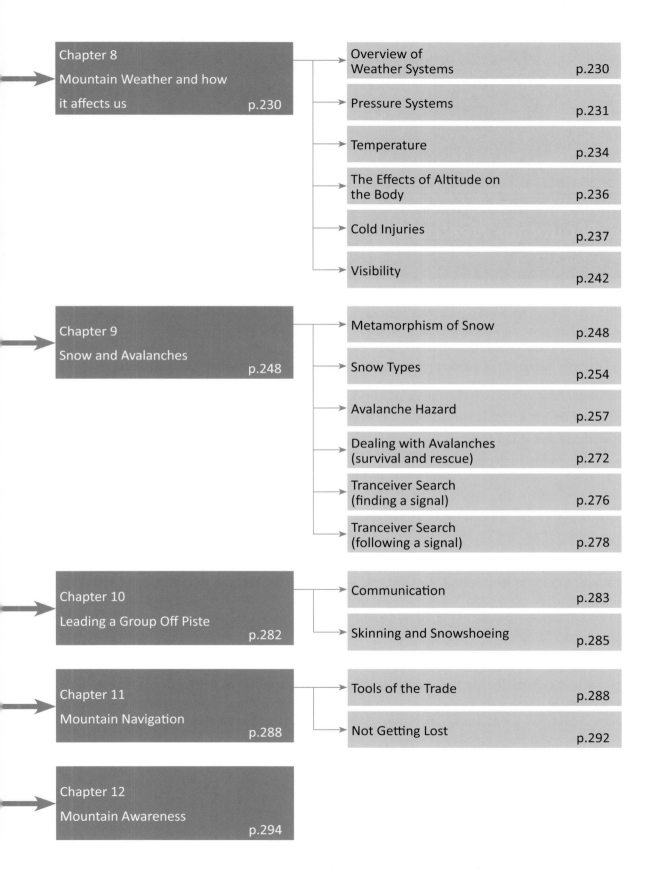

8. Mountain Weather

The weather plays a big part in the decision making process with regards to where we will lead a group, on piste as well as off. This may be choosing to work at a lower altitude to stay warmer, getting high so you are above the clouds or choosing a less committing off-piste tour. This section deals with the basics of weather forecasting and how the mountains influence the weather.

In particular it will look at the following areas:

- Temperature including wind chill and cold injuries
- Visibility and cloud cover
- Sunlight and its effects on us

Overview of Weather Systems

Weather forecasting is a complex business. Nowadays it is done by skilled professionals, with the aid of modern technology such as satellites and a string of automated weather information gathering stations throughout the land and sea. This technology can negate the need for us to understand the "why" and "what if's" surrounding forecasting. What follows is a brief description of how the planets' weather is formed and how in particular it affects us in Europe, to help us answer the "whys".

In global terms, Europe lies in an area of the planet where the air is rising. Rising air tends to give a wet climate (rather like a kettle boiling on a window ledge, as the steam rises and hits the window, it cools, condenses and drips back down). Europe lies in what is called a temperate zone. Equatorial zones are where it rains most days, forming the rainforests of the planet (also rising air) and desert regions are where it is dry and warm (descending air). Figure 8.1 shows the big loops of air in the Northern Hemisphere which help form the deserts, rainforests etc.

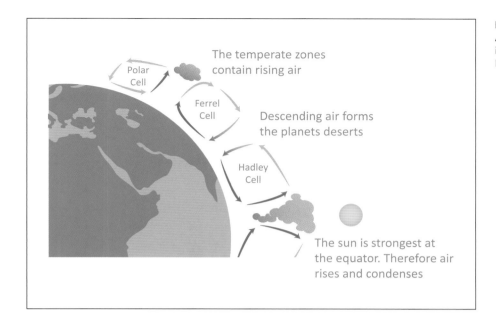

Figure 8.2:
Air movements in the Northern Hemisphere

The temperate zones contain rising air

Polar Cell

Ferrel Cell

Descending air forms the planets deserts

Hadley Cell

The sun is strongest at the equator. Therefore air rises and condenses

In addition, Europe's weather predominantly comes from the South West. The air masses bringing this weather have to cross the Atlantic in order to reach us. As these air masses cross the sea they pick up more moisture. As they reach the Alps or the UK, the air is forced up over the mountains. This rising air gives us precipitation and in turn a wetter climate.

Due to the fact that the air in Europe is predominantly rising, low pressure systems (rising air therefore less pressure) are produced. Again if we think back to the kettle example, rising air produces rain. In summary, the three things that mean Europe has a relatively wet climate are:

• Living in the temperate zone with rising and condensing air

• Weather arriving from the Atlantic with moisture in it, rising over the mountains

• Our positioning on the planet giving rise to low pressure systems

Pressure Systems

The weather chart in figure 8.2 shows low and high pressure systems and the three different weather fronts.

The circular lines are called isobars and they link points of equal pressure. As a rough guide, the wind runs along these lines and the closer they are together, the stronger the wind (rather like contours representing steepness on a map). In a low pressure system, due to the spin of the earth, the wind/air travels anti clockwise. The opposite is true of a high pressure system i.e. clockwise. It can be seen that the isobars are closer together in the low pressure system therefore it is windier than the relatively calm high pressure.

The fronts are a division between warm and cold air and generally produce more violent conditions. See figure 8.3. A cold front usually follows a warm front. The warm front approaches relatively slowly and can often be detected by the appearance of very high wispy clouds (Cirrus). As the warm front arrives the weather deteriorates, usually bringing an increase in temperature, prolonged rain and stronger winds. After the initial front has passed, the warm sector brings muggy wet conditions. The cold front is an altogether more violent phenomenon, bringing a drop in temperature, strong winds and sometimes thunderstorms.

The information in figure 8.3 shows the weather created by frontal systems.

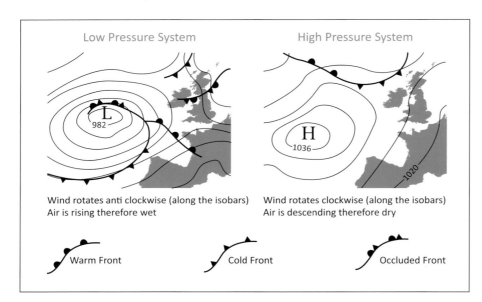

Figure 8.3:
Pressure Systems

If we travel to the Southern Hemisphere there will be differences. The winds will travel the opposite way around, low and high pressures and prevailing weather systems may come from a different direction other than the South West. Most southern ski resorts are in an area where air is rising so the wet climate is similar. It is advised that you gain knowledge of the above weather information in order to help you make an informed decision before venturing onto the mountains. Of course for the snow sports enthusiast, the wet climate that is continually mentioned in this chapter is an excellent one especially when combined with the temperature drop given by the height of the mountains and our northern latitude. This combination produces the snow that forms the basis of our hobbies and profession!

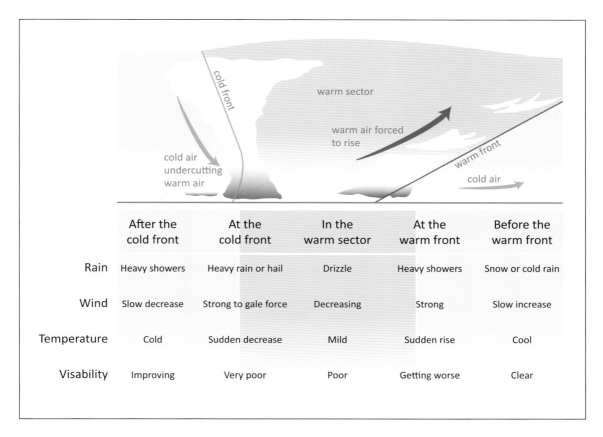

	After the cold front	At the cold front	In the warm sector	At the warm front	Before the warm front
Rain	Heavy showers	Heavy rain or hail	Drizzle	Heavy showers	Snow or cold rain
Wind	Slow decrease	Strong to gale force	Decreasing	Strong	Slow increase
Temperature	Cold	Sudden decrease	Mild	Sudden rise	Cool
Visability	Improving	Very poor	Poor	Getting worse	Clear

Figure 8.4: Cross section of a warm and cold front

Top Tips

A practical way we can gain information regarding mountain weather conditions particularly related to low pressure systems is called the "crossed winds rule"

- If you stand on a mountain top with your back to the lower wind and the upper wind comes from your left, then the weather is likely to deteriorate

- If you stand on a mountain top with your back to the lower wind and the upper wind comes from your right, then the weather is likely to improve

- If you stand on a mountain with your back to the lower wind and the upper wind is behind you or ahead of you, then there is likely to be little immediate change in the weather

The lower wind is blowing round the low pressure system and the upper wind is moving the low pressure system along i.e. the South Westerly air mass that affect Europe

Temperature

Even at resort level, the air temperature in winter can be very low. As altitude increases, it generally becomes colder still. The precise relationship between altitude and temperature depends on the prevailing weather conditions however, to help calculate it, we can use a formula called the Lapse rate. This helps us work out how the temperature changes with altitude.

On a clear day the temperature will fall by 1°C per 100m of ascent, if it is cloudy or wet then this becomes 1°C per 200m of ascent. From this we can see that as you ascend on a clear day with no moisture in the air, it gets much colder at altitude than on a wet or cloudy day. Of course with solar warming on a clear day it may feel warmer or certainly more pleasant than the relatively depressing cloudy wet day. This is illustrated in figure 8.4, assuming the temperature in the village to be -5°C.

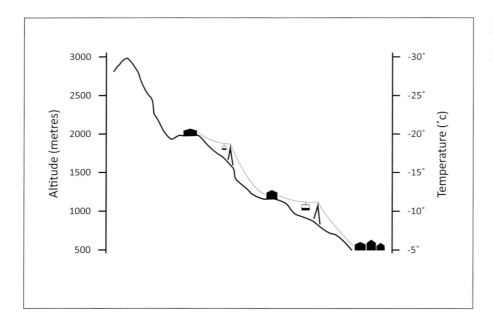

Figure 8.5: The effect of altitude on temperature

In the context of a ski resort, that means that with a village temperature of -5°C, 1,500 metres higher up the mountain it can be as low as -20°C. It is therefore important that one is prepared for the conditions that are likely to be encountered. On a clear, windless day, it may feel relatively warm in the village and yet be bitterly cold at the top of the mountain. Added to the drop in actual air temperature, there are several other factors which compound the effect.

The Effect of Wind-chill on Temperature

In the same way that a fan cools you in summer, wind increases the rate at which your body loses heat. This adds to the effects of altitude, and can make even a sunny winter's day an ordeal for all but the best equipped. The phenomenon is known as 'wind-chill' and is usually stated in terms of temperature. The wind-chill temperature is the equivalent temperature that would produce the same rate of cooling in the absence of a wind. For example in Figure 8.5, if the actual air temperature is -5°C, a 25km/hr (15mph) wind produces a wind-chill equivalent of -20°C. If the actual temperature is already down at -15°C, a 50km/hr (30mph) wind gives a wind-chill of -38°C. In other words, wind-chill can have a dramatic effect on our comfort and safety and that of our clients.

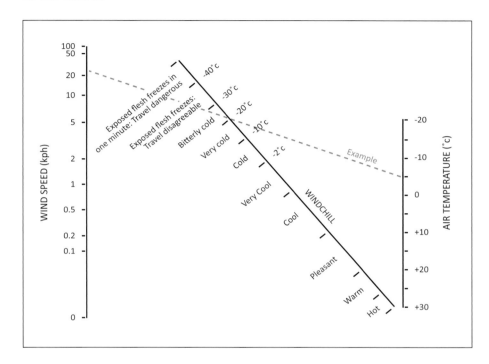

Figure 8.6: Wind-chill

To interpret Figure 8.5, place a ruler to link the actual (thermometer reading) air temperature and the wind speed. Where it crosses the diagonal wind-chill line, read off the equivalent wind-chill temperature.

The actual relationship is rather complex. As a guide, the lower the still air temperature (as indicated on a thermometer), the greater the effect of wind-chill. Also, the stronger the wind, the greater the wind-chill factor. This holds for wind speeds up to around 50km/hr (30mph). Above this wind speed, relatively little further cooling occurs. It should be borne in mind that these effects do not simply occur in windy conditions. Even on a still day, skiers create their own wind-chill by their rate of travel through the air. Descending at 30km/hr (20mph) has the same effect as standing still in a 30km/hr wind. The same applies when riding lifts - modern chairlifts travel at speeds of up to 15km/hr and can cause considerable wind-chill on a cold day.

Finally, remember that wind speed generally increases with altitude. The wind is roughly 2-3 times stronger per 1000m of ascent. It may seem calm in the valley, while a strong wind is blowing higher up the mountain. On a clear day, look out for tell-tale signs such as spindrift blowing off exposed ridges, the speed at which clouds are moving or lenticular clouds (lens shaped or flying saucers).

The Effect of Humidity on Temperature

Just as wind increases the body's rate of heat-loss, so does air humidity. The more moisture there is in the air, the higher the rate of heat loss. Once the body has become wet the moisture evaporates, cooling the body in a similar way to sweating. On a sunny day in the mountains, the air is often quite dry. But in mist, low cloud or during a snowfall, the humidity becomes much higher. While the air temperature usually rises at the start of a snow-fall, the rate of heat-loss will often be increased by the extra humidity. The effect can also occur during spells of dry, clear weather. In these conditions, 'temperature inversions' are common. This refers to a weather pattern in which the temperature is lower in the valley than it is on the mountain. As a result, it can remain clear and sunny on the upper slopes while the valley is shrouded in mist. It may feel warm in the sunlight, yet become bitterly cold on descending into the layer of cloud. In fact, three factors contribute to this sudden cooling - high humidity, reduced actual air temperature and the screening of the sun's rays by the cloud layer. Thus, it is important that mountain users always go out well prepared and equipped. Not only can the weather itself change dramatically over a short period, even in stable weather the conditions can vary widely at differing altitudes. In addition to its relationship with air temperature, altitude has several effects on the human body. While these may seldom affect your clients, it is important to bear them in mind when planning your sessions and in responding to problems which arise.

The Effects of Altitude on the Body

Air Pressure at Altitude and Cardio-Respiratory Overload

Atmospheric pressure decreases with altitude which increases the cardio-respiratory overload referring to the heart and lungs. At an altitude of 2,400 metres, the air pressure is 75% of its sea level value. As a result, the heart and lungs have to work harder to supply the body with oxygen. Snowsports professionals need to bear this in mind when dealing with clients. It is important to be sensitive to the fact that an increased load on the body's resources occurs at altitude and may lead to tiredness and lack of performance. It is advised to take more rest stops and descend to a lower altitude to help the body cope.

Altitude Sickness

In addition to cardio-respiratory overload, reduced air pressure can also give rise to a condition known as altitude or mountain sickness. Its symptoms include feelings of weakness and nausea, headaches, loss of appetite, dizziness and fainting. Most commonly, altitude sickness affects mountaineers, especially when climbing at high levels such as in the Himalayas. Although most people seldom experience it below about 3000 metres, it can occur as low as 1500 metres in certain situations. Anyone who suffers from anaemia, cardio respiratory complaints or hormonal imbalances is at increased risk of the condition. In an alpine environment, altitude sickness seldom causes serious problems and is easily treated. In the majority of cases, all that is required is descending from the higher slopes and rest. Occasionally the victim may need to descend to a lower altitude for a few days in order to recover. Unfortunately, an individual's cardio-respiratory fitness seems to have little bearing on the likelihood of their being affected by altitude sickness.

It generally takes several days for the body to adapt fully to living at altitude and the problems are more common among people visiting a high level resort (e.g. where their accommodation is above 1,500 metres).

Altitude, Humidity and Dehydration

In very dry air, a further hazard is that of dehydration. Because perspiration evaporates quickly in dry air, you can lose large amounts of body moisture without realising it. The rate of fluid loss is increased by altitude. Compared to sea level, you have to breathe more rapidly or deeply to obtain the same amount of oxygen. Moisture is therefore lost at a higher rate through the mouth, even when not perspiring. As a result, it is important that skiers take regular refreshment stops throughout the day. This is especially important for beginners, whose workload can be considerably higher than that of experienced skiers. Also, the higher temperatures in spring or summer (such as on a glacier) will greatly increase the rate of fluid loss, as will any sustained energy expenditure such as climbing, bumps skiing and so on.

Cold Injuries

Frostbite

Frostbite can occur on its own but in most mountain situations it will be associated with hypothermia. Frostbite is the freezing of fluid in the tissues of your body. If you are hypothermic, the body will have started to restrict blood flow to the extremities in an effort to keep the core warm. If no blood flows to places like your fingers or toes, then sooner or later in temperatures below zero, you will get frostbite. The flow of blood to your toes can also be restricted by wearing boots that are too tight. The rest of your body might feel warm enough but with no blood able to flow through your feet, the chances of getting frostbite are increased. We have all had cold feet or hands, however the pain associated with frostbite is much more severe. If the affected area feels cold or stiff and the skin appears waxy or colourless then this may be an indicator of frostbite.

The following steps can be taken to help prevent frostbite occurring:
- Do not get hypothermic
- Do not wear gloves that are too small
- Do not crank up your boot buckles too tight for too long
- Do not smoke or drink alcohol
- Cover exposed skin as much as possible, especially ears, nose and cheeks
- Watch each other, look for white patches appearing on cheeks, noses and ears

In most situations people will only have 'frostnip' which is the early stage of frostbite. If somebody has a white patch appear on their cheek, warm it up as soon as you see it by:
- Placing a warm hand over the patch of white
- Cover the affected area by putting on a balaclava or face mask
- Go somewhere less exposed to the wind

- Do some exercise if you have been standing about too long
- Put more clothing on to help increase the circulation of blood to the extremities
- Eat more food
- Have a hot drink, but no alcohol

If somebody complains of cold hands, help them to get them warm by:
- Exchange gloves, give them your warm pair for a while
- Put more clothing on the core, get it to overheat, then it will pump out blood to the extremities
- Arm swinging exercises
- Hand movement exercises

Warming up hands and toes can often produce severe pain, known as 'the hot aches'. Sometimes a person can feel sick or even faint with the pain. In severe cases, where somebody has no feeling of pain and the affected part feels hard to the touch, do not re-warm on the hill, head to the valley and see a doctor. If frostbite is re-warmed on the hill and then it freezes again, the chances of a good recovery are seriously reduced.

Hypothermia

A person has Hypothermia when they have a lower than usual body temperature (Greek: Hypo - less than and therme - heat).

How we Lose Heat

Radiation	Is the largest source of heat loss as the body continually radiates heat.
Evaporation	Sweating and evaporation heat loss from the skin and airway can account for up to 30% of heat loss.
Convection	Cold air in contact with the skin extracts heat as it tries to become as warm as skin temperature. When this warmed air is displaced by the wind or body movements, it is replaced by cold air which extracts more heat. This is an almost continuous process. Cold and wind = WINDCHILL.
Conduction	Heat is drained away from the body when it is in contact with a cold object, e.g., water, snow, rocks. Conductive heat loss increases when clothing is wet.

Signs and Symptoms of Hypothermia as Somebody gets Colder

Temperature °C	Effect on body
37	Normal body temperature
35	Feels cold, skin numb, shivering starts
	Minor muscular impairment, e.g. hands
34	Frequent stumbling and falling
	Cannot use hands
	Slow thought, slow speech
32	Shivering reflex stops
	Stiffness
	Cannot walk or stand
	Severe lack of muscular co-ordination
	Incomprehension
30	Semi-conscious
	Dilation of pupils
	No apparent heart beat and pulse
	Severe muscular rigidity
	Barely able to be aroused
28	Ventricular Fibrillation
	Deeply unconscious
26	Appears dead
17	Known recovery case

What Happens to the Body?

When your temperature drops, the brain automatically tries to maintain the correct temperature within the core of your body, so that all the essential organs can keep functioning. To do this it restricts the circulation of blood to your extremities. Toes and fingers are the first places to have the circulation impaired. They become pale, cold to the touch and stiffer. You find it more difficult to use your fingers.

Main Causes of Hypothermia

Wetness – Wet clothing does not insulate you as well. The air pockets which keep us warm in dry clothes reduce or disappear. Water conducts heat away from your body and evaporation of the water removes heat from the body.

Wind – A wind will increase heat loss through convection and working against a wind will use up more energy.

Cold - More heat is lost by radiation when it is cold and if combined with wind, then heat is lost very quickly due to the wind chill effect.

Tiredness

- Travelled too far or too fast
- Not eaten enough prior to going on the hill or whilst on the hill
- Not drinking enough fluids
- Carrying too much in the rucksack
- Over or under dressed
- Poor technique

Low Morale

- Not enjoying the journey
- Feeling like a burden on the rest of the group
- Safety concerns
- Problems at home or work
- One individual with low morale can easily spread and affect others in the group

Illness - If recovering from a recent illness a person will not function as well as normal, especially if the illness has left them dehydrated.

Injury - A person carrying an injury has to work harder and therefore uses up more energy.

Signs of Hypothermia

Always keep a watchful eye on your group, especially if you think hypothermia might become an issue. Normally, due to experience it is easier for you to keep warm, eat enough, drink enough and avoid hypothermia, but if you are feeling cold, the chances are your group is feeling colder.

Look out for the following:
- Shivering
- Fumbling with hands
- Slower to respond to questions
- Speech becomes slower and less clear
- Apathy, doesn't bother to put a hat on, zip up a jacket or eat something
- Pale skin

It may be that the person in your group states the following which should alert you to the potential for them to become hypothermic:
- I feel cold
- I am tired
- I can't work my compass
- I can't do my zip up
- I can't be bothered

If the problem starts to get more severe then the following may begin to happen:

- Shivering stops
- Cannot walk or stand
- Poor muscular co-ordination, appears to be very stiff
- Irrational behaviour
- Seems confused when answering a question

As hypothermia progresses, the casualty will become semi unconscious, their pupils will dilate and the heartbeat will be hard to detect. Eventually the casualty will become unconscious and die. Note: - No hypothermic person should be pronounced dead while the body is cold.

What to do if Somebody has Hypothermia

If somebody in your group has hypothermia it can lead you and your group into an ever more serious situation. Any number of things can happen, such as:

- Going slower, so you end up travelling in the dark
- Going slower, so everyone else is exposed to the elements for longer, they get tired and hungry
- Skiing less effectively so they have a fall and hurt themselves
- Skiing with less control so they ski onto dangerous terrain
- They drop a glove, but the spares are already in use
- They leave something important behind at the last stop, you feel you must go back

When you first see signs of hypothermia it is vital that you act immediately to prevent the situation worsening:

Clothing

- Put more on
- Remove wet clothing and replace it with dry if possible
- Wear the clothing properly
- Make sure it is not too tight, restricting blood flow

Food

- Put fuel in the engine, eat more
- Drink more to stop dehydration

Morale

- Make people feel happy, chat to them tell jokes
- Assure people, allay their fears
- Involve people in the planning
- Let them see the rational behind the plans

Plan

- Change your route
- Alter the pace
- Re-distribute equipment
- Phone ahead to say you will descend a different way
- Phone ahead to say you will be late

Rest

- Use the group shelter, insulate from the cold ground by sitting on rucksacks
- Give the body a chance to digest the food & drink, also time to recover from exertion
- Alter clothing in the shelter
- Benefit from the group heat in the shelter
- Go inside a mountain hut or restaurant

If you find somebody with severe hypothermia, move them as little as possible, stop further heat loss but do not re-warm them, protect them from the elements, seek help and monitor the casualty. It is believed that an Eskimo immersed in Arctic waters will die from hypothermia at the same rate we do. Their ability to live comfortably and survive in such a hostile environment is entirely due to the fact that they keep fit, dress well and are highly experienced in avoidance. This sums up all that we need to know about cold injury prevention. It is much better to avoid a case of exposure than to have to treat one.

Visibility

Compared to other landscapes, snow-covered terrain provides much more limited visual information. It can be much harder to see the terrain contours due to the uniformity of colour and the high level of reflected light. Strong, directional illumination gives the best visibility, such as on a clear sunny day. In contrast there are two weather conditions which produce especially poor visibility.

Flat Light

When the sky is overcast, the sunlight becomes diffused and comes equally from all directions. As a result, no shadows are cast by undulations in the snow surface, creating a condition known as 'flat light'. Even when the overall light levels are quite high, it can be very difficult to see the terrain contours. Skiing and snowboarding become both more difficult and also potentially more dangerous, especially on bumpy and varied terrain. The best remedy is to head for slopes which offer more directional lighting – for example, runs which are cut through the trees, or which have darker areas of terrain on one or both sides (e.g. rock faces or exposed vegetation). Any darker features adjacent to the run will help break up the uniformity of lighting, throwing the terrain into sharper relief.

White-out

In conditions of mist or low cloud, such problems are magnified further. When you are within the layer of cloud, the dividing line between snow and sky vanishes, creating what is known as a 'white-out'. It not only becomes hard to see the terrain but also to make out the slope angle or even to tell which way is up. In thick mist, visibility can be reduced to a few metres, so that reference points such as trees, lift pylons and piste markers disappear. This creates a sensation which can be likened to being inside a floodlit ping-pong ball. The problems which are experienced in white-out conditions include:

• Inability to see the terrain contours

• Difficulty in determining the slope angle

• Loss of information about speed and direction

• Disorientation and loss of balance (sometimes resulting in feelings of nausea)

Group Management in White-out Conditions

In white-out conditions, it becomes very easy for the group to get split up, for you to lose your way, or even to ski off the edge of the piste or over a drop-off. The best advice is to stop skiing until the conditions improve. If you have to manage your group in a white-out, there are several procedures which can help minimise the risks:

1. As in flat light, head for runs which go through trees or which have dark areas at their margins. This will provide some directional lighting and give added visual reference points for navigation and orientation.

2. Select a strong person to act as back-marker and travel down slowly with frequent stops to check that everyone is present. Tell the group to stay close together and to watch the person in front and call out if anyone falls over.

3. Try to follow reference points such as lift pylons, piste markers or lines of trees, making sure you do not stray off the edge of the piste. Remember in many resorts the left and right piste markers are different allowing you to know which side of the piste you are on or if you are off-piste. The sound of lift motors and even food or other smells from mountain restaurants can help you identify your location.

4. Always stop and assemble the group at points where the run divides to make sure that no-one takes the wrong turning. Make sure that the group are aware of any hazards such as exposed rocks, either by stopping before them or by giving a clear verbal warning.

5. When away from the marked pistes, white out can be a much more serious proposition. You may be reduced to following a compass bearing and leap frogging group members on this bearing (see navigation section).

One final point is that in bad visibility, the tendency is to focus most of your attention on trying to see. While it is clearly important to gain as much visual information as possible, it is also helpful to use other sources as well. For example:

- Listening to the sound coming from the snow can help you gauge the snow texture and determine your speed and direction (the sound is louder in the second half of the turn)
- Focusing on the soles of your feet can help you feel the terrain contours and identify changes of speed as you go through each turn
- Keeping your head level helps the balance organs of the inner ear to function effectively

There are also a number of techniques which can be useful in bad visibility:

- A pole-plant can help you identify the slope gradient and the texture of the snow - if necessary, between turns as well as at the start. A double (two-handed) pole-plant gives added stability at the start of the turns
- Use a plough parallel for added stability and precision when skiing slowly. Step rather than rotate the outer ski into the plough, to avoid catching it on unseen lumps and ridges
- Throw snowballs ahead of you (wi thin the limits of visibility) to make a mark on the snow surface and help you gauge its shape and gradient. If you are travelling slowly in soft snow, you can scoop up handfuls while on the move

Sunlight

The light reaching the Earth's surface consists of a range of wavelengths from infra-red (IR) through the visible spectrum to ultraviolet (UV). The ultraviolet part of the spectrum is further sub-divided into two types: UVA (longer wavelengths) and UVB (shorter wavelengths). Research on the long-term effects of sunlight increasingly emphasises the dangers posed by ultraviolet radiation. This concern is heightened by evidence of thinning of the planet's ozone layer, which filters out much of the UV light.

Ozone thinning was first detected over Antarctica, but now appears to affect many parts of the world.

Both UVA and UVB cause tanning and burning of the skin, but UVB is around 1,000 times more potent and is generally considered to carry greater risks to health. Many products such as sunscreens and sunglasses specifically state the protection which they afford against UVB rays. Recent research however suggests that prolonged exposure to UVA also carries some risk.

Short-term Effects: Sunburn and Snow-blindness

The most obvious short-term effect of UV exposure is sunburn, causing reddened, sore and peeling skin. Less common but no less painful is snow blindness, resulting from irritation of the eyes. A few hours after exposure the eyes start to water, feeling painful and gritty. At this point, even subdued lighting can cause discomfort. The symptoms usually appear 8 to 12 hours after exposure and last for 12 to 48 hours.

Despite being very distressing, snow blindness is simply treated by resting in a dark room, with the application of cold compresses over the eyes.

Long-term Effects: Skin Cancer, Cataracts and Pterygia

While the short-term effects have long been recognised, it is only recently that the long-term damage caused by UV radiation has been fully appreciated. The three key dangers are skin cancer, cataracts and pterygia:

- **Skin cancer -** This can take many years to develop, and generally takes the form of dark-coloured mole-like growths called melanomas
- **Cataracts -** These result from the lens of the eye becoming opaque due to UV exposure. This causes a progressive loss of vision, although not total blindness
- **Pterygia -** Pronounced 'terigia', these are thickened, yellow-coloured patches on the whites of the eyes caused by prolonged UV exposure. They can extend onto the cornea and impair vision, requiring surgical removal

In Europe, recent figures show that the incidence of skin cancer has quadrupled over the last 25 years. Because it can take over 20 years to develop, the risks are not immediately apparent. The evidence also suggests that people receiving occasional short exposures (e.g. a week or two each year) are at the highest risk.

The Effects of Snow and Altitude on Ultraviolet Radiation

Despite these facts, public awareness can sometimes be poor. Even less common is the recognition that snowsports enthusiasts are exposed to particularly high UV levels, even in mid-winter. Because the atmosphere acts as a filter, the intensity of ultraviolet radiation increases with altitude. In general, it rises by around 4% per 300 metres. At 2500 metres (the altitude of many alpine resorts), the UV level is therefore 33% greater than at sea level.

In addition, snow acts as a reflector, increasing the total amount of radiation falling on the skin and eyes. Because haze and thin cloud scatter the rays without absorbing them significantly, the effect is intensified by multiple reflections. As a result, the Alps in winter can have higher UV levels than a Mediterranean beach in summer. In summary, ultraviolet radiation:

- Increases with altitude
- Is reflected by snow, increasing net exposure
- Is not screened by cloud

Protection Against Sunlight

As a professional teacher, you may spend much of the year in a high-ultraviolet environment. You therefore need to protect yourself from its dangers. In addition, it is important to make your clients aware of the risks by offering sound advice and a good personal example. The two key forms of protection are sunglasses or goggles and sunscreens (skin creams). Provided they are used appropriately, modern sunscreens and sunglasses can provide very good levels of protection. The slogan "Slip, Slap, Slop!" can be used to remind us to "Slip on your sunglasses, slap on a hat and slop on the sun cream".

Sunscreens and Sun Protection Factors

Sunscreens generally protect skin against UVB radiation. Most display a numerical sun protection factor (SPF), which indicates the level of protection. For example, if the strength of UV is such that you can stay in the sun for no more than an hour without burning, SPF 2 allows you to stay out for 2 hours, while SPF 8 gives 8 hours of protection. These figures assume that the protective layer remains intact on the skin. Since many sunscreens are water-soluble, they are diluted by sweat, reducing the level of protection. For this reason, regular applications are necessary (about once every hour or two, and after every headlong fall into the snow). In any case, it is important to apply sunscreen thoroughly. Due to upward reflections from the snow, the ear lobes and the underside of the nose are particularly vulnerable. The scalp can also be burned, even through a full head of hair. Either wear a hat or use sunscreen for protection. It is worth bearing in mind that certain people can have allergic reaction to many of the sun care products available. It may be worth checking with the parents of a child before a lesson if they have such a reaction. In the Alps, a fair skinned person may only take 15 minutes to start burning, so that SPF 15 sunscreen will allow them less than 4 hours' exposure. By contrast, SPF 30 will give protection for over 7 hours. It is recommended that the snowsports enthusiast use a factor greater than SPF-15 and re-apply it every 2 hours.

UVA Damage to the Skin

With effective UVB protection, people can stay out in strong sunlight for long periods. However, there is now concern about the effects of prolonged exposure to UVA, which many sunscreens do not filter out.

It is known that UVA radiation causes premature ageing of the skin, and may also be linked to skin cancer. Some sunscreens do now state their level of UVA protection, and a standard system to describe this is currently being considered.

Just like the skin, the eyes need good protection from sunlight. Most good quality sunglasses should give adequate screening, but care needs to be taken over the following points:

- Sunglasses should protect the eyes from upward reflections as well as direct sunlight
- The outer corners of the eyes are vulnerable to burning. Wrap-around sunglasses or ones with side-shields give the best protection
- Sunglasses and goggles should have shatterproof lenses, either made of plastic or toughened glass
- Lenses should offer close to 100% screening of both UVA and UVB rays. Most good-quality ski glasses should achieve these levels. Dark lenses can actually damage the eyes if they fail to screen out UV radiation effectively. Because the pupils react automatically to the amount of visible light entering the eye, they dilate when wearing sunglasses. In the absence of effective screening, even more UV can therefore enter the eye than without the glasses

For people who need to wear spectacles, there are several options:

- Prescription sunglasses
- Clip-on lenses which fit over spectacles
- Contact lenses worn under normal sunglasses

Dark contact lenses which filter out UV radiation are also available. While these can provide effective protection for the cornea, lens and retina, they are not recommended as the sole form of protection, for two main reasons:

- Contact lenses do not cover the whole surface of the eyes. As a result, the whites of the eyes (sclera) and parts of the iris are exposed to UV radiation, leading to a risk of pterygia
- It is difficult to apply sunscreen to the skin immediately surrounding the eyes. In any case the cream often enters the eyes, causing irritation. As a result, the only effective protection for these areas is to use sunglasses

Looking after your Class

In relation to the above hazards, your main role as an instructor is to offer your clients sound advice on clothing and protection, and to check that they are suitably equipped at the start of each session. Beyond this, there are two additional points to bear in mind:

- Energy supplies are burned much faster in cold conditions, regardless of the level of exertion. As a result, it is important that everyone is well nourished
- Ensure that the group have regular refreshment stops throughout the day, to guard against dehydration

Finally, it is advisable for instructors to carry a few spare items for emergencies:

- First-Aid kit
- Spare hat
- Glove liners
- Scarf or face-mask
- Spare sunglasses or goggles
- Sunscreen
- Mobile phone

9. Snow and Avalanche

In a mountain environment, conditions are subject to rapid and often dramatic change. As discussed in the previous chapter, weather is the most obvious of these variables. In conjunction with other factors, weather patterns strongly affect both the snow conditions and the probability of avalanche. Both of these are important in ensuring the safety of your group:

Snow Conditions – Even on prepared pistes, the snow conditions can vary widely from one time of day to another. This has a strong bearing on the choice of appropriate terrain for your class - a slope which was well within their ability at one time may be much more demanding in different conditions. Equally, the selection of suitable tasks and exercises must be judged in relation to the current snow conditions - an exercise which was safe on one type of snow may become hazardous on another.

Snow Stability – When working off-piste, an assessment of snow stability is of prime importance. In making that assessment, you must take into account both the current snow and weather conditions, and the patterns of weather and snowfall over the preceding days and weeks. In addition, the snowpack's stability can vary dramatically over a short period. A slope which was stable at one time of day may be extremely dangerous at another.

The information in "Snow Conditions" applies both on- and off-piste. Since instructors generally spend most of their time teaching on prepared runs, an understanding of the different snow types and their properties is clearly paramount.

The section on Avalanche Hazard has obvious relevance when working off-piste. But even on-piste, people are occasionally caught by avalanches. While the resort's ski patrol does their best to minimise these hazards, they can never be entirely eliminated. You therefore need to be aware of the dangers, and be able to recognise potentially unstable snowfields or cornices which threaten the runs on which you are working. But finally, the most important source of information on snow and avalanche hazard is that available locally. In almost all cases, the resort's ski patrol or piste security service have the most detailed and up-to-date knowledge of the snowfall and weather patterns over the season. It is only with this information that an accurate assessment of hazard can be made. Wherever possible, local expert information should be consulted on avalanche conditions and weather forecasts before going to any potentially hazardous areas, whether on- or off-piste. Both on- and off-piste, snow conditions are affected by a number of factors. These include:

- The altitude of the slope
- The slope's aspect or orientation
- The gradient of the slope
- The current temperature
- The time of day
- The prevailing wind strength and direction
- The time of year
- The prevailing and preceding weather pattern

The Formation of Snow

An understanding of snow conditions is best approached through knowledge of how snow crystals form and change. What follows is only an outline of the processes involved - for a more detailed account see the references section. In certain conditions of atmospheric humidity and temperature, snow crystals will begin to form. At first they are very small and tend to remain suspended in the air. As the crystals grow, they begin to fall earthwards. Their eventual size depends among other factors on the time it takes them to reach the ground.

Figure 9.1:
Typical snow crystal shapes

Snow Conditions

All snow crystals have a basic six-sided structure, with shapes often resembling a six-pointed star (known as stellar or dendrites). Other six sided shapes are also found, such as hexagonal plates and columns, thin needle-like crystals, and various combinations of these basic patterns. The actual structure which is found depends on the atmospheric conditions at the time of formation. Whatever their initial shape, the structure is only retained provided the snow falls in reasonably windless conditions. In this state, freshly-fallen snow has a relatively low density, with over 90% of its volume made up of trapped air. It has a very light, fluffy texture and is known as powder snow.

The Effect of Wind on Snow

When snow falls in windy conditions, buffeting caused by turbulence breaks up the crystals into smaller particles. On falling to earth, these pack together much more densely than snow which has fallen in still air. Depending on the wind strength and degree of turbulence, the resulting snow consistency can vary from heavy powder to solid slab into which a ski pole will barely penetrate. In general, this snow type is known as windslab, and is further subdivided into soft and hard slab. Overall, the wind produces what is possibly the most difficult type of snow to assess the avalanche risk in. The degree of turbulence which occurs depends not only on wind strength but also on terrain features such as ridges and rock outcrops. Even in a moderate wind, these features can cause significant slab formation. Deposits of windslab are generally found on lee slopes, or in areas on the lee side of a ridge or outcrop - that is, on the side away from the wind. Even in calm conditions, features can often be seen which indicate the strength and direction of earlier winds. Three common features of this sort are cornices, sastrugi, and rime deposits as shown in figure 9.2

Figure 9.2: Shows a cornice, Sastrugi & Rime Ice

Cornices – These are overhanging lips of snow which run along exposed mountain ridges and around the heads of gullies. They are caused by the wind blowing snow over the ridge and depositing it on the lee side (the side away from the wind), building up an overhang. Cornices can also form on the side of a gully during side loading (cross loading) winds i.e. winds that blow across the gully.

Sastrugi – These are areas of deeply carved grooves and ridges in the surface, where the wind has etched away the snow (wind ripples being a gentler form) It is sometimes seen in combination with raised footprints or ski tracks standing proud of the surface, where the snow which has been compressed by the tracks has resisted erosion while the softer snow has been stripped away. With sastrugi, the wind direction is shown by the fact that the steeper faces (sometimes with points) of the etched ridges point into the wind.

Riming – Where a strong, moist wind has been blowing, it deposits rime on the windward sides of objects such as lift pylons, piste poles etc. Riming is commonly seen in the Scottish Highlands, but is less often found in the Alps since the colder temperatures reduce the moisture content of the air.

It should also be noted that windslab can form without a snowfall. If previously fallen snow is blown around, the turbulence can break up the crystals to create slab conditions wherever they are deposited.

For example, the prevailing wind in the Alps comes from the south-west. This generally produces the largest snow (and slab) accumulations on north-east-facing slopes. Provided the snow pack is not hard enough to resist erosion, a north-east wind may later produce a layer of windslab on south-west-facing slopes.

Metamorphism of Snow

Once it has fallen, the snow is subject to various processes of change known as transformation or metamorphism. These processes alter the physical shape of the snow crystals, as well as the degree and type of bonding between them. As a result, metamorphism has a profound effect on the stability of the snow pack. The metamorphism of snow is generally due to a combination of mechanical forces such as the pressure of overlying snow, and thermal effects due to the ambient temperature and humidity. Three distinct processes of transformation can occur, depending on the precise combination of temperature, humidity and mechanical effects:

Rounding – In the rounding process the grains become more blob shaped and bond to neighbouring grains

Squaring – In the squaring process, also called recrystallization or temperature gradient (TG) metamorphism, ice is deposited on the grains by the flow of water vapour through the snow.

Melt-freeze Metamorphism – Changes in crystal structure due to freeze thaw action.

Rounding

This type of metamorphism is the most common of the three processes of transformation. It occurs at all temperatures down to around -40° C. In the main, the colder and dryer the conditions, the slower the process becomes, at temperatures below around -40° C, it virtually ceases, so this process occurs over a wide range of temperatures. New snow crystals which have fallen in relatively cold and still air have a complex, star-shaped structure. The snow crystals gradually lose material from the tips of their branches, and gain material at the centre. Even at very low temperatures, moisture in the form of water vapour is present within the snow pack. This is due to a process called sublimation, in which water passes directly between the solid and vapour phases, without an intermediate liquid phase. It is a two-way process, so that the water vapour which is released by sublimation can resublime back into a solid, crystalline form. In rounding, this process results in a net loss of material from the tips of the snow crystals and a net gain at the centre, as the water vapour re-sublimes onto the crystal nucleus.

As a result, they gradually become more granular in shape, as shown in figure 9.3.

Rounding	Stabilising Simpler Shapes Settlement	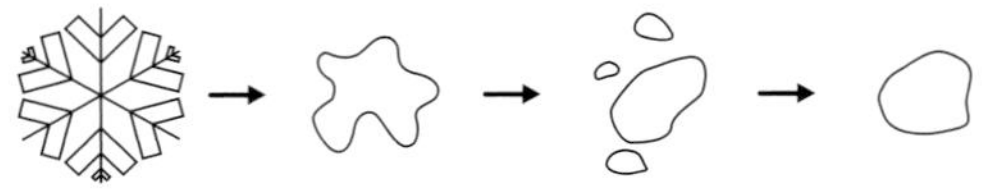 New Snow Partially Settled Round
(rounding continued)	Further settlement Necks Bonding to strong snow pack	
Squaring	Destabilising Crystal Growth Loose, doesn't bond, sugar Possible collapse Temperature gradient greater than 1°C/10cm	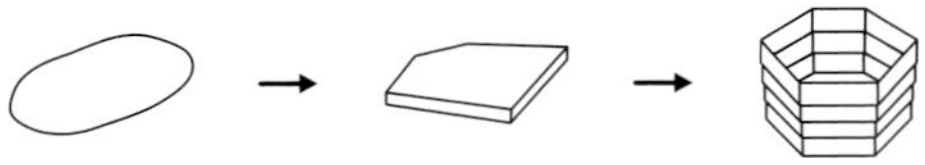
Melt-Freeze	Free water when melting Very safe when frozen Looks glassy	 Grain Cluster Melt Freeze Particle

Figure 9.3: Metamorphism of snow

These crystals pack together much more densely, bonding at their points of contact and making a firmer and generally more stable layer. At air temperatures above freezing (such as commonly experienced in Britain), newly-fallen snow transforms into a coarse granular consistency within a few hours. On a cold, high north-facing Alpine slope, the same process could take several weeks.

When it has just fallen, the fine branches of adjacent crystals interlock with each other, helping to bind the particles together. As the snow transforms, the crystals lose material from their extremities, so that the degree of interlocking of adjacent crystals gradually reduces and the snow pack becomes less stable.

Over the first few hours after a new snowfall, loose-snow avalanches occur due to this initial loss of stability (see Avalanche Types below). As the process of rounding continues however, the stability of the snow pack once more tends to increase. The increasingly granular crystals develop bonds at their adjacent points of contact, so that the snow becomes gradually denser and more cohesive.

Squaring

Except on glaciers and in regions of permafrost, the ground below the snow cover remains almost exactly at freezing point. In contrast, the snow surface may be many degrees below freezing due to the ambient air temperature. As a result, there is usually a temperature gradient through the snow pack – warmer at the base and colder at the top. The higher the temperature, the greater the amount of free water vapour present in the snow pack (see sublimation in previous paragraph on rounding). Due to the tendency of warm air to rise, the water vapour which is released from the lower layers in the snow pack tends to re-sublime higher up, creating a new layer of crystals. As a result, there is a net growth of these over-lying snow crystals at the expense of those lower down. These growing crystals have a very characteristic shape. Starting with a hexagonal plate, they form open, cup-like structures with six stepped sides. They are given various names - 'depth hoar', 'cup crystals' or 'beaker crystals'. Depending on the length of time they have been forming, they can be anything from a millimetre to a centimetre in length.

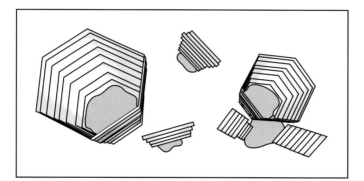

Figure 9.4:
Squaring

A crucial feature of depth hoar is that the crystals do not form bonds with each other. Instead they remain loose and separate, like a layer of ball-bearings within the snow pack. Their effect on the likelihood of avalanche can be dramatic. Even without any further snowfall, a previously cohesive and well consolidated snow pack can become highly unstable, due to the growth of a layer of these loose, un-bonded crystals. Because they usually lie deep within the snow pack (they can also form within the snow pack e.g. below crusts), their existence is also difficult to detect. The occurrence of squaring is influenced by two main factors:

- The ability of air to circulate within the snow pack. Very densely-packed snow (on prepared pistes for example) makes it less likely or at least slows down the rate of crystal growth. In contrast, vegetation increases the probability, since the stems and branches of plants create spaces within the snow pack, increasing the circulation of air

- The steepness of the temperature gradient. The bigger the temperature difference per unit of vertical distance through the snow pack, the faster the rate of growth of depth hoar. As a result, depth hoar is often found after a prolonged very cold spell, such as during a period of clear, sunny weather with low night-time temperatures. Its formation is especially likely when the snow cover is not very thick, such as in the early part of the season

Melt-freeze Metamorphism

This refers to changes in crystalline structure due to repeated thawing and re-freezing of the snow. Although it can occur at any time, it is most common in the spring. It produces the very coarse, granular snow crystals often referred to as spring snow (known as corn snow in North America). In the main it has a stabilising influence on the snow pack, but can also cause increased hazard in certain situations:

- Where a period of warm or sunny weather has produced a melt-freeze layer and this is then covered by cold new snow, the adhesion between the layers is low. As a result, the new snow is much more likely to slide off than where it has fallen on a softer underlying surface
- During a prolonged thaw, free water may start to percolate downwards through the snow pack. Where this water meets a hard melt-freeze layer, it tends to flow over the frozen surface, loosening the bonding of the overlying snow and increasing the likelihood of avalanche

Snow Types

As a result of these processes of change, a wide variety of different snow types and conditions are formed. It takes considerable experience to become familiar with their effects when skiing, and to recognise the signs of instability and avalanche hazard which they create. Rather than attempting to categorise the different snow conditions in detail, what follows is a fairly simple list of snow types as a basis on which this experience can be built. This section deals only with the general properties of the different types of snow. The specific avalanche hazards, along with advice on recognising and avoiding them, is dealt with in the section on Avalanche Hazard.

Powder Snow – As described above, snow which has fallen in cold and fairly still conditions has a dry, fluffy consistency. When it is packed down, it retains a soft and grippy texture. Depending on the precise atmospheric conditions, powder snow may range from a very loose, dry consistency to one which is relatively moist and cohesive. When it is newly-fallen, the crystals will in any case be more strongly bonded together than after rounding has started to take effect. While powder snow offers some of the best conditions for off-piste descents, it also presents some serious hazards. Apart from a high risk of avalanche, there is also the possibility of a person becoming trapped in deep powder snow, and even of asphyxiating if the face is buried. In addition, there is a high likelihood of losing a ski or snowboard in deep snow, with possibly serious consequences if the route back to the resort is long or difficult. Powder snow is easy to recognise by simply picking up a handful. If the top layer breaks away from its surroundings like a fragile plate, it is actually soft slab (see below). While heavy powder can be quite cohesive, it does not show a clear fracture but instead comes out as a slightly sticky mass. If the particles remain loose and separate, the snow is light. Squeezing it into a snowball gives a further test of its humidity - the wetter the snow, the more easily it forms a snowball, if it refuses to bind together at all, and instead trickles through the fingers like sand, it is very dry.

Windslab – As discussed briefly above, wind turbulence breaks up dendrites (snow crystals) into small particles. These have a much higher packing density than those of powder snow, and bond together to form a very cohesive snow type known as windslab. Depending on the wind-strength and degree of turbulence, the resultant texture can vary between one similar to heavy powder, to a rigid layer like brittle concrete. These two sub-divisions are known as soft and hard slab respectively. Windslab represents the most dangerous of all conditions with respect to avalanche. Its surface is often hard and unyielding, giving the impression of being very stable and well consolidated. But because of the strength of its internal cohesion, it lacks the flexibility of many other snow types. As a result, internal stresses can be set up as the snow pack attempts to settle, requiring only a small trigger to set off a large and very destructive avalanche. But even setting these risks aside, windslab also poses a number of additional dangers. When a layer of hard slab lies on top of softer snow, it may or may not support a person's weight. This slab often gives way in a random and unpredictable fashion, disrupting balance and control. The skis/board can also become trapped beneath the surface, compounding these difficulties. Where the slab is very hard, skiers may also suffer injuries from impact and leverage of the legs against the edge of the broken slab, even in the absence of a fall. Soft slab generally allows the equipment to sink into the snow surface. While there is no obvious hard layer, the snow is still very difficult to ski/ride, and is heavy enough to create increased risk of injury due to leverage against the legs. Soft slab is also very prone to avalanche, and poses the additional danger that at first sight it may be mistaken for powder snow.

While windslab is most likely to be found off-piste, it can also occur on pisted terrain, especially where wind-drifted snow has blown across a run, or has been deposited in the lee of a ridge or other terrain feature. Hard slab can usually be recognised by having a very matt, chalky appearance. It sometimes produces a hollow, booming sound when walked on, and tends to squeak when a ski pole is pushed into it and twisted round. In comparison, soft slab often looks very similar to powder snow. Here, the best sign is to push the flat of your hand beneath the snow surface and lift it upwards. While powder snow cascades off your hand leaving a conical heap, soft slab tends to remain in the form of a fractured plate of snow. The same test can be done by slicing the tip of your ski beneath the surface and lifting it up.

Breakable Crust – There are basically three processes which can produce a crust layer on the surface of the snow: wind, sun and warm air. The resulting snow conditions are known as wind-crust, sun-crust and melt-crust respectively.

Wind-Crust – When a layer of wind-crust is formed, the action of the wind is different from that involved in creating windslab. While the process is not fully understood, it appears to be due to the wind compacting the existing surface layer of snow, rather than depositing a new layer of fine particles. As a result it generally affects windward slopes, as opposed to the lee faces on which windslab is found.

Sun-Crust – Even while the air temperature remains below freezing, the snow can be melted by strong sunlight. As the sun moves or goes behind cloud, re-freezing occurs to leave a hard, icy layer. Because snow is highly reflective, the effect does not usually penetrate very deeply. In consequence, the crust tends to be very thin and fragile, like a highly glazed layer of eggshell.

Melt-Crust – As the air temperature rises above freezing, the snow begins to melt, starting at the surface and working downwards. If the snow subsequently re-freezes, a hard layer of melt-crust is formed. Compared to the action of sunlight, the effect of warm air usually penetrates more deeply, producing a coarser, thicker layer of crust. In itself, a layer of crust poses relatively little avalanche hazard compared to windslab. However, unless the crust layer is very thick, it usually breaks under a person's weight, especially where it overlies a layer of soft snow. As a result, it causes the same additional difficulties and dangers as noted above for windslab. Loss of balance and control as the crust gives way, trapping of the skis/board beneath the surface, impact and leverage of the legs against the edge of the broken crust. The major risk of avalanche occurs when new snow falls on top of the crust layer. Fresh snow gains very poor adhesion, especially on the glazed surface of sun-crust, and is therefore highly prone to avalanching at this weakly-bonded junction. Once more, while these types of crust are most often found off-piste, they also occur on prepared runs. Sun-crust and melt-crust are especially common, being found on slopes facing the sun and in late season respectively. In this case, there is little danger from the skis/board breaking through the crust layer, due to the firmness of the underlying snow. Instead, the major risk is of loss of grip and control due to the icy conditions, along with increased likelihood of injury when falling on a hard surface.

Sun-crust is very easy to recognise due to its glazed and often very shiny surface. Melt-crust may have a similar appearance, but depending on the degree of melting before re-freezing occurred, it may look indistinguishable from spring snow (below). Indeed, spring snow is produced by a prolonged period of melt-freeze metamorphism. The key difference is that while fully transformed spring snow has the same granular consistency right through the snow pack, melt-crust may lie on top of a less dense and less supportive layer. For all practical purposes, if stamping hard on the surface produces no significant cracking, it can be treated as spring snow.

Spring Snow – The process of melt-freeze metamorphism occurs most rapidly in the spring, turning the snow into the granular consistency known as spring snow. In warm weather it frequently re-freezes overnight before softening again throughout the day. Because of its rough texture, spring snow usually provides reasonably good grip even when frozen, despite its hard, icy feel. Spring snow is found both on- and off-piste, initially on slopes which face the sun, but eventually over the entire mountain in periods of warm weather. When frozen hard, spring snow has a very low probability of avalanching. But in conditions of major thaw, wet snow avalanches frequently occur (see Avalanche Hazard below). Setting this aside, there are two major risks when there is spring snow. The first is when ruts and lumps are frozen into the surface, making it both difficult and dangerous. The second is that in warm weather, the snow eventually becomes very wet and heavy. This makes it much harder to maintain balance and control, and greatly increases the leverage acting on the legs in a fall.

Heavy Snow – As snow begins to melt, it gradually changes from a slightly wet consistency to that of porridge. Even firmly compacted snow can soften to a point at which the skis/board sink into the surface, making them very hard to turn. A similar effect occurs when a layer of un-pisted powder snow is subjected to rapid warming. Where first it was light and fluffy, it becomes progressively heavier and more difficult. In either case, such conditions are dangerous as well as difficult. Because of the heaviness of the snow, not only is it harder to turn, the legs are also subjected to substantially greater forces, especially in a fall. The risk of avalanche also increases, especially when there has been a rapid temperature rise.

Ice – Strictly speaking, ice only occurs either on glaciers or where the snow has melted to the point of having free water on its surface before re-freezing. However, it is often used loosely to describe other sorts of very hard-packed and polished snow. Whatever its origin, icy terrain requires a combination of good technique and sharp edges. While ice is in itself extremely unlikely to avalanche (the exception being glacial serac collapse), it contributes to subsequent avalanche hazard in precisely the same way as crust (above). The harder and smoother the surface, the less adhesion it provides for any new snow which falls on top of it. On ice, the main danger is of injury (especially to the upper body) due to the absence of cushioning in a fall. A further hazard is that on steep terrain, one can slide out of control after falling, sometimes travelling many hundreds of metres before coming to rest. This poses the additional dangers of injury due to collision with rocks or other obstacles. As a result, even marked and open runs may become extremely dangerous in such conditions. Indeed, many people have died as a result of head injuries sustained while sliding uncontrollably on icy terrain.

Hardpack – While it does not refer to a specific type of snow, hardpack is the label generally applied where the surface is firmly packed (usually on-piste), with the exception of spring snow. It is distinct from ice or crust, and provides a consistent, grippy and responsive surface. To a lesser degree than on ice, there is some risk of upper body injury due to the absence of cushioning in a fall, and of sliding away for a considerable distance where the terrain is steep. Since it is usually found only on-piste, the risk of avalanche is extremely low. However, it should be noted that when off-piste, areas of hard windslab can easily be mistaken for hardpack, with all the consequent and serious dangers which that creates.

Avalanche Hazard

Avalanches represent one of the most serious of mountain hazards. All instructors, whether working on- or off-piste, should be aware of the potential dangers. Indeed, the best advice is for everyone to be able to recognise dangerous slopes and snow conditions, and to know what precautions to take. In addition, instructors need to be fully conversant with avalanche search and rescue techniques. This section simply provides an outline of the principles of avalanche hazard evaluation and rescue procedures. For more detailed information, see References section. Instructors are also strongly advised to attend a specialised avalanche course to build on this knowledge. The techniques of hazard evaluation and protection, along with search and rescue procedures all require practical training to be effective. While reading provides valuable background knowledge, this needs to be consolidated with practical hands-on experience.

Avalanche Types

The most common system for classifying avalanches uses a set of five criteria, each of which may show one of two basic characteristics, shown in the diagram below. Rather than representing ten separate and distinct types, avalanches can possess a combination of the above features, for example, full-depth, wet slab channelled avalanches are frequently found coming down gullies late in the season, surface dry-slab unconfined avalanches are often seen on open slopes throughout the earlier parts of the year.

1. Type of breakaway

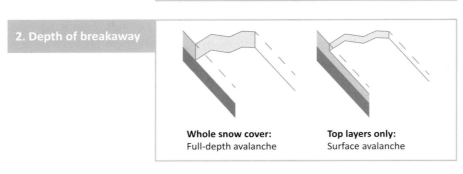

From a single point:
Loose snow avalanche

Extended across slope:
Slab avalanche

2. Depth of breakaway

Whole snow cover:
Full-depth avalanche

Top layers only:
Surface avalanche

3. Humidity of snow

Wet:
Wet snow avalanche

Dry:
Dry snow avalanche

4. Cross-section of slope

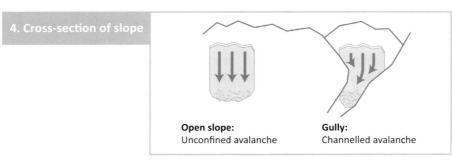

Open slope:
Unconfined avalanche

Gully:
Channelled avalanche

5. Form of movement

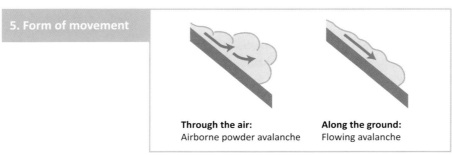

Through the air:
Airborne powder avalanche

Along the ground:
Flowing avalanche

Loose Snow Avalanches

Loose snow avalanches occur where the snow lacks cohesion. This typically happens in the first few hours after a new snowfall (see rounding), and when high temperature or rain has weakened the cohesion of the snow. Such avalanches start at a single point and pick up more snow as they run, so that from a distance their slide path takes the shape of an inverted V. As the name implies, the snow is loose and usually only involves surface or near surface snow. Their speed is dependant on slope angle and the moisture content of the snow. Depending on the conditions which gave rise to it, a loose snow avalanche may also be either dry or wet. While loose snow slides may often appear much less dramatic than slab avalanches, they nevertheless represent a very high risk to anyone who is caught. In cold, dry conditions, victims can easily suffocate due to inhaling large quantities of powder snow. Wet snow slides carry similar dangers, this time because of the small amount of air present in the debris, so that anyone whose face is buried is likely to suffocate.

Slab Avalanches

Slab avalanches can be difficult to predict and are also particularly dangerous and destructive, and therefore warrant a more detailed explanation. Throughout the winter, the snow pack accumulates in successive layers with each new snowfall, or by wind moving previously-fallen snow. If each layer has fallen in relatively still air, the process of rounding may gradually consolidate and stabilise the snow pack. But because of its structure and mechanical properties, windslab is potentially unstable, and can become even more so over time. On any sloping surface, the snow is constantly being pulled downhill by gravity. As a result, many types of snow actually creep or 'flow' slowly downhill. This is illustrated by the way in which the snow on a pitched roof eventually ends up overhanging the eaves, see figure 9.6.

This gradual movement helps to reduce the stresses in the snow pack, making it less likely to avalanche. But because windslab is relatively rigid and brittle, it cannot move or settle sufficiently to reduce the stresses caused by gravity. As the underlying layers of snow settle and stabilise,

Figure 9.6:
Snow creep on chalet roof

the slab layer becomes even more unstable, like a sheet of glass which is being bent. A small additional force like that from a ski track, footprint or pole-plant can be enough to trigger a fracture, which extends almost instantaneously across the slope (it takes a third of a second for a fracture 100m long to propagate). As noted above, windslab can vary from the consistency of heavy powder to a surface which is so hard that a ski or boot will barely make a mark. A slab avalanche occurs when the slab begins to slide on an underlying layer to which it is only weakly attached. Such avalanches vary in size from only a few metres wide to those covering whole hillsides. In hard slab, the snow immediately fractures into large blocks, which may gradually break up into smaller pieces as they slide and tumble downhill. Since these blocks may be anything up to several metres thick, the risk of death or serious injury to anyone caught in such an avalanche is extremely great. The fracture in hard slab may be a long way from the loading point i.e. well above you!

While soft slab initially fractures in much the same way, the snow generally breaks up into much smaller lumps and particles. It leaves debris similar to a loose snow avalanche, but with the clear, continuous fracture line characteristic of a slab release. As well as windslab, many other types of snow can form a slab avalanche. Basically, whenever a layer of fairly cohesive snow (such as that resulting from rounding) is weakly bonded to the layer beneath, it can release as a slab. This commonly occurs in several situations:

- Where there is an underlying surface to which the cohesive snow is poorly bonded, such as rock slab, long grass, ice or crust
- Where a layer of depth hoar has formed through squaring
- Where water percolates down through the snow pack to an impermeable surface, over which it then flows, weakening the adhesion to the layers above
- Buried surface hoar and graupel (ball bearing like snow formed in violent storm clouds i.e. cold front)

Full Depth Avalanches

These typically occur in heavy thaw conditions when the whole snow pack has become saturated, and free water weakens the bond between the snow and the ground surface below. This type of avalanche can often be spotted in snowsport resorts on grassy slopes, the grass providing a suitable sliding surface for the snow layers above. Full-depth avalanches also occur where other factors have weakened the adhesion of the base layer of snow. This is most common where a layer of depth hoar has formed close to the ground surface, due to squaring. Due to the generally larger amount of debris which they contain, full depth avalanches can be even more dangerous and destructive than surface releases. They may also contain rocks and boulders, further increasing the risks to anyone who is caught.

Surface Avalanches

Throughout the earlier parts of the season, these are characteristic of the majority of avalanches. The loose snow slides which commonly occur after each new snowfall are almost always surface avalanches, as are many of the slab releases described above It should be noted that the term 'surface avalanche' does not simply refer to those involving the topmost layer of snow, but includes any avalanche which does not involve the full depth of the snow pack. Surface avalanches can occur in any situation in which the bonding between adjacent layers of snow is weak.

Dry and Wet Snow Avalanches

Here, it is the humidity of the snow which is the defining characteristic. The snow may be either loose or in a slab, full-depth or surface. Dry snow avalanches are characteristic of those occurring during prolonged cold periods, whereas wet snow avalanches occur during sustained warm weather. It should be noted that while a sudden temperature rise often acts as a trigger, it may still result in a dry snow avalanche. The type of avalanche depends not only on the temperature at the time of release, but on whether the snow was already wet or dry. An additional danger posed by wet snow avalanches is that once the snow has come to rest, it tends to freeze into a solid mass. In such cases, probes and snow shovels are virtually useless, so that pick-axes and machinery may have to be used to recover the body of a buried victim.

Unconfined and Channelled Avalanches

In all of the above categories, the properties of the snow pack determine the type of avalanche which occurs. Here it is simply a matter of the shape of the terrain. Except where the snow's momentum carries it to the outside of a bend, avalanches will always take the most direct route downhill. Channelled avalanches therefore tend to follow the floor of a gully, whereas unconfined avalanches, especially slab releases, may extend for hundreds of metres across an open slope. In general, channelled avalanches tend to produce large depths of debris, since the snow cannot spread out over such a wide area as on an open slope. This has serious consequences for anyone who is caught, as survival chances are closely linked with the victim's depth of burial. This danger is magnified where an unconfined avalanche is then channelled into a gully further below.

Airborne Powder Avalanches

These are relatively uncommon, but have remarkable destructive power when they occur. They start as loose snow slides or more commonly as slab releases. If the slope is sufficiently steep, or the ground contours create sufficient turbulence in the moving snow, the avalanche can become airborne. Once this occurs, the avalanche can accelerate rapidly to speeds in excess of 200 kilometres per hour. Such avalanches throw up a powder or dust cloud in front of them, and are preceded by a pressure-wave with the power of an explosion. They can cause huge destruction of buildings and trees as well as seriously injuring or killing anyone caught in their path. Due to their speed of travel, airborne avalanches can continue for large distances over level ground, and have been known to continue for some way up the further side of a valley.

Flowing Avalanches

The majority of avalanches fall into this category. While both loose snow and windslab can become airborne in certain situations if the snow is sufficiently dry, all other snow types tend only to produce flowing avalanches. It should be noted that it is possible for an avalanche to flow for some way downhill, and then become airborne where a terrain feature such as a ridge or steep drop creates sufficient turbulence in the moving snow.

Factors Influencing Avalanche Occurrence

As outlined above, one major set of factors affecting the likelihood of avalanche is the nature of the snow pack:

- The snow's mechanical properties (such as the dense, brittle nature of windslab, or the lubricating effects of water within the snow)
- The snow's crystalline structure (affected by the weather conditions in which it was formed, and the subsequent processes of metamorphism)
- The bond strength between adjacent layers (affected by factors such as the existence of crust layers, and the percolation of free water through the snow pack)

In addition to these, several other factors have a strong bearing on the stability of a given area of snow. These include the nature of the terrain, and specific events which may trigger a release.

The Nature of the Terrain

1. Slope Angle

Avalanches are most common on slopes of 30° to 4 5° - the same slopes that offer some of the best off-piste conditions for the experienced skier/boarder. As a rough guide, a steep black run is about 30°. However, in extreme cases avalanches can occur on slopes as shallow as 15° - a gradient found on many blue runs - so that almost any slope can become hazardous in certain circumstances.

In figure 9.7 the colours are roughly the same as standard piste colours, some overlap can occur, for example a steep blue or easy red. The figures are based upon a distance of 100m and varying vertical drops. To work this out, find the vertical drop then count the number of contours. If using a standard UK Ordnance Survey map or most French IGN Top 25 series, then the contour interval will be 10m. Most Swiss maps have this interval at 20m. See the navigation chapter of this manual, the key of your map or the recommended reading for further info.

Horizontal distance	Vertical drop	Angle in degrees
100m	20m	12°
100m	30m	17°
100m	40m	22°
100m	50m	27°
100m	60m	31°
100m	70m	35°
100m	80m	38°
100m	90m	42°

Figure 9.7:
Slope angle

Don't forget, you can be avalanched standing on flat ground such as in the valley bottom, or worse still, whilst standing some distance up the other side!

The maximum slope angle on which avalanches are likely to occur is 60° (well above the steepest gradient which would normally be skied). Above this angle, the snow tends to slide (slough) off as it falls, so that too little can accumulate to form an avalanche hazard. For practical purposes, the best rule of thumb is that the steeper the slope, the more likely it is to avalanche.

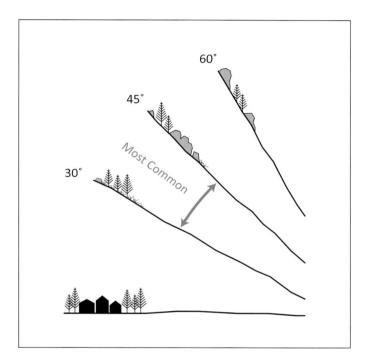

Figure 9.8: Avalanche likelihood and slope angle

2. Slope Profile

As noted in the section on slab avalanches above, wherever the ground is sloping, the snow pack is pulled downhill by gravity. The steeper the slope, the stronger this effect. As a result, slopes with a varying gradient are subject to different levels of stress at different points. On a convex slope, the snow lower down is being pulled more strongly than that higher up, creating tension in the region of maximum convexity. On concave slopes the opposite occurs, so that the snow higher up presses down on the more stable snow lower down.

The result is that a fracture is much more likely to occur on a convex area than where the profile is concave. This is not to say that concave slopes never avalanche. Rather, while the area where the fracture occurs is more likely to be convex, once an avalanche has started it will continue down the slope irrespective of the profile. In practise, the key point is to steer clear of convex areas, especially when traversing or turning a long way out of the fall-line. Finally, it is important to note that the profile which you see is not necessarily the same as the profile of the ground.

Snow accumulation can smooth out the contours, giving the impression of a smooth slope where in fact the ground undulates. In such cases, the ground is indeed smooth as far as the surface snow is concerned, with no variations in gravitational stress. However, stresses may remain in underlying layers, if these were deposited before the undulations were filled in. If settling and transformation has not eliminated these stresses, areas of weakness may remain despite the slope's apparently uniform gradient.

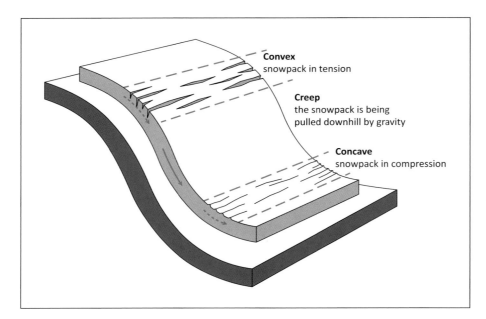

Figure 9.9:
Slope profile

3. Slope Altitude and Aspect (direction it faces)

Temperature effects have a strong bearing on the stability of the snow pack. For example, sunshine often triggers avalanches soon after a new snowfall, and also later in the season during the thaw. Conversely, once the initial period of instability has passed, sunshine or warmth can speed up the process of rounding, stabilising the snow more quickly than on a slope which remains at a lower temperature. Thus, the slope's altitude and aspect can have a large bearing on the likelihood of avalanche. In assessing the stability of a particular slope, it is therefore useful to look for signs of avalanche activity on other slopes of the same altitude and aspect. If any similar slopes have avalanched, the likelihood is that all others may be unstable. However, the converse does not hold true. The absence of avalanche activity on other slopes of similar altitude and aspect gives no guarantee that the present slope is stable. Not only may other, less obvious factors be at work, it may simply be that none of the slopes has avalanched yet. Yours may be the first.

4. Ground Cover

Seeing a slope in summer can give additional evidence of its tendency to avalanche. For example, a large, smooth rock slab provides far less adhesion for snow cover than rough scree. Similarly, long grass gives a much less stable anchor than does short stubble. Shrubs, bushes and trees also have a stabilising effect on the overlying snow, as do any ridges or terracing running across the slope. However, all of the features which can help to increase stability only have an effect on full-depth avalanches. Once they have been completely covered in snow, they will have no further beneficial effect in stabilising additional layers.

Indeed, as noted in squaring previously, the presence of vegetation can increase the likelihood of formation of depth hoar, therefore increasing the chances of avalanche. Finally, it is important to note that the profile which you see on the map is not necessarily the same as the profile of the ground.

5. Cornices

These can fracture well back from the edge of the ridge. They can deposit several tonnes of snow onto the slopes below. The lips of cornices point away from the direction of the wind which formed them, so that the snowfields beneath them generally consist of already-unstable windslab, compounding the degree of hazard. As a result, it is important not to travel along ridges on which a cornice may have formed (bearing in mind that they may be invisible from above), and to avoid slopes beneath them. Cornices may collapse spontaneously, and even if they do not trigger an avalanche on the slope below, they can send large blocks of snow tumbling downhill.

Avalanche Triggers

An area of snow may be potentially unstable due to a combination of its structure and the nature of the terrain on which it lies. In this situation, the only remaining factor which is required is something to trigger an avalanche. Triggers can be either natural or artificial. Examples of natural triggers include increased stress due to further snowfall, or decreased strength due to a build-up of depth hoar. Typical artificial triggers are the arrival of a skier or boarder, or the setting off of an explosive charge. Thus, some common triggers include:

- A skier/boarder or climber
- A fall of glacier ice or a serac
- An explosive charge
- The collapse of a cornice
- Rainfall
- Sun warming of the slope
- Further snowfall
- A rapid rise in air temperature
- Wind-drifting of the snow
- A prolonged spell of very low temperatures

In addition, sustained low temperatures prolong the risk of avalanche after a new snowfall, by slowing down the process of stabilisation which results from rounding. From the above, it can be seen that in already unstable conditions, only a small event may be necessary to trigger a slide. All too often, that small event is a skier/boarder appearing on the scene. Very few avalanches in which skiers/boarders are caught happen spontaneously. Rather, it is the people themselves who unwittingly set them off. As a result, the most important step which can be taken in avoiding exposure to avalanche hazard is to evaluate the stability of the slope.

Evaluating Avalanche Hazard

By a careful analysis of the relevant factors, it is possible to evaluate the risk of avalanche, both for the area in general and for specific slopes. But to do so requires not only a knowledge of the immediately visible factors such as slope angle and profile, but also of hidden factors such as ground cover, and of past events such as weather patterns. For accurate evaluation, the following information is needed:

• Slope steepness, profile, aspect and altitude

• Ground cover

• Structure of the snow pack

• Weather pattern throughout the season to date

These last two factors are intimately connected. While past weather is most easily established from weather reports, much can be inferred from the snow itself. For example, a period of very cold weather may be revealed by the presence of depth hoar, recent wind direction may be indicated by snow formations such as sastrugi, cornices, etc. Indeed the main significance of the weather is in its effect on the structure and stability of the snow pack. Knowledge of past weather patterns is simply a way of reducing the amount of time which would otherwise have to be spent studying the structure of the snow pack directly, as described below.

Snow Pits

The structure and stability of the snow pack can be most clearly established by digging a snow-pit, to expose a cross-section of the snow. Its stability is determined by the mechanical properties of the layers which exist, along with the strength of adhesion between them. The layers themselves are the result of past weather patterns. Just as the rings of a tree indicate successive growing seasons, so the layers in the snow indicate past weather events. Not all of these layers represent actual snowfalls however. Many are caused by wind, temperature change and sunlight.

Wind Effects – As noted in The Effect of Wind on Snow above, a layer of windslab may form without new snowfall, due to the wind shifting already fallen snow into new locations. Thus, a slope which was previously stable and free of windslab may become hazardous after a relatively short period of wind. Until it has been subjected to extensive metamorphism, such a slab layer will show up in a snow pit.

Temperature Effects – As described in squaring previously, a period of very cold weather may promote the formation of depth hoar. The resultant cup crystals may lie deep within the snow pack, and remain hidden and unchanged for weeks or even months. Thus, a slope which was stable before the cold spell may become highly unstable. Without digging a snow-pit, it is very hard to detect the presence of these crystals. It should be noted that because depth hoar forms some distance below the snow's surface, the snow-pit must be dug to the full depth of the snow pack (i.e. down to ground level) to fully establish the potential hazard.

Sunlight Effects – As described in Breakable Crust above, sun-crust can be formed even during cold weather. Considerable care must be taken when examining the snow pit, as once it is covered by new snow, sun-crust can be hard to detect due to its delicate nature. Because it has a smooth, glazed surface, very little anchorage is provided for a subsequent snowfall, leading to a substantially increased avalanche hazard.

Using Snow Pits to Evaluate Avalanche Hazard

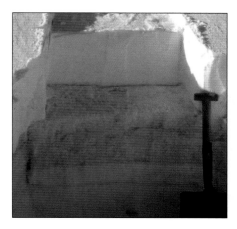

Figure 9.10:
A snow pit showing different layers

While a great deal of information can be obtained from snow pits, there are also limitations in their use. First and most significant is that it takes considerable experience to interpret what is found. That experience can only be gained through hands-on training. For that reason, this chapter does not attempt to give detailed advice on how to dig or analyse snow-pits, but simply aims to outline the procedures which are involved. The other two main limitations of snow pits is the time it takes to dig and inspect them and that once dug, the cross-section is only representative of the area around the snow pit. Indeed, the effects of localised terrain features such as gullies, ridges, rock outcrops and trees can substantially affect the pattern of snow deposition and the resultant snow profile. In consequence, snow pits tend to be used relatively seldom. Many skiers only use them for one of two purposes - either to obtain an overall picture of the season's pattern of snowfall and weather, or to check a particular slope over which they have grounds for concern. But in contrast, snow and avalanche specialists recommend digging pits on a regular basis while off-piste, in order to build up a detailed picture of the snow pack over the area. Finally, it should be noted that digging a snow-pit can itself be a risky activity. While the location should be representative of the slopes which are to be descended, it should also be sufficiently protected that if any serious instability is present, the person digging the pit is not at risk. Having dug a snow-pit, there are two main sources of information – the cross-section itself, and various types of shear test.

Interpreting the Snow-pit

The key factor when interpreting cross-sections revealed by a snow-pit is the relative hardness of adjacent layers of snow. Where there is a large difference in hardness (e.g. light powder on top of sheet ice), the adhesion between the layers is much weaker than where adjacent layers have a similar hardness. As a result, there is much more likelihood of avalanche in the former case. By contrast, a typical snow pack with a high degree of stability is one in which the layers show a gradual increase in hardness from surface to ground but where any two adjacent layers differ only slightly.

Figure 9.11:
A skiing Rutschblock

The Simple Shear Test

As well as examining the snow's cross-section, a simple shear test can be used to check the stability of the snow pack. Having identified a layer which appears to be bonded only weakly to the one below, the procedure is to isolate a block of it by cutting down on all four sides to the weak junction, then testing how easily it fractures away from its base.

Once again, where two adjacent layers are of very different hardness, the block is likely to fracture cleanly at the junction between the layers. Where the layers are of similar hardness the block should be more difficult to release. On occasions you will find that an easy shear occurs between two layers of very similar hardness. This could be for several reasons but one common reason is that a thin layer of buried surface hoar exists between the two layers. If the layers are strongly bonded, it will also tend to fracture unevenly to either side of the junction rather than releasing cleanly. It should be noted that shear tests are rarely conclusive, and it requires considerable experience to interpret their results. Once again, specialised training is recommended in order to become familiar with the various tests which may be performed.

Other Sources of Information

With practise in the analysis of snow conditions, a reasonably accurate evaluation can be obtained by direct observation and testing while on the hill. However, even the most experienced instructor or mountain guide makes use of additional sources of information and advice. The less experienced the individual, the more important these other sources become. Before even setting off, build up a picture of the avalanche hazard and which areas, if any, should be avoided. Sources of information include:

- Avalanche forecasting agencies – nowadays these operate in all of the major skiing countries and should be used as the primary source
- Local piste security services
- Local professional guides and instructors
- Weather reports from TV, radio, newspapers and the internet

The great majority of resorts now provide regular local avalanche forecasts and warnings. Over recent years this information has been presented in an increasingly uniform way, making it easier for skiers to understand and interpret.

The European Avalanche Hazard Scale

In late 1994, a standardised scale for reporting avalanche hazard was adopted throughout Europe. Since its introduction, the scale has also been adopted by Canada, and is likely to become accepted world-wide in the fairly near future. It uses a five-point scale which provides a simple but valuable rating of the overall level of risk. In its basic form, the scale contains three columns, Degree of Hazard, Snow pack Stability and Avalanche Probability. As originally proposed, the scale also includes two additional columns. Effects on Traffic and Residential Areas, and Effects on Off-Piste and Back-Country Activities. These last two columns are however not being used in all of the countries which have adopted the scale.

Degree of Hazard	Snow Pack Stability	Avalanche Probability	Effects on Traffic & Residential Areas	Effects on Off-Piste & Back-Country Activities	Avalanche Probability
1 Low	The snow pack is generally well bonded and stable	Triggering is possible only with high additional loads on a few very steep extreme slopes. Only a few small natural avalanches (sloughs) possible	No hazard from avalanches	Virtually no restrictions on off-piste and back-country skiing and travel	7% of recreational fatalities
2 Moderate	The snow pack is moderately well bonded on some steep slopes, otherwise generally well bonded	Triggering is possible with high additional loads, particularly on the steep slopes indicated in the bulletin. Large natural avalanches not likely	Virtually no hazard from avalanches	Generally favourable conditions. Routes should still be selected with care, especially on steep slopes of the aspect and altitude indicated	34% of recreational fatalities
3 Considerable	The snow pack is moderately weakly bonded on many steep slopes	Triggering is possible, sometimes even with low additional loads. The bulletin may indicate many slopes which are particularly affected. In certain conditions, medium and occasionally large sized natural avalanches may occur	Traffic and individual buildings in hazardous areas are at risk in certain cases. Precautions should be taken in these areas	Off-piste and back-country skiing should only be carried out by experienced persons able to evaluate avalanche hazard. Steep slopes of the aspect and altitude indicated should be avoided	47% of recreational fatalities
4 High	The snow pack is weakly bonded in most places	Triggering is probable even with low additional loads on many steep slopes. In some conditions, frequent medium or large sized natural avalanches are likely	Avalanches may be of large magnitude. In hazardous areas, closure of roads and other transport is recommended in some circumstances	Off-piste and back-country skiing and travel should be restricted to low angled slopes, areas at the bottom of slopes may also be hazardous	12% of recreational fatalities
5 Very High	The snow pack is generally weakly bonded and largely unstable	Numerous large natural avalanches are likely, even on moderately steep terrain	Extensive safety measures (closures and evacuation) are necessary	No off-piste or back-country travel should be undertaken	No recreational fatalities

Notes:

30°: Moderately steep (easy black run)

30°-35°: Steep

35°-40°: Very Steep

40°+: Extremely Steep

Figure 9.12: The European Avalanche Hazard Scale

Avalanche Evaluation En Route

Having consulted all available sources of information and conducted a thorough first-hand evaluation, the final step is to maintain a healthy sense of doubt. Don't be paranoid but question everything. Even with the best information and analysis, avalanche forecasting is an inexact science. When skiing off-piste, it is therefore important to keep a constant look-out for any signs of instability and danger, and to be ready to adjust your plans or even curtail the trip. Avalanche activity and debris are nature's biggest clues. Where present, these are a sure sign that other slopes of a similar aspect, altitude and gradient are highly unstable and should be avoided. It is also important to remain alert for possible avalanche triggers such as those listed above. If any are present, evaluate whether they are likely to affect the stability of the slope on which you are skiing/riding. For example, a skier/boarder on the opposite side of the valley is unlikely to present any hazard, one directly above you on a steep off-piste face is a very different matter. Other important clues to look out for are:

- Snow cracking or blocking around you
- Hollow sounding snow
- Settling noises ("whumphs")
- Balls of wet snow running down the slope
- Avalanche control work in nearby areas
- Easily released slides on small, steep test slopes

Vegetation also provides an indication of past avalanches and of potential slide paths. For example, you may see swaths of open ground cut through woodland, with trees broken and bent downhill. Even dense vegetation on a slope does not imply security. If an area of hillside is covered with 11 year old trees, the likelihood is that it last experienced a major avalanche 12 years ago.

Reducing the Odds

Having already evaluated the risk of avalanche, your route should have been planned to minimise exposure to danger. For example, terrain features such as ridges, valley floors, windward slopes and those which are heavily wooded offer more safety than gullies and steep lee slopes.

Safe Movement Off-piste

Whenever you are on avalanche-prone terrain, always minimise the number of people exposed to risk. The principle of safe movement is to ski one at a time, with the rest of the group watching the entire run from a safe vantage point. Once at the bottom, the skier/boarder should move to a safe location before anyone else starts their descent. Travelling one at a time also exerts the least amount of stress on the slope. Additional recommendations include:

- Building up to steeper slopes by visiting easier-angled ones first
- Entering the slope at the top rather than at the sides

- Travelling at the edge of the slope first, working inwards with each successive run
- Ridge lines or tree-covered hillsides offer more safety than bowls, gullies and cornice-rimmed slopes

These principles should be standard practise on every trip, even if the avalanche hazard is thought to be low.

Crossing Suspect Slopes

If you are faced with having to cross a suspect slope, stop and look for alternative routes which avoid the slope completely. Only if you have **no** other choice should you attempt to continue. In this case, there are several key points to minimise the risk. The two primary ones are:

- Cross one at a time - cross the slope one at a time while the rest of the group watches from a safe location. Move swiftly to minimise your exposure time
- Cross high - choose a crossing point as high up the slope as possible, and avoid the steepest ground

Other actions which should also be taken:

- Make sure everyone in the group is fully briefed on what is happening and what to do in the event of an avalanche (see below)
- Zip up and close all clothing. Cover mouth and nose with a scarf, loosen rucksack straps and undo waist belt. Remove ski pole straps and ski retaining straps (if fitted)
- Alpine ski bindings should be set low enough to kick out of. Telemark skiers can either unfasten the bindings or slacken the laces of their boots
- Other group members should cross in the same track
- If it is feasible to do so, anchor one end of a rope (e.g. to a rock or tree) and belay each person as they ski the slope. But before going on, consider the implications of an avalanche, especially its likely track - for example into rocks, over a cliff face or down a gully where large depths of debris will accumulate

Even with all of the above precautions, an avalanche on such a slope will almost certainly prove fatal for anyone who is caught. From that viewpoint, is there an alternative route?

Dealing with Avalanches (survival and rescue)

The central purpose of this chapter is to avoid exposure to foreseeable avalanche hazard. However, as noted above, avalanche forecasting is an inexact science. Not all avalanches can be predicted, sometimes because of inadequate information, sometimes due to the inherent uncertainties of the task. As a result, knowing what to do if an avalanche occurs is just as important as knowing how to minimise the risks. A key point to bear in mind is that when an avalanche releases, things start to happen very fast. Whatever actions that need to be taken must be pre-planned. Whether witness or victim, there is little chance of being able to take any useful action if you have to spend time thinking about it first. For this reason, the recommendations which follow are given as short, succinct points rather than detailed descriptions. Each point should be thought through and mentally rehearsed beforehand, so that in the event of an avalanche, it can be acted upon as quickly and automatically as possible.

Action if Caught in an Avalanche

- Shout out to attract attention
- Try to escape to the side of the avalanche
- If you cannot escape, get rid of gear like skis, poles and rucksack
- Try to grab hold of a tree or rock to stop your slide
- Activate your airbag backpack if you have one
- Attempt to stay on the surface by 'swimming' or 'rolling like a log'
- Close your mouth when under the surface
- As the avalanche comes to a stop, make a huge effort to get to the surface
- Cover your mouth and nose with one hand, thrusting the other to where you think the surface is
- Make a breathing space in front of your face
- If you cannot break free, try to relax and slow your breathing to conserve oxygen and energy while buried

Action if you Witness an Avalanche

- Keep the victim in sight all the time. If they disappear, make a mental note of their last position
- Check for further avalanche danger. Make sure you are not going to be caught in a second slide
- Appoint a lookout and select an escape route in case of further avalanches
- Mark the spot where the victim was last seen. If the group are carrying avalanche transceivers, switch them to receive and conduct a search
- If not, then make a hasty search of the debris below the point that the victim was last seen. Many people have been found quickly due to a protruding arm or leg
- Any pieces of equipment found on the surface may indicate the direction in which the victim has been carried
- Using probes, ski poles (with the baskets removed), skis or ice axes, probe the most likely burial points (uphill side of trees and boulders, hollows, terraces and at the toe of the debris)
- Failing that, a more thorough probe line should be organised
- Only send for help if numbers allow. The survival of the victim relies on a rapid and efficient search by as many people in the group as possible. After 1 hour the chance of a live recovery is down to only 20% (see Avalanche Survival)
- Do not contaminate the debris with food or urine in case a rescue dog has to be brought in
- Once the victim has been found, first aid treatment is likely to be required. First aid information is covered during the mandatory first aid course taken regularly in order to maintain BASI membership

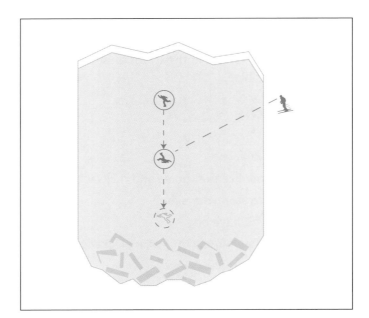

Avalanche Survival

Being caught in an avalanche entails many hazards which threaten injury or death. While in motion there are the risks of collision with rocks, trees and other obstacles, or being swept over a cliff, or being crushed and wrenched by the tumbling debris itself. Once stopped, unless the victim is lucky enough to be on the surface, the risks are of suffocation through lack of air, or the inability to breathe due to constriction of the chest. Victims may suffer hypothermia while buried, and are often in deep shock by the time they are rescued, having sustained multiple injuries. In other words, avalanches are a threat which should never be treated lightly. Even small slides are capable of killing or seriously injuring anyone who is caught. Apart from the gravity of any injuries which are sustained during the avalanche itself, the two main factors which influence survival are depth and duration of burial. The deeper a person is buried, the lower the chances of survival. This is largely due to the greater mass of snow constricting the abdomen and chest and the more limited supply of air. The relationship of survival probability to duration of burial is shown below. The actual values shown are for someone buried within one metre of the snow surface. At greater burial depths, the shape of the graph is the same, but shifted down the chances of survival axis.

As can be seen from diagram 9.14, once a victim has been buried for 15 minutes the chance of surviving the avalanche is greatly reduced. The chance of survival reduces further to around 20% after an hour. In other words, in the time it generally takes for the rescue services to be summoned and a full search to be put in place, the majority of victims will have died.

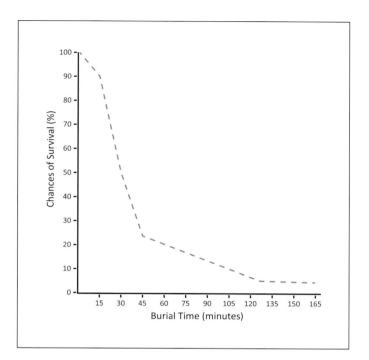

Figure 9.14:
Survival statistics in avalanches

Thus, the best hope for an avalanche victim is to be found by those on the spot. To do so promptly and efficiently requires specialist equipment. The items in question are unlikely to be owned by the majority of recreational skiers, but can generally be hired by the day or by the week. At the very least, all groups who are venturing off-piste should be equipped with the minimum of:

• Avalanche Transceivers

• Probe

• Shovel

• First Aid Kit

The transceiver, probe and shovel should be carried by each member of the group. Since it can be the instructor who is avalanched, teaching your group how to conduct a transceiver search is as important for your own safety as it is for theirs. The snow shovel is also important. To dig out a cubic metre of compacted debris using bare hands and skis takes about an hour. To do so with a shovel takes around 10 minutes. It is recommended that a metal shovel is used and nowadays they are almost as light as the plastic ones but much stronger. The only reliable method of locating a victim not wearing a transceiver is to use avalanche dogs. It should be noted that many of these items, while very expensive to buy, can be rented from various organisations. In addition to shops which offer a rental service, clubs such as the Ski Club of Great Britain and the Alpine Ski Club have stocks of avalanche transceivers for hire. For details, see Background Reading and Resources at the end of this section.

Avalanche Search Methods

The initial search involves a fast scan of the entire area where victims might be found (that is, from the last seen point, within the perimeters of the avalanche, and in the deposition areas). It concentrates on likely areas of burial in addition to listening for transceiver signals and looking for clues on the surface.

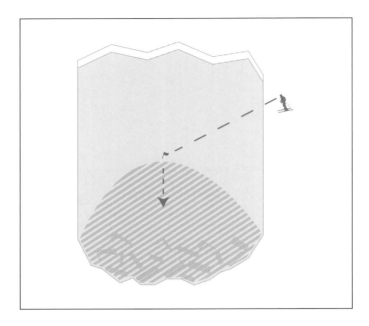

Figure 9.15: Last seen position and likely burial area

Initial searchers should be equipped with transceivers, probe, and shovel:

- Do a visual search for clues on the surface (that is, hand, foot, clothing, and equipment)
- Call out occasionally and listen for responses from victims
- Pull any items found out on the snow to see if a victim is attached
- Mark the location of found items and bring them to the attention of the rescue leader
- Listen for transceiver signals in these locations. (If victims were not wearing transceivers or it is unknown whether transceivers were used, quickly probe the area around found items.)
- If a transceiver signal is found, carry out a transceiver search. If there is more than one person buried, the initial search continues to look for visual clues, etc
- Probe likely burial areas

Transceiver Search (finding a signal)

Single Searcher on a Small Slide

Depending upon the size of the avalanche debris and the number of searchers available, various search patterns may be used in deploying searchers. If the slide path and avalanche debris is confined to a narrow area (typically less than 40 metres wide) a single searcher can search by moving down the slide path and onto the debris in a straight line in the middle of the slope.

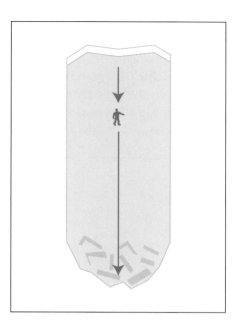

Figure 9.16:
Single searcher on a small slide

Single Searcher on a Large Slide

If there is only a single searcher and the slide path and debris covers a larger area, the searcher must zigzag down the slope, all the while ensuring that they never get more than about 20 metres away from the last track that they searched along. If the spacing between the zigzags is too large, the signal may be missed and the search will have to be started again, wasting valuable time.

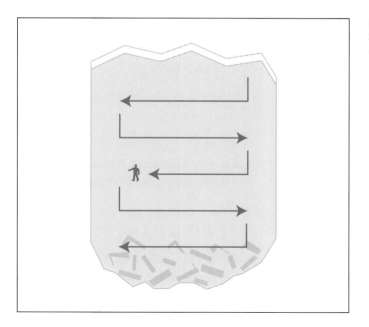

Figure 9.17:
Single searcher on a large slide

Several Searchers on a Slide

If there are several people searching on a smaller avalanche, the searchers can line up along the top of the slope and space themselves out evenly. The searchers should not be more than about 20 metres apart. They proceed directly down the slide path until a signal is heard. If the slide path is large and the group size is not sufficient to allow reasonable spacing between group members, then a combination of the two techniques just discussed may be required.

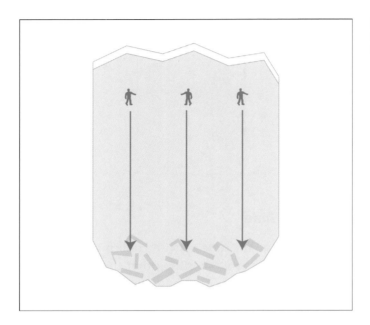

Figure 9.18:
Several searchers on a slide

Transceiver Search (following the signal)

Induction-line Method

Learning the induction-line technique is a practical skill and it should be practised several times a season or, better still, at the beginning of each outing.

In addition, at the beginning of each trip and at critical points thereafter, avalanche transceivers should be checked to ensure adequate transmit and receive range as well as to ensure that the batteries have not died.

The field of induction lines has a three dimensional shape. A cross section looks somewhat like an apple cut in two but with layers like you see in an onion, as shown in the 2 dimensional diagram.

An advanced version of the induction-line technique has the person stop to re-orientate the beacon after moving 10 percent of the distance setting currently shown on the transceiver.

For example, if the setting you are on is the 80 metre range, the distance you move is 8 metres. If the setting you are on is the 15 metre range, you only move a distance of 1.5 metres before scanning again. This adaptation has the advantage of recognising that you will likely have to turn more often and more dramatically the closer you get to the buried subject. In addition you are less likely to move too far and walk past the subject using this modification. Some digital beacons actually give a distance reading for how far you are from the subject and/or lights that direct you which way you should turn to find the best signal. The distance shown is not the actual distance but rather the distance along the "flux line".

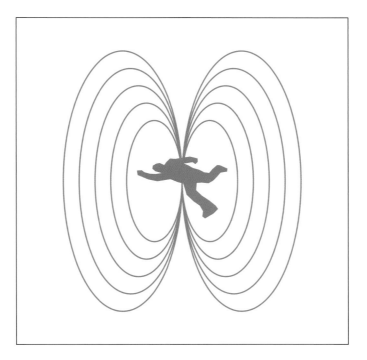

Figure 9.19:
Flux lines

Grid Pattern Method to Aid Pinpoint Recovery

The grid method of transceiver search has now largely been replaced by the induction method discussed above. Grid searching is usually slower and requires the searcher to cover more terrain before being able to pinpoint the final location.

The procedure used in the grid method is still useful when it comes to the pinpoint part of the search. When you have homed in on the general site of burial and the volume control is turned down to the lowest possible setting but a signal is still audible, do a grid search.

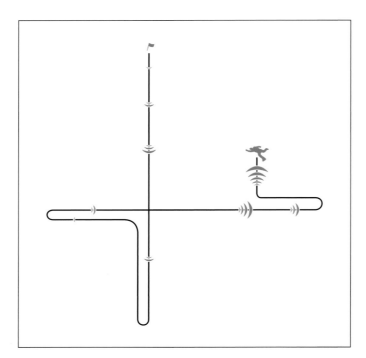

Pinpoint and Recovery

Once a searcher is using the lowest receive setting on his/her transceiver, the most experienced searcher who is readily available should quickly pinpoint the final location. Less experienced searchers should assist or continue the search for other victims.

Some Points to Keep in Mind when Pinpointing

- If using transceivers with loudspeakers, only one person should home in and pinpoint the signal
- When homing in on the victim's location, move as quickly as possible and turn the volume of your transceiver down whenever possible
- When pinpointing the final location, use a logical pattern (e.g. grid method) and slow down so as not to miss the strongest point
- Mark the area where the signal is strongest
- Probe the marked area using a logical pattern
- When the victim is hit with the probe, do not remove the probe
- Notify the rescue leader of the hit
- Note the approximate depth of the victim
- Begin rescue digging

Figure 9.21:
Fine search

Secondary Search Procedures - If a transceiver search is unsuccessful, secondary procedures must be used:

- Continue with initial search procedures
- Probe around likely burial areas (for example, around trees, around rocks, on benches, in gullies, in deep deposits) in the victim's known or suspected line of travel
- If probing around found items or in likely areas of burial is unsuccessful, an organised probe line may be useful if there are enough searchers to set one up. (A probe line needs at least 6 searchers to be efficient. If there are not enough searchers, continue to probe likely areas.)
- Probe likely areas of burial
- Mark probed areas
- When considering going for help, take into account:
  1. Safety of those going out
  2. How many will be left to continue searching
  3. Time before rescuers arrive
  4. Survival chances of victim in that time
- If going for help, write an 'Incident Report'
- Continue searching but make provisions for feeding, sheltering, and safety of searchers if an extended search is anticipated

10. Leading a Group Off-Piste

Going off-piste with a group that you are responsible for is quite an undertaking. There are many more hazards than you are exposed to on piste.

These hazards include:
- Bad weather
- Getting lost
- Falling over cliffs
- Breaking through the snow and falling into water
- Colliding into rocks and trees
- Setting off an avalanche that sweeps others down the mountain
- Being caught in an avalanche
- Snow that is very difficult to ski
- No help immediately available
- No shelter for your group whilst they wait for help

In order to be able to cope with the above hazards a competent off-piste leader will need to have the following skills:
- Good navigation in difficult conditions
- Have a good understanding of snow and how it changes
- Understand the effects of weather
- Be able to deal with emergencies
- Leadership skills

You need to be constantly observing, watching for changes and seeking new information such as:
- Where have avalanches occurred?
- Where is the good snow for skiing?

- Where is the bad snow to avoid?
- Is the weather changing?
- How are your skiers coping with the snow?
- Are members of the group getting tired?
- Are people enjoying the runs?
- Is the condition of the snow changing?
- What is above? Could rock, ice or snow fall on to your group?
- Who is below you? Are your movements a risk to them?
- Where are the terrain traps?

Keeping control of the group is vitally important so people don't get lost, expose themselves or others to more danger and so that the rare commodity of untracked snow is not ruined.

Leadership Tips

- Descend by a series of pitches, stopping to regroup and appraise the route in front
- Brief the group about the plan
- Travel one at a time so only one person is exposed to a serious hazard at a time. The next person does not start until the skier in front is in a safe and protected area
- Travel with an agreed spacing between everyone to minimise the risk where there is a small risk. Emphasise that the spacing must be maintained
- Describe a corridor that everyone must ski within e.g. between 2 sets of tracks or between 1 set of tracks and a natural feature such as a forest edge or only in the corridor made by the leader's track
- Dictate the speed maintaining a safe spacing and not allowing overtaking.

The following acronym can help when considering many of the decisions we need to take leading off-piste. C.L.A.P

> **C**ommunication
> **L**ine of sight
> **A**voidance is better than cure
> **P**osition of maximum usefulness

Communication

It is vital that we strike a balance between letting our clients know what is going on and not giving them so much information that it confuses them. A small amount of relevant information when it is needed is best. Take a familiar on piste scenario of describing to a group where you want them to stop e.g. 3 marker poles below the number 5 piste marker. I am sure this has produced many different results with some of the group heading for the correct point, some of them heading for what they think is the correct point, others questioning what you said and some just not listening. In the off-piste environment it is absolutely vital that our clients stop where we want, in order to avoid the many dangers, some of which may not be apparent to them. How we communicate this point without ambiguity needs to be considered. The best advice is unless there is an obvious point e.g. big rock, mountain hut, saddle etc then it is best to lead from the front so they stop where you stop. It is worth stressing to them to stop above you so as to avoid a catastrophe if you stop by an edge. Much of the vital communication can take place before a tour or big descent in a safe practise area where the clients can learn how they are expected to behave off-piste.

Line of Sight

Maintaining visual contact is a vital part of group safety. There may be some situations where a descent goes round a corner and you would like to head out of sight. Initially consider breaking the journey into smaller pitches. If this is not possible you could stop at the corner or dogleg and get one of your more competent clients to come to you. They can then stay at this point to relay messages to the rest of the group. Effectively you are always in sight of at least one member of your party. Appointing a back marker is also useful as then all you need to do when you look back is spot that person and you know the rest of the group are between you and the marker. If the terrain is not too serious or you have a large group then you can pair people up so now you only need to spot half of the group i.e. if you have 10 people then when you look up you only need to count 5 pairs which is easier. Pairing up is also good for group interaction and giving each person a buddy for safety (it is recommended to work on a 1 to 6 ratio for off-piste.)

Avoidance is Better than Cure

If there is any doubt in your mind then it is probably best to avoid getting into a hazardous situation. I am sure you have been on a descent that offers many possible lines. You know one of them and know it will work with your clients, the other lines may be better or worse... Do you take the gamble? Sometimes after careful consultation with your clients you may decide to go for it and take the risk. It is best at this stage to be honest and discuss the implications of the chosen line not working with your group. If there is any doubt in your mind about their ability or the potential hazards and/or time constraints of your chosen line, then avoidance is the best option.

Position of Maximum Usefulness

Try to foresee all eventualities and position yourself within the group where you can be of most use, not where the biggest catastrophe may occur. This will usually be at the front because of the many possible route finding difficulties and changeable snow conditions. It may be nice to let your group choose the line and head off to a designated meeting point while you are at the back. You will however have to be fairly sure of their abilities, the safety of the snow and the ease with which they will find the designated meeting point. One approach which can be used is to designate a safe stopping point and then stop half way to it. This gives clients the chance to ski a long or short pitch while still allowing the leader to assess the snow conditions and be on hand in the middle of the pitch if there is a problem.

Skinning and Snowshoeing

Travelling uphill brings new challenges. It is important to get to grips with new equipment, selection of line and stamina to name a few. The following points will help with uphill travel techniques.

Equipment

- Ski mountaineering bindings which can be released at the heel and can fit a ski crampon. Getting these with a brake as opposed to leashes makes them more versatile. The leashes are good for crevassed terrain
- Skins which fit the base of the ski leaving the edge exposed (if the skins are not shaped to the ski then grip will be reduced). Skins should be fixed at the tip with some having a tail fix (more difficult with twin tip skis). Ideally the skins should be sticky enough that they are difficult to separate in a warm room
- Ski crampons, also known as Harscheissen or couteaux
- Snowshoes are generally the preferred method of travel for snowboarders. They come in many shapes and sizes. It is worth spending a bit of money on them and avoiding the cheap supermarket ones. The size of the snowshoe depends on your size and weight which you can check at the time of buying or hiring. It is very important to check they fit your boot. Avoid some models with aluminium tubing around them, they are too big and cumbersome for many steep and potentially icy tours
- Good Points to look for in a snowshoe, crampon with front points, plastic or metal rails running the length of the snowshoe, a lockdown facility on the binding, heel lift bars

Technique

- Drag/slide the ski over the snow. Do not walk and lift the ski. Getting glide is best
- On steeper ground, set the skin by pulling slightly back on the ski just before you stand on it. Stand tall, do not lean forward
- Keep the ski as flat as possible to get maximum grip
- Kick turns uphill or downhill (several different ways which require on snow training)
- With snowshoes a wider stance is necessary, lifting the legs more in deep snow. This uses different muscles and can be tiring

Line

- Try to even out the changes in angle of the slope
- Avoid kick turns if not absolutely necessary, by going for longer curving turns or step turns
- If you have to do kick turns then make a turning platform and bash down the snow on the uphill side of the turning spot. Avoid doing them above cliffs and steep drops or under hazards from above
- Keep away from avalanche prone slopes
- Keep to snow that is deep to avoid rocks cutting the skins

- Snowshoeing requires the following subtleties. When travelling uphill engage the built in crampon avoiding leaning too far forwards or backwards. When travelling downhill it may help to lean slightly forward to help engage the crampon and during a traverse, pointing your toes slightly uphill will help the snowshoes bite
- As snowshoes can damage the skinning track for skiers, it is best to choose a different line or stick to the back of the group

Pace

- Make it sustainable, climb at talking pace
- Move at a speed that avoids sweating excessively
- Spread people out so they do not bunch up and lose rhythm at kick turns
- Step out of the trail to let faster people pass

11. Mountain Navigation

Tools of the Trade

- A map which has a scale of 1:25,000 or 1:50,000, laminated or kept in a flexible map case (Ortlieb)
- A compass with 360° and a large base plate e.g. Silva type 4/54
- An altimeter

Maps

Regardless of the scale of map you use, it is important to become familiar with the map, and one of the best ways of doing this is to refer to the key, sometimes known as the legend. Before venturing out and having to use the map in earnest, make sure you know the following:

- How many millimetres make a kilometre?
- How many millimetres make 100 metres?
- How far apart are the contour lines, 10m, 20m or something else?
- Is the contour spacing different on different parts of the map?
- Are there grid lines to take a bearing from?
- What is the magnetic variation?
- How is a grid reference given from the map?
- How are glaciers represented?
- Are cliffs shown on the map?
- How are depressions shown?
- How are ridges, gullies and cols represented?
- How are ski routes shown?
- How are lifts represented?
- How are water features shown?

One of the most important features of a map are the contour lines, spend a lot of time becoming very familiar with them:

- Contours close together = steeper ground
- Contours further apart = easier angled ground
- Contours missing = very steep ground
- Contour lines in bold = index contour lines, usually 50m or 100m apart

Contour lines help us establish how steep a slope is and this allows us to keep off slopes which are steep enough to avalanche. For example if you measure a horizontal distance of 100m on the map and over that distance the drop is 50m, the slope will have an average angle of 27°. If you refer to the Avalanche section you will see a diagram illustrating this.

Compass

A compass with a large base plate is easier to work with. It should have the following features:

- It can take bearings and back bearings over longer distances
- It doesn't get lost in a large gloved hand when following a bearing
- A magnifying glass to help with fine detail
- A roamer scale to make measuring distance and giving grid references easier
- Rubber feet to stop it slipping on the laminated map or map case

The compass should have a housing which is divided into 360°, military compasses with 6,400 divisions (mils) are not so easy to use in bad light/conditions.

Altimetres

When the weather closes in, altimetres can be a valuable tool for the skier travelling away from the piste. All altimetres use a barometer to measure atmospheric pressure and then from that calculate the altitude, giving a reading in metres or feet. They are now incorporated into many wrist watches and as such are relatively inexpensive but very useful.

International standards tell us that the reference atmospheric pressure for sea level is 1013 mb. Atmospheric pressure decreases with altitude, by approximately 1millibar (mb) for every 10 metres of ascent. Therefore, when the pressure is measured at sea level to be 1000mb, and you ascend to a place where the barometer in your watch says 600mb, if you switch the function to 'Altimeter' it will read an altitude of 4000 metres.

Due to the ever changing weather, the atmospheric pressure keeps changing, sometimes slowly, but on occasion very swiftly. It is vitally important if you are going to rely on the accuracy of the altimeter, that you set the altitude at every opportunity. On a day's ski tour, check the altitude reading on the altimeter against the altitude displayed at lift stations or on the map, and change it if there is a difference. In order to keep the altimeter as accurate as possible during the day, you should check and adjust if required at every known height you visit. These heights are found on your map and include:

- Lift stations
- Col or saddle
- Summit
- Mountain hut

If you have been diligent with calibrating your altimeter and the cloud rolls in on part of your descent, you will be able to rely upon it to give an accurate reading of your altitude. This may help you with a change in direction on a navigation leg e.g. Descend the valley until 2400m then turn up the East (83°bearing) slope till you reach the mountain hut at 2650m. At base, it is useful to observe the changing pressure shown on your watch. If overnight the pressure drops by 20mb, there is a very good chance that the weather for the day ahead will not be as good as the previous day. Likewise, should the pressure rise noticeably overnight, there is a chance the weather will be better.

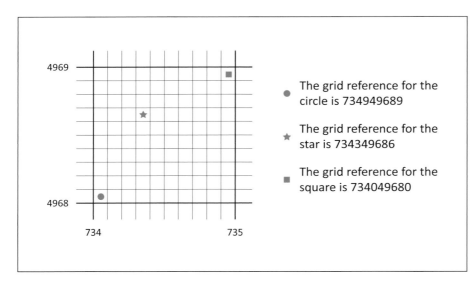

The grid reference for the circle is 734949689

The grid reference for the star is 734349686

The grid reference for the square is 734049680

Figure 10.1:
Example of a grid reference

Orientating the Map

In good visibility, orientating the map can help greatly when it comes to identifying where we are and what surrounds us:

- Place your map on a table with the compass on top
- Turn the map but not the compass until the grid lines are parallel with the magnetic needle of the compass, making sure that the north end of the grid lines are pointing in the same direction as the north end of the compass needle
- If there is too much metal in the table this won't work
- Use man-made features to help you orientate the map, such as lift lines
- Use natural features also, especially ones with straight edges, like valleys or ridges

When the map is orientated you can walk round it and eye-spy different features, dropping your eye to the map and following a line back to where you are on the map. The feature you are looking at will be close to this line.

When trying to work out what mountain that is over in the distance, count the number of valleys between it and you on the ground, then go to the orientated map and work away from your known point counting off the valleys and ridges in the direction of the mountain. This should bring you close to where the mountain is on the map.

Taking a Bearing

1. Place the compass on the map with the edge of the compass along the desired line of travel.

2. Rotate the compass housing until N on the dial points North on the map. Check that the compass housing red/black north/south lines are parallel with the map's meridians (north/south lines)

3. Hold the compass in your hand and turn yourself until the red end of the compass needle (North) coincides with the red arrow in the bottom of the compass housing. The front of the compass with the direction of travel arrow is now pointing towards your destination.

4. Depending on where you are in the worls, you might have to add or subtract a few degrees to account for the fact that the compass points to magnetic north and the grid on the map is aligned with grid north. This is known as 'magnetic variation'. Refer to the map you are using to find out what the variation currently is.

Not Getting Lost

Whilst navigating from one place to another, it is easy to get lost in poor visibility and then find yourself on a slope which might avalanche or skiing over a small cliff, which you had not expected to come across. To avoid getting lost, use as many navigation tools as possible.

Read the map carefully and interpret what it is telling you

- Will you go directly down the slope or slanting to the left at an angle?
- Will you be contouring the mountainside?
- The journey will be over flattish ground to start and then it will go steeply down?
- There will be a gully on the right halfway down?

Take a bearing

- Guess the bearing first to avoid going off in the wrong direction
- Remember to adjust for the magnetic variation if there is one
- Hold the compass base plate at right angles to your chest when following it
- Hold the compass away from your body so that it is not affected by other metals

Use the altimeter

- Make sure it is set to the correct altitude where you are
- Identify the altitude you are descending to

Read the ground

- On the descent, pay attention to what you see and feel
- I expected to see the gully on the left
- I did not expect to have a cliff on my right – Check the Map
- The ground is a lot steeper than I expected – Check the Map
- I have crossed a stream bed as expected

Use time

- It is very difficult to use timing on a descent, but at least have a cut off time. Don't just keep going in the hope you will get there

Other Tools for Ascent

Timing

- Calculate the time for the journey at 4km per hour initially
- Add on extra time for the ascent, try adding 1 minute for every 10 metres ascended
- Change both of the above if the formula is not working
- Stop when your estimated time has run out and appraise your location

Pacing

- This is not easy or often done on skis, but you can work out how many paces you take to cover 100 metres over different angles of terrain

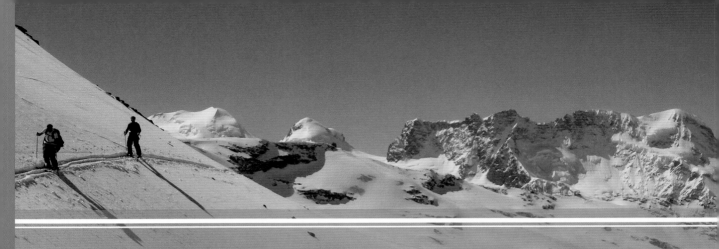

12. Mountain Awareness

To travel safely, with the most enjoyment, you need to be aware of the environment that you are operating in. Safety, enjoyment and learning are often referred to within the field of instructing, coaching and guiding.

Safety

Seeing
- The weather change
- Avalanches old and new
- Changes in the snow pack

Understanding what you see
- It's going to get stormy
- I am on a similar aspect of slope
- These roller balls often happen before single point avalanches

Acting upon what you see
- We'll finish early
- Let's go onto a different aspect
- If we go higher onto a northerly aspect it will be colder

Enjoyment

Knowing what surrounds you
- Locating the best snow
- Getting the best view
- Being in an environment surrounded by familiar things

Knowing how it works

• This will only be good in the morning

• It will cloud over as the day warms up, so enjoy the view whilst you can

• "This is here because..."

Learning

Being able to answer questions from your clients

• Every day we see these birds, what are they called?

• Why is the snow better here?

• I saw these animal tracks yesterday. What animal would be up here?

1. Why do we not ski over there?
2. This rock is really sharp. What is it?
3. What happens here in the summer time?
4. These trees are well spaced. What sort are they?
5. Why are we going down?
6. There is a beautiful purple flower over here, what is it?

Do you just take the thrill of skiing from the mountain? Is it just a place to take from? What do you give the mountain, noise, food scraps, litter and disturbance?

Or

Do you acknowledge that the mountains are home to many animals, birds and plants? The mountains are a valuable water, mineral and scenic resource and you are just one of many visitors that come for many different reasons to the mountains.

It is vital that we are aware of how our interactions with the mountain environment can affect this unique resource and in turn how we can protect it. Not only by educating ourselves, but educating our clients. The mountains give us so much but not least our enjoyment and livelihood so it is important to respect, understand and preserve this precious wilderness.

THE TOOLBOX

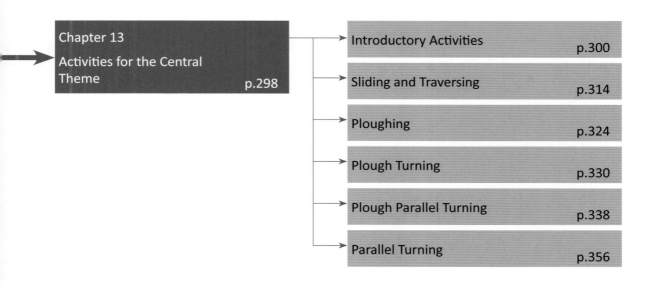

13. ACTIVITIES FOR THE CENTRAL THEME

INTRODUCTORY ACTIVITIES

Environment

The ideal terrain is a completely flat and level area, large enough for the class to move about freely while getting used to wearing skis. Snow conditions should be smooth and firmly pisted. Once pupils have learned to walk and turn on the flat, they will need a short and very gentle slope on which to learn to climb and turn around. This should have a good run-out, which ideally should enable skiers to run straight downhill for 5 to 10 metres and come to a halt naturally without any braking action on their part.

1 Introduction to Equipment

At this initial stage, it may be advisable to check that pupils have been issued with appropriate and correctly-adjusted equipment. The procedure varies from one ski school to another. However you should note that adjusting clients' bindings (as opposed to sending them back to the rental shop for adjustment by a technician) may leave you open to legal proceedings if clients subsequently injure themselves, either due to failure of the binding to release or due to premature release.

1.1 Boots

Explain that:

a) To minimise the risk of injury, boots should provide a snug fit, especially around the ankle and lower leg. Check for fit in the case of children.

b) All the boot clips should be done up while skiing, and that skiers should check that none have come undone after a fall.

c) To ensure effective release from the bindings, the boot soles should not be unduly worn, and that they must be free of mud, grit and snow.

d) Games and activities with boots only can aid learning e.g. Making a bow tie shape on the snow with the sole of the ski boot by rotating the sole of the boot on the snow, can teach leg and foot turning. Similarly walking around and feeling the sides of the boot can allow people to get a sense of edging.

1.2 Bindings

a) Give a non-technical account of the function of the brakes and bindings, including an explanation of the sideways release at the toe, the upward release at the heel, and the importance of correctly-functioning ski brakes for both safety and user convenience.

b) Explain the importance of correct binding adjustment (of both release and boot sole length settings) for their safe and effective operation. Emphasise that these should only be adjusted by a technician, and highlight the risk of injury through inadvertently taking the wrong skis, due to the binding settings being incorrect.

c) Show the class how to put on and take off their skis.

1.3 Skis

a) Explain the basic sliding and gripping properties of the ski base and edges, and the need to protect them from abrasion on stones and grit.

b) Explain that skis are designed not only to slide, but also to grip and turn. (N.B. at this stage, information on flex, camber and sidecut is unnecessary).

1.4 Poles

a) Explain the function of the ice point (i.e. to provide purchase in the snow while minimising the risk to the user and others) and the basket (i.e. to prevent the pole sinking too deeply into the snow).

b) When teaching beginners it is generally good practise to remove the ski poles to improve balance and increase the beginner's use of their skis to maintain control by. Whilst this should be done at the earliest opportunity, teachers should ensure that the students have sufficient control to maintain safe practise. Once the beginners have relinquished their poles then they can be used as markers to create slaloms and obstacle courses thus adding fun, challenge and excitement to their lesson.

c) Explain how to hold the poles (i.e. with the hand going up through the loop, then down to grip both handles and loop, for skiers with weak or injured thumbs, use the opposite grip, with the hand going down through the loop and gripping only the handle).

1.5 Carrying Skis when Walking

a) Demonstrate and practise how to carry skis and poles safely when walking, skis over the shoulder with tips in front and pulled well down when in open spaces, held vertically in confined spaces, poles held vertically with points down at all times. Children may carry their skis across their body or carry one ski.

1.6 Putting on and Taking Off Skis

a) Allow repeated practise of putting skis on and taking them off, including scraping snow from the boot soles, and ensuring that the heel binding is open before attempting to put the ski on. (N.B. time spent practising at this stage is often well repaid later in the lesson).

2 Activities on Flat Terrain

On ideal snow and terrain, ski poles may initially be more of an encumbrance than a benefit. It may therefore be preferable to discard them in the first few lessons. However, some of the exercises which follow require additional balance support. The poles can either be used at this stage and discarded later, or the exercises modified to be done without poles. All of the following exercises require completely level terrain. There should be enough space for pupils to perform them safely, without falling into each other if they lose balance.

2.1 Familiarisation with Wearing Skis

a) While standing on the spot, shuffle the skis gently back and forth to get used to their slipperiness. Aim to keep both skis on the snow, and to slide them in unison so that one moves forward as the other moves back.

b) Lift one ski off the snow and then the other. Practise making rhythmic stepping movements while keeping the skis pointing straight ahead, maintaining balance throughout the activity.

c) As before, but first lift only the tail, then only the tip, then the whole ski off the snow. Aim for accuracy in balancing the skis at the required angle when lifting, again keeping them pointing straight ahead.

d) Lift up one ski and tap its tip rhythmically on the snow on either side of the tip of the other ski. Aim for accuracy in turning the foot, so as to touch the snow a set distance (e.g. 6 inches) away from the other ski tip. Repeat with the other ski.

e) Rock from side to side and become aware of when feet are flat on snow and when you are standing on the edges of the skis.

f) Turn round a full 360°, pivoting around the tails of the skis and lifting only the tips (a 'clock' or 'star' turn). Repeat, this time stepping around the tips and lifting only the tails of the skis .

2.2 Development of Balance and Agility

All of the following exercises should be done while standing on the spot on smooth, level terrain.

a) From a slightly flexed 'ready' stance, gently stretch and bend the legs so as to move the body vertically. Aim to remain balanced over the centre of the feet, moving up and down by around 5 centimetres. Note that if skiers straighten and bend from the waist, their point of balance is likely to shift back and forth.

b) Crouch down to touch the boots, then stretch up tall, reaching the hands high above the head.

The BASI Alpine Manual

c) Rock the body gently forwards and back to discover the limits of support while wearing skis. Movements should be slow and gentle.

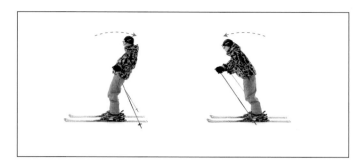

d) From a flexed, well-balanced posture, rhythmically slide both feet back and forward in unison. Both skis should slide in the same direction at once, moving back and forth beneath the body. Try to minimise changes to posture.

e) Jog gently on the spot, lifting first only the tails of the skis, then the whole ski. Aim to maintain good posture, remaining balanced over the skis with joints flexed.

f) Jump the tails of the skis off the snow. Aim for a two-footed jump so that both skis come off the snow together and land softly. Pupils should try to make 3 or 4 jumps in succession, maintaining an even rhythm.

g) As in (f), this time jumping the whole length of the skis off the snow. Again, aim for several rhythmic jumps in succession, each with a soft landing.

h) As in (f), this time jumping only the tips of the skis off the snow. Pupils should only jump the tips a few centimetres off the snow, to avoid stressing the knee joints and to minimise the risk of over-balancing backwards.

i) As in (f), rhythmically jumping the tails apart and together again, so that the skis alternate between an 'A' (snowplough) position and parallel.

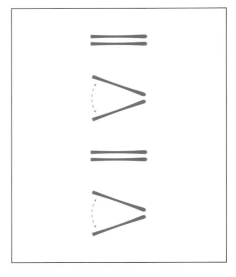

K) As in (i), rhythmically jumping the skis wider apart then closer together (but never closer than hip width apart), while keeping them parallel throughout.

l) As in (i), rhythmically jumping the tips apart and together again, so that the skis alternate between a 'V' (herringbone) position and parallel.

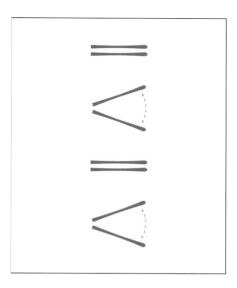

2.3 Moving on the Flat

a) Walk forwards in a straight line, sliding each ski forward in turn without lifting it off the snow. If poles are used, aim to develop a rhythmic arm action with the same co-ordination as in normal walking, using the poles to assist propulsion.

b) Walk around a curve by lifting the tip of the inside ski and turning it slightly into the new direction then bringing the other ski parallel to it. Make sure the skis are pivoted around their tails so that they do not cross over one another. This exercise can be done by having pupils walk around a 'figure of 8' circuit.

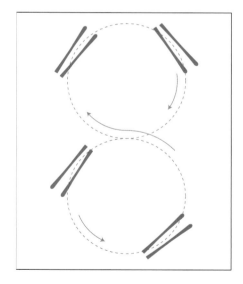

c) Make repeated sideways steps (as if side-stepping uphill), keeping the skis parallel at all times. Make sure that when stepping sideways, the ski which is being stepped off has enough grip to prevent it sliding sideways.

d) If the ski poles are available, push along in a straight line without using the legs. Using both poles in unison, make sure that the torso moves forwards during the push, rather than allowing the feet to move ahead of the body.

e) Stand with the skis in a 'V' shape and walk forwards in herringbone fashion. Make sure that pupils take sufficiently large strides and have a wide enough gait to avoid crossing the ski tails.

f) Negotiate an obstacle course which has been set on the flat (e.g. weaving in and out of ski poles, ducking under a 'bridge' made from 3 poles, stepping sideways over poles laid flat on the snow, etc.).

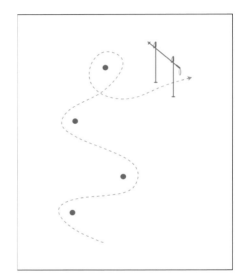

3 Climbing and Turning on a Slope

3.1 Side-stepping

a) Side-step a few metres up the slope, then side-step back down again. Point out to pupils that they have not only learned how to climb uphill, but also have a safe and controlled means of descending a slope down which they do not feel confident to ski.

Common Problems

Leaning the upper body into the hill, or allowing the downhill thigh to move outwards when side-stepping. In either case, the ski will be too flat on the snow to grip effectively. Correct by moving the hips gently sideways towards the hill

3.2 Herring Boning

Herringbone straight up a gentle slope for a few metres, maintaining a wide 'V' position the whole time. This method is faster but more demanding than side-stepping.

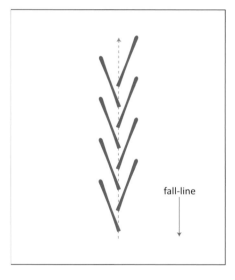

fall-line

3.3 Turning on a Slope

Having climbed a few metres up the slope, your pupils now need to learn to turn to face downhill without sliding away. This can be done either with or without poles. The starting point is with skis across the fall-line (i.e. ensure that the class has side-stepped rather than herring boned uphill).

a) Without poles, with the skis across the hill, step the uphill ski out into a wide snowplough position. Take a small step towards it with the downhill ski, keeping as wide a snowplough as possible. Repeat until facing directly downhill in a wide plough. To move off, stretch up and forwards and allow the skis to run parallel.

Top Tips	Common Problems
Ensure that the snowplough is wide enough for the skis to remain strongly on their inside edges, even when stepping the second ski towards the fall-line	Taking too big a step with the second ski, so that the plough angle becomes too small
Keep the hips lowered in a braking plough stance to maintain grip	Leaning the torso back so that the ski tips move apart taking a wide step, but opening the tips of the skis so that some of the plough angle is lost
If pupils have difficulty, take your own skis off and stand below them, holding their tips to prevent the skis sliding away until they are facing downhill and ready to go	

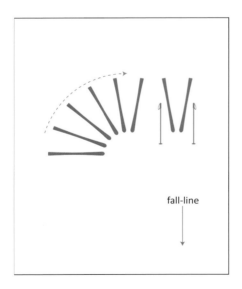

fall-line

b) With poles, with the hands over the tops of the pole grips, place the points in the snow about half a metre apart and one metre downhill of the skis (the distance varies with the skier's height and the slope angle). Step the skis round to point downhill, keeping the feet directly uphill of the poles.

The BASI Alpine Manual

Top Tips	**Common Problems**
'Lock out' the wrists and elbows so that they stay straight, keeping the arms directly in line with the poles. This ensures that it is the skeleton that takes the load rather than the muscles	Stepping downhill towards the poles while turning, which causes the arms to become bent and the muscles to take the load
When moving off, ensure that the poles are swung to trail backwards so that they cannot catch in the snow or endanger other skiers	Stepping forward while turning, so that the skis do not remain directly uphill of the poles
	Holding the poles in a normal grip rather than with the hands over the tops, putting the wrists at an awkward angle

3.4 Putting on Skis on Sloping Terrain

Once skiers have started climbing and turning on a slope, they also need to learn how to put their skis back on when the terrain is sloping. There are two main difficulties which people initially experience in this situation:

- The skis tend to slide away before the skier manages to step into the bindings
- If the ski is lying flat on the slope, the leg must be tilted at an awkward angle to get the boot engaged in the binding

The first and most important point is to ensure that the skis are placed exactly across the fall-line before attempting to put them on. Next, always step into the downhill ski first. The first ski is usually the easier one to put on. Thus, if the downhill ski is already attached, it helps to stop the uphill one from sliding away. However, there are two further tricks which also help:

- If the snow is soft enough, pack down a flat platform for both skis before attempting to put them on
- In all cases, stand below both skis before starting to put them on. The downhill leg must therefore be crossed over the uphill one when putting on the first ski. While this may initially seem awkward, it ensures that the legs can more easily be tilted to the correct angle if the skis are lying on a slant

Adjustments for Snow and Terrain

The introductory activities above may have to be modified where the snow or terrain are less than ideal. Problems may arise in the following situations:

- The practise area is sloping
- The snow is hard or icy
- The snow is soft or wet

Sloping Practise Area

While it may normally be preferable not to use poles in the first few lessons, they are indispensable when taking an introductory lesson on sloping terrain. Not only do they assist with balance, the poles also help pupils avoid sliding away. In addition, there are three key abilities which pupils need to acquire as a first priority in this situation:

- Reading the terrain in order to see the direction of the fall-line
- Placing the skis accurately across the fall-line
- Gripping with the edges when standing and moving across a slope

Pupils must first learn how to put their skis on when standing on a slope, which is covered above. From this point, several of the above exercises may be used as they are, or modified for sloping terrain. In general, many basic exercises can be done while wearing only one ski, so that the other foot provides grip and support in the early stages.

Hard or Icy Snow

Here, the two key priorities are to reduce the risk of falling on the hard surface, and to ensure that skiers have enough grip while performing the activities. Once again, the poles may be used to assist with balance and provide additional grip and support. All of the Introductory Activities above may be used, but bearing in mind that exercises involving jumping the skis off the snow may involve greater risk of falling over and sustaining injury. Also, the skis should only be jumped one or two centimetres off the snow to minimise the impact of landing on a hard surface. Where the skis are brushed or jumped apart, ensure that they do not continue to slide further apart at the end of the movement.

All the exercises involving grip or propulsion from the ski edges and all those in this section are significantly more difficult in these conditions. As a result, a higher level of edge control and awareness must be developed before these activities can be performed successfully.

Soft or Wet Snow

There are two main problems which arise in these conditions:

- Increased risk of injury due to greater leverage forces on the legs in a twisting fall if the skis become trapped in the soft snow
- Difficulty in performing exercises in which the skis are slid or brushed sideways, due to the build-up of snow

First of all, provided the snow is not too wet, it can usually be compacted to create a more suitable practise area. This can be done as part of the introductory activities, by having the group side-step the area to pack it down into a firm, level surface. If the snow is very wet and heavy, the skis may still sink into the surface. In these conditions, ensure that the skis are lifted high enough to clear the snow surface where exercises involving stepping are used. Exercises which involve sliding or brushing the skis out to the sides should be used with caution, due to the risk of catching edges.

The BASI Alpine Manual

SLIDING & TRAVERSING

Environment

The ideal terrain is a smooth, well pisted slope with a very gentle gradient and good run-out. The slope profile should enable skiers to run straight downhill for 5 or 10 metres and come to a halt without any braking action on their part. The overall gradient should be shallow enough that skiers travel no faster than walking speed when straight running.

4 Straight Running

Once skiers are facing straight downhill, they simply need to release their support to begin sliding downhill. Before attempting any additional exercises, skiers should have several practise runs to gain confidence and familiarity with the sensation of sliding downhill. At this stage, the main focus should be on developing good posture with reference to the Central Theme section of this manual. Once pupils are comfortable with the activity and are showing moderately good posture while straight running, various exercises to develop confidence, balance and agility can be introduced.

4.1 Development of Confidence and Awareness

Nervous or timid pupils often lack confidence in simply letting the skis carry them downhill. Initial fears tend to be of the skis sliding uncontrollably away. This anxiety is also reflected in their awareness of what is going on around them. Especially over their first few descents, skiers may suffer from a kind of 'tunnel vision', in which they stare at a fixed point (often either the tips of their skis or an object at the foot of the slope which they are afraid of running into), and remain oblivious of everything around them. These problems normally resolve themselves fairly quickly, and are minimised by suitable choice of terrain. However, there are various exercises which can be done while straight running to help reduce skiers' anxiety:

a) Place a marker such as a glove or ski pole on the run-out, a few metres past the point where the slope flattens out. Over several descents, skiers should attempt to judge their starting point so as to come to rest with their feet directly level with the marker, without having to make any attempt to brake or speed up. This exercise improves skiers' awareness of how far the skis will travel from a given starting point on the slope, and helps improve the confidence of timid skiers. By becoming focused on the actual distance travelled from a given starting point, the skier's attention is distracted from any fears of sliding away.

b) Stand at the foot of the slope and as each skier descends, throw a glove, bean-bag or ball for them to catch. Initially the object should be thrown directly to them, so that the skier only needs to move their hands in order to catch it.

This exercise develops skiers' awareness of what is going on around them, and counteracts any tendency to focus on a single point. In addition, it encourages them to make small body movements while sliding, instead of remaining in a static or rigid posture.

4.2 Development of Balance and Agility

As noted in the Introduction, all of the following exercises mirror those introduced in Introductory Activities. All of the exercises should be done while travelling slowly downhill, initially from a starting point somewhat lower than was previously used for straight running.

a) Starting from the normal straight running stance, gently stretch and bend the legs so as to move the body vertically. Aim to keep the point of balance over the centre of the feet, moving up and down by a few centimetres. If skiers straighten and bend from the waist, their balance is likely to be disrupted.

b) Crouch down to touch the boots, then stretch up tall, reaching the hands high above the head. While the point of balance may move back and forth during the movement, ensure that stability is maintained.

c) Rock the body gently forwards and back while sliding downhill. The movements should be slow and gentle, without approaching the limits of balance.

d) While sliding downhill, shuffle the skis slowly back and forth while keeping them on the snow. Aim to slide both skis simultaneously, so that one moves forward as the other moves back.

e) While sliding downhill, lift one ski off the snow and then the other. Practise making rhythmic stepping movements while keeping the skis pointing straight ahead and maintaining balance throughout.

f) From a well-balanced position, rhythmically slide both feet back and forward in unison. Both skis should slide in the same direction at once, moving back and forth beneath the body but without disturbing the flexed, rounded shape of the torso.

g) Jump the tails of the skis one or two centimetres off the snow. Aim for a two-footed jump so that both skis come off the snow together and land softly. Pupils should try to make 3 or 4 jumps in succession, maintaining an even rhythm.

h) As above, this time jumping the whole length of the skis off the snow. Again, aim for several rhythmic jumps in succession, each with a soft landing.

i) Make repeated sideways steps (as if side-stepping uphill), keeping the skis parallel and pointing directly down the fall-line the whole time. Make sure that when stepping sideways, the ski which is being stepped off has enough grip to prevent it sliding sideways.

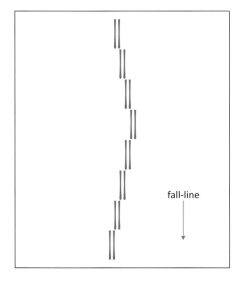

fall-line

Adjustments for Snow and Terrain

Where the snow or terrain is less than ideal, various modifications may have to be made to the above activities. Problems may arise in the following situations:

- The practise area is too steep
- The run-out is inadequate
- The snow is hard or icy
- The snow is soft or wet

Steep Practise Area

Provided there is an adequate run-out, it may be possible to have the group use only the very bottom of the slope. In this situation, all of the activities can be used. However, if the maximum safe descent is very short, it may only be possible to perform one or two repetitions of some of the movements. In this case, it may be necessary to increase the number of times that each activity is performed in order to ensure that everyone has sufficient practise.

Where the practise area is too steep for pupils to set off straight downhill in safety and comfort, use the modifications described under Inadequate Run-out below.

Inadequate Run-out

In this situation, more drastic changes are required. Instead of doing the exercises while travelling straight down the fall-line, they have to be done in a traverse. If the available slope is flat across its width, skiers will initially need to learn to come to a stop by making small scissor steps to bring the skis across the fall-line.

If the slope is hollow across its width (i.e. in the form of a broad, shallow gully), it may be possible for skiers to stop naturally by running up the side of the gully. However, unless the change in angle is fairly gradual, there is a risk of injury through skiers falling backwards as they come to a halt. In this case, it is preferable to work on a more uniform area of terrain and use scissor steps to stop.

In either case, pupils should first be taught to control their speed and direction in a traverse. Once everyone can traverse and stop safely, all of the balance and agility exercises in section 4.2 can be practised in a modified form. Note however that these exercises are considerably more difficult when performed in a traverse as opposed to running straight down the fall-line.

Hard or Icy Snow

As with the activities on flat terrain, the two key priorities are to reduce the risk of falling on the hard surface, and to ensure that skiers have enough grip while performing the exercises. All of the exercises in sliding may be used, but bearing in mind that exercises involving jumping or stepping the skis off the snow may involve greater risk of falling over and sustaining injury. The skis should only be jumped a centimetre or two off the snow to minimise the impact of landing.

Where the skis are stepped sideways, they should be displaced only a very small distance to minimise the risk of their sliding further apart. Overall, apart from the general issue of ensuring the group's safety, there are two key areas of performance to be developed in this situation:

- Good shock-absorption. The legs need to be supple to minimise vibration when sliding over icy undulations, and to avoid any jarring when jumping the skis off the surface
- Good edge awareness. Even when straight running, the skis can easily slip sideways or twist round, especially when performing stepping exercises

Soft or Wet Snow

As with activities on flat terrain, the main problem in these conditions is the increased risk of injury due to leverage against the legs. This occurs principally if the skis become trapped in soft snow during a twisting fall. There is also an increased risk of catching edges when performing sideways stepping movements. If the snow is very soft, it is best to avoid such exercises.

As noted earlier, it may be possible to pack the snow down to create a more suitable practise area. However, if it is very wet and heavy the skis will still tend to sink into the surface. In these conditions, the skis should be lifted clear of the snow surface when performing stepping exercises to avoid catching edges. Also, any exercises involving jumping the skis should be used with caution and avoided if there is significant risk of pupils having a twisting fall, for the reasons given above.

5 Traversing

Traversing is an important technique. Rather than coming at a set point in a skier's development, it should be introduced when needed – for example:

- As a means of negotiating specific areas of terrain (e.g. pistes or trails which run diagonally to the fall-line)
- As an exercise to develop edge awareness and control (e.g. prior to learning skidding or side-slipping)
- As an alternative to straight running where the terrain is too steep (i.e. where there is no terrain suitable for a conventional beginners' lesson)

The way in which traversing is taught depends on the skier's existing technical level. Skiers who are already competent plough or plough parallel turners should have little difficulty in performing a reasonably effective traverse straight away. In this case, they may be able to go straight into the activities in section 5.2 below. In contrast, beginners who have not yet learned straight running will require a much more gradual introduction. The activities described in section 5.1 below are designed for pupils in this category.

5.1 Development of Agility and Edge Control

Before attempting any sliding activities, skiers need to have developed very good agility, edge awareness and control. The best approach is to extend the session on flat terrain until the entire class can successfully perform even the most challenging exercises on flat terrain. Considerable time should then be spent practising side-stepping. This should be done repeatedly, stepping both up and down the slope until everyone can grip securely on every step while keeping the skis pointing accurately across the fall-line.

At this stage, several additional exercises can be used:

a) Make a series of quick, small side-steps while climbing uphill, skipping rapidly from foot to foot. Aim to develop good grip and accuracy while stepping at this faster tempo.

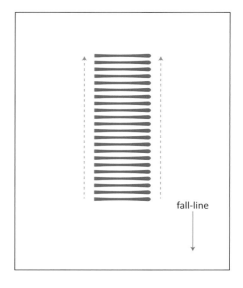

fall-line

The BASI Alpine Manual

b) Start by facing across the hill, then step both skis to point slightly downhill and immediately step them back across the fall-line. When stepping both towards and away from the fall-line, the first step is made with the uphill foot. The uphill ski is stepped into a shallow plough before stepping the downhill ski parallel to it. Then the uphill ski is stepped back across the hill with a scissor action before bringing the downhill ski parallel once more. The whole action should be performed quickly enough that the skis have only just started to slide before they are stepped back across the hill.

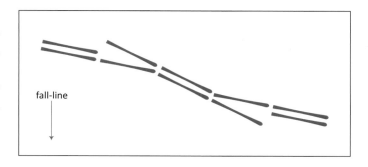

fall-line

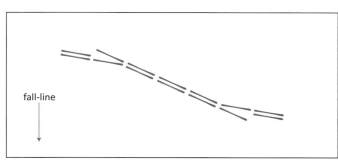

fall-line

c) As in (b), but this time allow the skis to traverse progressively further across the hill before they are stepped back across the fall-line to stop. Make sure that everyone maintains good edge grip as they traverse. If necessary, emphasise the action of moving the hips gently towards the hill to increase the skis' edge grip.

d) As in (c), but this time take two or more steps towards the fall-line to set off, then a series of small scissor steps to stop. If the slope is very steep, it may be necessary to limit the exercise to a single step towards the fall-line to avoid building up too much speed. Even so, as people start travelling faster, they may need to make several scissor steps back across the hill in order to come to a controlled stop.

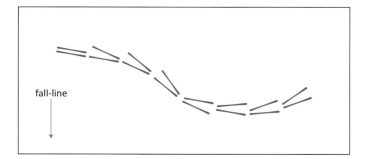

fall-line

5.2 Development of Posture and Balance

Once skiers can traverse across the slope, the manoeuvre should be practised to both sides to develop confidence and familiarity. Over this period, the main focus should be on good posture. Compared with straight running however, traversing differs in two key respects:

- The uphill ski may be slightly advanced (up to 15cm)
- There is more weight on the downhill than on the uphill ski (this is more pronounced as terrain gets steeper)

Some additional exercises can be used to develop these aspects, as well as improving overall edge control and balance:

- a) Holding the downhill pole normally, reach it downhill to touch the snow below the skis, just in front of the toes. This exercise helps to develop a slight downhill ski bias for pressure
- b) As in (a) above, vary the distance and position of the pole to find good lateral balance and effective separation
- c) Make two or three uphill side-steps while traversing, ensuring that the downhill ski does not slide sideways when stepping off it. This exercise improves precise edge grip, and improves agility

Once skiers have developed reasonably good posture and balance when straight running, and are confident at making small body movements while in motion downhill, they are ready to begin learning to plough. Once more, most of the exercises for developing balance and agility repeat those which were used earlier in straight running.

Top Tips

Use different joints to change the edge angles on the skis. Which movements are most effective?

Ask pupils to pick a target on the further side of the slope, and see whether they can hold their line while traversing towards it

For increased awareness of the quality of their edge control, ask pupils to look back at their tracks after they have stopped - do they show a clear, sharp line or are they smudged because the skis have slipped sideways?

Common Problems

The torso may be turned to face uphill, often in an effort to prevent the skis from slipping sideways in the traverse and as a reaction to standing on a slippery slope. Since facing the hill tends to push the hips away from the hill, it actually increases the likelihood of the skis slipping. Instead, emphasise a slight outward (i.e. downhill) facing of the upper body or being completely square

PLOUGHING

Environment

At this stage, the same terrain can be used as for straight running - ideally a smooth, well-pisted slope with a very gentle gradient and good run-out. Once skiers have learned to plough reasonably well, they may need a slightly steeper or longer slope due to the greater resistance which ploughing creates. At this stage, the slope profile should enable skiers to plough straight downhill for 10 to 20 metres and come to a halt without any additional action on their part beyond maintaining a narrow gliding plough. The overall gradient should allow skiers to travel at around walking speed when plough gliding.

6 Plough Gliding

By this stage, skiers may already have done some activities in which the skis were displaced into an 'A' or snowplough stance. This prior experience can now be built on while sliding downhill. For the first few attempts, pupils should start from a point somewhat lower than was used for straight running.

6.1 Introduction to Ploughing

Starting with the skis parallel, run straight down the fall-line in a basic stance, then rotate both legs in unison into a narrow gliding plough. Initially, skiers should only attempt to start ploughing at the point where the slope flattens out. The plough can then be initiated progressively earlier in the descent, until eventually the skier can sustain a plough for the entire descent. At this stage, skiers should practise starting from a stationary plough as well as setting off with skis parallel and immediately getting into the plough.

Initially, emphasise that the skis should only be displaced at a very shallow angle

Whilst the focus of movement at this stage is the rotation of the skis, the skiers may need to extend the legs slightly to achieve a plough shape

At first, skiers may only be able to create a brief plough, with the skis immediately running parallel to each other again. This is quite common, as the slight resistance caused by ploughing tends to push the skis parallel again. Pupils should attempt to sustain the plough for longer periods, and progressively stretch and rotate the legs earlier and earlier in the descent. Emphasise that a continuous gentle effort must be maintained in order to hold the plough

Provided the terrain is not too steep, skiers should not attempt at this stage to create any significant braking effect from the plough. Rather, the aim is to produce a narrow, gliding plough as a basis for learning to steer

Be aware that if skiers tilt the skis actively as they rotate them, the skis may be over–edged and the skier may become braced in an uncomfortable position. Allow the edge angle to build naturally due to the lateral displacement of the feet. Only adjust if there is a problem

Some skiers tend to stand with more weight on one foot, while pushing the other forward at an angle and bracing against it. Emphasise that the ploughing action should be done simultaneously with both legs. If the problem persists, have the pupil try the action with the opposite foot forward before attempting to adopt a symmetrical stance

If pupils lack confidence or have difficulty in controlling the plough, stand facing them on the downhill side and snowplough backwards while holding the tips of their skis. By gradually relaxing your grip over a few descents, pupils should develop sufficient confidence to control the plough by themselves

6.2 Development of Confidence, Agility and Control

Before starting to learn plough turning, pupils should consistently be able to perform a gliding plough. They should be able both to maintain their plough while descending a slope, and to regain the plough whenever the skis run parallel.

On unfavourable terrain it may be necessary to introduce plough braking at this stage, as described in Adjustments for Snow and Terrain below. However, if possible this should be delayed until pupils are already confidently controlling their speed by turning. Otherwise, they may start to use plough braking instead of steering to control their descent, inhibiting their technical progress.

Once again, several of the exercises involve similar movements to those already used in straight running:

a) While travelling straight down the fall-line, rhythmically push the skis out into a shallow gliding plough. As soon as the skis are ploughing, allow them to run parallel again then repeat the stretching action into the plough.

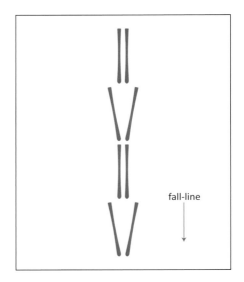

fall-line

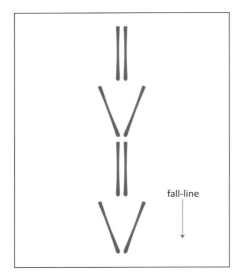

fall-line

b) Without opening the skis into a wide, braking plough, rhythmically vary the plough angle. The skis should not be allowed to run parallel, but alternate between a wider and narrower angle.

c) As a refinement of exercise (b), set a corridor of ski poles down the fall-line. Place alternate pairs of poles wider apart and closer together, as markers for pupils when varying the width of the plough.

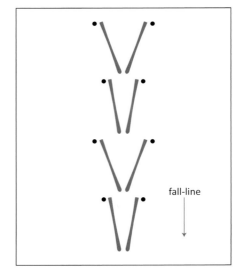

fall-line

d) While maintaining a constant width of plough, gently stretch and bend the legs to move the body up and down by a few centimetres, keeping the point of balance over the centre of the feet. Aim to develop accurate control over the plough angle during the exercise.

e) While ploughing, move the body fore and aft over the feet, changing the point of balance.

Adjustments for Snow and Terrain

On unfavourable snow or terrain, a number of changes may have to be made to the above activities. In some situations they need only be modified slightly, while others require more drastic change. The following situations typically cause problems:

• The practise area is too steep or the run-out is inadequate

• The snow is hard or icy

• The snow is soft or wet

Steep Practise Area or Inadequate Run-out

If the slope is steeper than ideal, it may be possible to use only the very bottom section, provided there is an adequate run-out. In this situation, all of the activities in ploughing can be used, but with the same proviso as before: if the maximum safe descent limits the number of repetitions of the movements, increase the number of times that each activity is performed in order to ensure that everyone has sufficient practise.

In order for pupils to progress however, they eventually need to make longer continuous descents while ploughing. At this point, plough braking may have to be introduced to enable skiers to control their speed on steeper terrain. Since a means of braking is also required where the run-out is inadequate, the overall approach is the same in both cases.

Plough braking is described in detail below. Once everyone is consistently able to control their descent in this way, all of the exercises described in the ploughing section may be practised in an adapted form, using a braking instead of a gliding plough.

Hard or Icy Snow

Again the key priorities are to reduce the risk of falling on the hard surface, and to ensure that skiers have enough grip while performing the exercises.

All of the activities in ploughing may be used, but bearing in mind that exercises involving jumping the skis off the snow may involve greater risk of falling over and sustaining injury. The skis should only be jumped a centimetre or two off the snow to minimise both the impact of landing and the risk of their sliding further apart.

In general, skiers should have developed reasonably good control over the plough before attempting any agility exercises. Otherwise, there is a danger that the tips of the skis may slide apart on icy snow, leading to a headlong fall between the skis.

As with straight running, the two key areas of performance are:
- Good shock-absorption
- Good edge awareness and control

Soft or Wet Snow

Again, the main problem is the increased risk of injury due to leverage against the legs. Also, because soft snow creates considerably more resistance than a firm surface, more effort is needed to initiate and sustain the plough. If possible, the snow should be packed down to create a more suitable practise area. Where skiers are varying their width of plough during a descent, mounds and ridges of snow may build up. If this happens, you should smooth out the surface by side-stepping the slope, or by going down in a wide braking plough.

Exercises in which the skis are jumped off the snow should be used with caution and avoided if there is significant risk of pupils suffering a twisting fall.

7 Plough Braking

Plough braking is an extremely useful technique, enabling skiers to negotiate narrow tracks and to control their speed in confined spaces such as lift queues. However, there is a risk that if plough braking is introduced too early, skiers may rely on braking instead of steering to control their descent. As noted below, plough braking also requires skiers to balance further back on their skis than when gliding and turning. Thus, if plough braking is used extensively at an early stage, it can inhibit skiers' technical progress. It is therefore best introduced after plough turning, except where the terrain is too steep or there is an inadequate run-out. The principle behind plough braking is this:

When straight running with skis parallel, both skis point in their direction of travel and therefore create minimal resistance. When ploughing, each ski is turned at an angle to its direction of travel, increasing the resistance. Two factors influence the amount of resistance which is created:
- The angle of the skis to their direction of travel – the wider the plough, the greater the resistance
- The amount by which the skis are edged - the more they are edged, the greater the resistance

In a gliding plough, the aim is to have the skis at a sufficient angle for effective steering, while creating minimal resistance in a straight line. The plough angle is therefore shallow and the skis only gently edged. For effective plough braking, the skis are rotated more, the feet are displaced wider and the hips will move backwards in response to greater resistance from the snow.

7.1 Introduction to Plough Braking

From a shallow gliding plough, gradually push the tails of the skis out to a wider angle. Aim to create a smooth increase in resistance, so that the skis come to a gradual stop.

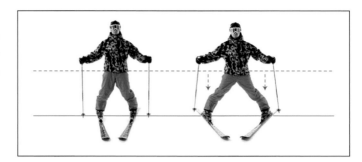

Many skiers experience difficulty or discomfort in braking to a complete standstill except on very gentle terrain. Often this is due not to a failure of technique, but rather because the skier has insufficient hip joint mobility to create an effective braking angle. Provided sufficient speed control can be achieved on the available terrain, this is not a problem. In general, women have less difficulty than men with plough braking, due largely to having greater hip joint flexibility

In a gliding plough, the skier's point of balance should be over the centre of the feet. But when plough braking, the hips must move back slightly in order for the skier to remain balanced while resisting the force from the snow. In addition, braking is more effective if the pressure is shifted slightly back along the skis. Thus, while it is normally undesirable to stand with the weight over the heels, in plough braking it is positively helpful. This is one of the reasons why, in ideal circumstances, it is preferable not to introduce plough braking until skiers have already become well practised in balancing over the centre of the feet while sliding, ploughing and turning. By practising plough braking at an early stage, there is a risk that this 'weight back' stance becomes habitual in their skiing

Common Problems

If the skis are pushed out too quickly or are edged too hard, they may judder instead of braking smoothly. Ensure that the action is gradual and progressive, easing off if the skis start to vibrate

Pupils may simply push the skis wider apart without increasing the plough angle. Although the skis become more strongly edged as the feet move further apart, the braking effect is less than if the skis are also turned at a wider angle. Ensure that the distance between the ski tips remains constant, with only the tails moving wider apart

PLOUGH TURNING

Environment

Once skiers can maintain a consistent and controlled gliding plough, they are ready to begin plough turning. To ensure effective progress, they should already have developed reasonably good posture and balance, which will allow them to be agile. Any substantial weaknesses in these areas can seriously inhibit future learning and should, if necessary, be dealt with at this stage.

Until skiers have learned to control their speed and direction by plough turning, they still need a slope with a good run-out. The same terrain can be used as before – a smooth, well-pisted slope with a gradient which allows skiers to travel at around walking speed when ploughing. Once skiers have learned to steer reasonably well, they will need a longer and slightly steeper slope. Ideally this should have a short drag-lift, allowing a greatly increased rate of practise as well as reducing the effort which is involved. Guidelines on teaching pupils how to use a draglift are in the safety section of the teaching content.

8 Introduction to Plough Turning

Even before learning to turn, skiers have in fact already developed a rudimentary use of all three steering elements and can create and control a gliding plough. When ploughing directly downhill, both skis are in fact skidding diagonally. To continue travelling in a straight line, all three steering elements must therefore be in balance, with a symmetrical application of edging, pressing and rotating to both skis. As soon as this symmetry is disturbed, the skis will tend to turn. In principle, any one of the steering elements could be used to initiate a change of direction. Within the framework of the Central Theme, the first element to be used for this purpose is control of rotation.

8.1 Starting to Steer - Control of Rotation

a) While ploughing directly downhill, gently point both ski tips into the desired direction. As the ski turns further across its existing direction of travel, its resistance increases and deflects the skier round a shallow arc.

b) Set a short series of open gates using ski poles. These need to be quite widely spaced, and should initially have a direct, fall-line route through the middle. In this way, skiers who are still having difficulty in turning can get through the course, while those who can steer more effectively can deviate from side to side by varying amounts.

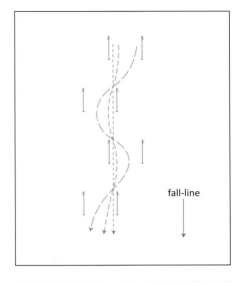

fall-line

Top Tips

Rather than attempting to turn the skis a long way from the fall-line, aim to make only a slight change of direction at this stage. If skiers attempt to make a large direction change by using leg rotation alone, the outer ski will tend to skid excessively

As soon as skiers have succeeded in making even a small change of direction, encourage them to try linking several small turns together, to follow a gently snaking path

Because most people have a dominant leg (usually the right leg for those who are right-handed), there is a natural preference for turning one way (because it is the outer ski which controls the turn, right-handed skiers generally prefer to turn left). By practising to both sides from a very early stage, there is less risk of skiers becoming excessively one-sided

Common Problems

At first, skiers may rotate the whole body instead of only the legs and skis. While the ski may pivot, it also tends to lose edge grip as the hips do not stay inside the base of support. As a result, it simply slides sideways instead of deflecting the skier round an arc

As the body rotates, the inside ski may also become 'locked' on its inside edge, adding to the problem

To correct this fault, emphasise that the leg action can be separated from the action of the body. Next, aim to keep the torso facing directly downhill while making small, linked turns

8.2 Development of Steering - Pressure Control

a) As their skis begin to change direction, pupils will notice a build up of pressure against the outer ski. This is the natural consequence of the skier's momentum trying to continue in a straight line as the skis begin to change direction. The skiers should be encouraged to recognise this feeling and resist the pressure without bracing the outer leg.

b) Set an easy slalom course with ski poles, but this time with slightly more of an offset from gate to gate. By again making each gate fairly wide, skiers of varying abilities can choose an appropriate route.

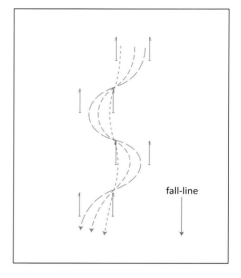

fall-line

Top Tips

Make sure that the outer leg retains some flex in the joints and does not become braced against the ski. Equally, there is no need to over flex the leg in order to control the pressure, this does not directly control pressure in the central theme. See exploring the fundamental elements

Aim to link several turns in a rhythmic sequence to allow a stepping or pedalling feeling to develop

As skiers begin to travel faster, more pressure is created against the outer ski. This allows each turn to be continued further away from the fall-line, enabling skiers to make more rounded, longer arcs. As a result, although travelling slightly faster their speed can be controlled more effectively using the arc length, and they can gradually move onto slightly steeper terrain

Common Problems

Bracing the outer leg will lead to an inability to rotate the leg and the skier will also lose any shock-absorption from the joints. Keep naturally flexed in the ankle, knee and hip, and maintain good posture. Slight bouncing movements can free up these joints for the skier

In an effort to maintain pressure against the outer ski, pupils may lean out sideways from the waist. While this action was taught many years ago in some ski schools, it is of very limited value as a basis for future learning. Apart from disrupting balance, it is fairly ineffective in controlling pressure. Instead, ensure that the upper body remains 'quiet', with the controlling actions being performed largely by the legs

The BASI Alpine Manual

8.3 Development of Co-ordination - Rhythm and Control

In order to negotiate the easy slopes of a resort with plough turning, skiers need to develop adaptability. They must learn to deal with changing gradients and contours, to vary their line to avoid obstacles, and to modify their speed in relation to the traffic and terrain. The main aspects of performance which need to be developed are:

- Co-ordination and rhythm: being able to turn at varying tempos to suit the terrain and to avoid obstacles
- Control of speed and line: being able to vary the turn shape, in terms of both the radius of the turns and the length of each turn's arc

A variety of exercises and activities can be used to develop these abilities:

a) Link the turns rhythmically, without any pause or traverse between the end of one turn and the beginning of the next. This can be aided by counting through the turns - "**Turn,** two, three, four, **turn,** two, three, four ..." By varying the count (**"Turn,** two, three, **turn,** two, three..."), the ability to vary the rhythm can also be developed.

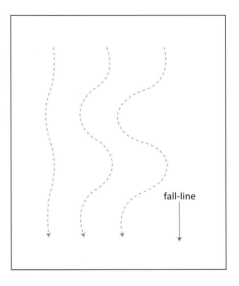

b) Use the image of pedalling to focus on the rhythmic application of pressure against alternate skis. As one foot settles against its pedal, the pressure comes off its partner. By pedalling continuously (no 'freewheeling'), the turns become linked, by altering the tempo of pedalling ('changing gear'), the rhythm of turning is altered.

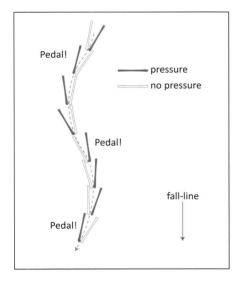

c) Set a single-pole slalom course for skiers to negotiate, initially with a fairly large vertical distance between each gate. Gradually tighten up the course to develop the skiers' ability to vary their rhythm and line.

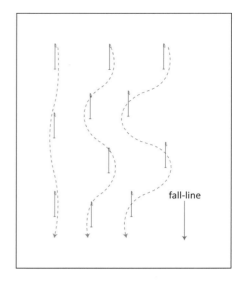

d) Pair up class members and have them take turns in leading each other down a short descent. The leader's task is to make round, smoothly-linked turns, while the follower aims to keep to that line as accurately as possible. While the follower must be able to see the leader's line, at this stage they should not get closer than about 4 metres to minimise the risk of collisions.

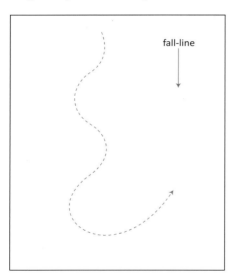

e) Make two or three linked turns, then continue the next turn far enough away from the fall-line to bring the skis to a stop. Initially this final turn should only be done where the gradient is very gentle, but with practise it can be attempted on progressively steeper sections of terrain.

f) Have pupils take turns in following your line down a short descent. Vary your speed and line so as to gently stretch their degree of control. If the entire class follows in a line, make sure to rotate the order in which they follow so that every member has a turn directly behind the instructor.

Adjustments for Snow and Terrain

As before, the above activities may have to be modified where the snow or terrain is unfavourable, typically because:

- The practise area is too steep or the run-out is inadequate
- The snow is hard or icy
- The snow is soft or wet

Steep Practise Area or Inadequate Run-out

Where the slope is only slightly steeper than ideal and has an adequate run-out, it may still be possible to use all of the activities in plough turning. To ensure pupils' safety, use only the lowermost section of the slope, to ensure adequate practise, increase the number of repetitions of each activity. If the maximum safe length of descent is limited to two or three turns, activities to develop co-ordination, rhythm and control are unlikely to be effective. Where the choice of terrain is seriously limited, it may ultimately be necessary to introduce plough braking for additional speed control, to enable skiers to practise over a longer descent. Provided that only a moderate braking plough is sufficient for speed control, all of the activities can be adapted for use. But if the terrain is so steep as to require a wide braking plough, an entirely different approach becomes necessary. Instead of making linked turns down the fall-line, pupils must first learn to traverse.

Hard or Icy Snow

Here, the key priorities are to reduce the risk of falling on the hard surface, and to ensure that skiers have enough grip to steer effectively. All of the activities in ploughing can be used, but in addition it may prove necessary to improve skiers' edge control. If the skis tend to skid excessively when turning, the following exercises may be of benefit.

8.4 Development of Edge Control

To reduce the amount of skid when steering on icy snow, the outer ski may need to be tilted further onto its edge but more probably, the skier needs to be more precisely balanced on top of the skis , both laterally and fore/aft. To help pupils get the feel of this action, various exercises can be used:

a) Reach the outer hand out and downwards while turning to balance better laterally on the outside ski.

b) Hold the poles across the body like bicycle handlebars. Using the 'handlebars' as a frame of reference, monitor their degree of tilt while turning. Generally they will tend to tilt towards the centre of the turn (i.e. in the same direction as on a real bicycle). Instead, aim to keep the bars level, or even to tilt them towards the outside of each turn.

c) Try to feel where on the foot the skier is balanced. The skier should be encouraged to move their balance from ball to heel and from inside to outside. Where is the "sweet spot" which gives them the best feeling of control of their skis?

Soft or Wet Snow

Once more, the main problem is increased injury risk due to greater leverage against the legs. If the snow is soft enough that the skis sink into its surface, turning becomes much harder in two key respects:

- More effort is required, both to maintain the plough and to steer the skis
- The skis tend to get 'tram-lined' in the snow, disrupting balance and control by crossing or catching edges

Both of these problems are solved if the snow can be packed down into a firm surface. But if it is wet and heavy, the skis will still tend to sink in. In this situation, the tendency of the skis to catch in the snow can be reduced by making the turns less skidded. Note that if the turns are less skidded, additional difficulties may arise:

- By skidding less, skiers will initially have more limited speed control. As a result, the terrain must be very gentle, and skiers should be encouraged to continue each turn further past the fall-line
- To begin with, skiers may only be able to make fairly large radius turns. For this reason, it is important that they do not attempt to 'rush' the turns, but allow the skis to follow their natural arc
- The less skidded the turn, the more precise must be the skier's steering and balancing actions. As a result, longer periods of practise are likely to be needed at each stage of learning

PLOUGH PARALLEL TURNING

Environment

Before starting to learn plough parallel, skiers should be able to perform rhythmically-linked plough turns on moderate (blue) terrain. At this stage, they should also have good posture when plough turning, with no tendency to rotate the torso or hips in advance of the skis. Finally, they must have the control and confidence to ski at a brisk jogging pace. In order to perform plough parallel effectively, skiers need to have enough momentum for the skis to skid easily. The manoeuvre becomes much more difficult at slow speeds, increasing the likelihood of inappropriate movements such as rotation of the hips and torso being used to help turn the inner ski.

The terms 'matching' and 'closing' are both sometimes used to refer to the action of steering a ski parallel to its partner. But in plough parallel, the skis do not come close together even during the parallel phase. Instead, they remain around hip-width apart for balance and control. As a result, the phrase 'closing the skis' should not be used in this context. Rather the action is described as 'matching the skis'.

At this stage, the ideal slope is a reasonably long, smoothly-pisted blue run. With suitable terrain, progress is generally faster when pupils have the opportunity to ski long sequences of continuously-linked turns, rather than practising one or two turns over a short distance. By this stage, skiers should all be able to use a drag-lift (see Teaching Safety section).

9 Introduction to Plough Parallel

9.1 Revision and Preparation

Before introducing any new actions, several aspects of plough turning need to be revised and consolidated:

a) Speed of travel - in order to steer the inside ski parallel, skiers must be supported principally by the outer ski. This becomes easier as speed increases, as there is a stronger centrifugal effect pressing the skier against the outer foot. In preparation, skiers should practise skiing at a brisk jogging pace while making continuously-linked plough turns (10 - 20 turns, over distances of 75 - 150 metres).

b) Width of plough - the wider the plough, the harder it is to flatten the inside ski in order to pivot it. Skiers should therefore practise steering while using a relatively narrow plough. For adult skiers of average height, the feet should be no further than 40 - 50cm apart when plough turning.

c) Rhythm of turning - the evolution from plough to plough parallel turning is much easier if turns are linked rhythmically without traversing, compared to having a pause between one turn and the next.

d) Active transfer of pressure - for ease of progress from plough to plough parallel turning, skiers should already be transferring pressure actively to the outer ski to initiate each turn using a pedalling motion. This can be introduced or revised using the activities above.

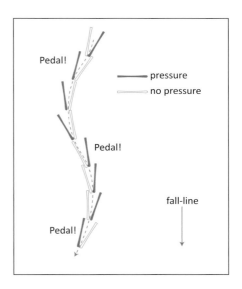

9.2 The Steering Elements

In this section, plough parallel turning is approached from the three separate perspectives of control of pressure, edging and rotation. However, all three elements must be developed before the inner ski can be steered effectively. For this reason, rather than working exhaustively on a single exercise until it has been mastered, it is preferable to work on a range of activities which includes all three of the steering elements. In this way, pupils can develop the appropriate blend of elements for steering the inner ski.

Pressure Control

a) Focus on taking the pressure off the inner ski so that it 'skims' over the snow surface. Imagine that the inner ski is 'gliding on eggshells' throughout the turn.

b) Starting with rhythmically-linked plough turns, use the pedalling action introduced in activities for plough turning above. This causes the pressure to build up against the outer ski while simultaneously diminishing against the inner one. Provided it is done positively over a distance of at least 10 to 20 turns, the inner ski may begin to steer as a result of this action alone.

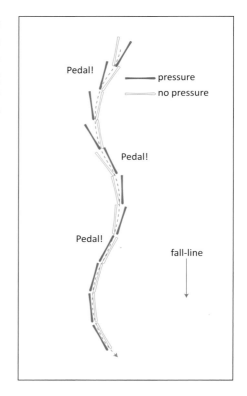

Edge Control

c) The inner ski must flatten against the snow before any leg rotation can occur, otherwise the ski edge will snag. To achieve this, gradually rock the inner foot from its inside (big toe) to its outside (little toe) edge during each turn.

Control of Rotation

d) While plough turning, rotate the inside leg to bring that ski parallel to its partner towards the end of the turn. The ski should be pivoted beneath the foot so that the ski tips move apart. Once the ski has been steered parallel to its partner, it must be pivoted into the direction of the following turn to re-establish the plough.

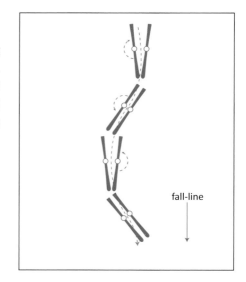

e) Use a rhythmic chant to help develop the co-ordination and timing of the rotary movements: "Turn one, turn two... turn one, turn two..." The aim is that the outer ski begins to be steered on the "one", the inner ski on the "two".

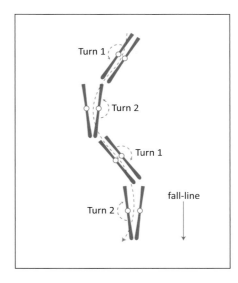

Top Tips

Focus on awareness as well as action. Rather than simply concentrating on making the required movements, encourage pupils to feel what is happening beneath their feet

Pay specific attention to what is happening with the inner leg and foot. Feel the inner foot go light and 'skim' over the surface, feel it rock from big toe to little toe, feel it pivot into the direction of the turn

There is a 'natural' point at which the inner ski turns easily - the point at which the skier's momentum is supported against the outer foot. Encourage skiers to feel for this moment rather than trying to force the inner ski to turn too early. As the outer ski grips more positively earlier in the turn, so the inner ski will tend to turn earlier

As the inner ski begins to steer parallel in the second half of the turn, a new feature emerges. During this latter part of the turn, both legs are now starting to work in unison, with progressive and symmetrical leg-lean, as both legs incline inwards to control the skis' edging (both skis more or less equally edged)

Common Problems

If the inner ski is pivoted around its tip rather than beneath the foot, the skis come close together, impairing balance and limiting edge control

If the hips are rotated too far into the turn, the inner leg automatically straightens. This makes it impossible to rock from big toe to little toe edge, preventing the inner ski from being steered unless it is lifted off the snow

Adjustments for Snow and Terrain

Typically, the above activities may have to be modified because:

- The practise area is too steep
- The practise area is too shallow
- The snow is hard or icy
- The snow is soft or wet

Steep Practise Area

The development from plough to plough parallel is based on gradually modifying pupils' movements while they make continuously-linked turns. Most of the learning comes from making changes to performance while on the move, rather than from doing discrete exercises on a small area of terrain. Where the practise area is too steep however, this situation is reversed.

To use the activities in this section, skiers must feel confident in letting the skis run fairly freely, at least during the first half of the turns. If the terrain is so steep as to encourage a wide, defensive plough, the entire process will be undermined. In this situation, an entirely different route must be taken, described in Skidding and Side-Slipping.

Shallow Practise Area

For the first time, the situation may arise where the terrain is actually too shallow for effective learning. Skiers need to be travelling at a brisk jogging speed in order to have enough momentum for the skis to skid easily while turning.

If the terrain is very shallow or the pupils' skis are running very slowly, steps must be taken to ensure they have enough speed when attempting to make skidded turns. Provided the slope is reasonably long, the easiest approach is to run straight downhill for some distance before starting to turn. Skiers should set off straight downhill and run for 10 metres or more, pushing with the poles if necessary to gain speed. Provided enough speed can be built up to make two or three turns, some progress can still be made.

If the terrain is so shallow that the extra speed is lost as soon as the skier starts to turn, it may be better to work on swinging to the hill (see Skidding and Side-Slipping below). In this case, repeatedly practise a single swing to the hill, alternating between left and right so that pupils do not become one-sided. Even on a very gentle slope, it should be possible to build up enough speed to perform a single, skidded swing to the hill.

Hard or Icy Snow

Once again, the main problem is the increased risk of injury. Make sure that progress is gradual, allowing pupils to become comfortable with each activity before moving on.

Provided the slope is smooth, a hard surface can actually make steering the inner ski easier. However, pupils are likely to be put off by the limited grip, and may attempt to compensate by

The BASI Alpine Manual

using a wider plough. If the terrain is very hard and icy, it may be safer and more effective to work on swinging to the hill, described in Skidding and Side-Slipping below.

Soft or Wet Snow

Here, the problems are identical to those for plough turning: increased injury risk due to greater leverage against the legs, and greater difficulty in maintaining control when turning. Again the difficulties of control encompass two main aspects:

- More effort is required to steer both outer and inner skis.
- The skis tend to get 'tram-lined' in the snow, disrupting balance and control by crossing or catching edges

Once more, these problems can be solved by packing the snow down into a firm surface. But if the snow is so wet and heavy that the skis still sink in, the best solution is to make less skidded turns. As with plough turning, this can be done by pressing the outer ski more and rotating it less. Also, the inner ski should be rotated smoothly and gradually, to minimise any tendency for it to catch in the snow. With these modifications, all of the activities described in this section can be used.

Once again, it should be borne in mind that if the turns are less skidded, the same difficulties may arise as in plough turning:

- By skidding less, skiers will initially have more limited speed control. As a result, the terrain must be fairly gentle, and skiers should be encouraged to continue each turn further past the fall-line
- To begin with, skiers may only be able to make fairly large radius turns. For this reason, it is important that they do not attempt to 'rush' the turns, but allow the skis to follow their natural arc
- The less skidded the turn, the more precise must be the skier's steering and balancing actions. As a result, longer periods of practise are likely to be needed at each stage of learning

Additional Activities (skidding and side-slipping)

Skidding and side slipping are very useful activities for developing edge-awareness and control. Skidding can also be used to provide an alternative pathway towards parallel skiing, when the route offered by the Central Theme is inappropriate. In addition, it is an extremely important technique in its own right, as a means of slowing down and stopping, and as the basis for coping with steep and narrow sections of terrain.

Environment

All of the activities in this section require smooth, firmly-pisted snow. Especially in the early stages, any activity which involves sideways motion of the skis poses the risk of catching a downhill edge. This can result in a potentially dangerous headlong fall. As a result, areas of loose or heavy snow should be avoided or packed down smooth. The activities should not even be attempted on rutted snow.

The gradient which is needed depends on the specific activity. However, none of the exercises require a gradient steeper than that found on the majority of blue runs.

10 Skidding

The key difference between side-slipping and skidding is that side-slipping relies on gravity, whereas skidding requires momentum. In other words, the skier must already be in motion in order to skid. By then rotating the skis across the direction of travel, the skis skid sideways due to the skier's inertia. The skis remain edged throughout, so that the skier slows to a stop. The amount of edging that is used depends on several factors:

• The slope angle

• The snow conditions

• The speed of travel

• The intended rate of deceleration

• The skier's level of ability

Skidding is an integral part of all turns from plough to parallel, and must be used skilfully in order to control the line taken by the skis and modulate the amount of resistance. Much of that skill can be acquired through normal skiing, by varying the line, turn shape and speed of descent. But skidding may also be practised separately to, amongst other things:

• Help the matching stage of Plough Parallel

• Improve control of speed and Line

• Aid stopping

• Eliminate one-sidedness

Activities

a) On a very shallow piste, slide straight downhill with the feet apart. Push one ski out into a plough or wedge shape, so that the ski skids diagonally sideways. Allow that ski to come back parallel, and then repeat the action to the other side. The action can be practised repeatedly during a single descent.

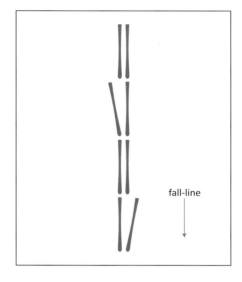

b) On a moderate gradient, plough downhill at a brisk walking pace. Start steering one ski parallel to its partner, and as the skis start skidding, continue rotating both legs so that the skis turn across the direction of travel into a skid to stop. This exercise is often known as a 'plough swing' or 'plough skid'.

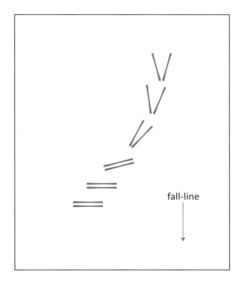

c) Set off on a moderate traverse (steep enough for the skis to travel at around jogging speed). Keeping the skis parallel throughout, rotate them across the direction of travel (i.e. pointing the tips uphill) while allowing the body to continue along its original line of descent to create a skid to stop.

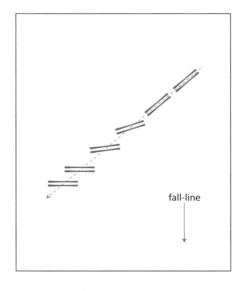

d) On a moderate slope, skid to a stop from a fairly steep traverse. Practise the action to both sides, varying the speed and steepness of descent as confidence and control improve. Vary the degree of resistance, so that at one extreme the skis come rapidly to a halt, while at the other the skid can be sustained indefinitely.

e) On a fairly long, moderately steep slope, start by making a sustained skid using fairly low resistance. By gently shifting the point of balance back and forth along the skis, the direction of the skid can be controlled, causing the skis to swing to either side of the fall-line during the descent. This activity is sometimes known as the 'falling leaf'.

f) On a very smooth, moderate slope, visualise two parallel lines around 30cm apart drawn straight down the fall-line. Set off downhill with one foot on each line and rotate both skis in unison so that they pivot from side to side like windscreen wipers. Each foot should remain on its imaginary line, with the ski being pivoted under the foot.

10.1 Swing to the Hill

Most of the activities in section 12 above have involved skidding in a relatively straight line. By varying the blend of steering elements (principally by slowing up the rate of leg rotation in relation to the application of pressure and edging), the skis can also be steered around a skidded arc. This is often known as a swing to the hill or an uphill swing. Essentially it can be thought of as the second half of a plough parallel or skidded parallel turn. Like most of the skidding activities in section 12, it can only be done as a single (non-linked) manoeuvre. Since the second half of the turn is the speed controlling phase, slope gradient poses much less of a problem than when doing complete turns. Thus swing to the hill is most frequently used to develop plough parallel or parallel turning where the terrain is too steep for the Central Theme. By starting to learn swing to the hill from a shallow traverse and gradually increasing the steepness of the line, pupils can eventually learn to make a controlled swing to the hill from the fall-line.

a) Gradually increase the angle of the traverse from which the swing to the hill is initiated. Make sure to practise the manoeuvre to alternate sides, to avoid the risk of becoming one-sided.

Where pupils can already do plough parallel, the activity can be taken all the way to the fall-line. In order to continue into complete turns, a safe and secure means of turn initiation is needed. For confident and agile pupils, this can be achieved with a strong, positive unweighting. If necessary, the unweighting action can be practised in garland form before introducing the complete manoeuvre.

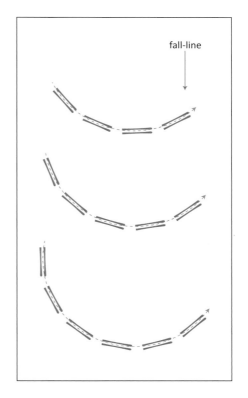

b) Start by practising unweighting on a traverse, with legs flexed, make a quick powerful extension of both legs to jump the skis clear of the snow. Then from a steep traverse use this action to pivot the skis into the fall-line, continuing with a swing to the hill to complete the turn. By gradually making the starting traverse shallower and pivoting the skis towards the fall-line during the unweighted phase, a complete parallel turn can be developed.

c) Start by ploughing steeply downhill. Turn away from the fall-line while steering the inner ski parallel to its partner, so as to finish with a parallel swing to the hill as before. Gradually increase the steepness from which the initial plough is performed. If the slope is not too steep, pupils should eventually be able to make complete turns, with the plough phase taking them into or beyond the fall-line, then finishing with a parallel swing to the hill.

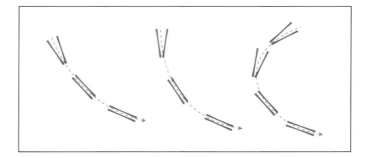

11 Side-slipping

Side-slipping can be used as a means of losing height, for example to descend a slope which is too narrow or restricted for turning. It is also a great way to develop edge awareness and sensitivity.

How to side-slip and common problems are covered in the Central Theme as part of Mountain Skills.

a) A variation on straight side-slipping is to perform the falling leaf drill as mentioned in the skidding section. For this to be a true side-slip the skier needs to accelerate rather than brake as they would when skidding.

Plough Parallel to Parallel Turning

In progressing through the Central Theme, each step so far has introduced a new component or action. For example the steering of the inner ski, when moving from plough turning to plough parallel. In going from plough parallel to parallel however, no new actions need be introduced. All the actions involved in performing a parallel turn are already present in plough parallel.

The only aspect which changes is the timing. The relationship between the steering of the inner and outer skis shifts from being sequential to simultaneous. In plough parallel turning, the outer ski starts to steer before the inner one, whereas in parallel turning, both skis are steered in unison.

Environment

Given appropriate terrain, virtually the entire evolution from plough parallel to parallel skiing can be accomplished through doing fairly long, continuous runs rather than brief, intermittent exercises. As a result, the ideal slope is similar to before - a long, smoothly-pisted run of moderate (blue) gradient.

The BASI Alpine Manual

12 From Plough Parallel to Parallel

12.1 Development of Rhythm and Co-ordination

a) Once pupils have developed the ability to steer the inner ski, they should practise over reasonably long, continuous runs. By focusing on a smooth, linked rhythm and allowing the skis to travel reasonably quickly, the inner ski should begin to steer progressively earlier in the turns as confidence and co-ordination improve.

b) Using a counting task, focus on the overall rhythm of the turns. Aim to maintain a fairly constant rhythm, with no pause or traverse between turns.

c) Using a chanting task, focus on the timing of steering the outer and inner skis. Aim to gradually reduce the time-lag, so that the actions eventually become simultaneous.

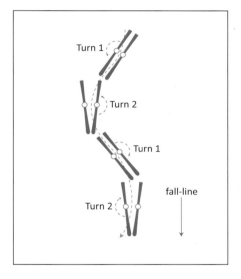

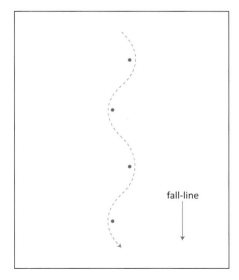

d) Set an open, flowing slalom course (preferably with low level markers rather than full-sized gates). The course should promote medium-sized, rounded turns, and encourage pupils to ski towards (but not beyond) the faster end of their comfort zone.

e) Visualise a parallel-sided 'corridor' between 3 and 5 metres wide, running directly down a smooth, uniform slope. Practise skiing within its margins, so that the turns just touch the edges of the corridor. The aim is to develop symmetrical, rhythmic and accurate turning. In fact, the corridor can either be imaginary, or set out using low-level markers such as small flags.

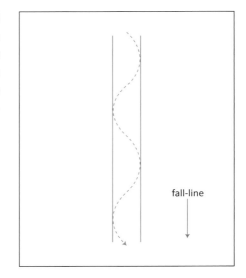

fall-line

Top Tips

In general, the aim is for skiers to gradually steer the inner ski earlier and earlier in the turns. This occurs as a resul t of:

- Increasing confidence
- Improved co-ordination and timing
- Earlier pressure on the outer ski
- Improved edging movements

Common Problems

As the inner leg leans into the turn and the ski is steered parallel, skiers may overbalance onto this inner foot. To counteract this tendency, focus on keeping the outer hand low. This helps skiers to remain balanced against the outer ski

Adjustments for Snow and Terrain

Typically, the above activities may have to be modified because:

- The practise area is too steep
- The practise area is too shallow
- The snow is hard or icy
- The snow is soft or wet

Steep Practise Area

As when going from plough to plough parallel, the development from plough parallel to parallel turning involves a gradual modification of pupils' movements. Using the activities described above, this again involves skiing fairly long, continuous runs.

As before, this requires terrain on which pupils feel confident to let the skis run fairly freely. If the terrain is too steep, a different approach must be used. With pupils who have a reasonably high level of confidence and agility, it may be possible to take them all the way to parallel skiing using swings to the hill. With less confident or agile pupils, it may be necessary to delay the introduction of parallel skiing until more suitable terrain is available. Instead, it may be more beneficial to work on improving skiers' speed control within the parallel phase of the plough parallel. On steep terrain, this can best be done by working on skidding to stop.

Shallow Practise Area

In order to ski parallel we need sufficient momentum to skid easily. If the terrain is too shallow or the skis are running too slowly, additional speed must be gained - by straight running, pushing with the poles or both - before attempting to make skidded turns. This can be effective provided enough speed can be built up to make at least two or three turns. If the extra speed is lost as soon as skiers start turning, a better approach is to work on single swing to the hill turns. Make sure that pupils do not become one-sided by alternating between left- and right-hand turns.

Hard or Icy Snow

Apart from the increased risk of injury, the main problem is due to the skis' more limited grip. As before, a smooth, hard surface can actually make steering the inner ski easier. To improve pupils' edge control and allow them to gain confidence when skidding, a useful activity is to practise skidding to stop. If the terrain is steep as well as icy, it may be preferable to use swings to the hill.

Soft or Wet Snow

As before, the same two general problems arise: increased injury risk and difficulty in maintaining control when turning. In parallel skiing however, there is an added difficulty at the point where the new turn begins. Up until now, skiers have had two main aids to stability when initiating turns:

• Wider base of support - the outer ski is first steered out into a plough
• Sequential edge-change - the outer ski changes edge before the inner ski

Both of these aids disappear as soon as the skis are steered in unison. Without some additional help, it requires a high degree of precision to initiate a pure parallel turn in soft or wet snow. For reasonably athletic, agile skiers, that additional help is best provided by jumping or unweighting the skis at the start of each turn. By lifting both skis clear of the snow surface, a clean, positive turn initiation can take place with little risk of catching edges.

Where skiers lack the necessary agility, the best approach is to delay the introduction of parallel skiing until more suitable terrain is available.

13 Stemming

Stemming is the action of displacing a ski out into a plough or 'A' shape. The key difference between stemming and the start of a plough parallel is that in plough parallel, the ski has pressure on it as it is displaced, whereas in stemming the ski is light, generally being lifted or gently slid out into the 'A' shape. In plough parallel, the direction change starts as soon as the outer ski begins to be displaced. In stemmed manoeuvres the ski is generally fully displaced before any pressure is applied. This allows the amount of edging to be adjusted prior to initiating the change of direction.

13.1 Stem Swing

The stem swing is normally performed at fairly low speeds - from a slow walk up to brisk jogging pace. It can either be used as an exercise, or as a technique for specific conditions:

• As an exercise, stem swing is generally used for developing more precise and positive edging at the start of the turns. For this purpose it is most appropriately used with pupils who can already ski parallel

• As a technique, stem swing is very effective for dealing with variable or difficult conditions - deep or heavy snow, breakable crust, rutted snow and poor visibility. It is ideal for difficult off piste conditions and is used by rucksack-laden ski mountaineers the world over

In either context the ski should be precisely edged before pressure is applied to it, to ensure a positive and accurate turn initiation. When done as an exercise, the ski can be slid or stepped out into the stem, as a technique for variable conditions, both outer and inner skis should generally be stepped, to prevent either ski from catching in the snow or snagging on unseen ruts.

a) Displace the outer ski by sliding or stepping it across into a stem. As its edge starts to grip and provide support, the inner ski is stepped or slid parallel. A pole plant may be used to trigger the action of bringing the inner ski parallel. In this case, the pole is prepared at the same time as the outer ski is stemmed.

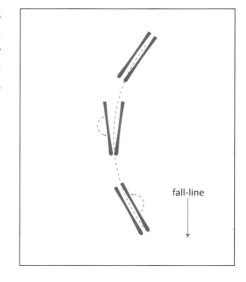

fall-line

13.2 Stem Step Turn

The stem step turn is very similar to the stem swing except that it is normally performed at higher speeds and with a more pronounced stepping action. It is used for a quick and precise edge- and direction-change.

a) Travelling across the slope at a brisk jogging pace, step the new outer ski into a stem. Place the ski onto its edge, as soon as it starts to grip, apply pressure by lifting the inner ski and starting to bring it parallel. A pole plant may be used at the point when the inside ski is about to be stepped parallel, to aid timing and give extra support.

13.3 Lower Ski Stem

The lower ski stem is another useful technique in its own right. Because the stemming action puts the lower ski very strongly on its edge, it gives a firm platform from which to initiate the next turn. It is useful on steep ground, in wet snow conditions and on various other types of terrain where grip at the beginning of the turn is vital. It can also be used as an exercise, to develop the ability to perform an edge-set (check) and rebound, as in short swing.

a) Set off slowly across the slope. Push the lower ski down into a stem, pivoting the ski around a point near its tip. Allow the body to 'fold' as the ski is stemmed, creating increased angulation. As well as turning further away from the fall-line, the ski is therefore tilted more strongly onto its edge, giving added resistance and support.

By 'rebounding' off the extra support from the stemmed lower ski, a very quick and positive initiation can be obtained for the new turn. Planting the pole just on the rebound helps stabilise the body so that the legs and skis can be pivoted positively into the new direction.

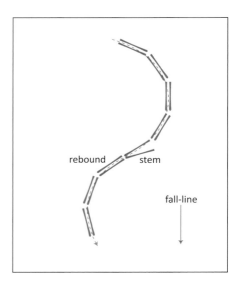

PARALLEL TURNING

Once pupils have learned to ski parallel, they have reached a level from which they can start to tackle a much broader range of skiing - higher speeds, steeper terrain, bumps, and variable conditions (e.g. fresh snow). These are all areas of skiing which lie beyond the Central Theme and are dealt with elsewhere. But before moving into these areas, there are certain aspects of basic parallel skiing which should first be explored and developed. These include the control of speed and line, the edge-change, and the introduction of pole-planting.

Environment

Although skiers should now be able to cope with a fairly broad range of terrain, the activities which follow are best attempted on reasonably easy slopes. In the main, appropriate runs would normally encompass blues and gentle reds.

14 The Development of Parallel Skiing

Along with the technical changes which take place when going from plough parallel to parallel turning, there are also factors which affect the skier's emotional state - the level of confidence and commitment they feel in relation to the activity. Two key issues which have a strong influence on confidence are control of speed, and the skier's state of balance, especially at the start of the turns. These two factors are in fact closely connected, and are dealt with in the following two sections.

14.1 Control of Speed and Line

At all levels of technique, there is a natural tendency for the skis to accelerate in the first half of each turn and decelerate in the second. This happens because the skis follow a progressively steeper line as they approach the fall-line, then a progressively shallower one as they turn away from it. However, the acceleration is less marked in plough parallel than in parallel skiing. By steering the outer ski into a plough at the start of the turn, extra resistance is created just when the acceleration begins.

Conversely, as the size and duration of the plough are reduced, the degree of acceleration becomes more marked. In consequence, skiers may start to feel that their speed control is deteriorating as they move from plough parallel towards parallel turning. The result is often a reluctance to abandon the plough phase due to the additional speed control which it provides. It is therefore important for skiers to recognise that this acceleration is normal. It belongs quite properly in the first part of a parallel turn, and is not the result of loss of control. Equally, the feeling of slowing down belongs in the second part of the turn, when the extra speed can again be lost.

a) To help skiers get used to this feature of parallel turning, try 'wheee...! - whoaa...!' turns. Call out 'wheee...!' during the acceleration phase and 'whoaa...!' when decelerating. The words keep pupils focused on this feature of the turns, but in a positive, light-hearted way. The activity captures the emotional rather than the technical content, encouraging pupils to seek the exhilaration of acceleration and the security of slowing down again.

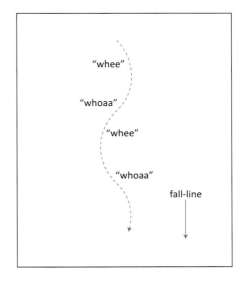

At this stage, pupils should also be starting to use turn shape for speed control. Rather than simply increasing the amount of skid in order to slow down, each turn can be continued further past the fall-line:

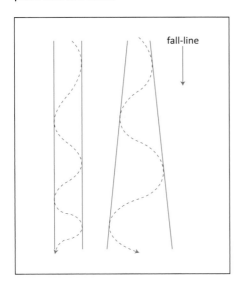

b) On a moderate gradient, make a series of linked parallel turns while minimising the amount of skidding. Then, without allowing any additional skidding to occur, try to slow down over a sequence of 5 to 10 turns. In other words, try to magnify the 'whoaa...!' phase of the turns, but without increasing the degree of skid. In order to achieve the task without any increase in skidding, the arc length of the turns must be increased, either within a constant corridor width, or by expanding the corridor.

14.2 The Crossover Effect

As the size and duration of the plough diminishes, a new feature emerges - the 'crossover'. This effect transforms the way in which the edge-change takes place at the start of the turn. When turning, the skier's hips (more accurately, the Centre of Mass) follow a path inside that of the outer ski in order to maintain balance. The faster the skier is travelling or the tighter the turn, the further the hips must move inwards to balance against the centrifugal effect.

This has two main consequences:

- Technically, the crossover leads to an earlier, more simultaneous edge change, as it causes both legs to incline towards the centre of the new turn. As a result, it further helps to eliminate the plough phase

- Emotionally, the crossover may at first be rather intimidating. Because the body is in effect toppling across the skis ('falling' downhill into the new turn), pupils may feel anxious about committing themselves to it. They must develop confidence in the sensation before anxiety can become transformed into exhilaration

This second point closely mirrors what is discussed in the previous section on Control of speed and line.

Common Problems

Many skiers have difficulty in eliminating the plough phase from the start of their turns - they always have a small 'stem'. Some exercises which may help are:

a) As the uphill leg stretches, transferring pressure onto the new outer ski, the body is usually displaced in an upward direction. Focus on this displacement and try to make it diagonal, across the path of the skis, reinforcing the crossover and accelerating the body into the new turn

b) Focus on the pressure against the outer ski while turning. Due to the combination of forces acting on the skier, it usually reaches a maximum towards the end of the turn. Just as it reaches its maximum value, relax that leg (at this point, the downhill one) so that it no longer provides any support and simultaneously stretch the new leg as explained in the previous example. The direction taken by the body is diagonally downhill, resulting in a crossover and re-initiation of a new turn. This last exercise has several interesting benefits:

- Provided the skier relaxes the leg at the point of maximum pressure and stretches the new leg simultaneously, it ensures that there is no pause between turns

- It harnesses the forces already present in the turn to create the crossover

- It provides a 'low-effort' means of turn-initiation. It is a particularly useful exercise for skiers who rely too much on raw strength

- It helps eliminate any residual stem. A stem or plough requires muscular effort from both legs to create and sustain it. Relaxing one leg implies the absence of muscular effort, so that the more effectively the leg is relaxed, the less likelihood there is of a stem

Skiers must be made aware of these emotional barriers to progress. To overcome them, they need to spend time practising on relatively easy terrain. They must develop confidence and learn to enjoy the sensation of flowing across the path of the skis as they accelerate downhill

Technically, the crossover is precisely what enables the skier to remain balanced against the skis as they accelerate into the new turn. Emotionally, fear of acceleration may be compounded by the sensation of the crossover itself.

14.3 The Pole-plant

Up until now, no mention has been made of the pole-plant. Throughout the Central Theme, the activities and manoeuvres have relied on leg movements to control the skis. Apart from pushing along on the flat and turning around on a slope, the poles have played no part.

Given appropriate terrain, there is no need for the pole-plant in working through the Central Theme. Indeed the poles can be more of an encumbrance than a help and are often best discarded in the early stages of learning. But at this point, after pupils have learned the rudiments of parallel skiing, the pole-plant can become a valuable aid. It has several purposes in turn initiation:

- **As an Aid to Timing** – While most of the movements of skiing should have a smooth, flowing quality, the pole-plant provides a brief, clear 'punctuation mark' to trigger the start of the turn

- **As a Balance Support** – In smooth, rounded turns the pole-plant provides added stability as the skier's Centre of Mass crosses the path of the feet, in turns with a pronounced check or edge-set, it aids balance at the moment of maximum deceleration of the skis

- **To Aid Leg Rotation** – To enable the legs to be rotated positively into the new direction without disrupting posture or balance, the pole-plant provides a momentary anchor between the skier's body and the ground

The key to an effective pole-plant is to have no unnecessary movement of the arm, shoulder or body. To start with, the action can best be practised on a traverse:

a) Traverse across the hill, repeatedly and rhythmically planting the downhill pole while ensuring there are no undue movements.

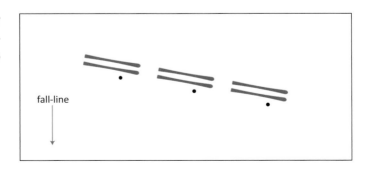

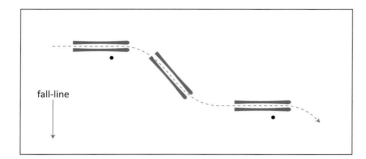

b) This can be further developed by using garland manoeuvres. This allows the pole-plant to be incorporated into the turn initiation without having to perform complete turns.

c) A common initial difficulty is remembering which pole to plant. One approach is to imagine the pole is a direction-indicator for other skiers - planting the left pole indicates a left turn, planting the right pole indicates one to the right. Without concern for accuracy or timing, simply practise planting the appropriate pole. The task can be aided by saying "Turning left . . .turning right!" just as each turn begins.

d) Once the correct pole is being planted, the next objective is to get the timing right. One method is to ski downhill making rhythmically-linked turns, saying "Now!" just as each turn begins. Focus on getting the timing of the words accurately linked to the actions, then try to plant the pole on every "Now!"

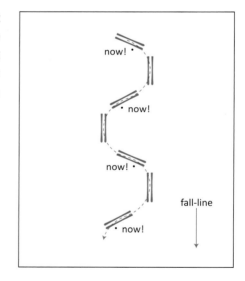

15 Garlands

Garlands are turns performed while moving diagonally across the slope. On initiating a turn, the skis approach the fall-line. But before reaching the fall-line, the skis are turned back onto a shallower traverse again. Because the skis never actually cross the fall-line, garlands can be used on terrain which is too steep for making complete turns. For example when traversing from left to right, the skier turns left to approach the fall-line, then turns right to return to the shallower traverse. Thus, a left turn initiation is practised alongside a right turn completion.

The beauty of garland turns is that they allow repeated practise of a part of a turn. Any type of turn can be practised as a garland, from snowplough, through to plough parallel, up to parallel and short swing. They are also valuable in providing repeated practise of a particular action or manoeuvre to one side, such as unweighting, stemming or pole-planting. Garlands can also be used to practise turning to the pupil's less-favoured side.

Garland manoeuvres have three main values. They enable practise to be maintained in the following circumstances:

- Where the terrain is too steep for the skiers' level of ability
- Where the slope is wide but very short
- Where pupils lack the confidence to make complete turns through the fall-line

In addition, garlands enable skiers to negotiate runs which cut across the natural fall-line, and to lose height safely on wide, steep slopes.

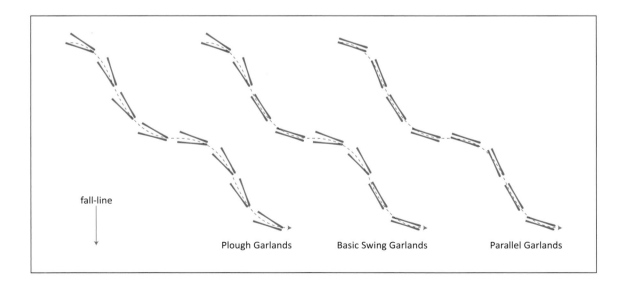

fall-line

Plough Garlands   Basic Swing Garlands   Parallel Garlands

14. THE TOOLBOX - DRILLS

THE DRILLS TOOLBOX

The drills listed are a collection of drills gathered from the training body and are presented here as examples of drills that can help to develop skiing skills throughout the five strands.

To make full use of the drills the skier must:

- Ensure that the terrain is suitable and safe to carry out the drill
- Perform the drill with accuracy and precision
- Assess how they perform the drill and what the drill gives them. What is it they need to do in order to achieve the drill (TTPPEE)
- Work on the drills they dislike as well as the ones they are good at

The drills listed below are by no means exhaustive. There are thousands of drills that can be performed. Steal drills from other Instructors and Coaches and have the confidence to make new ones up.

Some drills, may have an effect on your skiing or your client's skiing that was not foreseen. Be confident enough to judge for yourself what the drill does for someone, tweak it as necessary or leave it alone if it doesn't work for an individual. It is not just a question of going through the drills, use the performance link to assess what is happening, what you want to happen, why it is happening, and then find a solution to get there. This approach will make the drills more effective.

The drills are structured around four levels, which roughly correspond to the four levels within the BASI instructor hierarchy. This is a rough guide only, it does not mean that Level 1 candidates should not try Level 4 drills, and equally many Level 4 Instructors would benefit from some Level 1 drills. There is no assessment attached to these drills and the ability to perform these does not guarantee success at any level. These drills should form just a part of anyone's training and development, as that is what they are for 'development'.

The table is a guide to which strands each drill is good for, and also which skills each drill works on. It is a guide only and some drills may work on other skills not highlighted in the table.

DRILL NAME	STRAND					SKILLS						
	Piste Performance	Bumps	Steeps	Variable	Freestyle	Alignment	Lateral Balance	Fore-Aft Balance	Steering Skills	Posture/Stance	Separation /Inclination	Timing /Co-ordination
A Dolphin Ate my Stork			✓			✓	✓	✓	✓			
Airborne Edge		✓		✓		✓						✓
Angles	✓						✓				✓	
Body Tilts	✓			✓				✓			✓	
Flatland					✓			✓	✓		✓	✓
Level Leaps	✓		✓			✓		✓				
Longs 1	✓								✓			
Longs 2	✓						✓					
Rails					✓				✓	✓		
Ridgeback Jumping		✓						✓				✓
Ridgeback Riding		✓		✓				✓				✓
Ropes	✓		✓	✓		✓				✓		
Shorties	✓						✓		✓			
Shorties 2	✓	✓	✓			✓			✓			✓
Shorties 3	✓	✓	✓				✓					✓
Sliders		✓							✓			
Tea Tray Cliché Drills	✓	✓	✓							✓	✓	
The 2 Step	✓					✓				✓		✓
The Big Dipper		✓			✓			✓		✓		✓
The Blender	✓		✓						✓			✓
The Chopper	✓			✓		✓			✓	✓		✓
The Corkscrew	✓	✓	✓					✓			✓	✓
The Hopper	✓					✓						✓
The Rollercoaster	✓			✓	✓	✓	✓			✓		
The Shuffle	✓			✓			✓					
The Slipper	✓		✓			✓			✓		✓	
The Up and Over	✓								✓	✓		✓
Transitions					✓			✓				
Cowboys and Indians	✓	✓		✓					✓	✓		
Who Needs Boots	✓			✓		✓		✓		✓		
Lost a Ski	✓					✓	✓				✓	
Thousand Step Turns	✓			✓							✓	✓
Back to Bracquage	✓	✓	✓				✓	✓	✓		✓	
Equine Twist	✓			✓					✓		✓	✓

A Dolphin Ate My Stork

Goal

To develop agility, sliding skills and the ability to retract the legs as is required in bumps skiing

Terrain

Piste getting progressively steeper, blue to black

LEVEL 1

- Hop turns on one leg, outside ski, pivoting under foot
- The same but on a slightly steeper slope, this should mean the skier has to turn the ski more to control speed
- No poles

LEVEL 2

- One leg skiing in a 2m corridor, outside ski, skis stay on the snow
- The same but do it slower, this demands more precision
- No poles

LEVEL 3

- The same as level 2 but with more active steering (a little more edge)
- On a steeper slope
- No poles

LEVEL 4

- One leg dolphin turns, the tip leaves the snow first and lands first
- The same but in chopped up variable snow
- No poles

Airborne Edge

LEVEL 1

- The skier jumps the skis off the ground in between turns
- No poles
- Take off on one foot and land on the other

LEVEL 2

- The same as level 1 but the skier now changes edges in the air
- Make the gap between jumps shorter
- No poles

LEVEL 3

- The same progression as level 2 but with both skis horizontal in the air.

LEVEL 4

- The same as level 3 level but on steeper terrain and in a narrower corridor
- Look for terrain to assist with the jump – this will change the rhythm
- No poles

Angles

Goal

To develop lateral separation essential for an efficient cross-over skiing

Terrain

Piste getting progressively steeper

LEVEL 1

- The skier traverses across the slope with no poles. The downhill hand rests on the downhill hip and pushes the hip up the hill. There should be no flexion at the waist only a lateral movement
- The same but only on the downhill ski, uphill ski lifted
- Keep the tip of the uphill ski pressed onto the snow

LEVEL 2

- The same 3 progressions as level 1 but during turns on a blue run. The hip should be pushed to the inside of the turn during the last third of the turn. The torso also needs to separate rotationally in order to face the centre of the next turn

LEVEL 3

- The same as level 2 but faster and using carved turns

LEVEL 4

- The same as level 3 level but with no poles

Body Tilts and Touch Down

Goal

To tilt the skis by inclining different parts of the body during a turn

Terrain

Varied pistes

LEVEL 1

- Shallow traverse on the uphill edge of the uphill ski. Joints aligned for maximum strength
- The same but this time skier makes small flexing and extending movements whilst traversing, using ankle, knee and hip
- The same but on a much steeper slope so that the skier has to work harder to balance on an edge (steep red or black)

LEVEL 2

- Carving without any angulation
- Try to carve a full circle – you need lots of speed for this. The inclined position maintains strength and edge grip
- Best done on a slalom ski, try to touch the snow on the inside of the turn without compromising the stacked position. No flexing at the waist

LEVEL 3

- One ski carving on the same ski. Show inclination of ankle, knee and hip. Avoid inclining the upper body but not the leg. Perform drill on both legs
- Make the arc length longer so that the skier has to tilt more progressively
- Try in chopped up or variable snow

LEVEL 4

- White Pass Turns. Start the turn on the little toe edge of the inside ski, outside ski airborne Place outside ski onto the snow just after the fall-line, then allow the body to crossover and incline into the next turn
- Put the outside ski down later and have a quicker cross-over
- No poles

Flatland

LEVEL 1

• Skier jumps and turns 180 degrees to land skiing backwards, with the skis roughly parallel

• Try this from forward to backwards and then backward to forwards

• Make the gap between jumps shorter

LEVEL 2

• Skier performs an Ollie

• Skier performs a Nollie – the reverse of an Ollie!

• Skier links several Ollies together

LEVEL 3

• Level 1 but faster

LEVEL 4

• Level 3 but even faster with your trousers round your ankles dude!

Level Leapers

Goal

To develop the ability to remain centred on the skis whilst on steep terrain. Skiers should experience the feeling of not only jumping up but also out from the slope to remain balanced

Terrain

Red/black piste & steep off-piste

LEVEL 1

- Ski down the fall-line on a red run, make 4 hops where both skis remain at the same angle as the slope whilst in the air. The skier's body should be perpendicular to the slope and skis
- The same but with poles in the snow to jump over. Do not touch the poles
- Make the gap between the poles shorter

LEVEL 2

- On a black run, skier takes off in the traverse and lands in the fall-line. Body must remain perpendicular to the slope when airborne. Repeat on both sides
- Skier makes a check or edge set before jumping
- No poles

LEVEL 3

- Repeat the progression for level 2 but link turns together on steep offpiste. The traverse is replaced by a controlled scrape. The body remains perpendicular to the slope in the jump phase. The skis are at the same angle as the slope when airborne

LEVEL 4

- Ski down the fall-line on a steep a black run make 4 hops where both skis remain at the same angle as the slope whilst in the air. The skier's body should be perpendicular to the slope and skis
- Hop into the turn and then make a second hop whilst in the fall-line before scraping to control speed
- No poles

Longs 1

LEVEL 1

- Traverse with skis on their edges, flatten the skis and then edge again
- Use only the ankles and knees to find an edge in a carved turn on a green run
- Move the knees and the hips inside the skis in a carved turn

LEVEL 2

- In a high tuck position make long turns on a green/blue run using lower leg angulation. Fists should remain facing downhill at all times
- The same but carving cleanly
- Shorter arc, more direct, more speed

LEVEL 3

- Skier begins carving and follows markers/brushes that oblige the skier to tighten the radius
- Set the markers so the course gradually forces the skier to tighten the radius more and more until the clean carve breaks down
- No poles

LEVEL 4

- Cloud burst drill. At the end of a carved turn the skier rotates the skis downhill at 90 degrees to the path of the carve, creating a side-slip across the slope. The skis are then brought back approx. 60 degrees onto the new carving edge to start the next turn. When coming back 60 degrees, skis should stay on the same edge and not revert to the previous turn. Red piste minimum
- Hold the side slip for longer
- Use GS skis as well as slalom skis. GS skis will make the side-slip feel safer but there will be much more speed to deal with if the skier maintains a clean carve

Longs 2

Goal

To develop the ability to influence the radius of a carved turn

Terrain

Varied pistes

LEVEL 1

- Skier makes a J turn from the fall-line, both skis carving cleanly
- The same but on one ski
- No poles

LEVEL 2

- Skier makes medium radius carved turns on one leg. Green run
- The same but the transfer from one ski to the next is done with a hop
- Both 1 & 2 but with no poles

LEVEL 3

- The same as level 2 but on a blue run

LEVEL 4

- Skier makes medium radius carved turns on one leg on a blue run with the other ski removed Practise on both legs
- More dynamism so the skier influences the radius of the arc
- No poles

Rail

Goal

To develop the ability to ride a rail in balance

Terrain

Blue/red piste and park. Too shallow a slope and level 1 drill is harder

LEVEL 1

- Skier hops and lands with skis across the fall-line and side-slips down the slope
- The same again but the skier hops again before turning back into the fall-line. E.g. Slide down the fall-line, hop & turn 90 degrees, side-slip, hop, side-slip
- Place a pole on the snow for the skier to clear

LEVEL 2

- Skier grinds a hard snow ridge
- Skier grinds a hard snow ridge and stops dead on the ridge, tips and tails clear of the snow
- Skier grinds a hard snow ridge and jumps clear to ski away

LEVEL 3

- Skier grinds a flat box, level with the snow
- Skier grinds a flat box, slightly raised accessed from a ramp
- Skier grinds a flat box, slightly raised accessed from a small kicker

LEVEL 4

- Skier grinds a flat rail, level with the snow
- Skier grinds a flat rail, slightly raised accessed from a ramp
- Skier grinds a flat rail, slightly raised accessed from a small kicker

Ridgeback Jumping

Goal

To develop timing and co-ordination of edge changes and pressure control in conjunction with the terrain

Terrain

A snowy ridge. Often between marker posts on the edge of a piste

LEVEL 1

- Skier uses the ridge to jump. The tips are the first part of the ski to leave the ground and the first part to land, enabling a soft, quiet landing. Skier regains control, turns and tries another jump in the opposite direction
- Touch the outside of the boot in the air
- Minimise the noise of the landing

LEVEL 2

- Same as level 1 but build in a smoother turn. Skier should flow down the ridge changing edges in the air, landing, turning, jumping, edge change etc. Gentle gradient, medium speed
- Cut back onto the ridge so that skis are less in the fall-line at take-off, this will result in more airtime
- No poles

LEVEL 3

- As level 2 but much faster, on a steeper run

LEVEL 4

- Take this into the bumps, skier should take off on one bump and land on the backside of a different bump. Done correctly this should be a smooth effortless manoeuvre
- The same but with the jump more in the fall-line
- Two jumps on one run

Ridgeback Riding

Goal

To develop timing and co-ordination of edge changes in conjunction with the terrain

Terrain

A snowy ridge. Often between marker posts on the edge of a piste

LEVEL 1

- Skier makes medium radius turns over the ridge, keeping skis in contact with the snow at all times. The timing of the edge change is dictated by the ridge

LEVEL 2

- Same as level 1 and using same ridge tighten the turn radius and increase speed. Maintain ski/snow contact

LEVEL 3

- Same ridge as levels 1 & 2. Increase the speed and make the turns grippier. Skier should compress the ridge to maintain ski/snow contact. Take this into easy open bumps field. Blindfolded is fun too

LEVEL 4

- Add in a ridge slide to check speed, along the length of the ridge, skis perpendicular to the length of the ridge. Skier should be able to stop dead on top of the ridge, tips and tails clear of the snow. Take this into a medium open bumps field

Ropes

LEVEL 1

- Pass a 2m length of rope under the buttocks and hold an end in each hand, pull the rope tight. In a straight run on a shallow slope pull the rope forwards so that the hips in turn move forwards and align over the feet
- Make the same movement but from a traverse. Pause whilst the hips re-align over the feet and then move into a turn
- The same but link 10 turns together pulling the hips forward during each transition

LEVEL 2

- The same rope drill but making medium to long radius turns on a blue run
- The same rope drill but make the turns and the pause shorter
- Eradicate the pause but make the same movements. Try to link everything together to get a flowing movement pattern

LEVEL 3

- The same as level 2 but on variable terrain or a steeper piste

LEVEL 4

- The same rope drill but in a cleanly carved turn. Allow the hips to follow the direction the skis are facing when pulling on the rope
- This time pull the hips more into the middle of the next turn so that they move across the skis rather than staying in line with them
- Experiment with these two types of cross-over. The first is better for building a solid balanced platform at the top of the turn, the second allows for a faster cross-over potentially increasing velocity. The second one can go wrong if not executed from a solid platform

Shorties 1

Goal
To develop edge control in short turns

Terrain
Varied pistes

LEVEL 1

- Short javelin turns, the skier makes short arcs and finishes every turn with inside ski lifted
- When the ski is lifted, cross it over the other ski
- No poles

LEVEL 2

- Rail both skis from edge to edge using ankle and knee tilt without actively using the hips. Short arc length, easy gradient
- The same but hold the poles like a handlebar, at eye level, arms out stretched. This helps to strengthen the core
- No poles, hands on hips. This allows the skier to feel if the hip is being used or not

LEVEL 3

- On a shallow gradient, skate downhill gradually transforming the skates into carved turns. Allow the hip to be used as well as the ankle and knee
- Use terrain so that the run gradually gets steeper. Once the skier is turning, try to maintain the same performance on the steeper slope

LEVEL 4

- Fun carving on slalom skis. Use whole body to maximise the use of the ski's side cut
- Try to lay the body out on the snow to extend the skiers comfort zone. Touch the snow with the inside hand without compromising a strong position
- Change the rhythm during a run

Shorties 2

LEVEL 1

- With the upper body facing downhill let the skis straight run then rotate the skis 90 degrees to the direction of travel and side-slip for as far as possible
- The same but link, to make a series of bracquage turns, body stays facing downhill
- The same again but with poles balanced on the back of the hands

LEVEL 2

- Double pole plants. With an open arm carriage the skier plants both poles directly down the hill below the skis whilst performing controlled short turns
- The same but on a steeper slope. The skier will turn the skis more across the hill using a greater degree of upper/lower body separation
- Use undulating terrain but maintain constant speed so the skier is forced to change the arc length

LEVEL 3

- 10 rhythmical short swings, lifting both skis completely off the snow
- Challenge the skiers to perform the 10 turns in as short a distance as possible, maintaining good form
- Short swings with no poles

LEVEL 4

- On a shallow gradient (blue) make short turns with a visible pause in between turns where the skier stacks for the next turn
- The same but make the pause shorter. The skier should still feel it and can use a trigger word to focus on the stacking phase e.g. "stack"
- The same but on level 4 short turn terrain, maintain the trigger word.

Shorties 3

Goal

To develop lateral balance and co-ordination in short turns

Terrain

Varied pistes

LEVEL 1

- Skier lifts inside ski at turn initiation and then completes the turn from fall-line on 2 skis
- Skier holds the inside ski off the snow for longer
- Skier does the whole turn on one ski

LEVEL 2

- Slightly crouched, the skier imagines there is a medallion hanging from his neck between the knees, then sets off in a straight line rolling knees across until the outside knee comes below medallion. Turns should be carved
- Move the knees until the outside knee goes passed the medallion
- Move into a tuck position and perform the same task – ankles now also need to be used

LEVEL 3

- Skier makes slow steered short turns with 2 pole plants with same pole between turns
- The same but using more edge in the turn
- The same but with high performance short turns

LEVEL 4

- Skiers hop laterally from outside ski to outside ski whilst in the fall-line landing on the big toe edge each time
- Ensure that both skis remain level with the slope – both tip and tail off the snow to the same degree
- No poles

Sliders

Goal

To develop agility, sliding skills and the ability to retract the legs as is required in bumps skiing

Terrain

Groomed red piste

LEVEL 1

- Skier stands across the fall-line, jumps and on landing side slips in balance maintaining skis as 90 degrees to the fall-line. Continue to punctuate side slip with a jump every 3 metres
- Define a 2m wide corridor in the snow inside which skiers must stay
- Build in a 'windscreen wiper' swish during the side slip phase. Tips up the hill and then tails up the hill, body remains downhill

LEVEL 2

- Skier starts with a straight run down the fall-line then jumps and turns skis 90 degrees, lands and side slips. Then jump back into fall-line, repeat every 3 metres. Repeat on both sides
- Build in an edge check before each jump back into the fall-line
- Mix the two. Two with an edge check two without etc

LEVEL 3

- Skier starts with a straight run down the fall-line then jumps and turns skis 90 degrees, lands and side slips. Then jump the skis through 180 degrees to face in the opposite direction before side slipping again. Repeat the jump every 3 metres
- Define a 2m corridor in the snow inside which skiers must stay
- No poles

LEVEL 4

- The same as Level 3 level but when the skier jumps through 180 degrees the direction of rotation should be uphill not downhill. This requires a greater degree of leg retraction to ensure the skis remain clear of the snow
- Define a 2m corridor in the snow inside which skiers must stay
- No poles

Tea Tray Cliché Drills

Goal

To develop separation and upper body control. Old school but important

Terrain

Groomed piste – steeper can be easier

LEVEL 1

- Skier makes short skidded turns down a corridor 2m wide whilst holding poles in front. Poles remain facing down the hill at all times
- Increase the tempo
- Vary the tempo: Slow – Fast - Slow

LEVEL 2

- Same as level 1 but with poles balanced across the back of the hands rather than held. Drill should be performed with more speed, grip and active steering
- Same progression as level 1

LEVEL 3

- Short swings with air under both skis, no poles, hands out in front. Take this upper body control and reintroduce poles into moderate bumps
- Take away poles

LEVEL 4

- Short swing dolphin turns, 2m corridor, no poles. Take this upper body control and reintroduce poles into rut line
- Take away poles

The 2 Step

Goal

To develop a stacked position on the skis at the start of the turn

Terrain

Variable terrain that is not too bumpy. Or smooth piste if working on precision

LEVEL 1

• The skier stamps one foot and then the other in quick succession in between turns. Groomed terrain

• The skier makes more steps between turns to allow longer to get stacked

• The skier focuses on feeling the skis flat on the snow during the steps and can say out loud the trigger word "flat" to reinforce this process

LEVEL 2

• The same as level 1 but on variable terrain

LEVEL 3

• The same as level 2 but on a gradient greater than 25 degrees

LEVEL 4

• The same as level 3 level but carving the skis through the turn, no skid

The Big Dipper

Goal	
To develop balance and co-ordination in the air	

Terrain	
Up to 10 groomed waves or rollers that are approx. 2m apart	

NB. Instructor must be firm with students and use a professional judgement as to who is capable of which level. These drills can result in injury if not closely supervised and managed by Instructor.

LEVEL 1

- Skier jumps off the last roller. The skier is in balance at take-off, in the air and on landing
- Mark a place on the snow as a target for the skier to land. This will help to build confidence
- Build in more of a pop on take off. Skiers can use the trigger word "pop" to help focus on this process

LEVEL 2

- Skiers jump off the last roller and aim to touch their boot at shin height in the air. Skiers do not reach down to the boot but pull legs up into a tuck in order to make the touch
- Hold the boot for a count of 2 or 3 rather than just touching it
- The same but hold or touch both boots at the same time

LEVEL 3

- Jump from the second last role and land on the back of the last role. The skier must be in balance at take-off, in the air and on landing
- No poles

LEVEL 4

- The skier makes a succession of jumps down the length of the rollercoaster, taking off on one roller and landing on the back of the next. This requires perfect balance and timing. This can only be done if the rollers are close enough to make it safe
- No poles

The Blender

Goal

To develop a blend of the steering elements and improve coordination and rhythm in short turns

Terrain

Varied pistes

LEVEL 1

- Short turns down a convex slope. As the terrain gets steeper the skier must smoothly slow down his descent without altering corridor width
- Make the corridor wider
- No poles

LEVEL 2

- Instructor stands at bottom with pole in the air. Skier turns in time with the rhythmical movements of the pole
- Change the rhythm to challenge the skier
- Agree a sign with the pole that means stop. Build this into the middle of the routine so the skier has to stop dead and then start again

LEVEL 3

- Ski down an inverted hourglass moving from sharp rotary turns to turns using more edge and pressure. This widens the corridor, then return to rotary turns and a narrow corridor
- Try the opposite, carved short turns to skiddy rotary turns and back to carved turns
- Use brushes or cones to set a course which forces the use of different blends of the steering elements

LEVEL 4

- Skier skis a sequence of turns. At the end of one turn, skier pops into the air as a result of pressure built up under the ski. Next one exit smoothly, next one pop, next smooth
- Make 5 turns as explained above and then change the side on which the pop happens for another 5 turns, without breaking the rhythm of the run
- Build in two pole plants on the smooth turn

The Chopper

Goal

To develop edge control and a stacked position

Terrain

Blue/red piste

LEVEL 1

- The skier stands facing across the fall-line and balances on the uphill edge of both skis. The skier makes a lateral jump down the hill and lands cleanly on the same edges. Check the tracks to measure precision
- Make 3 jumps, each leaving clean tracks
- No poles

LEVEL 2

- The same as level 1 but whilst travelling across the hill in a traverse. For every 3 metres traversed, the skier jumps laterally down the hill and lands on the uphill edge of both skis and continues traversing
- Pair up and watch. Are both skis leaving the snow and landing at the same time?
- No poles

LEVEL 3

- The same as level 1 but instead of hopping both skis at the same time the skier hops one then the other. There should only ever be one ski on the snow at any given time
- Skis should be level at all times
- No poles

LEVEL 4

- Make the same hopping movement as the level 3 but during a carved turn. Sometimes known as 1000 step turns – pure carve on an easy slope
- Tighten the radius of the turns
- No poles

The BASI Alpine Manual

The Corkscrew

Goal

To develop control of rotational separation in slow skidded turns on steep terrain

Terrain

Groomed red/black run

LEVEL 1

• Braquage turns in a narrow and defined corridor (2m)

• Boots open

• No poles

LEVEL 2

• Braquage turns but with a double pole plant below the skier during the transition from one turn to the next

• Speed it up

• Make the corridor wider (4m). Skiers try to use the full width of the corridor whilst still making a double pole plant

LEVEL 3

• Braquage turns on one ski. Skiers remain on the same ski throughout the drill using both edges. Repeat the drill on the other leg

• Skiers must remain in a 2m corridor

• The same drill but slower

LEVEL 4

• The same as the level 3 but without poles. This is very difficult!

The Hopper

LEVEL 1

- Ski down the fall-line on a green run, make 4 hops where both skis remain at the same angle as the slope whilst in the air
- The same but on a blue run
- No poles

LEVEL 2

- Skiers jump over horizontal slalom poles 8m apart. Skiers should not touch any of the poles
- Add in two tunnels (slalom poles, drilled at an angle so they cross) that skiers duck under
- No poles

LEVEL 3

- The same as level 2 but with shorter distances (4m) and on a steeper slope (blue/red run)
- Add in two lateral jumps to make a more complex course
- No poles

LEVEL 4

- The same as level 2 but change the rhythm by setting some poles with a short distance (4m) and some with a longer distance (8m)
- Make the start line further away from the first obstacle to induce more speed
- Continue to change the course and challenge the skiers until it is at the limit of people's capability

The Rollercoaster

Goal

To develop a dynamic balanced position and allow the body to flex smoothly

Terrain

Up to 10 groomed waves or rollers that are approx. 2m apart

LEVEL 1

• Ski over the last three/four rollers in a straight line, flexing and extending to maintain contact with the snow

LEVEL 2

• Ski over all 10 rollers, flexing and extending to maintain contact with the snow

LEVEL 3

• Starting outside the area to generate some speed, the skier makes a long gradual turn through two or three waves down the length of the rollercoaster. Maintain ski snow contact

LEVEL 4

• The same as level 3 but the skier makes a turn in between every roller, cones/brushes can be used as gates

NB. Trainer must be firm with students and use a professional judgement as to who is capable of which level. These drills can result in injury if not closely supervised and managed by the Trainer.

The Shuffle

To develop a centred, stacked position

Groomed green/blue piste

LEVEL 1

- The skier stands on a flat section and whilst remaining in the same place, shuffles both skis slowly backwards and forwards. Equal length of shuffle for both legs, hips remain centred over the skis at all times
- The same but on a slope with the skis across the fall-line, boots undone, repeat facing in both directions
- Boots fastened

LEVEL 2

- The same as level 1 but travel across the slope in a traverse whilst maintaining the quality of the shuffle, boots undone
- Boots fastened
- Take this into shallow turns on a green/blue run

LEVEL 3

- The same as level 2, but link rounded steered turns down a blue run
- Boots undone
- No poles

LEVEL 4

- The same as level 3 level but with carved turns
- Boots undone
- No poles

The Slipper

Goal

To develop edge control and a stacked position. All drills should be performed on both sides

Terrain

Steep, smooth red or black piste

LEVEL 1

- Skier maintains parallel position, side slipping down the fall-line with a constant speed. Body faces across the slope rather than in the direction of travel to maintain maximum strength
- The same but in a defined 2m corridor
- The same but with more speed

LEVEL 2

- Using edge angle, the skier should slow the side-slip and then increase speed again. Use brushes to set markers for slowing and speeding up in a 2m corridor
- Skiers make falling leaf turns (facing the same way all the time) from side to side round cones/brushes, constant speed
- Skiers make 180 degree turns (brackage) in the same corridor. Use lots of brushes so skiers can see if they touch one and drift out of the corridor

LEVEL 3

- The same as level 2 but faster and with more precision

LEVEL 4

- The hockey stop. Straight run on a red run for approx 30m (long enough to be travelling at a speed that makes you a little worried!) then stop smoothly and in balance in an area of no more than 10m long by 2m wide. Mark out the stopping area with brushes, the skier should not travel across the hill at all. Do this on both sides
- No poles
- Change the distances to make it more challenging until you reach the limit of what is possible!

The Up and Over

Goal

To develop a stacked position at the top of the turn

Terrain

Groomed piste getting progressively steeper

LEVEL 1

- The skier traverses across the slope. Every 3 metres the skier extends the uphill leg and rides purely on the little toe edge of the uphill ski. The leg should be fully extended
- On a shallow slope (green) the skier makes the same extension of the uphill leg but on the third extension allows the ski to roll from the little toe edge onto the new turning edge. The skier can then complete the turn on two skis
- The same but on a blue run

LEVEL 2

- The same as level 1 but with no poles

LEVEL 3

- Make the extension of the uphill leg as before and roll the ski into the turn. Complete the turn on one ski and remain on one ski, the outside/turning ski. Blue run
- Red run
- No poles

LEVEL 4

- The same as level 3 level but faster and with greater precision
- The same on variable terrain
- No poles

Transitions

Goal

To develop the ability to jump in balance

Terrain

Piste and Park

LEVEL 1

- With skis removed, skier practises jumping and landing softly in ski boots on snow. This can be done on the flat and then on a slope
- With skis on, the skier makes the same jumping movement whilst on the move down a shallow slope
- Skier jumps over a series of poles lying across the fall-line in the snow. This develops the ability to 'pop' and builds confidence

LEVEL 2

- Jump over a small kicker or ridge on the side of the piste
- Skier performs a tuck jump o ver a small kicker
- Skier touches the boot at shin height whilst in the air. This is done by bringing the feet up and retracting the legs rather than reaching down with the body

LEVEL 3

- Skier jumps a blue kicker in balance at take-off, in the air and on landing
- Skier performs a tuck jump over a blue kicker
- Skier touches the boot at shin height whilst in the air. This is done by bringing the feet up and retracting the legs rather than reaching down with the body

LEVEL 4

- Same as for level 3 but off red kicker

Cowboys and Indians

Goal

To develop the ability to change the width of stance and feel a different blend of the steering elements

Terrain

Groomed blue/red piste

LEVEL 1

- Skier makes cowboy turns keeping skis and shins parallel within a set corridor 3m
- The skier keeps the same corridor and skis with the feet together as close as possible developing stability and rotary skills
- Skier takes both these stances and skis a much wider corridor

LEVEL 2

- Funnel shape from wide corridor to tight corridor in each of the stances
- Upside down funnel
- Hourglass shape

LEVEL 3

- Skier skis tight corridor and changes stance every two or three turns depending on space available
- Skier does the same with a wide corridor
- Skier does the same with the funnel and hourglass shapes

LEVEL 4

- Same as for level 3 but faster with more ski performance

Who Needs Boots?

Goal

To develop balance and feel on the skis. Care must be taken with this drill not to exceed the ability of the skiers. Skiers should only progress when they are sure of success. If in doubt, do not proceed

Terrain

Groomed green/blue piste

LEVEL 1

- Skier skis on gentle terrain and imagines they have no boots on. What do they feel through their feet?
- Go a little faster
- Mix up the turn shapes and corridors

LEVEL 2

- The skier loosens the boots and repeats level 1

LEVEL 3

- The skier undoes the boots completely and repeats level 1

LEVEL 4

- The skier keeps the boots undone and then tries some different terrain

Thousand Step Turns

Goal

To develop balance, agility and coordination between the two feet. Finding a place on the ski where the skier can move in every direction whenever they wish

Terrain

Groomed piste, steeper as the levels progress

LEVEL 1

- In a skidded turn, the skier steps towards the centre of the turn and keeps stepping inside throughout the arc. Go into the next turn and do the same
- Ski funnel and upside down funnel shapes doing the same as above
- Do the same in an hourglass shape

LEVEL 2

- Same progression as level 1 but stepping to the outside of the turns

LEVEL 3

- Perform level 1 and 2 progressions in carve turns

LEVEL 4

- Show versatility by changing from skidded turns to carve turns whilst performing step inside turns
- Show versatility by changing from step inside to step outside turns in skidded turns
- Change from step inside to step outside turns whilst making carve turns

Back to Braquage

Goal

To develop rotary skills to turn the skis and highlight how both lateral and rotational separation can aid lateral balance

Terrain

Flat, hard red/black piste

LEVEL 1

- On a steep, smooth piste, the skier side slips then rotates the skis through 180 degrees back in to a side slip. Repeat, staying in the fall-line
- Make sure that the skis do not drift forward or backwards during this manoeuvre. This requires that the timing of the edge (minimal but present) is delayed until the skis are across the fall-line

LEVEL 2

- Repeat level 1 progression. Try to keep the hips facing down the fall-line. How does this feel and how does it affect the edging and rotation of the skis?
- Allow the hips to stay square to the skis and keep the shoulders down the fall-line. Same questions as above
- Keep the whole body square to the skis. Same questions as above

LEVEL 3

- Braquage as before but this time the skier has to stop at the end of each turn and balance on the downhill ski only
- Hips square, how does this help/hinder?
- Whole body square, how does this help/hinder?

LEVEL 4

- Same as level 3 but vary the speed of descent. Go faster and also go as slow as possible

Equine Twist

Goal

This drill requires the ability to separate rotationally, and requires the skier to be able to change the timing of their movements to the inside. This can help when trying to set a platform at the start of the turn

Terrain

Flat smooth blue/red run

LEVEL 1

- In a fast traverse, the skier twists the skis across the direction of travel and tries to power slide across the slope
- Do this on both sides
- How far can you travel across the slope rather than being dragged down the hill by gravity?

LEVEL 2

- In the same traverse the skier twists the skis and then twists them back again to the same traverse. Try not to lose any speed
- Do the twist in the other direction

LEVEL 3

- The skier goes in to a power slide with the skis inside the turn (downhill). The skier then applies the edge and starts to come forward out of the turn
- Carry enough speed out of the turn in order to link these power slides together
- When the skier applies the edge they complete the turn in a carve

LEVEL 4

- At the end of a carved turn, the skier rotates the skis downhill at 90 degrees to the path of the carve, creating a side-slip across the slope. The skis are then brought back approx. 60 degrees onto the new carving edge to start the next turn. When coming back 60 degrees, skis should stay on the same edge and not revert to the previous turn. Red piste minimum
- Vary the time at which the edges are re-applied. At the fall-line, before the fall-line and after the fall-line

APPENDICES

15. BIOMECHANICS IN EQUIPMENT DESIGN

Skis and snowboards are designed to allow you to slide and turn on a bendable board attached to your feet. Largely, the design works by tilting an hour glass shaped flexible board that has two edges that can grip into the snow. Modern skis are much wider, especially at the tip, due to advances in technology, borrowed largely from snowboarding, that enable greater torsional stiffness (resistance to twist about its long axis). A ski with high torsional stiffness is less prone to twist and lose edge grip in response to high loading. Conversely, a ski with low torsional stiffness is more forgiving and you are less likely to catch an edge. A stiff board tends to be better on ice, whereas a softer flexing board is generally preferable in soft snow where the larger tip and tail help to bend the board into the arc required for turning. The flex pattern and shape will also affect its performance.

The way we control boards is via the interface of boot and binding that attaches us to our sliding platform. Problems often occur when the alignment of the foot and leg does not result in an effective line of force transmission. With higher and stiffer boots and when using lifter plates, the appropriate alignment becomes even more important to optimise performance. An additional consideration is optimising women's performance which often requires different boot, binding and ski combinations to those used with men. This is due to the typically narrower heel, wider calf, wider hips and the more rearwards and lower position of the centre of gravity in women. In snowboarding, there is clear asymmetry in the potential of the body to angulate toe versus heelside, plus a difference in mechanical advantage with the highback binding. The differences in left and right turns for both male and female skiers, suggests that the optimal solution for most skiers could be different for the left and the right leg. There is often no easy solution for asymmetry and when making interventions to a client's technique as instructors we should be aware that perfect symmetry is not always a realistic goal. Poor technique is often blamed when asymmetry and set up are the real culprits and in many cases this is something impossible to overcome in the short term.

Current thinking is often that ski boots should be tight fitting, locking the foot in place and that a foot orthotic should solidly support your foot in the neutral position. However, a locked foot with a limited range of movement inhibits sensitivity and the ability to make adjustments for balance and for subtle edging movements. Bode Miller for example, adjusted his boots to allow some extra foot tilting movement. In snowboarding, a well fitting boot should have a snug cuff and with strap bindings the lower leg and boot cuff should rest against the entire highback to facilitate transmission of movements to the board. However, there are few rules here, individual ability to balance and flex (all the relevant joints) effectively is key.

A commonly made suggestion is that heel lift helps you stay forward, as does boot forward lean. However, such an adjustment will potentially have the opposite effect to that desired. Increasing the forward lean will in turn increase knee flexion and actually move the hips back. Increasing ramp angle reduces ankle flex rather than promoting it and can negatively affect the ability to tilt the foot. In production, boot-board heights are unchanged, regardless of boot size, this can also have a noticeable yet often over-looked impact on a skier's ability to perform and make changes. However, the distance between the two points varies, resulting in a significant change in the actual ramp angle. Ramp angle simultaneously increases boot forward lean as can short leg-length and high calf-size, angling the tibia away from the rear spoiler. Total ramp angle (delta angle - binding, boot and orthotic combined) can be >8 degrees whereas practise based evidence suggests 3-4 degrees to be optimum (for males and females). The manufacturers sell what they believe the public will buy. This does not always mean the science behind the product is precise. One thing to consider in set up with a footbed is what are the angles of the baseboard in the boot?

It is generally assumed that the marked boot position on the ski, which was introduced around 1980, is an exact science that ensures the ski is set up to fit everyone. However, the characteristics of each individual skier are of more importance. The performance of elite racers has been shown to alter by small adjustments of binding position, in fact racers are sometimes mounted ahead of the standard manufacturers mark. Alain Baxter for example, moved his binding plate forward, and adjusted his ramp angle, but kept the standard boot position. Factors such as, skiing technique, muscle strength, skeletal alignment, anthropometric measures and motor control asymmetries, will all have an effect on the optimum boot placement and binding set-up on the ski. Despite the larger sweet spot of modern ski technology, practise has shown improvements in balance and control by experimenting with a position of between 1 to 3.5cm forward of standard. Although an appropriate method to determine this "optimal" binding position exactly is still not available, it is worth experimenting with different set-ups and keeping an open mind in both skiing and snowboarding.

16. EQUIPMENT

Equipment is one of the performance threads and is referred to in the strands section of this manual. Without proper equipment the safety, enjoyment and performance of the skier are compromised.

This appendix does three things:

1. It explains the main properties of ski equipment

2. It provides guidelines for its appropriate selection

Bindings

In simple terms, ski bindings are spring-loaded clamps which attach the boots to the skis. As well as the toe and heel units, the other key components are the anti-friction device (AFD) and ski-brake

Figure 15.1:
Ski binding

Binding Selection

Not only must the bindings keep the boots securely attached to the skis, even more important is that they must release when needed in a fall. Considerable care should therefore go into their selection. When making a decision, it is essential to establish the skier's correct setting – the number shown in the binding setting window, which indicates the force required to open it.

Adjustment Range

A binding which is appropriate for a particular skier ideally has that persons' setting number somewhere within the middle third of its range. For example, if a skier requires a setting of 6, the bindings should have a range of something like 3 - 9. Although they will still function when set near the top or bottom of their range, most bindings work best around the middle.

Adjustment for the Boot

There are three separate features which may need to be adjusted:
- Toe height
- Toe width
- Forward pressure

The absence of one or more of these adjustments on a particular model does not imply that it is unsatisfactory. Rather, it will have been designed to compensate automatically. But if the adjustment is there, it must be correctly set.

For the correct retention and release of the ski boot from the binding, all of the above settings need to be correct. Whilst there are many similarities between binding function and settings across brands, skiers must not assume that they can set bindings themselves. Any setting of bindings needs to comply with the manufacturer instructions and should be carried out by a trained professional with reference to the specific settings for that particular skier.

In conclusion, ski teachers should understand both the need for correct binding adjustment and the principles which underlie them. However, where adjustment is needed you should send your client to a qualified technician (i.e.in a ski shop or rental facility), rather than attempting to do it yourself.

Boots

Comfort plays a key part in the selection of ski boots. Apart from a snug fit with no pressure points or rubbing, boots should give good lateral and rear support and have a smooth, progressive forward flex. That is, the boot should progressively resist the forward movement of the lower leg, rather than coming to an abrupt halt. How stiff this flex should be is based on several factors:
- The skier's ability
- The skier's height and weight
- The type of skiing being done

Different models of boot have different systems of closure and adjustment. Whatever the system, it should allow independent adjustment of the fit around forefoot, ankle and lower leg. A good fit is needed for three reasons:

- **Safety** - Too loose a fit can allow the leg and ankle to move within the boot. In a fall, instead of the forces being transmitted directly to the binding so that it releases, the skier's leg can absorb some of these forces, resulting in needless injury
- **Control** - The boot is the steering linkage between the leg and the ski. Too loose a fit can cause excess play, leading to reduced steering accuracy and edge control
- **Comfort** - Too loose a fit can result in chafing and blisters, too tight a fit can cause pressure-points, bruising, cold feet and loss of sensation

In addition to adjustments for fit, many boots also have features such as variable stiffness, variable forward lean and canting adjustment. These features increase the cost of the boots and the need for them should be evaluated before purchase. Provided the boots fit well and offer the skier an appropriate amount of support, these additional adjustments become less important the lower the ability level of the individual.

After choosing a model, it is very important that the foot is correctly aligned within the boot. Each ankle bone should be an equal distance from the inside of the shell. This can be adjusted by wedging the heel on one side or the other, between the liner and the shell. The arch of the foot should also be supported, to prevent it collapsing under load.

Finally, a range of custom-fitting adjustments can be made. These adjustments can be performed on virtually any boot, and include:

- Fitting custom-moulded foot beds
- Selectively padding around different parts of the foot
- Cutting or grinding away some of the existing padding of the inner boot
- Stretching the boot shell to alter its shape
- Cutting or grinding areas of the shell to alter its' flex or fit
- Having custom-moulded (e.g. foam injected) inner boots fitted

In other words, skiers should seldom have to put up with sore feet. Provided they are the right size and performance range, the comfort of virtually any boots can be improved. What can be achieved is limited more by the knowledge and ability of the boot technician than by the boot itself. But when choosing boots, it is still best to select one which gives a good fit before any modifications are made. In this way, eventual comfort will be less dependent on the (often rather variable) skill of the boot technician.

Skis

"What length ski should I use?" is usually the first question which skiers ask. The answer depends on several factors, including the person's ability and the design of the ski.

The main factors that govern the performance of skis are:

• Sidecut

• Overall geometry

• Flex pattern

• Torsional rigidity

• Swing weight

• Damping

Different designs may achieve similar skiing properties while using different blends of these factors.

Sidecut - The curved shape of the side of the ski. Except for some very specialist off piste skis, all skis are narrower at the centre than at the shovel or tail, giving them a waisted shape. Other factors being equal, the more pronounced the skis sidecut, the smaller the skis "natural" turn radius, and the more tightly it will be able to turn without skidding.

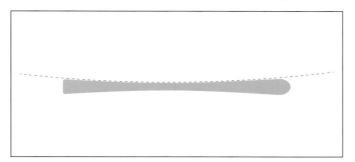

Figure 15.2:
Sidecut

Overall Geometry - As well as the sidecut, other features of the shape of the ski will influence its' its performance greatly. A wide ski will tend to float better in soft snow, but will be slower to change edge to edge. A wide ski overall will tend to float for its' its whole length whereas a ski which is wider at the tip will tend to lift the tip more and may allow the ski to switch edges easier on the piste.

Flex Patter - The shape the ski assumes when flexed, governed by variation in stiffness along its length. While skis vary in overall stiffness, they also differ in their flex distribution. Some have a fairly even flex throughout length, while others are very soft at the extremities while having a stiff mid-section. The effect of this factor is complex. When picking a ski, you should take it from the rack in the ski shop, place one hand in the middle and one at the tip and then force the ski to bend in order to test its flex pattern. This rarely helps but by nodding sagely and staring at the ski, a good impression is always made.

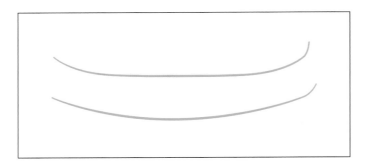

Figure 15.3:
Flex patterns

Torsional Rigidity - The ski's ability to resist twisting (where the force tries to twist the ski into the shape of an aircraft propeller). When a torsionally stiff ski is edged, the whole length of the ski presents the same angle to the snow, a ski which is torsionally softer tends to twist at tip and tail, reducing the effective length of edge gripping the snow. Torsionally stiff skis tend to be livelier and less forgiving than those which are torsionally softer.

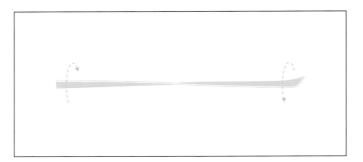

Figure 15.4:
Torsional stiffness

Swing Weight - The amount of the skis overall weight which is distributed nearer the tip and tail. The heavier the swing weight, the more effort it takes to make the ski pivot, thus increasing the skis stability in a straight line. Skis for high speeds generally have a higher swing weight than those designed for quick turning.

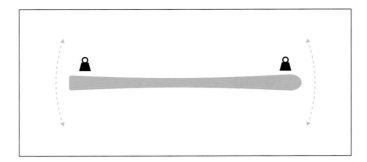

Figure 15.5:
Swing weight

Damping - The ability of the ski to deal with vibration from a rough surface. Edge grip can be drastically reduced by vibration, if the ski is insufficiently damped. Highly damped skis tend to be very smooth, but can sometimes feel a little 'dead''.

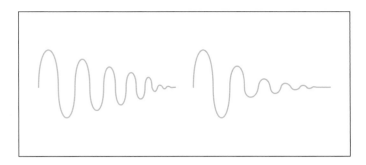

Choosing and Buying Ski Equipment

The correct equipment will enhance safety, enjoyment and performance. Manufacturers make ski equipment for all types of skiers and it is important to buy equipment that suits the skier and their needs, rather than trying to buy the top of the range model.

When choosing equipment the skier should consider the proposed use of the equipment as well as their ability, physical condition and attitude (ranging from gung – ho to timid).

To buy boots the skier should put aside a considerable amount of time to get things right and should only buy boots from a shop which is prepared to make adjustments to them after sale. Having willing and knowledgeable staff is more important for boot buying than saving a few pounds on price.

Buying skis will also benefit from salespeople who know their onions. Most manufacturers cover the full range of ski types but you may not be familiar with all the brands. The buyer must be realistic with their requirements when choosing skis. There is no such thing as a ski that does everything very well. The best all round ski will probably do everything rather averagely. If you wish to have the benefit of performance in one strand or another, then it is best to buy a ski that is suited to that strand. Race skis do not go in to deep off piste very well, fat boy twin tips will not help in a race course and very light weight touring skis are pretty awful for any type of performance skiing

Skis for Ski Teachers

The key aspects of ski performance are grip and stability. Fast skiing requires a stable, grippy ski, whereas for plough turning on nursery slopes, both are relatively unimportant. Indeed, a high performance race-tuned ski can make it hard to perform slow, skidded manoeuvres on gentle terrain.

Clients learn a great deal from clear demonstrations performed at an appropriate speed. As a professional ski teacher, you need to be able to focus on your clients, not on forcing your demonstrations because of inappropriate equipment.

Either you can have several pairs of skis to suit your various classes, or use one all-round pair. Some of your own performance skis may not be appropriate to teach on.

Equipment Maintainance

As a ski teacher, your image reflects your professionalism. This applies not only to your ability and behaviour, but also to your appearance. While clothing reflects the image of the Ski School, the condition of your equipment reflects your attitude towards yourself and your clients.

Dilapidated skis and boots with broken clips can present an aura of indifference. While your clients may know little about ski equipment, they may also know nothing about car engines yet still be able to spot shabby bodywork.

Professional Ski Teachers need to keep their equipment in first class order, but not just for appearance. Your equipment – especially your skis – must work effectively in a wide range of situations. Since the skis' condition directly affects their performance, their care should form part of your daily routine.

This is especially true when preparing for a training course or assessment. For assessment, you may need all the help you can get – including well maintained and appropriately-prepared skis. Effective ski preparation has several benefits:

• Reduced effort and energy when skiing

• Enhanced ski performance

• Increased working life of skis

In the extreme, poorly maintained skis can also increase the risk of injury, such as when attempting to negotiate steep or icy terrain on skis with blunt edges.

Modern skis are precision-made tools with in-built turning and gliding characteristics. And like any tools, care and maintenance are vital to prolong their life and maximise their performance.

What follows does not go into the detailed techniques of ski maintenance but provides an overview of the principles and procedures which are involved.

Ski Care

As the parts of the ski in contact with the snow, the base and edges are susceptible to damage. In terms of performance, both are extremely important:

• The base gives the ski its gliding characteristics, affecting the ease with which it slides and turns

• The edges provide grip, affecting the turning response and 'feel' of the skis

Routine care can keep the base and edges in first class condition. To maintain and repair your skis, use this three step approach.

The Three-stage Approach

Step 1 - Repair the Base

In order to glide and turn easily, the ski base must be free of cuts, scrapes and gouges. The base should also be flat across its width and flush with the edges, especially beneath the ski-boot. 'Railing', whether due to gouges or because the base is concave, makes the ski unpredictable and hard to turn.

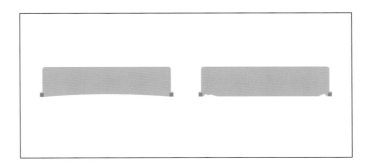

Figure 15.7:
Railing

A convex base is also undesirable, as it makes the ski unstable and reduces edge response. The aim is to fill in any gouges in the base and restore the ski's gliding properties. As a good 'rule of thumb', any gouges on which you can catch your thumb-nail should be repaired. Ski bases are made from various forms of polyethylene (polythene), usually known as P-Tex. Repair strips and 'candles' made of this material are available from ski shops.

Molten or semi-molten P-Tex is applied to the damaged area, then shaved down and smoothed level with the original surface. If the ski base is badly damaged, it may need to be patched. This is best done by a properly equipped ski technician or repair shop.

Equipment Needed

Tools and materials	Application
Workbench and clamps	Holds skis firmly for filing and waxing
Brake clip, or strong elastic band	Holds ski brakes clear of base
True bar or straight edge	To establish if the base is flat and true.
Plastic wax scraper	To take wax off bases
Hot wax	To apply to bases or use for cleaning bases
Waxing iron	Melting wax and ironing into base
Base cleaning fluid	Cleans old wax and dirt from base
Metal scraper and rough file	To remove excess P-Tex

Preparation

1. Use a brake retaining device or strong elastic band to hold the ski brake clear of the base and edges. Some bindings have removable brakes.

2. Clean the base using a proprietary solvent to remove old wax and dirt. Alternatively, wax the base and scrape it down again immediately to remove dirt and old wax.

3. Assess the extent of damage and the necessary repairs, and establish whether any thing needs to be done by a professional workshop.

4. Check that the ski base is flat, using a metal straight-edge. With the base upper most and facing the light, look along the ski and draw the straightedge towards you. The light between the straight-edge and the base will indicate one of the following:

Figure 15.8:
Railed base

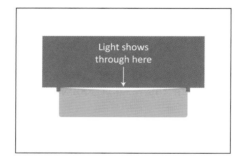

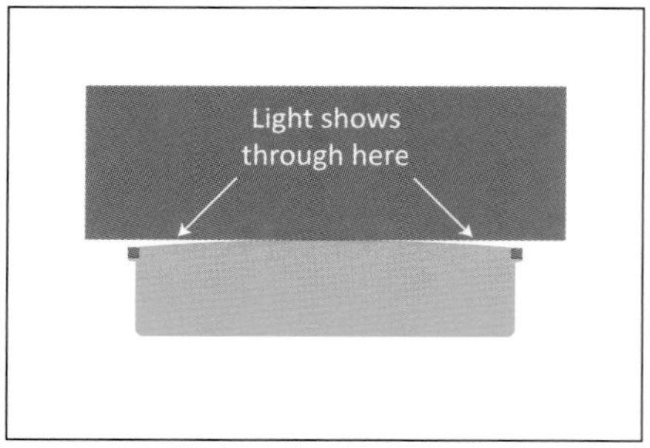

Light shows through here

Figure 15.9:
Concave base

Light shows through here

Figure 15.10:
Flat base

No light shows through

The ski in figure 15.8 is railed, making the ski hard to turn. Due to its concave shape, the edges catch on the snow surface.

The ski figure 15.9 is convex, making the ski hard to control. The ski must be tilted further be fore the edge begins to grip, making it drift and lack directional stability.

The ski in figure 15.10 is as it should be,forming a flat, level surface.

The bases in figures 15.8 and 15.9 can be rectified in two ways. Either flat file them yourself, or have them professionally serviced. If they are seriously concave or convex, have them machined by a repair shop on a stone grinder or belt sander.

Modern manufacture generally ensures that new skis have accurately machined, level bases. However, it is still worth checking them prior to purchase.

Base Repair

For a lasting repair, the base must be clean and dry. Any moisture or contamination in the base will prevent P-Tex and wax from adhering properly. If possible, keep the ski in a warm room for several hours before starting work. Begin by removing any P-Tex that is proud of the base by flat-filing or scraping with a steel blade, then clean the area.

There are two main methods of applying P-Tex to the base at home:

1. P-Tex candle:
- Ignite one end and let it burn until any carbon impurities have dripped off
- Hold it close to a metal scraper to keep the flame small and prevent carbon build-up
- Then keep the candle close to the ski while dripping molten P-Tex onto the base until the gouge is filled proud of the surface

2. Repair strip or granules:
- Use a gas iron to melt the P-Tex into the base
- Check that the correct temperature has been reached by touching the repair material against it before use - the P-Tex should begin to evaporate
- Fill the gouge proud of the surface, keeping the iron moving to avoid overheating the base

When all the gouges have been filled, leave the ski to cool completely. Any surplus material should be removed using a scraper blade or base file, cutting the repair back flush with the surface. Finish by rubbing the area down with fine emery paper to blend it with the rest of the base.

Flat Filing

The purpose of this stage is twofold:
- To remove any burrs on the base edge, so that the base can be repaired and scraped down without snagging or damaging the scraper blade
- To correct a concave or convex base. If it is severe, have the ski machined

If the ski is in good condition, do the minimum amount of filing necessary to remove the burrs, to preserve the factory-finished base.

1. First, clamp the ski securely into a vice or workbench. Holding the coarse file diagonally across the base, maintain even pressure while flat-filing.

2. It may be easier to control the file by drawing it towards you rather than pushing it away (make sure the file is the right way around as files only cut in one driection).

3. Do not press too hard on the file, but allow the file to cut along the length of the ski. If the file does not cut then the edges are case hardened, the file is not good or the file is being used in the wrong direction.

4. The edges should be cut by the file as long as the base is no longer proud of the edges. Material will come off the edge and the edge will be given a texture by the file.

5. If the file skips across a section of the ski without biting, and leaves a highly polished area of edge, the edge has become case-hardened and needs rubbing down before you continue filing.

6. Finish by taking two or three long sweeps over the entire length of the ski, drawing the file lightly towards you.

To bevel the base edge (creating a 'hanging edge'), use a purpose-designed adjustable sharpening tool. While ski technicians may prefer to use a handheld file, it needs considerable practise.

Step 2 - Prepare the Edges

Tools and materials	Application
Workbench and clamps	Holds skis firmly for filing and waxing
Brake clip, or strong elastic band	Holds ski brakes clear of base
Diamond file, emery paper or stone	To remove case hardened areas of edge
Base edge file guide – bevel guide	To hold the file when bevelling the base edges
Side edge file guide	To hold the files when sharpening side edges
Files of varying fine-ness	To set and fine tune the edge angles
Fine diamond/stone/gummy	To polish and detune the edges

The skis' edges provide lateral resistance or grip, which is vital for the effective control of speed and direction. It would be unwise to descend a steep mountain road in a car with bald tyres and no brakes. The same is true of skiing with poorly maintained edges.

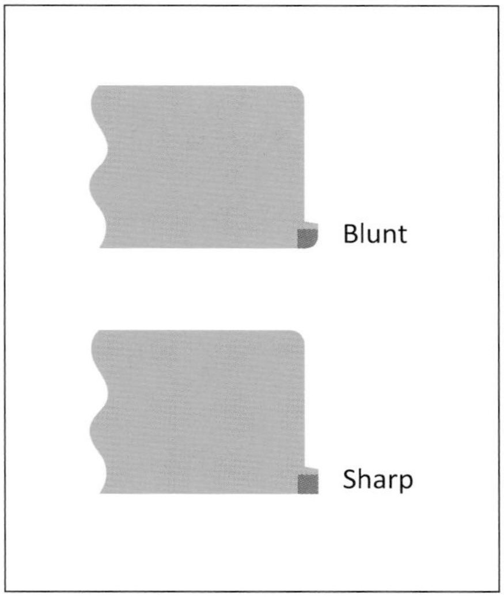

Figure 15.11:
Sharp or blunt
edges

Blunt

Sharp

The ski edge has two surfaces – the base and side edges – which form an approximate right-angle. An edge sharper (i.e. less) than 90° gives better grip, but blunts more quickly. At greater than 90°, it is more hard wearing but provides poorer grip. Figure 15.12 shows an angle of 90°, with the base edge flat with the sole of the ski.

Figure 15.12:
A "flat 90" edge

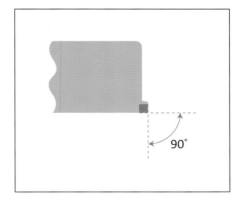

90°

This is a starting point for changing the edge angles and can be referred to as "flat 90". This means there is no change to base angle (the base edge lies flat with the base of the ski) and the side edge angle is at 90 degrees to the ski. Do not assume that a new set of skis will arrive with a "flat 90" set up.

Many manufacturers, ski workshops and keen skiers tune their skis by changing the ski edge angles away from the "flat 90" position. This modifies the ski's characteristics, and allows skiers to adjust the way their skis pivot and grip according to their preferences.

The Base Edge

Taking the base edge away from flat makes the ski easier to turn and pivot. Too much base edge adjustment will make the skis feel like they are slow to engage the edge and they may pivot too easily.

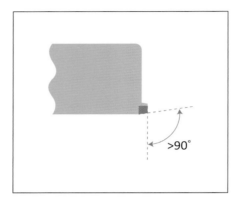

Figure 15.13:
Base edge bevel or "hanging edge"

The base edge is normally adjusted from flat between 0 degrees (no adjustment from flat) to 2 degrees. Zero degrees can make the ski very catchy and difficult to control. Two degrees will allow the ski to pivot easily and it will create confidence that the ski will not catch, however edging will be less responsive. Most all round services apply 0.5 degrees to 1.0 degrees of base bevel to the skis. This is something worth experimenting with to establish what you prefer.

The Side Edge

Making the side edge angle more acute makes the edges sharper and they will grip better on ice. The more acute the angle the quicker the edge will lose its sharpness.

Figure 15.14:
Changing the side edge angle

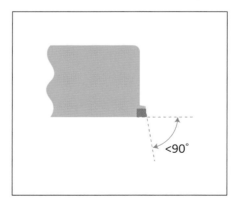

The range of side angle will go from 0 degrees to 5 degrees. The most acute angles will require the most maintenance and are only used by racers. Common settings for non racers are from 0 degrees to 3 degrees. Often the side edge angle is talked in the inverse sense. 0 degrees is called

90 degrees, 3 degrees would be called 87 degrees. It doesn't matter which reference is used as long as it is clear that the reference is to the side edge.

Sharpening the Edges

Ski edges are normally sharpened with a file. Before doing this however, any burrs and localised areas of hardening should be removed with a small sharpening stone, a diamond file or a piece of fine emery paper. Even without filing the edges, regular de-burring helps maintain the ski's performance. It only takes a minute or two and can even be done between runs if you keep a small stone in your pocket.

Check for damage after each day's skiing by gently running your finger along the edges to feel for any roughness or burrs. If there are no burrs, check the sharpness by lightly scraping a fingernail across the edge – if it leaves a fine shaving, the edge is acceptably sharp.

The main problem when repairing and sharpening edges is that the metal often becomes hardened. Steel is hardened by heating followed by rapid cooling. This is precisely what happens when the edge hits a rock – a small, microscopically-thin area of edge becomes hardened and resists all efforts to file it. These areas are harder than the file, and will quickly blunt its teeth. The answer is to rub down the edges, using a carborundum stone, diamond stone or emery paper wrapped around a file. This removes the hardened spots and enables the file to do its job.

Apart from flat-filing, the base edge requires little maintenance other than to set or restore the bevel angle (if any) from time to time. To do this, follow this procedure. Any repairs or flat filing must be done first:

1. Clamp the ski with the base up and the brakes secured or removed.

2. Choose the base angle you wish to set or maintain and fit the medium/fine file in to it.

3. Work the file along the edges making sure it is biting properly and ejecting material.

4. Change files for a fine diamond or stone and continue to use the guide to polish and finish the edges.

Side edge sharpening is carried out more frequently and makes the ski edge sharp.

1. Clamp the ski with the edge-uppermost, and rub it down with carborundum or emery to remove any hard-spots. If using an edge sharpening tool or file guide, set it to the required angle and draw it towards you using light pressure.

2. Use a larger file to set the edge angle and then a finer file for sharpening the edges.

3. After a few passes of a file, the edge should be sharp.

4. However, filing also leaves a slight burr which must be removed. This is done by gently rubbing along the base and side edges with a buffing pad or fine emery paper.

Once sharp, the edges should finally be tuned. This consists of:

1. Dulling them at tip and tail to stop the ski being too grabby or twitchy.

At the very least, the edges should be dulled from tip and tail as far as the contact points with the snow. Experiment with how much de-tuning you prefer on your skis.

Step 3 - Wax the Bases

Tools and materials	Application
Workbench and clamps	Holds skis firmly for filing and waxing
Brake clip, or strong elastic band	Holds ski brakes clear of base
Plastic wax scraper	To take wax off bases
Hot Wax	To apply to bases or use for cleaning bases
Waxing iron	Melting was and ironing into base
Base cleaning fluid	Cleans old wax and dirt from base
Nylon brush	To remove the last of the wax and make it look nice

Waxing a ski base serves two main functions:

1. To enhance the ski's glide properties.

2. To protect the base from wear and oxidation.

On its own, P-Tex has reasonably low friction on snow. But this can be greatly improved by waxing. Many skiers believe that extra speed is the only benefit, and therefore see waxing as irrelevant or even undesirable. But reduced friction also allows the skis to turn more easily, ultimately giving improved control.

One factor of particular relevance to ski teachers is that properly waxed and well maintained skis require less effort, and make it easier to produce consistent, clear demonstrations. By reducing friction, waxing also lessens the rate of wear, and can considerably prolong the life of the base.

Finally, when skis are stored for any period, the P-Tex base oxidises due to exposure to the air. This gives it a white powdery, 'dry' appearance. The oxidised layer generates increased friction, and wears faster than unoxidised PTex. A layer of wax protects the base from the air, and inhibits oxidation.

There are three types of wax - Hot, spray and rub-on. The best method is hot waxing, which provides the most long-lasting and effective result. Done regularly (every few days of use, and finally before storing for the summer), the skis' performance and durability will be greatly improved.

Most waxes are designed for specific air temperatures and snow conditions. Each covers a particular temperature range, sometimes with variations to cope with differing snow hardness or age. It is simply a matter of choosing the best wax for the conditions.

The most common method is with an iron, ideally a specialist waxing iron with a temperature control in degrees. This allows the temperature to match the recommendations for the specific wax.

1. Slowly coat the ski, using enough wax to 'wet' the entire base, but without having it running off the sides.

2. To avoid overheating the base, keep the iron moving the whole time.

3. Continue ironing for 2 - 4 minutes to allow the wax to soak into the P-Tex.

4. Allow the ski to cool slowly to room temperature.

5. The base should then be scraped using light, even strokes with a smooth-edged plastic scraper. Aim to scrape almost back to the P-Tex, so that only the thinnest film remains.

6. After cleaning any wax off the side edges, finish by buffing along the length of the base with a nylon brush.

When waxing the skis before storage (e.g. over the summer months), the choice of wax is immaterial. Indeed, ordinary (uncoloured) candle wax is perfectly adequate. In this case however, quite a thick layer of wax should be applied, covering both the base and edges. Make sure the edges are completely coated so as to prevent rusting. After the skis have been waxed, they should not be scraped down.

Summary

Sharpening and tuning skis can be a very technical and complicated process. The procedures listed above should be considered the basics for ski maintenance. For very high level skiing the focus and attention paid to the ski preparation increases dramatically.

For recreational skiers it should be remembered that ski preparation works on the principle of diminishing returns. This means that if most of the work can be done in half an hour then most of the benefits will be felt too. By taking another half an hour the skier will see more benefit, but not as much as the first half hour provided etc...Do not become attached to the work bench for hours every evening, do a little amount of maintenance as often as you can. Find yourself a ski shop whose servicing is consistent and do not be afraid to us them in order to re-set the base and deal with larger repairs.

www.swixsport.com provides video tutorials on how to tune skis for every type of skier. They will also be able to provide you with the equipment needed to do it.

www.Toko.ch are a major player in the wax an tuning market. They too provide guidelines on how to use their products in relation to alpine skiing.

17. PHYSICAL PERFORMANCE THREAD:
Background Information and Further Reading

The physical thread is enormously important in alpine skiing. From a beginner needing to be able to get up on their own after falling over, to an advanced skier making a fall-line descent of the bumps, physical condition plays a key part in the ability of the skier to perform the task. Physical condition will also play a part in the ability of the skier to repeat these tasks within a run, on the day and within the same week.

The subject of physical training is an enormous topic. Even if BASI wanted to, it would be very difficult to cover every facet of physical preparation within this manual, and that is not our aim here. Our aim is to highlight a few areas in which physical condition will affect the performance of the skier and to provide references for further learning for those who wish to pursue it.

Short Term Management v Long Term Development and Training

For most skiers the time frame in which we perform is relatively short, it may be one run, an hour, a day or a week. Therefore we often have to accept the level of fitness that we have and focus on managing this to maximise our potential, rather than expecting to be able to significantly improve it in such a short time frame.

Preparation - To perform close to our best the body needs to be warm. This gets the cardiovascular system working ready for activity and activates the muscles and tissues which will be needed for the activity. A good warm up will prepare the body and help to prevent injury.

Dehydration - Especially at altitude where the air is dry, dehydration can affect performance very significantly. For example studies across many different sports typically show that 2% dehydration can result in a 10% drop in performance. The solution for optimal performance is more complex than "drink plenty of water", but it is a good starting point.

Energy Levels and Nutrition - In order to perform anything physical, the body needs energy. When skiing this can be used to just keep us warm as well as to power the muscles for physical

The BASI Alpine Manual

effort. Eating enough of the right foods at the optimal times will allow skiers to perform on the hill without feeling low in energy or experiencing the dreaded "wibble" or "bonk".

Recovery - When performing it is important to be able to repeat an optimal performance over the course of a day or a week. For the demands of a sport like skiing the body needs to be allowed to recover in between these efforts. A good night's sleep would be the starting point for any recovery programme. Beyond this, a warm down and stretch may help performance the next day and avoid soreness in the muscles. Good management of hydration and food will also play a large part in the skier's recovery.

Fatigue - Physical fatigue is what we are fighting against in the short term and is caused by not managing the points above. By managing the food and water going in to our bodies and ensuring that recovery is a part of the program, skiers give themselves the best chance of achieving their optimal performance in the short term.

Long Term Development and Training

Physically we can optimise what we already have to ensure that our performance in the here and now is as good as it can be. In order to maximise our performance in the future, physical gains need to be planned and developed over a longer time frame.

Below is a summary of the physical attributes which can be trained effectively and can make a real difference to your skiing (and other performance sports).

Aerobic Capacity and Stamina - OK, so a run in skiing is rarely more than a couple of minutes and is often a lot shorter. Skiers still require a base fitness of aerobic capacity as it allows us to recover quicker from any effort and is a base requirement for any training program.

Anaerobic Stamina - Do you get exhausted by the end of the run in the GS or in the bumps? If so, then training this could make all the difference.

Speed - Are your movements not fast enough to cope with the rut line? Do you straddle during the flush of the local slalom race?

Strength - Do you find long turns at high speed on hard snow difficult to cope with? Do you get pulled off balance easily in heavy snow?

Power - Combine speed and strength and your become more powerful. Be able to make bigger moves in a shorter space of time. Cope with changing conditions easily.

Flexibility - It is nice to have a full range of movement in all of the joints. Strength, speed and power are only going to make a useful difference to skiing performance if the skier is able to move freely enough to utilise these physical attributes.

Co-ordination/Agility/Balance - This is an enormous area for development which can benefit every strand in skiing. We can always improve our performance in these areas and the training can be diverse and lots of fun.

Training Program

In order to get the best effects from longer term physical training it is essential that the training itself is structured and planned so that you optimise physical gains. Some of the areas for physical development listed above do not complement others if trained at the same time. Others can be used in combination to great effect.

Every person requires a different approach to their training and each person should have their own training program which takes in to account their strengths and weaknesses as well as their commitment and time available. This training program needs to be skiing specific. What type of skiing is the performer training for? How long is the effort phase? What type of loads will the body be encountering? How many repetitions are required in order to train effectively? Are there any special environmental conditions that need to be prepared for?

The program may just mean that the individual modifies or augments a program that they already pursue for another sport. Alternatively, you may start with a testing program in order to determine where the strengths and weaknesses lie in the first place, and then put together up to a year long program in order to peak for the following year.

Follow the basic principles of physical preparation, set some realistic goals for your physical development and create yourself a program. It can make all the difference to performance.

Further Reading

In order to make changes in your performance or the performance of you clients you will need to base any physical preparation on sound scientifically proven theories and methods. The literature in this field is huge so below is a short list to get started. The common theory course run by BASI covers a lot of this material and will provide a background in this area.

www.pponline.com

A journal based website with access to up to date information on all types of fitness and performance training. Subscription required.

Strength and Conditioning for sport: *A Practical Guide for Coaches. Clive Brewer. Revised 2008*

This would be the first reference book to get your hands on if you wish to start to train the physical thread or understand more about the physical thread and how it affects performance. There is a lot of information in this book and a lot of it is practically applicable.

The complete guide to sports nutrition. Bean A. 2003

There is a lot of misinformation about nutrition and diets. This book does not go in to much detail on this topic and this book would fill that gap.

www.coachesinfo.com

This website has information for coaches, runs education programmes and allows you to read articles online for free.

www.1st4sport.com

This provides access to a large number of sports education and training titles.

www.brianmac.co.uk

Lots of information available freely on this site but beware that only the appropriate information is going to be useful and this site does not guide you through a program.

18. PSYCHOLOGICAL PERFORMANCE THREAD:
Background Information and Further Reading

As with any sport, psychological preparation in skiing is key to performing well. From timid beginners taking their first slide down the nursery slope to elite athletes preparing for a run in the Olympics, 'being in the right place' mentally is extremely important and learning how to get there (whichever mental situation you are aiming to be in) is a useful skill to have.

Sport psychology is a huge topic and not one that we are able to cover in its entirety in these pages. Instead there is a brief overview of some of the common themes from this thread that apply to alpine skiing and there is a bibliography at the end of this section for further reading.

Principle Concepts

- Visualisation/Mental rehearsal
- Arousal curves
- Focus of attention
- Psychological thresholds

Mental Rehearsal

Have you ever seen the racers on the television making curves with their hands whilst keeping their eyes shut? This is visualisation. Being able to walk through a performance in your mind's eye will give you a greater depth and understanding of the performance you are about to give. Visualisation can be done from within where the skier rehearses what the performance will feel like as they do it, and it can also be done from a distance where the performer sees them self giving the performance from various angles as though they were someone else.

To get good at using this technique, performers should rehearse what they are about to do, do it then review their performance mentally to compare the two. In time the skier can then start to accurately forecast what the performance will feel like before it happens which gives a psychological advantage and can be used to enhance performance.

Arousal Curves

To perform well in any sport you need to be in the right place on the spectrum between mentally calm and excited to perform well. Sprinters and boxers will often find themselves with a high arousal level for an explosive, possibly aggressive performance, whereas golfers and snooker players typically need to remain calm under pressure to play their best game. For skiers, it is going to be somewhere between the two and it is going to vary from person to person depending on the needs of the performer. Knowing where you need to be on the scale to perform at your best is something with which you can experiment.

Achieving the right arousal level then becomes a skill in its own right. Various measures such as breathing techniques can be employed to raise and lower your pulse rate. Short sharp breaths will quicken the pulse rate and raise your arousal level, whereas long slow breaths will lower the pulse rate and calm you down.

Management of your arousal level is also key to the performance. It is impossible to be high on the scale for long periods so performers need to be able to time their peak mental state for when they need to give a performance and then learn to lower the arousal level, relax and switch off when not required to perform, since they will otherwise expend a good deal of energy. It is also possible to go too far on the arousal curve through over-excitement which then has a detrimental effect on the performance. Depending on the sport and the personality of the performer, it is possible to 'overcook' the performance through being too 'revved up'. Achieving a balance – the right place on the arousal curve – and timing that for giving the optimum performance is a good skill to practise.

Focus of Attention

It is natural for our minds to wander and we can end up thinking about non-skiing related topics at moments when skiing and the performance we are giving should be the only thing on our mind. Try skiing down a hill and then at the bottom review what you thought about on the way down. If the weather, what you are having for tea and whether United beat Chelsea features at all then you are said to have a wide focus of attention.

Being able to narrow your focus of attention, albeit for short periods of time, to exactly what you are trying to achieve will help you achieve it. That focus may be on the snow conditions, pressure in the curve or anything that you are currently working on, but being able to focus solely on a single point, or two points maximum, will aid your performance.

Psychological Threshold

Everyone has a point at which they become nervous or even frightened. For some people, this point will not prove to be a block to a performance since there will be technical, physical and tactical blockages that appear before they can reach this point. But a lot of people will become apprehensive or frightened about the gradient of the hill, the speed they are travelling at, the size of the bumps etc which will prove detrimental to their performance. Overcoming this is a priority over the need to focus on technical issues.

Learning to extend your psychological threshold or that of your clients to a point where there is no longer a block to performance is hard to do but will pay dividends if it can be achieved.

There are various ways in which this can be tackled but one approach is to use drills and exercises to make the task more difficult, with a view to making the whole performance seem easier when revisiting it. Skiing bumps on one ski, taping up the lower part of your goggles so that you cannot see the snow in front of you, skiing without poles or with your boots undone. All these exercises make the task harder so when you return to 'normal' skiing, it should seem easy by comparison.

For lower level skiers who suffer from a lack of confidence, it is a good idea to mark their progression. They may well be hitting the psychological threshold each time they go out, it is good to make them aware that skiing the nursery slopes used to seem steep and now it is a blue run that seems steep. They may well still be hitting their threshold but it has been extended to more difficult terrain and there is empowering confidence that can be gained from this realisation.

Finally, it is always important to set realistic goals. If a task is unachievable even with an optimum level of performance, then the scene is set for failure. It is a real skill to be able to set goals which will stretch a performer yet will equally be achievable. Successfully finding this balance will allow a person's psychological threshold to be pushed forward little by little.

Conclusion

Having a strong psychological approach to your skiing and knowing what works for you will make a big difference to your level of performance, particularly if there is a blockage which is preventing other elements of your skiing from moving forward, so try to focus on careful mental preparation for important performances.

Further Reading

Sport Psychology. *Richard H. Cox, 2006*

Applied Sport Psychology: *A Case-based Approach (Wiley SportTexts). Brian Hemmings and Tim Holder, 2009*

Foundations of sport and exercise psychology. *Robert S. Weinberg and Daniel Gould, 1995, Revised 2007*

Physiology of Sport and Exercise. *Jack H. Wilmore, 1994 revised 2008*

The Mental Game Plan. *S.J. Bull, John G. Albinson and Christopher J. Shambrook, 1996*

19. TEACHING WORK STATION

This diagram is intended to be used as a way to provoke discussion. Each teaching style is presented in such a way as to make a link to other areas of teaching. As we know the teaching styles are intended to offer the teacher opportunities to present information in different ways, each one will be more beneficial than another in certain circumstances.

What is important is not whether the links made on the diagram are 100% accurate, rather that you take time to consider and discuss the effects of a teaching style on the outcomes listed. Ask yourself these questions:

- Does this style develop understanding or performance, or both?
- Does this style develop the team or the individual?
- What kind of feedback is this style likely to produce?
- Who takes most responsibility when using this style, the teacher or the learner?
- Does this style help to attend to certain parts of the TIED model more than others?
- Would this style help performers who are in certain stages of skill acquisition?

See if you agree with the diagram and try to justify your reasons. By talking through this information and understanding how the choices you make as a teacher will affect the outcomes will enhance your understanding and help you to become more skilful with your delivery.

Self - Check T I E D

Develop Understanding — Develop Performance
Builds Team — Builds Individual
Intrinsic Feedback — Extrinsic Feedback
Teacher Led — Learner Led

Cognitive | Associative | Autonomous

Divergent T I E D

Develop Understanding — Develop Performance
Builds Team — Builds Individual
Intrinsic Feedback — Extrinsic Feedback
Teacher Led — Learner Led

Cognitive | Associative | Autonomous

Command T I E D

Develop Understanding — Develop Performance
Builds Team — Builds Individual
Intrinsic Feedback — Extrinsic Feedback
Teacher Led — Learner Led

Cognitive | Associative | Autonomous

Self Teach T I E D

Develop Understanding — Develop Performance
Builds Team — Builds Individual
Intrinsic Feedback — Extrinsic Feedback
Teacher Led — Learner Led

Cognitive | Associative | Autonomous

Reciprical T I E D

Develop Understanding — Develop Performance
Builds Team — Builds Individual
Intrinsic Feedback — Extrinsic Feedback
Teacher Led — Learner Led

Cognitive | Associative | Autonomous

Learner Design T I E D

Develop Understanding — Develop Performance
Builds Team — Builds Individual
Intrinsic Feedback — Extrinsic Feedback
Teacher Led — Learner Led

Cognitive | Associative | Autonomous

Practise T I E D

Develop Understanding — Develop Performance
Builds Team — Builds Individual
Intrinsic Feedback — Extrinsic Feedback
Teacher Led — Learner Led

Cognitive | Associative | Autonomous

Guided Discovery T I E D

Develop Understanding — Develop Performance
Builds Team — Builds Individual
Intrinsic Feedback — Extrinsic Feedback
Teacher Led — Learner Led

Cognitive | Associative | Autonomous

Inclusion T I E D

Develop Understanding — Develop Performance
Builds Team — Builds Individual
Intrinsic Feedback — Extrinsic Feedback
Teacher Led — Learner Led

Cognitive | Associative | Autonomous

Learner Initiated T I E D

Develop Understanding — Develop Performance
Builds Team — Builds Individual
Intrinsic Feedback — Extrinsic Feedback
Teacher Led — Learner Led

Cognitive | Associative | Autonomous

Discovery Threshold

Lesson Plan

General Information	No of pupils:	Age Range:	Sex:	Lesson Duration:	Class standard:
	Special Requirements				

Overall Goal (lesson aim)	Intermediate Goals (lesson objectives)	
Terrain for lesson		
Warm up activities	Revision activities	

Lesson Activities

Exercise/Activity	Purpose	Explanation/Demonstration	Teaching Methods

Fault Correction

Likely major faults	Corrective exercises and activities

OUVERT
OPEN

FERMÉ
CLOSED

LIAISON
TIGNES
FERMETURE A

RESENTE

20. THE MOUNTAIN ENVIRONMENT:
Accident and Emergency Procedure & Further Reading

Prevention

There is no doubt that prevention is better than the cure. Try and answer the following questions before you go to ascertain if you have planned appropriately.

Is the planned trip appropriate for the fitness of the group?

Is the group correctly equipped? (this is more appropriate to touring and off piste)

- Transceiver, probe, shovel
- Map and compass
- Bindings adjusted
- Skins that fit and are sticky enough
- Adequate clothing
- Sun protection
- Taking enough food and drink
- Personal 1st aid kit
- Spare clothing
- Pencil and paper

Do you have all the correct group kit?

- Group shelter
- Mobile phone or VHF radio
- Spare parts and repair kit
- First Aid kit
- Does everyone know how to use the gear they are carrying
- Are people travelling as light as possible

Do you know the route, if not have you obtained as much info as possible?

What has the weather been like?
- What is the forecast for today?

What has been happening to the snow pack recently?
- What is the avalanche hazard for today?
- What are you expecting the snow to be like?
- Where do you foresee problems arising if care is not taken?

Are you and the group insured appropriately?

Make sure somebody in the valley knows where you are going and when you will be back at the latest.

Find out the phone numbers to call in an emergency, and put them into your phone.

On the route, remember to stay vigilant and continue to be aware of all the conditions around you:
- Continually observe the weather and snow conditions
- Take heed of what you see, don't ignore the danger signs
- Be flexible, change your route to improve safety
- Select safe but enjoyable lines up and down the mountain
- Keep a track of where you are, refer to the map regularly
- Spread the group out where required to minimise the number of people exposed to the potential hazard
- In avalanche terrain, remove hands from pole wrist straps, undo waist and chest straps on rucksacks, remove powder leashes
- Ski the best snow: it is less tiring and less likely to injure people
- Operate at sustainable pace, eat, drink and rest to avoid injuries from fatigue
- Have challenges, but avoid taking people beyond their comfort zones

If you have an incident, remember to look after yourself then the group then the casualty.

Yourself

- Stay calm, do not rush
- Make sure you stay warm, eat and drink
- Delegate
- Avoid putting yourself at risk

Rest of Party

- Ensure that no others become casualties
- Utilise the expertise within the group if required
- Attend to their needs as well, reassure them etc
- Prevent the group from hypothermia, use a group shelter

The Casualty

- If it is safe, approach the casualty
- Provide 1st Aid
- If it is necessary remove the casualty to a safer place
- Prevent the casualty from hypothermia, use a group shelter

Sending for Help

- Use a mobile phone
- Use a VHF radio
- Send the most appropriate person / people in the group for help
- If none of the above are an option then use your whistle or torch, 6 blasts/flashes at minute intervals till rescued!

Incident Report

- **Who** is calling
- **What** has happened
- **Where** is the accident location
- **When** did the accident happen
- **Number** of victims
- **Number** on site helping
- **Weather** in the area

Working with Helicopters

Helicopters are used in many mountain rescues especially in the Alps. They present an additional hazard for all concerned

If you need help fro m one stand like this with your back to the wind facing the helicopter:

- Dress warm, the downdraught can shift a lot of snow
- Remember to zip up clothing and put goggles, hat and gloves on
- Make sure all your kit can't be blown away or sucked up into the helicopter engine
- Keep the group at a safe distance
- Only approach the helicopter when directed to do so by the crew
- If the helicopter lowers a winch cable down, let it touch the ground to discharge the static electricity before touching it
- Keep your head low: rotor blades can sag and the ground can rise
- Give an incident report to the crew

Figure 20.1:
Signalling a helicopter

Books and Videos

Avalanche Safety for Skiers and Climbers. *Tony Daffern ISBN 0-906371-26-0.*

The Avalanche Handbook. *David McLung and Peter Schaerer   ISBN 0-898863-643.*

Avalanche. *Robert Bolognesi (Cicerone ISBN-13 978 185284 473 8)*

Avalanche and off piste safety DVD (avalancheawareness.co.uk)

Off Piste Essentials DVD. *The BMC   ISBN- 978-090390813-9*

Staying alive in avalanche terrain. *Bruce Tremper ISBN 978-1-59485-084-4*

Snow Sense. *Jill Fredston and Doug Fesler ISBN 0-9643994-0-7*

Weather for hillwalkers and climbers. *Malcolm Thomas ISBN 0-7509-1080-1*

Hypothermia frostbite and other cold injuries. *Wilkerson, Bangs and Hayward ISBN – 0-89886-024-5*

Mountaincraft and Leadership. *Eric Langmuir ISBN 1-85060-295-6*

Mountain Navigation. *Peter Cliff ISBN 1-871890-55-1*

Off Piste. *Wayne Watson ISBN 1-873668-04-X*

Alpine Ski Mountaineering Vol. 1 Western Alps. *Bill O'Connor ISBN 1-85284-373*

Alpine Ski Mountaineering Vol. 2 Central & Eastern Alps. *Bill O'Connor ISBN 1-85284-374 8*

Off Piste and Ski Touring Guide Books with very useful Safety Guidance, produced by Vamos www.editionsvamos.com

Val D'Isere-Tignes Off Piste. *Jean-Luc Steiger & Guy Bonnevie ISBN 2-910672-10-7*

Chamonix Off piste. *Francois Burnier & Dominique Potard ISBN 2-910672-10-7*

Mont Blanc Ski tours. *Eric Delaperriere & Franck Gentilini ISBN 2-910672-08-5*

Les 3 Vallees Off Piste. *Philippe Baud & Benoit Loucel ISBN 2-9106723-12-3*

L'Alpe d'Huez, Les 2 Alpes, La Grave Off Piste. *Francis Ginet & Fabrice Villaret ISBN 2-9503673-6-4*

21. REFERENCES

Teaching Section

The Learning Process

KOLB D A (1984) Experiential Learning: experience as the source of learning and development New Jersey: Prentice-Hall (0 13 295261 0)

Smith, M. K. (2001). 'David A. Kolb on experiential learning', The encyclopaedia of informal education. Retrieved from www.infed.org/b-explrn.htm.

HONEY P and MUMFORD A (1982) Manual of Learning Styles London: P Honey

Goal Setting

Doran, G. T. (1981) "There's a S.M.A.R.T. way to write management's goals and objectives", Management Review, Vol. 70, Issue 11, p35-36, 2p.

Skill Acquisition

John Shedden, Skilful Skiing, EP Publishing, 1982. ISBN 0-715808-00-1

Fitts, P.M., & Posner, M.I. (1967). Human performance. Belmont, CA: Brooks Cole

Teaching Styles

Mosston, Muska (1965). Teaching Styles. A Spectrum. N.C.P.E.A.M. 69th Proceedings, December.

Mosston, M. (1966) Teaching Physical Education. Columbus, OH: Merrill.

Mosston, M., & Ashworth, S. (1994). Teaching physical education (4th ed.). New York: Macmillan.

Structure of Practise

Dail, Teresa K. Christina, Robert W. 2004. Distribution of practise and metacognition in learning and long-term retention of a discrete motor task. (Motor Control and Learning, Research Quarterly for Exercise and Sport).

Climate Setting

Starr, L. (2004). Creating a climate for learning. Effective classroom management techniques. Education World.

Knowles, M. S. (1980). The modern practise of adult education. From pedagogy to andragogy. Englewood Cliffs: Prentice Hall/Cambridge

Enjoyment

Wankel and Kreisel (1985) Factors underlying enjoyment of youth sports. Sport and age group comparisons.

Review

Adair, J. (1988). Effective Leadership Pan. New Ed edition